HAPPY AND
GLORIOUS

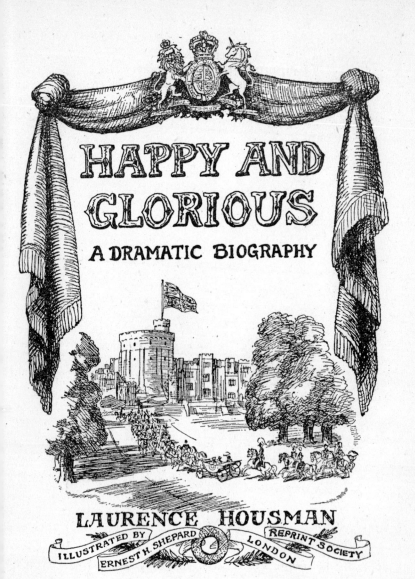

HAPPY AND GLORIOUS

A DRAMATIC BIOGRAPHY

LAURENCE HOUSMAN

ILLUSTRATED BY ERNEST H. SHEPARD

REPRINT SOCIETY LONDON

THIS EDITION 1943
PUBLISHED BY THE REPRINT SOCIETY LTD.
BY ARRANGEMENT WITH JONATHAN CAPE LTD.

822
3657

PRINTED IN GREAT BRITAIN IN THE CITY OF OXFORD
AT THE ALDEN PRESS

CONTENTS

CONTENTS

PREFACE

THE Victorian era has ceased to be a thing of yesterday; it has become history; and the look of age, which now grades the period, grades also the once living material which went to its making.

With this period of history those who once shared its life can deal more intimately than those whose outlook is later. We Victorians can write of it as no sequent generation will find possible; for we are bone of its bone, and flesh of its flesh; and when we go, something goes with us which will require for its reconstruction, not the natural piety of a returned native, such as I claim to be, but the cold, calculating art of literary excursionists whose domicile is elsewhere.

When I started to plan this series, a friend asked why I should trouble to resuscitate so dead an age. My answer was because I myself am a Victorian, and because, for me, the Victorian age can never seem dead. Here I have endeavoured to put on record the living interest which it must always have for me.

Some day, no doubt — though not yet — all these plays will be available for public performance in the country of their origin. I began to write them in the year 1920; twenty-one years later I finished writing them.

As they were published in succeeding volumes, I submitted them to the Lord Chamberlain for a stage licence, but until the year 1935 it was refused to all of them: the Lord Chamberlain did not consider them fit for public representation. In 1935 a Higher Authority, of blessed memory, intervened, and a licence was granted to nine of them. Since then eleven more have been licensed, while to three others (which are inconveniently truthful) a licence has been definitely refused. Intending producers should, therefore, take note that twenty-seven of the plays here presented are still waiting to obtain official recognition. I have no doubt it will come some day — when the censorship has learned to operate more sensibly; but I shall not live to see it. The law still permits a single official to deprive an author of the reward of his work on no better ground than his own private judgment. Though these plays are neither indecent, nor libellous, nor blasphemous, nor liable to cause a

7

breach of the public peace (which are the grounds on which the censorship is supposed to operate) I have no right of appeal against a decision which has cost me, and will continue to cost me, many hundreds of pounds. Even when he refuses me a licence the Lord Chamberlain demands a fee for the damage he does me; and when he reverses his unjust judgment — as he has done over twenty-two of my plays up to date — he demands another. I state these facts because I am quite sure that anything which helps to discredit the present censorship of plays is a benefit to the English stage.

L. H.

COMING EVENTS

1837

*The chamber is lofty but not large; its proportions, windows, doors,
furniture, all suggest that it has larger connections than its floorspace
alone would indicate. This often happens to the smaller apartments of
great houses; proportionate breadth denied, height is thrust upon them
by the architectural design of the main building. The result here is a
spindly pretentiousness, modified by age; for the hangings, once
splendid, are faded and shabby; the crimson carpet is worn, and the
red of the curtains has had its day. In the centre of this too aspiring
chamber sits a young maiden, fair and of fresh complexion; submissive
in attitude, diminutive in stature, she seems nevertheless a figure of
more importance than the large lady her companion, who, deferentially
strict, sits directing her studies — for this is the* PRINCESS VICTORIA,
so soon to become QUEEN. *The* GOVERNESS *has at her side a small
table; on it lie books and needlework. Her pupil occupies an upright
chair with gilt legs, too high to be comfortable; upright as the chair she
sits, straight and symmetrical, holding a book in both hands.*

GOVERNESS   You have read enough for to-day, Princess.
Begin your recitation.

> (*She takes a book from the table, opens it at a marked page; and the*
> PRINCESS, *who has watched her with waiting eye, receives the
> signal to begin.*)

PRINCESS   'Hope deferred maketh the heart sick: but when
the desire cometh it is a tree of life.

'Whoso despiseth the word shall be destroyed: but he that feareth
the commandments shall be rewarded.

'The law of the wise is a fountain of life to depart from . . .'

GOVERNESS   No, Princess, no! After the word 'life' there is
a pause. Say it again!

PRINCESS   'The law of the wise is a fountain of life. . . . To
depart from the snares of death.'

GOVERNESS   You see — it makes a difference!

9

PRINCESS   'A wicked messenger falleth into mischief: but a faithful ambassador is health.

'Poverty and shame shall be to him that refuseth instruction: but he that regardeth reproof shall be honoured.'

(*The door opens; a lady of stiff dignity enters.* GOVERNESS *and pupil rise and curtsy; for this is* H.R.H. *the* DUCHESS OF KENT; *and though a widow of restricted means, she holds her narrow court with a rigour of decorum that requires everything. The* DUCHESS *seats herself, and by a gesture indicates that the others may sit also. She and the* GOVERNESS *both speak with a foreign accent.*)

DUCHESS   What are you doing?

GOVERNESS   The Princess was reciting her Scripture, Madam.

DUCHESS   Continue.

PRINCESS   'He that walketh with wise men shall be wise: but a companion of fools shall be destroyed.

'A good man leaveth an inheritance to his children's children: and the wealth of the sinner is laid up for the just.'

DUCHESS   My dear, sit up, and sit straight!

PRINCESS   I *was* sitting straight, Mama!

DUCHESS   Never answer your Mother, my dear!

(*The* PRINCESS *struggles with her emotions. Habit is powerful: she controls herself.*)

GOVERNESS   Go on, Princess.

PRINCESS   'He that spareth the rod spoileth the child: but he that loveth him chasteneth him betimes.

'The righteous eateth to the satisfying of his soul: but the belly of the wicked shall want.'

DUCHESS   Lehzen!   The Princess should not have been permitted to learn *that*!

GOVERNESS   It's in the Bible, Madam.

DUCHESS   There are things *in* the Bible, as well as out of it, which are not seemly on the lips of a young girl ... I hope you do not allow the Princess to read *all* the Bible?

GOVERNESS   There are parts of it I do not read myself, Madam.

DUCHESS Very proper of you, I'm sure. Victoria, bring me your diary.

(*The* PRINCESS *does so; her Mother turns the pages.*)

DUCHESS When did you write in it last?

PRINCESS This morning, Mama.

DUCHESS You have not put the date. Nor have you entered the fault for which I corrected you yesterday. Go and do it at once.

PRINCESS Which fault, Mama?

DUCHESS *Which!*

PRINCESS There were so many!

DUCHESS My dear, that is almost like answering me again! Do you pretend not to remember how, when I questioned you about certain things, you lost your temper . . . Do not lose it again *now*!

PRINCESS No, Mama.

DUCHESS There, take it to the table . . . Mind! Do not leave anything out!

PRINCESS No, Mama.

(*The* PRINCESS *goes to a table near the window and begins writing.*)

DUCHESS Lehzen!

GOVERNESS Madam?

(*By a gesture the* DUCHESS *draws her toward her for a confidential exchange of words.*)

DUCHESS You have the history lesson prepared, as I told you?

GOVERNESS Yes, Madam.

DUCHESS You have marked the passage? You have put in it — the — ?

GOVERNESS Yes, Madam.

DUCHESS You are sure that you have made it *quite plain*?

GOVERNESS Yes, Madam. I have numbered the names of all heirs to the succession in order, and have underlined them in red ink. Under the Princess's name I have made *three* underlinings.

DUCHESS That is as I wished it . . . Have you heard how the King is to-day?

GOVERNESS No, Madam.

DUCHESS They never let *me* know anything — that they can help.

GOVERNESS I heard yesterday that he was a little better. He had taken a good turn, they said.

DUCHESS They told *me* that yesterday — to annoy me. It was not true.

GOVERNESS Indeed, Madam? Then your Royal Highness has had news?

DUCHESS I have means of information about which *they* know nothing.

GOVERNESS That is very fortunate, Madam.

DUCHESS It is not a question of *fortune*. It is the respect that is due to me. They seem to forget that some day *I* shall be the Queen-Mother.

GOVERNESS They will soon find themselves reminded, Madam.

DUCHESS They will. Victoria, have you done?

PRINCESS Yes, Mama.

DUCHESS Read it!

PRINCESS Yesterday, at breakfast, after the Chaplain had read prayers, Mama said to me, 'Victoria, did you fold up your night-gown?' 'Yes, Mama,' I said. 'Did you clean your teeth?' Mama then inquired. 'Yes, Mama,' I said. Her next inquiry —

DUCHESS '*Mama's* next inquiry.' Alter it!

(*The* PRINCESS *makes the alteration.*)

PRINCESS Mama's next inquiry was whether I had said my prayers. I answered, 'You know quite well that I said them, Mama; for you were there!' My dear Mama told me not to answer like that; and I lost my temper. This was wrong of me. Mama then kindly explained that she asked all these questions — not because *she* wanted to know, but in order to get me into the habit of asking them of myself, which I always do.

DUCHESS Those last four words had better be erased. If true, it is unnecessary to say so. If not true, they sound a little like defiance.

PRINCESS They *are true*! Why mayn't I write the truth?

DUCHESS The truth, when it means answering your Mother defiantly, is not a suitable weapon in the mouth of a young girl . . . Not another word, Victoria! You will now do your history lesson.

(SIR JOHN CONROY, *the* DUCHESS'S *major-domo, enters and comes confidentially towards her. He brings her a letter.*)

Ah, my good Sir John, so you have returned. You have news for me?

CONROY A letter, Madam. It has just come.

(*He hands it.*)

DUCHESS Ah! I will see you again, when the Princess has finished her lessons — alone.

(*In the last word there is an implied intimacy of understanding.* SIR JOHN *goes: he looks back; she is looking at him. Their eyes meet. Yes, there is an understanding between them. Meanwhile, the* GOVERNESS *has begun the history lesson.*)

GOVERNESS We were reading yesterday, you will remember, Princess, about the House of Hanover. Why was it so called?

PRINCESS It was so called because my three-times great-grandfather came over to conquer England for the Protestant faith.

GOVERNESS Not exactly to *conquer* it, Princess. He was called constitutionally, to establish the Protestant succession, and keep out all Papist pretenders.

PRINCESS Are *all* Papists pretenders?

GOVERNESS Yes, Princess. No Papist can sit on the throne of Great Britain.

PRINCESS Or Ireland?

GOVERNESS Or Ireland.

PRINCESS The Irish are pretenders too, aren't they?

GOVERNESS 'Are they not' — not 'aren't they . . .' They are Papists and rebellious — a very troublesome and disagreeable people.

PRINCESS   Then I need not like the Irish, need I?

GOVERNESS   Only those who live in the north, in Ulster. They are industrious, and loyal, and deserving. For the rest you can have only pity.

PRINCESS   And try to convert them?

GOVERNESS   *Pray* for their conversion, Princess. That is all you can do.

PRINCESS   I will do so to-night.

DUCHESS   The dear King is worse, much worse, they tell me. Victoria, you must remember to pray to-night that his precious life may be spared. That is far more important than the conversion of the Irish. I do not think they would ever make good Protestants.

PRINCESS   Very well, Mama.

GOVERNESS   Begin your reading, Princess: page 273.

PRINCESS   (*opening the book*) Oh, what is this?

GOVERNESS   That is a chronological table, Princess, showing the succession to the crown at the present day.

PRINCESS   Oh, how interesting! I have never seen this before. Am I in it?

GOVERNESS   Your Royal Highness's name is there — with others.

PRINCESS   What is the red ink for?

GOVERNESS   That is to show, Princess, the order of inheritance, in the last — and in the present generation.

PRINCESS   I see my Father's name.

GOVERNESS   Yes, Princess. Had your Royal Father lived, he would now have been heir-presumptive to the throne.

PRINCESS   Why 'presumptive'?

GOVERNESS   On the presumption that His Majesty the King has no children.

PRINCESS   Oh, but Cousin George told me the other day that he's had lots.

(*There is a moment of painful embarrassment. Then the* DUCHESS *speaks.*)

DUCHESS   They have all died, or have passed from the succession in other ways.

PRINCESS *(a little puzzled)* Oh? . . . Then it would have been my Father?

GOVERNESS   Undoubtedly.

DUCHESS *(consequentially)* Of course it would have been your Father, my dear! And *I* should have been Queen.

PRINCESS *(genuinely astonished)* La! Mama! How you surprise me! . . . Then now it is one of my uncles?

DUCHESS *(with asperity)* *None* of your uncles, Victoria. They do not come in, I'm thankful to say.

PRINCESS   Then . . . do *I*?

DUCHESS   You have the table there, my dear. Study it.

PRINCESS *(after further examination)* Oh! Oh! I didn't know . . . I never thought I was quite — quite — no near as that. Oh, Mama, Mama!

DUCHESS   What is it, my dear? It is nothing to be upset about.

PRINCESS   Oh, now I know why you have always been — so — so — Oh, I will be good! I will be good!

DUCHESS   Indeed I hope so! For that a great deal depends on *both of us*. It has been *my* care hitherto. In the future it will have to be yours.

PRINCESS   Oh, Mama, forgive me if I ever — ever seemed — ungrateful! I am so young for it!

DUCHESS   I shall always be there, my love. You will be Queen. But I am your Mother. I shall not go away and leave you.

PRINCESS   Oh? . . . No, of course not.

(Disappointed, she weeps.)

DUCHESS *(soothingly)* Of course not.

GOVERNESS   Why, of course not, Princess! There, there! Don't cry!

DUCHESS   Let her cry, Lehzen! It will be good for her. After all it's only natural; a great shock. It was time she had it.

PRINCESS It's so sudden!

DUCHESS Not as sudden as it might have been. Considering his age, the King must have a very strong constitution. It is wonderful how it has lasted. So now I must go and see after my black, to be ready in case anything happens.

GOVERNESS Is the last news very alarming, Madam?

DUCHESS Everyone had given up hope yesterday, they tell me. And now he has given it up himself.

PRINCESS Is he conscious, Mama?

DUCHESS No, not conscious, my dear. He has given that up too. Perhaps that is as well. I fear he did not lead a good life.

PRINCESS But he was *married*, Mama!

(*This causes shock.*)

DUCHESS My dear! All married people do not lead a good life — not all.

PRINCESS Oh, I thought they did!

DUCHESS Victoria, you shock me! Who has been talking to you?

PRINCESS Talking to me?

DUCHESS Yes, about marriage, and — and things of *that* sort.

PRINCESS No one . . . only Cousin George. The other day he asked me to marry him. He said it would make him good.

DUCHESS Your Cousin George!

PRINCESS Yes; he said that all my uncles wished it, and the King wished it too. So that was why he asked me.

DUCHESS Yes. I daresay they do . . . I daresay they do! But I can tell them *this* — and I tell you too — you are not going to marry your Cousin *George*. *He* is not going to be King.

PRINCESS No, Mama, not if I am to be Queen.

DUCHESS Kiss me, my dear! Ah, you do not know the dangers from which I have protected you. I hope that you will never have to know. . . . That will do, Lehzen, for the present. You may go. The Princess will finish her lessons later.

(LEHZEN *curtsies and retires.*)

My child, listen to me! It's time that you knew — *this* at least. Ever since you were born, I have been fighting a battle to save you from the hands of *wicked men*.

PRINCESS   Oh, Mama!

DUCHESS   Yes. They wanted to get hold of you; but I would not let them. They wanted to choose a husband for you — your Cousin George, and then to make *him* King instead of you. But I saw what they were after. I saved you from *that*. That is why I never left you alone — never let you go out of my sight, except sometimes when we were at Windsor, and it could not be helped. That is when your Cousin Goerge spoke to you, I suppose? . . . What did you say to him?

PRINCESS   Of course, I said he must first ask Mama!

DUCHESS   My own darling child!

PRINCESS   And that didn't seem to please him.

DUCHESS   No, I daresay not!

PRINCESS   He said that in that case it was 'all up'!

DUCHESS   That is the sort of language I should expect from him! — 'All up!' He has been learning English from his uncles — and other things as well, I'll be bound! So marrying you was going to make him *good*, was it? . . . Oh, my darling, now that you see from what I have saved you, I only ask you to remember, and be a little grateful. You are so young, so inexperienced — and such a child! But I know, oh, I know *things*! . . . But Mama is still with you, my child; always will be with you. Trust Mama! Come to Mama about *everything*!

(*The* PRINCESS *stands dutifully attentive, wistful, interested, a little alarmed, and yet self-possessed; and when the* DUCHESS *at last pauses for her to speak, it is a portent of coming events that she does not say,* 'Yes, Mama', *as perhaps she was expected to do; but stands looking out — into the future. The door opens.* SIR JOHN CONROY *enters, and stands looking at mother and daughter.*)

DUCHESS   Go, now, for your walk with Lehzen.

(*The* PRINCESS *curtsies and retires.* SIR JOHN *holds open the door, shuts it, and advances toward the* DUCHESS. *Oh, yes, there is an understanding between them. She puts out her hand, and he takes it.*)

THE SIX O'CLOCK CALL

1837

It is still dark; for in the entrance hall of Kensington Palace the shutters have not yet been unclosed. Behind a wide archway at centre burns a dim light: there is the staircase lobby. To the left of the archway one sees the foot of the stairs.

In the dark emptiness goes the clanging of a bell, followed by knocks. A FOOTMAN, *not quite dressed as he should be, enters carrying a light. He crosses from left to right, and passes out of view. You hear unchaining and unbolting of a door; then, indistinctly, voices, which grow louder as the visitors enter and become visible. Heavily cloaked,* LORD CONYNGHAM *comes in, followed by the* ARCHBISHOP OF CANTERBURY.

CONYNGHAM Tell them to take the message at once! Say the matter is urgent.

FOOTMAN Yes, my Lord. But Her Royal Highness isn't up yet, my Lord.

CONYNGHAM 'Up?' Of course she's not up at this hour! Send Her Royal Highness's maid to call her.

(*The* FOOTMAN, *having the only candle, is busy now lighting others. But the urgency of his lordship stops the business half-way, and only one set of candles gets lighted before he goes.*)

FOOTMAN Yes, my Lord.

CONYNGHAM And say His Grace the Archbishop of Canterbury, and Lord Conyngham are here to see Her Royal Highness on important business.

FOOTMAN Yes, my Lord.

CONYNGHAM Hurry, man! Hurry!

FOOTMAN Yes, my Lord; but I'll have to call the maid first.

CONYNGHAM Well, call her!

FOOTMAN Yes, my Lord; but the maids sleep where I'm not

supposed to go, and the door up to it is locked. I shall have to throw up at the window.

CONYNGHAM Isn't there a bell?

FOOTMAN Yes, my Lord; in her Royal Highness the Duchess's room there is a bell.

CONYNGHAM Well, go and ask that it may be rung!

FOOTMAN (*aghast*) I daren't go to Her Royal Highness the Duchess's room, my Lord: not now. Her Royal Highness the Princess is there too.

CONYNGHAM Well, go and do the best you can. But say Her Royal Highness *must* come —

FOOTMAN Yes, my Lord.

(*Exit* FOOTMAN.)

CONYNGHAM (*finishing his sentence*) — at once! . . . Good Lord! What a house! Sleeps with the old Cat, does she?

ARCHBISHOP (*corrective, but suave*) I beg your pardon?

CONYNGHAM I — I beg yours! Yes; I suppose one oughtn't to say that now. But your Grace knows that the Duchess has been a difficulty all along.

ARCHBISHOP The Duchess is a determined character.

CONYNGHAM Yes.

ARCHBISHOP It has had its advantages.

CONYNGHAM They have escaped my observation, I'm afraid.

ARCHBISHOP The Princess has not seen a great deal of her uncles. Her education has been — safeguarded.

CONYNGHAM (*extenuatingly*) Well, of course, I know — I know — I know.

ARCHBISHOP (*less extenuatingly*) Yes, my Lord, we *know*.

CONYNGHAM Had we not better sit down? We may have to wait. If that man's stone-throwing is not good — we may have to wait a long time . . . So this is how history gets written!

ARCHBISHOP *This* won't get into history, my Lord.

CONYNGHAM No ... Your Grace? — may I? ...

(He offers a flask-cup, after filling it.)

ARCHBISHOP Ah, no. I thank you.

CONYNGHAM It's a chilly hour to be up. I never go about, late at night, or early — without *something*.

(Drinks.)

ARCHBISHOP For you, my Lord, very wise, I've no doubt. But I never go out at night, you see; at least, not late.

CONYNGHAM Ah! I often wish I didn't, when the night is over.

ARCHBISHOP That is — understandable.

CONYNGHAM (*missing the note of sympathy*) It's only human nature, your Grace.

ARCHBISHOP Yes, I suppose so. I don't know ... My office ... There is a good deal of human nature that I have to avoid.

CONYNGHAM Rather difficult to avoid at the Court of the Regency, wasn't it?

ARCHBISHOP Oh, of course, sometimes I had to — well — look the other way. Still, I attended so seldom; only when called on officially.

CONYNGHAM Your Grace has officiated on a similar painful though auspicious occasion, I believe?

ARCHBISHOP Yes. Yes. I announced his accession to His late Majesty King William. But he was only in the next room waiting.

CONYNGHAM Ah! How did he take it?

ARCHBISHOP With alacrity ... 'Bless my soul! you don't say so! were his first words. And then — 'Well, well, though I'm less of a figure-head, I shall make a better King than poor George.'

CONYNGHAM But he didn't, you know.

ARCHBISHOP No; a better character, but not a better King. That sometimes happens, I'm afraid.

CONYNGHAM Yes, kings often manage to do quite well without morals. Brain is more important.

ARCHBISHOP Not too much of that either, I should have thought. Don't those with brain give much more trouble to their ministers?

CONYNGHAM Oh, they manage to do that without any! His late Majesty was a conspicuous example of it. You wouldn't believe — no, you wouldn't believe the trouble we sometimes had with him. They say you can make a donkey go by tying a carrot in front of its nose. Well, he was like a donkey with a carrot tied to its tail.

ARCHBISHOP Really?

CONYNGHAM Just like that. Over the Reform Bill, you know, we almost had a Revolution — almost. Not *his* fault that we didn't.

ARCHBISHOP (*discreetly*) Was he just a little — like his Father, you know?

CONYNGHAM Mad, eh? No, not mad. It was the shape of his head, I think. It was pear-shaped, you know — just like a pear. 'The weakest fruit drops earliest to the ground,' says Shakespeare. Well, his head was weak fruit distinctly — amazing how it *hung on*: one can't exactly say 'lasted'.

(*The* FOOTMAN *re-enters.*)

Well? What have you done?

FOOTMAN I've called the maid, my Lord. Would your Lordship like more light?

CONYNGHAM Oh yes; a little more light would, I suppose, be better. (*Then to the* ARCHBISHOP) For so auspicious an occasion.

FOOTMAN The windows, my Lord?

CONYNGHAM No, no, not the windows, I think. *The blinds — the blinds* must stay down at any rate.

(*The* FOOTMAN *lights more candles.*)

ARCHBISHOP (*confidentially*) Very sad, very sad, you know! Good old King George — such a large family — so many sons, and not one of them what he should be.

(*Exit* FOOTMAN.)

CONYNGHAM (*grimly*) And she — the daughter of one of them.

ARCHBISHOP Ah, but women are different — so different, you know. Let's hope! Let's hope!

CONYNGHAM Well, we must get her married, and then — married to the right man — the difference won't so much matter; her Cousin, Prince George of Cambridge, would be very suitable — same age, and can talk English now, so I'm told, like a native.

ARCHBISHOP Over that you will have difficulty with the Duchess.

CONYNGHAM Oh, yes; the Duchess is going to be difficult whatever's proposed. She will regard this as her own accession almost.

ARCHBISHOP (*wisely*) It almost will be.

CONYNGHAM That is what we must *prevent*.

ARCHBISHOP The Duchess has privately planned a marriage more to her own liking, I'm told.

CONYNGHAM Eh? Who?

ARCHBISHOP She has two nephews — through her brother the Duke of Saxe-Coburg — Prince Ernest, and Prince Albert.

CONYNGHAM But that won't do! Tainted blood! Tainted blood!

ARCHBISHOP Indeed!

CONYNGHAM (*disgustedly*) Ye-es: bleeding skins — haemophilia. It's in the family. Cousins. No; it won't *do*.

ARCHBISHOP But Prince George is her cousin, also.

CONYNGHAM Ah, but it's not on that side. It's on the mother's — the Coburgs. And, you know, it comes through the women. The males have it: the women don't; but they pass it on. Do you know her brother, the Duke, once nearly bled to death?

ARCHBISHOP Dear me! Is that so?

CONYNGHAM Marrying her daughter to *his* son would be fatal! You know, it's all very well, in one way, Royalty to make itself a class all by itself. But it's a German notion: 'tisn't English. And when it leads to so much inbreeding, it gets dangerous. English kings have married commoners in the past; they'd better do it again — or into the peerage. Do you know — if the Duke of Wellington had been — well, twenty years younger, I'd have married her to him.

ARCHBISHOP You don't mean it!

CONYNGHAM I do. 'Twould have been very popular; and a foreign marriage won't be. (*He looks at his watch.*) Tut, tut! That girl's a very long time coming!

ARCHBISHOP (*correctively*) The Queen?

CONYNGHAM (*plausibly covering his mistake*) No, no; I mean the maid. I'm wondering whether she has called her . . . It's a pity, you know, a pity! I don't know what to think of it!

ARCHBISHOP 'It' meaning what?

CONYNGHAM A female on the throne; a King would have been so much better.

ARCHBISHOP I don't know, my Lord. Heirs male of the last generation have not been a conspicuous success.[1]

CONYNGHAM No English King has been a conspicuous success since Edward I.

ARCHBISHOP Yet the monarchy has — gone on.

(*Enter* MAID-SERVANT.)

CONYNGHAM Yes; but it's gone off.

MAID I beg your pardon, my Lord.

CONYNGHAM Yes? Well?

MAID Her Royal Highness, my Lord. I went in, but Her Royal Highness was asleep.

CONYNGHAM Well, you must wake Her Royal Highness up, then.

MAID Such a beautiful sleep, my Lord: I didn't like to.

CONYNGHAM Even the most beautiful sleep must give way to affairs of State. You know who I am?

MAID Yes, my Lord.

CONYNGHAM You know His Grace?

MAID Yes, my Lord.

---

[1] This remark having been ruled out of one of my plays by the Lord Chamberlain, now goes into another.

CONYNGHAM Then go at once: wake Her Royal Highness, and tell her that we are here, waiting — for an audience.

(*Awestruck and submissive, the* MAID *goes. A clock strikes.*)

Six o'clock. There is to be a Council at ten.

ARCHBISHOP Where? Here?

CONYNGHAM At St. James's, I imagine. 'No, perhaps it will have to be here. She musn't appear in public yet. 'Twouldn't be quite decent. People might cheer.

(*Enter the* DUCHESS OF KENT: *she is robed rather than dressed; but her heavy négligée has a certain dignity about it. She enters, a conscious 'Presence'. They rise and bow.*)

DUCHESS Your Grace, my Lord Conyngham, you have news for us?

CONYNGHAM For her Royal Highness the Princess, we have news, Madam.

DUCHESS Ah! The King then — ?

CONYNGHAM Is dead.

DUCHESS Then my daughter is now — ?

CONYNGHAM Queen.

DUCHESS It has come, then — at last! And I — I am the Queen Mother!

CONYNGHAM No, Madam: your Royal Highness is not the Queen Mother.

DUCHESS (*affronted*) Not?

CONYNGHAM Your Royal Highness is the Queen's Mother; that is the distinction. Only had your Royal Highness been Queen in the first place, would that other title now follow.

DUCHESS Then, if it is not mine by your laws, she shall give it me.

CONYNGHAM That, Madam, I fear, will be impossible.

DUCHESS Ah! I will go myself and speak to her at once. That shall settle it!

CONYNGHAM Madam, we are here to see Her Majesty the Queen on urgent business; and we must not be delayed. Your presence at the interview, Madam, will not be required, unless Her Majesty sends for you.

DUCHESS Ah! This is not to be borne!

ARCHBISHOP (*conciliatory*) Madam, this is a very historic occasion. We are here officially only. Etiquette and immemorial tradition prescribe certain rules which have to be observed. Your Royal Highness would not wish to break them.

CONYNGHAM (*at centre*) Your Grace, she's coming!

ARCHBISHOP Then, Madam, for a moment — for a moment only!

(*He opens a side-door and bows the* DUCHESS *through it. She goes, compelled, but reluctant. The shadow of* QUEEN VICTORIA *is projected upon the wall of the lobby as she descends. She enters: the* ARCHBISHOP *and the* LORD CHAMBERLAIN *kneel and kiss her hand. The side-door opens again; the* DUCHESS *thrusts in her head; she watches spell-bound.*)

CONYNGHAM Your Majesty, it is our painful duty to announce to your Majesty —

DUCHESS (*not waiting for the sentence to finish*) Ah! my daughter, she is Queen — Queen!

(*The curtain slowly descends; after a few seconds it rises again.* VICTORIA *stands alone at the foot of the stairs. Away to the right, ceremoniously backing from the Presence, the* ARCHBISHOP *and the* LORD CHAMBERLAIN *make their last bow and go. Into this solemn scene no* FOOTMAN *intrudes; they let themselves out. At the sound of the shutting door, the side-door opens fully: the* DUCHESS *enters, and advances rapturously to claim her daughter's homage.*)

VICTORIA (*still a little mazed at the wonder of it all*) Mama!

DUCHESS (*embracing her*) My child! My child! Oh, my child!

VICTORIA They came to tell me that I am Queen.

DUCHESS Yes: you are Queen at last!

VICTORIA But really Queen — *now*: before I have been crowned?

DUCHESS Yes, now, at once! The King is dead: you are Queen!

VICTORIA Then my reign has already begun? I can do — as I like?

DUCHESS Yes; as you like! Do not mind what anyone says. If you want to do it — do it!

VICTORIA Oh! . . . Then . . . Mama. There is something I would like.

DUCHESS Ah, yes! Say it! It shall be done.

VICTORIA How strange that it should have all come — so suddenly!

DUCHESS Yes, so suddenly — after we have waited so long. But now, my love — do not stay here to catch cold. Come back to your own Mother's bed!

VICTORIA No, Mama dear. As I may now do as I like, I wish in future to have a bed, and a room of my own.

DUCHESS (*stupent*) *Of your own?*

VICTORIA Yes — please, Mama.

DUCHESS Oh! so you have been waiting — for *that*!

VICTORIA I should be glad, if you don't mind — now that I am my own mistress. Yes, I would rather be alone.

(*She does not wait to hear more.*)

DUCHESS Mind! . . . Glad! . . . Alone! . . . O God! What is going to become of me?

(*She stands and watches, while* VICTORIA, *mistress henceforth of her own destiny, turns and goes quietly upstairs again, having imposed, even now, her wish to be alone for a while.*)

'POOR MAMMA!'

20th June 1837

The clock at Kensington Palace is about to strike ten. And in the ante-room to the Council Chamber there are signs of ceremony. Before a closed double-door stand two Attendants. From another door THE QUEEN *enters, robed in black, toweringly followed by the* DUCHESS OF KENT, *in black also. After her come two Ladies-in-Waiting and* SIR JOHN CONROY, *who halt within the door of their entry. An Attendant opens one half of the closed door just sufficiently to admit a* COURT OFFICIAL, *then closes it again. The* COURT OFFICIAL *bows, advances toward* THE QUEEN, *and bows again.*

COURT OFFICIAL If it please your Majesty, your Majesty's Privy Council is now in attendance.

THE QUEEN It is already the time?

COURT OFFICIAL The hour is now striking, your Majesty.

THE QUEEN Very well. Will the ceremony, my lord, take long?

COURT OFFICIAL Oh, no, your Majesty. A matter of a few minutes only. Your Majesty makes the statutory declaration, and signs the Oath. That is all.

THE QUEEN Thank you.

(*The* COURT OFFICIAL *bows her toward the door.* THE QUEEN *turns.*)

THE QUEEN Good-bye, Mamma.

DUCHESS Am I not to come with you?

THE QUEEN Not now, Mamma. To meet my Privy Council I must go alone.

DUCHESS (*icily*) Very well.

(THE QUEEN *moves toward the doors, which the Attendants throw wide. 'Her Majesty the Queen' is announced. There is a sound of rising. The doors close again.*)

DUCHESS (*turning to* SIR JOHN CONROY) You see?

29

(*He comes towards her.*)

SIR JOHN Does your Highness intend to wait?

DUCHESS Yes. I must wait. That is my duty. Tell those two women that they can go outside.

> (SIR JOHN, *with courteous movement and gesture, fulfils the order. The two Ladies curtsy and retire.* SIR JOHN *and the* DUCHESS *are alone, except for the two Door-keepers — automata, who cannot be removed. The* DUCHESS *comes down the room, followed by* SIR JOHN, *and sinks to a settee.*)

DUCHESS Sir John! See how she has changed already! She is no longer the same person.

SIR JOHN (*extenuatingly*) At that one can hardly wonder, your Highness. It is a great change for her.

DUCHESS Yes; but why should she change to *me*?

SIR JOHN Just at first, perhaps, she feels strange to everybody. Presently she will come back to you, and be natural again.

DUCHESS No. My little Vicky has gone — for ever! I feel it. I am sure. Now I shall be alone always.

SIR JOHN But, Madam, to preside at the Council it was necessary that she should go without you.

DUCHESS (*clutching at hope*) Was that so? You say? You are sure? You are not deceiving me?

SIR JOHN I am quite sure, Madam. A State function: it would have been impossible — against all rules for it to have been otherwise.

DUCHESS (*returning to her grievance*) And she knew *that*, and did not tell me till she came — to the door!

SIR JOHN Perhaps she assumed that your Highness knew already.

DUCHESS Oh, Sir John, you are now trying to comfort me with words — inventions. But my own heart tells me! In there my Daughter is getting rid of me.

SIR JOHN Her Majesty is taking the Oath, Madam, before the members of the Council, and is receiving theirs of allegiance in return. It is all a formality — but necessary.

DUCHESS   Are her Uncles in there — too?

SIR JOHN   Undoubtedly, Madam. Everybody must be there who possibly can be. Their Royal Highnesses — the Lord Chancellor — the Prime Minister — and all others who hold office under the Crown.

DUCHESS   The Prime Minister? Ah! He hates me. So do her Uncles — all of them. Everyone there is my enemy. They are going to take her from me.

SIR JOHN   I think they will not succeed, Madam. Her Majesty, though young, has a will of her own.

DUCHESS   Oh! So *you* have found that out too?

SIR JOHN   Dear Madam, was it not always apparent?

DUCHESS   No! She concealed it from me — until to-day. I did not know that she ever wished to think differently from what *I* wished. Oh, and I have tried so hard to make her all that she should be! But now, there she is — without me — in the hands of my enemies, of those who all her life have been trying to steal her from me. You know how always I have defeated them, even when it was the King — yes, even the King! — because I had Parliament and the law behind me. I was her Guardian by law, and they could not take her from me. But now that is over; she is her own mistress; and if she goes from me herself, I can do nothing — nothing — nothing!

SIR JOHN   Do not distress yourself, dear Lady, unnecessarily. What you fear may never happen. The change will not be so great as you now make yourself imagine. Certain changes under the new circumstances — in things ceremonial and official — there will have to be; they are unavoidable. But whatever happens, Madam, you have a great position; and it is still yours . . . Also, dear Lady, your life is now your own; with many years yet to come, in which you will have leisure — and freedom. You will be less tied than you have been. Is that not something that *we* can look forward to?

DUCHESS   Oh, dear Sir John, you are very kind to me; and I will try to believe what you say. . . .

(*She breaks off, and sits listening.*)

Why does she not come back? Why have they not done with her? They are keeping her from me, her own mother!

SIR JOHN Ah, no, Madam. It is all over; for I can hear. The Council has risen. She will be with you again in a moment.

(*There is a pause. The* DUCHESS *rises in agitation, and moves away.*)

DUCHESS Ah! What is going to happen to me? Sir John, let me see her alone. And tell the women not to come back — just yet.

(*The stroke of an Official's wand from within gives the signal. The Attendants open the doors.* SIR JOHN *goes out.* THE QUEEN *enters and advances quietly towards the* DUCHESS.)

THE QUEEN Mamma, dear, how good of you to wait for me!

DUCHESS I could not go away! I could not! I was so anxious for you, my dear! Did all go well? Was everything done properly?

THE QUEEN Oh, quite, Mamma. Everyone has been very nice to me. They made things so easy — when I did not quite know what to do.

DUCHESS And what do you think of it all, now that you are Queen?

THE QUEEN Of course, at first, it was a little strange, Mamma. But I am sure that presently I shall get used to it. Taking the Crown Oath and receiving the formal homage of so many whom I already knew — including one of my Uncles — made it all very solemn and impressive. I wish you could have seen it, Mamma.

DUCHESS (*whom this speech has mollified*) Yes, if that had been possible . . . Well, I shall see you crowned, my dear. I shall be allowed to see that, shall I not?

THE QUEEN Why, yes, Mamma, of course!

DUCHESS But in there I was not allowed. No! Why?

(*Before* THE QUEEN *can answer, the* COURT OFFICIAL *has come through the door and again stands before her, waiting permission to speak. By a gesture it is accorded.*)

COURT OFFICIAL If it please your Majesty, His Majesty the King of Hanover and His Royal Highness the Duke of Sussex request permission for a short audience of your Majesty.

B

THE QUEEN Oh, yes. Ask them to come in. And tell the Attendants to go.

DUCHESS (*significantly*) Your Uncles! What do they want with you now?

(*The folding doors are fully opened to admit Royalty. As they close them again the Attendants retire within. The two Dukes enter, side by side. They are dressed in black, but, for the occasion of State which has brought them, they are wearing their Orders. Of all the Royal Dukes the* KING OF HANOVER *is the least well-favoured; beside him his quite plain brother, the* DUKE OF SUSSEX, *looks almost handsome. But they are both said to have 'the Royal manner', and are now on good behaviour. Whatever else may be said against them, they do not pull long faces, or pretend a grief they do not feel.*)

SUSSEX (*coming cordially to the point*) Very good, my dear, very good! Couldn't have done it better! Not if you'd been born to it!

THE QUEEN But, my dear Uncle, I was born to it, as you know.

SUSSEX Ah, yes; but a good many years to wait for it, hadn't you? Well, well! — made your old Uncle proud of you. Here's His Majesty, your Uncle Ernest, come to say the same thing.

THE QUEEN How very kind!

HANOVER Yes, Niece, it's going to be all right. You've got the trick of it. You came in just as if — well, just as if you were *me*! Of course, you haven't your poor Uncle George's style — a wonder he was! — but you don't need it, your own way's better. Stick to your own way, my dear, in all things. Don't let anyone —

THE QUEEN Uncle Ernest, Uncle Augustus, here is Mamma.

THE UNCLES (*in mixed greetings*) Ah, yes, to be sure. How do you do, Duchess? Good morning. Hope we see you well.

(*In response to their greetings, the* DUCHESS *curtsies silently. And the two Dukes, having been forced to recognize her presence, waste no more time on her.*)

SUSSEX Well, Victoria, my dear, circumstances have prevented me from seeing much of you till now. Hardly know each other, do we? Never kissed your Uncle yet, have you? Never! Circumstances — call 'em that — have prevented. Almost strangers, you and I. Not my fault, my dear, not my fault; nor my wish either. Now I hope we shall see more of each other — you being now your own mistress.

THE QUEEN I am sure, Uncle Augustus, I shall always be pleased to see you — at any time.

HANOVER I suppose you know, my dear — you heard your Uncle call me 'His Majesty' just now — that I have become King of Hanover — reigning sovereign, like yourself. 'Sire, my brother', you've got to call your old Uncle now, when we meet on ceremony. That's why I had to keep out of it just now; couldn't take the oath of allegiance to you, you know — being a reigning sovereign myself. 'Twouldn't have done. Well, you and I have divided the inheritance between us, and we shan't quarrel about it: kingdom's divided — honours equal. Your poor Uncle, King William, was the last to hold both. Perhaps it's better as it is now. What does England want with Hanover? Or Hanover with England, for that matter? I only came over to say good-bye to him. You didn't see him, did you? No. But he spoke of you — more than once. He was fond of you, my dear: said he hoped you'd know how to be your own mistress — without interference from anyone. And I hope you do.

THE QUEEN It's very kind of you, Uncle, to say so. But quite unnecessary. I hope that some day I may be able to come and visit you — in Hanover. And now, my dear Uncles, if you will excuse me; for I have much to do. But, please, before you go, there is just something I want to say to you as now representing the Family. I want, in your presence, to thank my dear Mamma for all that she has done for me in the past. I want to say that no one could have done more. I wish you both to know how very much I owe to her, and how grateful I feel.

(*This testimonial to the woman they detest puts the Uncles somewhat out of countenance. But between them they manage to say what, under the circumstances, they are obliged to say, since* THE QUEEN, *in her quiet mastery of the situation, has made it impossible for them to say otherwise.*)

HANOVER Ah, yes, yes! Very right and proper of you, I'm sure, and like a dutiful daughter. And I hope Her Royal Highness, your Mamma, appreciates it, as I am sure she ought to do.

SUSSEX Very handsome of you, my dear, very! You couldn't have said more, could you? Well, Ernest, now I think we'd better be going. And I hope you'll have a happy reign, my dear, and everything in the proper time to make the succession safe for others after you.

HANOVER Yes, Niece, you'll have to marry, and the sooner the better. Choose well! Good-bye.

(*They go together to the door. Then the* DUKE OF SUSSEX *returns and says a last kind word.*)

SUSSEX Don't worry about the funeral, my dear. We shall be there: but you won't be expected to go. 'Twouldn't be the thing. Ah, your poor Uncle! Now he's gone, only three of us are left. But there, there! Life doesn't last for ever: never did, never will! Good-bye.

THE QUEEN Good-bye, dear Uncle. Thank you so much for coming to-day.

SUSSEX Thank *you*, my dear. Thank you. It was a pleasure to see you do it. Good-bye, Duchess.

(*And, with a grunt at having to say good-bye to 'that woman', off he goes.*)

DUCHESS Those are your Uncles — two of them. Now you have *seen* them.

THE QUEEN Yes, Mamma.

DUCHESS What do you think of them?

THE QUEEN They were both very kind, Mamma.

DUCHESS Kind! Kind! Oh, take care of yourself, my child! Take care of yourself! Kiss me, Vicky! Kiss me! Do not ever forget what I have done for you!

THE QUEEN Mamma, dear, you are tired: you were up so early. Go and lie down!

DUCHESS And what are you going to do?

THE QUEEN I am going to write letters, Mamma.

DUCHESS Who to?

THE QUEEN To so many people. To my Uncle, King Leopold, for one.

DUCHESS Ah, yes! Write to *him*: tell him *everything*!

THE QUEEN I must also write to the poor Queen — Queen Adelaide, I mean. I am going to tell her that she must not leave Windsor till — till she wishes.

DUCHESS Then when do you mean going to Windsor yourself?

THE QUEEN Not for some time, Mamma. I have not yet decided. I shall first consult the Prime Minister.

DUCHESS It seems to me that, in your mind, you have arranged everything.

THE QUEEN Almost, Mamma; not quite. Now go and lie down and rest.

DUCHESS That is the first time, Victoria, that you have given an order to *me*.

THE QUEEN Mamma dear, you know that I only do it for your good.

DUCHESS *(turning away)* Oh, yes; it is for my good, I suppose. Oh, I am so tired — so tired of everything.

(She goes out, leaving the door open. Tentatively, one of the Ladies-in-Waiting enters and, after curtsying, stands to attention.)

THE QUEEN Ah, Lady Charlotte, will you, please, open those doors?

(LADY CHARLOTTE goes and throws wide the doors leading into the Council Chamber.)

Thank you. That will do. You may leave me.

(LADY CHARLOTTE curtsies and retires. THE QUEEN remains alone. She goes slowly towards the doors, enters, stands within the doorway, and looks round on the large empty chamber in which the first ceremonial event of her reign has taken place. She turns back and, recrossing the threshold, halts, and speaks.)

THE QUEEN So. Now I am Queen. And my reign has really begun . . . Poor Mamma!

A HEAVY CHANGE

1837

It is the first time that Leopold, King of the Belgians, has paid a visit to his niece, Queen Victoria, since her accession to the throne. THE KING *and his sister, the* DUCHESS OF KENT, *are together in one of the private apartments at Windsor.*

DUCHESS Has she said anything to *you*?

LEOPOLD No, we have not yet been alone together. I am here now to meet her, by appointment.

DUCHESS. Then I will go. She must not know that you have seen me. You have had my letters, and now I have told you everything . . . Oh, I am so unhappy!

LEOPOLD My dear sister, do not distress yourself. Now that I am here again, all will presently be well. As you know, Victoria has always listened to my advice in the past, and she will still do so, I am sure. Often she has even asked for it.

DUCHESS When did she last do that?

LEOPOLD I do not quite remember; but in reply to my last letter of advice, I was still her 'Dearest Uncle', and she thanked me most gratefully. I don't think that she cares for her other uncles as she does for me.

DUCHESS No, Leopold, that is true. Her other uncles I have tried that she shall not know. You know what they are . . . Well, if you think you can manage her, to you I leave it. Now I go.

(*As she goes to the door, one of the* QUEEN'S GENTLEMEN *enters, stands aside, and bows as she passes out.*)

GENTLEMAN Her Majesty bids me inform your Majesty that she has been unexpectedly detained by a visit from the Prime Minister. She begs your Majesty will excuse her for keeping your Majesty waiting.

LEOPOLD Pray tell Her Majesty that I beg her not to be concerned on my account: I am entirely at Her Majesty's disposal. Is the Baron Stockmar still in attendance?

GENTLEMAN He is here, your Majesty.

LEOPOLD Ask him to come in.

(*The* GENTLEMAN *retires.* THE KING, *with thoughtful self-impor-
tance, moves to the window, and stands looking out. Presently the*
BARON *enters.*)

Ah, Baron, I want you. I have just been talking to Her Highness,
the Duchess. What she tells me decides me to do as I had already
proposed to you. Things here just now are a little difficult, but
nothing to be alarmed about. It is only natural; Her Majesty is
new to her position. She needs the advice of someone she can
trust — someone of independent judgment — one whom I can trust
also. And so, as you have already, it seems, made yourself acceptable
to Her Majesty, I shall arrange that, when I leave, you will remain
here permanently.

STOCKMAR That, Sir, relieves me of a difficulty; for Her Majesty
has already indicated to me that she wishes me to remain — should
your Majesty be willing to spare me.

LEOPOLD (*not too well pleased*) Oh, indeed? Well, I think that she
should have consulted me first. However, it does not matter. It
shall be arranged . . . And now, Baron, about the marriage. When
do you think it will be advisable to make the first suggestion of what
we have in mind for her?

STOCKMAR If I may be allowed to advise, Sir, I would say — not
yet. Her Majesty is at present greatly enjoying her independence.
It is new to her, and she insists on having it. That, Sir, is where the
difficulty has been. Naturally Her Royal Highness the Duchess
finds it hard to — to adapt herself to so great a change.

LEOPOLD That is quite understandable. Nor would I wish Her
Majesty to remain too much under her mother's influence. It will
be quite sufficient if, on all matters of real importance, she continues to come to *me* for advice as she has done in the past. I believe
that she will.

STOCKMAR I trust, Sir, that she may.

LEOPOLD How much does she come to you for advice?

STOCKMAR For advice hardly at all, Sir. She asks me many

questions on matters of fact — etiquette, rules of procedure, her relations to Ministers, and such like. Also on events in history and in diplomacy, about which she has not yet informed herself. But for advice — no.

LEOPOLD   Still, Baron, if she asks for information on matters of diplomacy — recent diplomacy — advice may naturally follow — don't you think?

STOCKMAR   It *may*, Sir; but I have to be careful.

LEOPOLD   Indeed; dear me! . . . She has remarkable self-confidence in one so young.

STOCKMAR   She has indeed, Sir.

LEOPOLD   That may become a danger. She is, I understand, on very good terms with her present Ministers.

STOCKMAR   With her Prime Minister, Lord Melbourne, on very good terms, Sir.

LEOPOLD   She accepts his advice — readily, you think?

STOCKMAR   I fancy he is very tactful in his way of giving it, Sir. She sometimes tells me how *she* has advised *him*.

LEOPOLD   He's not treating *us* very well just now, Baron. The interests of Belgium are not receiving all the consideration they ought to receive.

STOCKMAR   No, Sir, I fear not.

LEOPOLD   Well, that is one of the things I am here for: I must see to it . . . And now about this marriage question; which of the two Princes do you think it is likely to be?

STOCKMAR   I gather, Sir, that she thinks Prince Albert the more handsome.

LEOPOLD   About that there can hardly be any doubt.

STOCKMAR   Of their two portraits, which came recently from Saxe Coburg, I have only seen her looking at one. If looks could decide the matter one might have good hopes; but for the present Her Majesty prefers freedom to marriage.

LEOPOLD   (*deeply meditative*) Ah, I see.

STOCKMAR But there is, Sir, a much more serious difficulty — elsewhere.

LEOPOLD Indeed. What?

STOCKMAR Lord Melbourne has somehow become informed of the matter; and is strongly opposed to it.

LEOPOLD Indeed? Why?

STOCKMAR On medical grounds, Sir; cousins — Coburg cousins — marrying.

LEOPOLD Ah, yes, that one can understand. But *that* can be got over.

STOCKMAR I'm not sure, Sir. It was indicated to me — in order perhaps that your Majesty should know — that if the proposal were pressed to an acceptance he might feel himself obliged to resign.

LEOPOLD Oh, indeed? Indeed? Well, in that case we *may* have to take Lord Melbourne into our confidence. (*significantly*) It might then still be Prince Albert.

STOCKMAR I suppose your Majesty knows that the Duke his father very much wishes it should be Prince Ernest.

LEOPOLD He would — naturally. Still, she must be given the choice.

STOCKMAR Yes, Sir.

LEOPOLD How would Melbourne take it — if he knew the facts?

STOCKMAR I don't know, Sir.

LEOPOLD Because — if he persists in opposing — he may have to be told.

STOCKMAR It would be a great risk, Sir.

LEOPOLD Yes . . . yes. So we must hope to avoid it. Still . . .

(*At this moment* THE QUEEN *enters.* STOCKMAR *stands back, and a moment later, at a look from* KING LEOPOLD, *bows himself out.*)

VICTORIA My dear uncle, I am so sorry to have kept you waiting. Had it not been that Lord Melbourne wished to consult me rather urgently, I should not have permitted such a thing to happen.

LEOPOLD My dear Victoria, no excuse is necessary. You are

now Queen, and affairs of State must necessarily come first. How nice it is to meet you again, for the first time, alone. We shall have much to say to each other. Tell me, my love, how do you like being Queen?

VICTORIA Dearest uncle, it pleases me very much; for with all the instruction and advice that you have given me in the past, I am really able now to understand things more than they expected me to; and when I find it necessary, I think I shall be able to manage my Ministers quite well.

LEOPOLD How do they treat you?

VICTORIA They are all very kind to me; nothing could be kinder.

LEOPOLD (*a little disapprovingly*) Kind?

VICTORIA Yes; but of course, they are also very respectful. You mustn't think that I allow them any familiarity, or to treat me as if they were my equals.

LEOPOLD That is quite right, Victoria. You must never forget your position.

VICTORIA I am sure, dear uncle, I never shall. You have trained me too well.

LEOPOLD There was also your Mother. You owe much of your good training to her.

VICTORIA Oh, yes; but that was different. Mama trained me as her child, and tried to keep me a child — too long, I think. But you trained me to be a Queen, and to think for myself, which now I always do; and Mama finds that a little difficult to understand.

LEOPOLD Just at first, perhaps. You must try to be kind to her, and patient.

VICTORIA I always am.

LEOPOLD Perhaps not quite so patient, my dear, as you might be.

VICTORIA Has she been complaining to you?

LEOPOLD (*cautiously*) Not complaining, no; you must not think that; but your poor Mama feels the change in her position. Until you became Queen, she had the sole care of you. You were everything to her. And now she feels, I think, that she has become almost nothing — that the Baroness Lehzen receives more of your confidence than she does.

VICTORIA Yes, Lehzen is now my Private Secretary. Mama could not possibly be that. So naturally Lehzen knows more of what I am doing every day than Mama does. Also I have to give Lehzen orders. I could not think of ordering Mama.

LEOPOLD Well, let us leave that for the present, though I think we shall have to come back to it . . . How do you get on with Lord Melbourne, your Prime Minister?

VICTORIA I could not possibly wish for a better. We have become quite friends, for I can really trust him. And he is so amusing: he makes everything quite interesting.

LEOPOLD He has the reputation of being somewhat lazy and careless. He does not always deal as promptly as is sometimes advisable with the questions which come to him to decide. For instance, there is that last matter about which I wrote to you — telling you of my desire for the renewal of the formal guarantee by the Powers of Belgian neutrality, now that Holland and Belgium have been separated. I had hoped that I should hear, before I came, what you were prepared to do in the matter.

VICTORIA That, my dear uncle, we have now quite decided. Lord Melbourne consulted me, and though I told him of your wishes, we neither of us thought what you proposed would be quite the best way of dealing with the matter.

LEOPOLD Indeed? What, pray, was your objection?

VICTORIA That, uncle, I would rather not discuss with you at present. The matter is now in Lord Melbourne's hands, and I shouldn't wonder if your Ministers have not already heard from him as to what we have decided.

LEOPOLD And can you not tell me, Victoria, what you have decided?

VICTORIA No, my dear uncle; I think, if you don't mind, that the matter should now be left to our Ministers. I am, of course, always glad to hear your opinion about — almost about everything, and so far as I can, after having had the advice of my Ministers, to meet your wishes if that is at all possible. But I am obliged, of course, to consider the interests of my own country first. The interests of a small country like Belgium cannot be allowed to weigh against those of my own country, which is so much greater, and to which I owe my first duty.

LEOPOLD I should not have supposed that there was any difference between the interests of our two countries, Victoria. The independence and well-being of Belgium are essential to the interests of Great Britain. I do not think that I have ever suggested anything, in the advice I have given you, which could in any way conflict with the best interests of the country over which you now rule.

VICTORIA I am quite sure, my dear uncle, that you would never have thought of such a thing for a moment; but though I have always been most grateful to you in the past for all your advice and instruction, I now have to think for myself — is it not so? And if, as sometimes may happen, we differ as to the best course to be taken, it is for me and my Ministers together to decide.

LEOPOLD Of course, Victoria, under the British Constitution, you cannot act without the advice of your Ministers; but I regret to find that now, for the first time, there should be any difference of opinion between you and myself as to what ought to be done. You know from experience that I never ask anything of you. I prefer remaining in the position of having rendered services without wanting any return for it but your affection.

VICTORIA Dearest uncle, I shall never have any doubt of your affection, nor must you have any doubt of mine. But in politics I must not let my feelings of affection have any influence whatever.

LEOPOLD Then, perhaps you will allow me to see Lord Melbourne, myself — and make my representations to him. . . .

VICTORIA Oh, no, my dear uncle, I do not think that will be possible; for the matter has now been decided. . . .

(*At this moment a* GENTLEMAN *enters, and stands waiting for permission to speak.*)

Yes?

GENTLEMAN May it please your Majesty, Lord Melbourne has

now returned, and begs that he may again have audience of your Majesty.

VICTORIA   Oh, my dear uncle, I am so sorry that I must leave you; but Lord Melbourne has come about a very important matter, on which he wants my advice, so I must not keep him waiting. (*To the* GENTLEMAN) Will you say to Lord Melbourne that I will be with him immediately?

(GENTLEMAN *retires*)

So now, dear uncle, you see I really must go; but I shall see you again as often and for as long as I can. Only please, during this very short time that you are here, don't let us talk too much on politics. There are so many other, and such much pleasanter things that I want to talk about. I shall want you, when we have time, to tell me all about Ernest and Albert. I am looking forward so much to seeing them both if a visit can be arranged. So now good-bye for the present.

(*She goes.* LEOPOLD *stands in moody meditation. He goes to the window and looks out, pursuing his lips and drumming upon the panes. The* DUCHESS OF KENT *enters.*)

DUCHESS   Well? You have seen her?

LEOPOLD   I have seen her.

DUCHESS   And you have talked to her?

LEOPOLD   Rather less than she has talked to *me*.

DUCHESS   What did she talk about?

LEOPOLD   I might almost say, mainly about herself.

DUCHESS   Ah; and what do you find?

LEOPOLD   She has changed . . . changed.

DUCHESS   You find that?

LEOPOLD   Yes. I find now not only that she has changed, but that we are in changed relations. Things are going to be difficult. I hadn't expected this.

DUCHESS   No? Then now you see what has happened to me also. You and I have become two *nobodies*. She belongs only to herself.

SUITABLE SUITORS

1838

THE QUEEN *is still in mourning but she does not mourn. Animated and happy, she sits listening to what, in earlier youth, she was never allowed to hear — the conversation of a gentleman of breeding, worldly, witty, and to a certain extent wise. This she thoroughly enjoys. And* LORD MELBOURNE, *her Prime Minister, enjoys talking to her. She is not clever; she cannot say clever things; but the mingled strain of artlessness and self-possession, of dignity and simplicity, which he finds in his Royal Mistress's character — a character which he is artfully moulding, not so much to his own ends as his own convenience — attracts and delights him. They are now on such intimate terms that* THE QUEEN, *when he comes for an audience, does not keep him long standing. They are seated now; and as an indication of their pleasant relations,* THE QUEEN *is going on with her woolwork.*

VICTORIA   How do you begin the day, Lord Melbourne?

MELBOURNE   Begin it, Ma'am?

VICTORIA   Yes. What do you do first — you, who have so many things to do in the day? I find it difficult to know myself where to begin.

MELBOURNE   Well, starting at the very beginning, Ma'am, I breakfast — if I may be allowed to say so — in bed.

VICTORIA   Oh! I should never have thought of that!

MELBOURNE   Try it, Ma'am, try it! It makes an invaluable break between sleeping and waking. Sleeping is one thing: it takes time. Waking is another: it takes more time. Working is another: and takes more time than all the others put together.

VICTORIA   And after breakfast, what then?

MELBOURNE   Well, let me think! . . . First, I rise, Ma'am. Over that I need not go into details.

VICTORIA   No?

47

MELBOURNE Or — would you like me to, Ma'am?

VICTORIA (*a little disappointed*) No, oh, no. You rise?

MELBOURNE I rise from my bed. Then I ride in the Park; when I come home I write. So I begin with the three R's.

VICTORIA But 'write' begins with a W.

MELBOURNE I am corrected, Ma'am. 'Write' *does* begin with a W. You Majesty is right, as usual.

VICTORIA (*laughing*) Oh! you are funny, Lord Melbourne.

MELBOURNE Funny?

VICTORIA So witty, I mean. You always say something amusing. Yes; please go on!

MELBOURNE That, Ma'am, is all the beginning of my day. When that is done, the day is half over.

VICTORIA And when do you say your prayers, Lord Melbourne?

MELBOURNE My prayers? Oh, I say them whenever I have time for them.

VICTORIA (*a little shocked*) But — Lord Melbourne!

MELBOURNE As often, and as long as possible.

VICTORIA That seems to me a little irregular.

MELBOURNE Did your Majesty never hear the story of the holy monk who had a Vision vouchsafed to him: a Vision of — well, of a very high character? And just as the Vision appeared, the chapel-bell began ringing. Duty — discipline — required the monk to leave the seraphic Vision and go into chapel with the rest: a function which, in these circumstances, was so like praying to the Vision behind its back, that it seemed almost foolish. It was a hard thing to do; but the monk did it. In great anguish of spirit, he left the Vision to itself, and went and did his duty. The service seemed intolerably long; he was dying to get back to his Vision. At last he was able to do so. The Vision was still there; and as he fell down before it in renewed adoration, the Vision made this remark: 'If you had not answered that bell, I should not have stayed' — or words to that effect. Ma'am, my position as Prime Minister is

very similar to that of the pious monk. I am constantly having to leave the vision to answer the *bell*.

VICTORIA   I thought, Lord Melbourne, that visions were rather superstitious things.

MELBOURNE   They are, Ma'am. In these days they are! Do your best to avoid them. They savour too much of Roman Catholicism. And so, Ma'am, with your Majesty's permission, let me, for the moment, leave visions and come down to facts, and the affairs of State. There are certain things which will have soon to be decided, and one or two in which delay — delay of preparation at all events — is inadvisable.

VICTORIA   Oh, yes; there are many, I'm sure.

MELBOURNE   There is one especially, which your Majesty graciously deigned to mention the other day. You then said, Ma'am — with a courage which I thought remarkable in one so young — 'Some day we must marry' . . . Has your Majesty given that matter any further thought?

VICTORIA   Oh, yes, Lord Melbourne, I have thought of it a great deal.

MELBOURNE   Is your Majesty prepared yet to take me into your Majesty's gracious confidence?

VICTORIA   You mean?

MELBOURNE   As to the possible recipient of so overwhelming an honour.

VICTORIA   Oh, I have not thought of any person — in particular. I mean, I have made no decision.

MELBOURNE   I am relieved to hear it, Ma'am. Then your Majesty has still an open mind!

VICTORIA   An open mind? Oh, *of course*, I shall make my own choice, Lord Melbourne.

MELBOURNE   Why, of course, Ma'am. I would not suggest otherwise, for a moment.

VICTORIA   But there are certain things as to which I am quite resolved.

MELBOURNE As for instance?

VICTORIA My marriage, Lord Melbourne, must be a marriage of affection.

MELBOURNE That, I am sure, Ma'am, can be arranged without difficulty.

VICTORIA Someone, I mean, whose character I can respect: one whom I can love and look up to.

MELBOURNE Look up to?

VICTORIA Yes, Lord Melbourne, it may sound strange to you; but I must have as my husband one whom I can eventually look up to — when I have trained him for the position he will have to occupy.

MELBOURNE Oh, quite so, quite so. I trust that such a person will be found. And as your Majesty has owned to an open mind on the subject, I have here with me a list of — of possibles.

VICTORIA Oh, Lord Melbourne, how interesting! ... How many?

MELBOURNE Well, at present, Ma'am, only five. But more are coming.

VICTORIA Coming?

MELBOURNE That is, I am making inquiries about them.

VICTORIA What kind of inquiries?

MELBOURNE All kinds of inquiries, Ma'am: my bounden duty. I would not wish to present your Majesty with one to whom there could be any possible objection.

VICTORIA And you have already found *five*! Lord Melbourne, how clever of you!

MELBOURNE 'Possibles', I said. The inquiry is still going on; I am making it now. After inquiry of your Majesty, possibly there will be only one left.

VICTORIA I would like to see your list, Lord Melbourne.

MELBOURNE If your Majesty will pardon me a moment. When I have fully explained the considerations which guided me in my selection, I will submit my list for your Majesty's judgment, and (as I hope) approval.

VICTORIA   I cannot approve all five!

MELBOURNE   Just as a preliminary, Ma'am, why not? From five in the running select your favourite — the winner.

VICTORIA   Perhaps I shall not choose one for a long time. But go on; I am quite interested and excited.

MELBOURNE   The conditions, Ma'am, for a suitable consort to your Majesty's throne are necessarily special and particular — I might even say, peculiar. He must, of course, be of Royal blood; on the other hand, he must not be the direct or likely heir of any foreign king or reigning prince.

VICTORIA   But why not, Lord Melbourne?

MELBOURNE   Political complications might arise, Ma'am. The crown of Hanover has passed from your Majesty to another, because of the law which limits the succession to males only: a circumstance which I regard as fortunate. We want no more crowns of Hanover; the country is better without them. To proceed, then: he must be a Prince of some Royal House, not too petty, not too important. We must avoid entangling alliances. He must also be of the Protestant faith.

VICTORIA   Oh, yes, *I couldn't* marry a Papist.

MELBOURNE   You could not, Ma'am. The Act of Settlement forbids it. He must be sufficiently young to be a suitable life-partner to your Majesty. He must know, or be capable of learning the English language; capable also of adapting himself to English customs, habits, and prejudices. The last is the most difficult of all, since the English have a prejudice against foreigners.

VICTORIA   But, Lord Melbourne, that makes it impossible!

MELBOURNE   No, Ma'am. It only rather restricts the choice. Someone must be found who, once naturalized, is able to share the prejudice. I've known it done. Your Majesty's cousin, Prince George of Cambridge, for instance, is rapidly acquiring a thoroughly British outlook. In another five years or so he will have learned to dislike foreigners as much as we do.

VICTORIA But do *you* dislike foreigners, Lord Melbourne?

MELBOURNE No, Ma'am, no: of course not! But sometimes, for political reasons, one has to pretend to.

VICTORIA Well, and what more?

MELBOURNE It would be well, Ma'am, if he had some means of his own; though they need not be large. Parliament will provide whatever addition is necessary. He must have presence suited to his station; also a certain amount of brain, but not too much. He must not expect to interfere in politics.

VICTORIA Indeed, no! I should never allow it.

MELBOURNE Finally he must have health, and a sound constitution; he must — that is to say — come of good stock. And that, Ma'am, has been our main difficulty. Good stock, in the Royal Families of Europe, is rare.

VICTORIA Please explain, for I don't quite understand. 'Good stock' — I thought that meant cattle.

MELBOURNE It does, Ma'am, in certain connections. But it also means — what comes from father to son. You find it referred to in the Second Commandment where we are told that the sins of the fathers are visited on the children: also their virtues. In certain Royal lines the sins and the virtues have been mixed; and one has to be careful that they shall not be more mixed. For that reason the marriage of Royal cousins is generally inadvisable.

VICTORIA Oh.

MELBOURNE Generally, I say. In the case of a certain branch of your Majesty's family connections it is unfortunately true in a rather special degree. For that reason, in the list I am about to submit, I have not included — though it was suggested to me — two of your Majesty's cousins, who might otherwise have been desirable candidates — their Royal Highnesses Prince Ernest and Prince Albert of Saxe-Coburg Gotha.

VICTORIA But they both looked quite strong and healthy when I last saw them two years ago.

MELBOURNE Apparently, Ma'am. But appearances are sometimes deceptive. It is, of course, a delicate — even a painful subject. But, acting under medical advice, and with a due sense of my responsibility, I have not included either of those young Princes in the list which I have now the honour to present to your Majesty.

(*He rises, and puts the list into her hand: hurriedly she glances down the names.*)

VICTORIA   Oh, but do I know any of them?

MELBOURNE   Your Majesty knows one of them very well.

VICTORIA   Oh — I didn't see. But Prince George is my cousin too.

MELBOURNE   By another branch, your Majesty. There is not there the same objection.

VICTORIA   Oh, but I couldn't marry my Cousin George! He is so — so —

MELBOURNE   Nobody wishes to decide your Majesty's choice. There are others.

VICTORIA   But, as I say, I don't know any of them.

MELBOURNE   That, Ma'am, can easily be remedied. You ask them to your Court in turn, saying nothing. And you let them go away again — saying nothing; or you *do* say something; and then — either they stay, or they come again.

VICTORIA   But it is for me to decide, is it not?

MELBOURNE   It is for your Majesty to decide. Your Majesty need not marry at all.

VICTORIA   Oh, but I must marry. Mama always said so.

MELBOURNE   So I have been told. But, in so important a matter, even devoted filial affection should not be allowed to influence your *choice*. I have merely indicated, Ma'am, that were any attempt to be made to influence your choice in a certain direction, that choice — for reasons already given, I should have to oppose.

VICTORIA   Lord Melbourne, I should not allow any opposition in a matter of that kind. It would not influence me for a moment.

MELBOURNE   No?

VICTORIA   Indeed, rather the other way.

MELBOURNE I see. I understand, Ma'am. I sympathize. I shall say no more. I will only commend the matter to your Majesty's good sense — and conscience.

VICTORIA Oh, how kind you always are to me, Lord Melbourne! What a lot you are teaching me!

MELBOURNE What a lot you are teaching *me*. I have served under older sovereigns — under two. But I have never served under one who listened to advice so wisely or so well.

VICTORIA (*rising*) Good-bye, Lord Melbourne. Will you keep the list, or shall I?

MELBOURNE By your leave, Ma'am; let what I have said be either remembered or forgotten. (*He tears the list and throws it into the fireplace.*) The choice must be your own.

VICTORIA Yes; but you haven't yet shown me — any portraits.

MELBOURNE Portraits, Ma'am? Why portraits?

VICTORIA I can't decide about anyone — till I know what they are like. It wouldn't be fair to them — or to me.

MELBOURNE But your Majesty can send for them, and see.

VICTORIA Oh, no. I'm not going to send for any, if I don't like the look of them.

MELBOURNE Portraits are sometimes deceptive, Ma'am.

VICTORIA Yes; I saw a portrait of my Cousin George of Cambridge the other day: quite handsome he looked.

MELBOURNE I can get their portraits, Ma'am, if you wish. But Court Painters, like Prime Ministers, know their duty; and they only do what is expected of them. If they can't do that, they have to go.

VICTORIA (*going toward a table, on which stands a framed portrait*) Here is a portrait that was sent to Mama, the other day — of my Cousin, Prince Albert.

MELBOURNE (*who has followed to the table*) Oh! Ah! Yes. H'm.

VICTORIA Surely *he must* have grown very handsome! It would not be possible for a Court Painter to imagine anyone like that.

MELBOURNE You never know, Ma'am, you never know.

Imagination sometimes goes a long way. Well, the list having gone, am I now to make a collection of portraits for your Majesty?

VICTORIA   Oh, no, Lord Melbourne. I wasn't speaking seriously when I said that.

MELBOURNE   No more was I, Ma'am. But I do ask your Majesty to *think* seriously. The future welfare of this country is now in this little hand.

(*He stoops and kisses it.*)

VICTORIA   Indeed, Lord Melbourne, I pay great attention to everything that you say. And I shall continue to take your advice, whenever I find it — possible. Good-bye.

(LORD MELBOURNE *bows himself out. She goes and takes up the portrait and kisses it.*)

Albert . . . Albert . . . Albert . . . will you marry me?

A STATE SECRET

1838

LORD MELBOURNE, *the Prime Minister, sits in his writing-room at Downing Street. With him is* MR. TUDOR, *British Minister at the Court of Saxe-Coburg Gotha, now on home leave. The Prime Minister lolls indolently at ease; so far the official report has not much interested him.* MR. TUDOR *sits upright in his chair, precise and respectful. He is much the younger man; but already he has been taken into the confidence of persons of importance; and is not without a certain sense of his own.*

MELBOURNE Yes? Well? What also have you to report?

TUDOR The Court of Saxe-Coburg is a little anxious, my Lord, because nothing has been said lately about the possible arrangement — of a marriage.

MELBOURNE (*his interest awakened*) Ah?

TUDOR The Court is anxious, my Lord, because the Princes are now of marriageable age; and it doesn't want to let good chances slip.

MELBOURNE Are any other brides in the market then?

TUDOR For His Royal Highness Prince Ernest there is the prospect of a very eligible offer. But a rumour of this other possibility has got about; and they won't make the offer if it is going to be refused.

MELBOURNE So they want the coast cleared for Prince Ernest, eh? What about Prince Albert?

TUDOR I have reason to believe that they would prefer it should be Prince Ernest.

MELBOURNE And I have reason — very grave reason — to prefer that it should be neither. Anyway, let Prince Ernest go. Tell 'em to give him away to anybody as quick as they like. That'll be one off my mind, at any rate.

TUDOR Your Lordship does not now favour the proposal, then?

MELBOURNE I never did. It was the Duchess with her damned interference. She seems to think this country was invented entirely for the benefit of her own family. 'Twas she made the match, as far as it could be made.

TUDOR Is Her Majesty greatly under the influence of Her Royal Highness the Duchess, my Lord?

MELBOURNE Not now; no, not now. But she is greatly under the influence of her own feelings. And it so happens that — before I could be there to prevent — the thing was done. She has seen both of them. Oh, yes; she'd have liked Prince Ernest well enough, if Prince Albert hadn't been there also.

TUDOR At Saxe-Coburg they do not wish it to be Prince Albert, my Lord.

MELBOURNE What they don't wish is not going to count. I'm afraid, I'm very much afraid she will go her own way in this matter. She's in love with him. She kisses his portrait, I'm told. And it's very serious — very serious indeed. Cousins of that stock marrying may be *fatal*.

TUDOR If your Lordship wishes to prevent the marriage with Prince Albert, it can be done quite easily.

MELBOURNE I've been trying all I know how. And it's God damn difficult. She shut me down — as if I were nobody. I've tried more than once.

TUDOR It need not be difficult, my Lord. You have merely to state certain facts, and — the match will be off.

MELBOURNE Well, now you do interest me exceedingly! Already morganatically married to some German wench, eh?

TUDOR Oh, no, no. Nothing of that sort. The Prince has a blameless character. The same cannot be said about his late mother, the Grand-Duchess.

MELBOURNE No, so I . . . His parents separated over something, I believe.

TUDOR They separated when the Prince was five years old. She

went to live in Paris; he never saw her again. The *cause* of the separation was of *more* than five years' standing, my Lord. (*This is said with meaning.*)

MELBOURNE (*rising, with sharp interest*) Heh? . . . You don't say so!

TUDOR After five years the parties forgot to be prudent: the thing got about.

MELBOURNE (*sitting down*) Who was — the *other* party?

TUDOR One of the Court Chamberlains: a very charming and accomplished person; but a commoner, and of Jewish extraction.

MELBOURNE (*pondering deeply*) Dear me! Dear me! . . . *Healthy?*

TUDOR Oh, quite . . . You have only to tell Her Majesty that her cousin, Prince Albert, is not quite so much her cousin as she imagines, and I apprehend that you will have no further difficulty.

MELBOURNE (*following his own line of thought*) The *Mother* was healthy, was she not?

TUDOR Well, she produced two fine boys. But *Prince Albert is the finer.*

MELBOURNE Then only Prince Ernest is really related?

TUDOR That is so.

MELBOURNE And the Duke can't be the father of Prince Albert?

TUDOR Unfortunately, no.

MELBOURNE You are sure?

TUDOR I have confidentially been shown documents which put the matter beyond dispute. In the deed of separation the facts were fully admitted.

MELBOURNE Why were you shown them?

TUDOR I imagine, my Lord, because at Saxe-Coburg there is a wish that Prince Ernest should be Her Majesty's choice — not Prince Albert.

MELBOURNE (*rising, in a tone of deep satisfaction*) Ah! . . . Mr. Tudor, I am enormously obliged to you — *enormously* obliged to you. Your information is a godsend! And — if my term of office holds for a while, as I think it will — I can promise you promotion.

The next suitable vacancy will be yours. Understand: you have done your country a great service.

TUDOR (*who has risen at the same time as his chief*) My Lord, I thank you.

MELBOURNE I thank *you*! Good-bye.

(MR. TUDOR *bows over his hand with deep respect, and goes.* MELBOURNE *rings, and walks about excitedly. A* SECRETARY *enters.*)

MELBOURNE Has Lord Conyngham waited?

SECRETARY Yes, my Lord.

MELBOURNE Then ask his Lordship to be good enough to come in.

(*The* SECRETARY *goes.* MELBOURNE *sits down, writes, gets up again, rubs his hands. He is as happy as a schoolboy. Enter* LORD CONYNGHAM.)

MELBOURNE Conyngham, we've done the trick! We are going to marry her to Prince Albert.

CONYNGHAM (*aghast*) Good Heavens! You don't say so! ... But —

MELBOURNE (*going up to him, and speaking with an intensity of significance which at last has its effect*) It's all right! ... It's all right! ... *It's all right!*

CONYNGHAM But, my dear Mel, what has made it — 'all right', as you say?

MELBOURNE *Human nature.*

(*And at last the* LORD CHAMBERLAIN *comprehends.*)

CONYNGHAM Well! It seems almost like — Divine Intervention.

MELBOURNE It was, Conyngham, it was! It isn't only *marriages* that are made in Heaven. Liaisons are made there too. Thank God!

STRAINED RELATIONS

1838

The DUCHESS OF KENT *sits in her old apartment in Kensington Palace, to which new splendours have recently been added. Before her stands* LADY CHARLOTTE, *one of her Maids of Honour.*

DUCHESS So; she said you were to go? What did you say?

LADY CHARLOTTE Madam, I only said that my appointment was to the Household of your Royal Highness.

DUCHESS Ah! You said that! Good! And she — what?

LADY CHARLOTTE She said that, when your Royal Highness had a separate household of your own, there would be no further objection.

DUCHESS 'Separate!' ... 'Separate!' She has not yet said that to *me*; but she has meant it. It has been coming, from the first day: her own bed, her own room — now it is her own house. Presently it will be her own country that I am not to share! (*Enter* VICTORIA.) So! You are sending me away!

VICTORIA Mama!

DUCHESS You are turning your own Mother out of doors.

VICTORIA Lady Charlotte, go, please!

DUCHESS Why is she to go? She is mine: she is not yours.

(*But without further word, the look of direct authority has been sufficient.* LADY CHARLOTTE *disappears.*)

VICTORIA Mama, I wish you would not speak to me like that before — servants.

DUCHESS Servants? Lady Charlotte is my friend, one of the few I have left.

VICTORIA You pay her for her service.

DUCHESS. *You* are paid for *your service* too — the country pays you. Does that give it the right to dismiss you at a week's notice?

VICTORIA   Mama dear, don't be foolish.

DUCHESS   Oh, what has happened to you? You are no longer the same!

VICTORIA   How can you expect me to be? I belong now to myself. I find that a great change.

DUCHESS   And who made you be — yourself? What had you done *for yourself*, till you got rid of me?

VICTORIA   Very little, almost nothing. For eighteen years I was not even allowed to go downstairs without somebody to hold my hand. But I did it sometimes, when no one was looking.

DUCHESS   Behind my back?

VICTORIA   Yes. I would look out from the room. If there was a servant-in-waiting, I would send them on an errand. Then — when I was quite sure that no one could see — I would run down — down and up again, as fast as I could go. That was about my only chance of doing anything, *for* myself, by myself.

DUCHESS   Then you were deceitful.

VICTORIA   Had you asked me, I should have told you. I have never told you an untruth, Mama; and I am not going to begin now.

DUCHESS   Then now tell me the truth — quick! Do you any longer love me?

VICTORIA   Of course I love you, Mama.

DUCHESS   Though you take from me everything that is mine.

VICTORIA   On the contrary, dear Mama. I am going to give you something more than you have ever had before. Often now I have to leave you alone.

DUCHESS   Yes.

VICTORIA   But not so much alone, in one sense, as you would like to be. You and Lehzen do not get on well together.

DUCHESS   We do *not*. Why do you keep her? She was only your governess. Send Lehzen away.

VICTORIA   No, Mama.

DUCHESS 'No, Mama!' 'No, Mama!' It is always 'No, Mama', now to everything I ask you.

VICTORIA When you said you did not wish to go to Windsor last week, did I make you go?

DUCHESS No, but you only put it off. I do not like Windsor. It reminds me of your Uncle too much. It was there that he insulted me before everybody.

VICTORIA You need not go to Windsor now, unless you like, Mama.

DUCHESS Need not go? If you go to Windsor, I must.

VICTORIA No, Mama. It is not necessary now. Should I need you, I can send for you.

DUCHESS But — you are not going to Windsor without *me*! It would be in all the papers.

VICTORIA I want you to have a change, Mama. It will do you good; and I am sure that, when you have tried it, you will like it. I have given directions that in future you are to have your own suite of apartments at Buckingham Palace, with a separate service of your own. Next week, when I go to Windsor, it will be ready for you.

DUCHESS I do not like Buckingham Palace. I am not going there ... I say that I am not going there ... Do you hear me? I am not going to Buckingham Palace, I am going to Windsor.

VICTORIA You are mistaken, Mama dear. You are not going to Windsor, for I do not invite you. I will do so later. When Ernest and Albert pay their promised visit, it will, of course, be necessary that you should be there.

DUCHESS Then I will not come!

VICTORIA I don't think we need discuss the matter any further: the date is not yet fixed. And now, Mama, about Lady Charlotte; for I see that she has been speaking to you. When you have a Household of your own, I shall not interfere. If you wish then to have Lady Charlotte as one of your Maids of Honour, she can come back to you again. Here, for reasons with which I need not trouble you, I do not wish her to remain.

C

DUCHESS So!

VICTORIA And if you stayed with me, Mama, there would have to be *other* changes.

DUCHESS What do you mean?

VICTORIA I would rather not say. I hope that, in the short time you are still with me, it may not be necessary.

DUCHESS Oh, why is there always now this — this opposition? This *battle*? It never happened before.

VICTORIA Often, Mama. But *then* you always got your way. If it is painful to you now when I decide things for myself, think how painful it used to be to me, when I was never allowed to.

DUCHESS You throw my training of you back into my teeth, eh? You would have liked better to be with those wicked Uncles of yours, with their wine, and their women, and all!

VICTORIA Mama, don't forget yourself.

DUCHESS Forget myself!

(*Enter* LEHZEN.)

VICTORIA Ah, Lehzen dear, is it already time for me to come?

DUCHESS Let that woman go! I have not said yet all that I want to say!

VICTORIA Good-bye, Mama.

DUCHESS Victoria, I am your Mother, and I command you to stay!

(*But* VICTORIA *and* LEHZEN *have gone. The* DUCHESS *sits down to weep.*)

DUCHESS To think that this should have happened to me, of all people!

(*Enter* SIR JOHN CONROY.)

CONROY Dear Lady, what is the matter?

DUCHESS My daughter is the matter.

CONROY I met Her Majesty just now, with the Baroness.

DUCHESS Did she say nothing?

CONROY   Nothing.

DUCHESS   Did she look at you?

CONROY   Yes: she looked at me.

DUCHESS   You bowed: did she return it?

CONROY   Hardly.

DUCHESS   You are going to be the next — if she can manage it. But I shall not let it be. No; she shall not send you away — my friend.

CONROY   What has happened?

DUCHESS   To-day she takes from me one of my friends. Lady Charlotte is to go. Yesterday I was not to dress myself as I liked.

CONROY   Not dress?

DUCHESS   No! . . . I had my dressmaker there. I was going to leave off some of all this stuff and nonsense which I am wearing for a man that hated and insulted me. She said the dates for change of mourning were all in the Court Circular, and must be obeyed. And when I asked her if I was expected to consult the Court Circular, she said yes, as long as I stayed at the Court; which was almost like telling me to go away. And when I asked was she still in deep mourning for having become Queen, she said, 'Don't talk nonsense, Mama dear!' That — to *me*! Whenever she has anything unkind to say to me now, she puts 'Mama dear' at the end of it. I always made her say it when I punished her for anything. Now she says it to punish *me*.

CONROY   Why do you still stay with her? Aren't you free now to go where you like?

DUCHESS   Oh, how can I go away from my own life? She was everything to me. And now to her I am nothing! There is only one thing now left me to work and hope for. When that is done I shall just go away to my own country — and die.

CONROY   What is that, dear Lady?

DUCHESS   Just to see her married to Albert or Ernest. I planned it from the day she was born. But I'm beginning to be afraid even that won't happen now. Oh, what a miserable woman I am! And I thought I was going to be so happy!

CONROY   Dear Lady, don't make me feel that I am useless.

DUCHESS   You? What can you do? She won't take advice from *anybody* now, except that wicked Melbourne. And he hates me. It is all *his* doing. She could not have changed to me like that, unless someone had come between.

CONROY (*embracing her*)   My dear Lady, and mistress!

DUCHESS   Oh, my friend! I am so utterly alone!

CONROY   Alone? No: not while you have *me*.

DUCHESS   Oh, yes, I have *you*. But if she knew — or even guessed — it would be all over. She has no pity for anyone. Human nature means nothing to her — nothing!

CONROY (*renewing his embrace*)   While to us it means so much! Everything.

(*Enter* VICTORIA. *They break apart.*)

DUCHESS   I thought you were going out with Lehzen.

VICTORIA (*coldly*)   Have I returned sooner than you expected, Mama?

DUCHESS   Oh, it does not matter.

VICTORIA   No? (SIR JOHN, *meanwhile, is making for the door.*) Do not go, Sir John. I have something I wish to say. I am making certain alterations in the arrangements of my Household. You have been told of them, perhaps, and were taking your leave of Her Royal Highness when I came in. As I do not wish that there should be any delay in the matter, let it be so. You will see the Comptroller before you go. I have given directions that a solatium shall be paid to you in recognition of your past services. You will leave to-day.

DUCHESS   You are sending away my friend?

VICTORIA   I did not know he was your friend, Mama.

DUCHESS   You shall not! This is unheard-of. It is monstrous!

VICTORIA   No, Mama; not monstrous, only wise.

DUCHESS   I will not allow it! I will not allow it! If he goes, you kill me.

VICTORIA   Mama! Sir John Conroy, will you retire?

DUCHESS Do not! Do not move! (*She rushes to the central door and stands barring it.*) He shall not go!

(*Undiverted, the* QUEEN *points quietly to another door, which has no tragic figure standing before it.*)

VICTORIA *That* door, Sir John.

(*Such perfect common sense commands the situation. Without hesitation he goes.*)

DUCHESS (*coming away from the door, her defence of it now useless*) Oh, you — you — you, that was once my little daughter! That I taught to be so good!

VICTORIA You, my Mother, that I was taught to think so good.

DUCHESS What do you mean? What do you say?

VICTORIA Nothing — that needs repeating.

DUCHESS Oh, you have no heart in you! You are harder than a stone wall. If you can no longer respect me — have you no pity?

VICTORIA Pity?

DUCHESS Yes; what is my life without you? What has my life been for? Why did your Father and I marry? For you to be born. He did not love me: I did not love him. It was for *you*. No, *he* did not do it for *you*. *He* wanted a son. When you came, he was disappointed. But I — I was not. He died, and you were everything to me. And ever since, I have been alone — *except for you*. Then you became Queen, and you are mine no longer; all at once you are your own, and I am *nothing*! And I am to live without love, and to have no friend? You see a little love offered to me — nothing wrong — just friendship, kindness, and you take it away from me, you drive him away. But he shall come back to me — he shall come back!

VICTORIA Mama dear, when you have a Household of your own, you will have in it whoever you like. I said so before; if it will be any comfort to you, I say it again. I have had to send Sir John Conroy away because here, it seems to me, he does not know his place. What his place is likely to be in the future, when the matter is in your own hands, I see only too clearly.

DUCHESS Victoria, you forget yourself!

VICTORIA   No, Mama; the forgetfulness is yours.

DUCHESS   I forget *nothing!*

VICTORIA   Then, please to remember, Mama dear, that you are now my subject.

DUCHESS   (*hardly believing her ears*)   Your *what?*

VICTORIA   If you wish me to repeat the word, I will. All my duty of obedience to you is over. It is now rather the other way.

DUCHESS   Oh! Oh! This is too much! — This to be the end of all my care of you! Have I become the mother of a revolting daughter?

VICTORIA   Of a reigning Queen, Mama.

(*She seats herself at the writing-table.*)

I am going to write some letters now, Mama; and I would prefer to be alone. I am going to invite Ernest and Albert to come and stay at Windsor early next month; and I shall want you to be there, so please make no other engagements.

DUCHESS   (*to herself*)   Ernest! Albert! Ah, then I am not quite dead yet. So you are writing to them? Very well. My love to both of them — especially to Albert.

(*She goes out. A* FOOTMAN *enters.*)

FOOTMAN   If it please your Majesty, Lord Melbourne asks if he may see your Majesty.

VICTORIA   Ask Lord Melbourne to come in.

(*She continues writing, till* MELBOURNE *enters. Then goes to meet him.*)

Dear Lord Melbourne, I am so pleased to see you.

MELBOURNE   That is kind of you, Ma'am: but your Majesty is always kind. I also am pleased — more pleased even than usual — to see your Majesty; for I have come to inform your Majesty of a happy circumstance.

VICTORIA   Yes?

MELBOURNE   In a matter where I feared we were going to differ somewhat seriously, we now see eye to eye.

VICTORIA   About what, Lord Melbourne?

MELBOURNE As regards your Majesty's proposed marriage —

VICTORIA But, Lord Melbourne, I have not proposed marriage to anyone.

MELBOURNE Matrimonial intentions, then, let me say — (*Very respectfully he takes up the portrait of* PRINCE ALBERT *and looks at it.*) I now withdraw all opposition. In fact I cordially agree. I think your Majesty's choice is excellent. In your hands the future welfare of the country is safe.

VICTORIA Oh, that is very kind of you, Lord Melbourne; and I am glad to hear it. But I feel bound to tell you that, even had you *not* agreed, it would have made no difference at all.

MELBOURNE No, Ma'am. The facts being what they are, it *would* have made no difference at all. Not the least!

VICTORIA I wanted you to know that, Lord Melbourne.

MELBOURNE (*bowing acknowledgment*) And the Prince comes — when, Ma'am?

VICTORIA Next month, I hope.

MELBOURNE Next month, let us all hope! And what, Ma'am, does Her Royal Highness the Duchess think about it?

VICTORIA Mama will be pleased, I'm sure.

(*She takes the portrait from his hand and kisses it. But — she does not know — the facts!*)

MELBOURNE 'Mama' ought to be very pleased, indeed — with such a daughter! So they married and lived happily ever after. And the world said —

VICTORIA Oh, Lord Melbourne, you are funny!

MELBOURNE Your Majesty is right as usual. The world said 'Oh, Lord Melbourne, you are funny!'

THE BED-CHAMBER PLOT

In the room at Buckingham Palace where she receives her Ministers,
THE QUEEN *sits writing: and the zest with which she does it indicates
that something is afoot of more than ordinary importance. In the
background stands the* BARONESS LEHZEN, *once the Queen's governess, now her Private Secretary; and though she stands at a respectful
remove, awaiting orders, there is just a suggestion that this guardian
angel of Her Majesty's youth has retained in her new position
something of the directing authority which she exercised of old.*
THE QUEEN *signs her letter, places it in an envelope, directs it,
seals it with a determined gesture, and then without turn of head
summons her secretary to her side.*

THE QUEEN Lehzen . . . (*she waits for* LEHZEN *to come*) See that this
letter goes to Sir Robert Peel — at once.

(LEHZEN *takes the letter, rings a hand-bell, and moving half-way
to the door, stands waiting. At the ringing of the bell,* THE QUEEN,
*about to extinguish the taper on her writing-desk, pauses for a
moment and looks at her beloved* LEHZEN *a little critically. A*
GENTLEMAN *in attendance enters.*)

LEHZEN (*reproducing the commanding air of Majesty*) See that this
letter goes to Sir Robert Peel — at once.

(*The* GENTLEMAN *takes the letter, bows, and retires. Meanwhile*
THE QUEEN *has put out the taper, and now sits, a little on her dignity,
waiting to say something.*)

THE QUEEN I think you should have *taken* it, Lehzen.

LEHZEN (*also upon her dignity at finding her self corrected*) Did your
Majesty not wish to hear your orders given?

THE QUEEN Had I meant you to ring, Lehzen, I should have said
so. (*And then, seeing her dear* LEHZEN's *look of annoyance*) Oh, but it
doesn't matter. I'm so worried, Lehzen dear. It *is* so difficult
having to decide — though I *have* decided — when one is all alone,
as I am now.

LEHZEN Not alone, your Majesty.

THE QUEEN I mean, without anyone to advise me, now that dear Lord Melbourne has gone. Though this morning he comes once again, just to say good-bye. And I shall tell him everything. Those wicked Tories are only doing this to annoy me. They are just trying it on. Take away all my Ladies, indeed; I shouldn't think of it! And give me others of their own choosing, I suppose, whom I don't even know. They think they can make me forget that I am Queen.

LEHZEN They will find their mistake, Ma'am.

THE QUEEN Yes; when Sir Robert Peel gets my letter he will find that I know my place in the Constitution better than he knows his. Queen Anne didn't give up her Ladies to please her Ministers, so why should I?

LEHZEN No, Ma'am. Nor would Queen Elizabeth have given up either her Ladies *or* her Gentlemen to please anybody. No one would so much as have dared to think of it. These English have to be taught what they have forgotten, that a Queen is the same as a King. Your Majesty from me has learned history. And now — for them again — you *make* history. And in this — your Majesty shall have the last word.

THE QUEEN Yes, Lehzen; I am not going to give in to anybody.

(*A* GENTLEMAN *enters and bows.*)

GENTLEMAN If it please your Majesty, Lord Melbourne is in attendance to know whether it is your Majesty's pleasure to receive him.

THE QUEEN Oh, yes. Ask Lord Melbourne to come in. (*The* GENTLEMAN *bows and retires.*) And now, Lehzen, you may leave me. But as soon as Lord Melbourne has gone I shall want you again.

(*The* GENTLEMAN *returns, accompanied by* LORD MELBOURNE.)

GENTLEMAN Please, your Majesty — Lord Melbourne.

(*As* LORD MELBOURNE *enters,* LEHZEN *retires, the* GENTLEMAN *follows.* THE QUEEN *rises and gives* LORD MELBOURNE *her hand. He bows and kisses it.*)

THE QUEEN Oh, Lord Melbourne, I am so glad you have come!

MELBOURNE For the last time, Ma'am, I fear.

THE QUEEN Oh, no; please, don't say that. If it were true I couldn't bear it.

MELBOURNE For the present, at any rate.

(THE QUEEN, *having seated herself, motions him to sit down also.*) I had your Majesty's gracious message last night telling me that Sir Robert Peel has been able to form his Ministry. I trust that gives your Majesty satisfaction?

THE QUEEN Indeed, no, Lord Melbourne; far from it. Sir Robert Peel has made a demand which it is quite impossible for me to accept. He requires me to change my Ladies.

MELBOURNE Change them, Ma'am; in what way?

THE QUEEN For others, about whom I know nothing — not even their names yet, for when he gave me the list I refused to look at them. He tells me that with a new Ministry I must have new Ladies also — of the same Party. Lord Melbourne, did you ever hear of such a thing?

MELBOURNE I'm not sure that I ever did, Ma'am. Queens in this country are rare events; and I am no historian.

THE QUEEN But Queens, in relation to their Ministers, are just the same as Kings. Did my uncle, King George, change *his* Ladies, when there was a change of Ministry?

MELBOURNE He did not, Ma'am; not when there was a change of Ministry.

THE QUEEN Then neither shall I.

MELBOURNE But he did, Ma'am, change his Ladies — when he chose.

THE QUEEN And I shall change mine, when *I* choose, and not before . . . But tell me, Lord Melbourne, why did *he* change his Ladies at all?

MELBOURNE He liked them to be fat, Ma'am. When they began to grow thin, their Court-service was over.

THE QUEEN How very funny!

MELBOURNE (*with judicious humour*) Yes, Ma'am, it was — funny.

THE QUEEN (*made wise by his tone*) Oh, now I begin to understand. You mean that my Uncle George didn't *have* Ladies — not of *my* sort?

MELBOURNE No, Ma'am, not of your sort — not your sort at all. In fact — if I may be permitted to say so — a *sort* which, at your Majesty's Court, would now be sought in vain.

THE QUEEN Oh, my dear Lord Melbourne, what amusing things you do say! Even when things are most annoying, you always manage to put me in a good temper again.

MELBOURNE A most invaluable gift, Ma'am, for a Crown's adviser. For when Kings lose their tempers they generally do foolish things.

THE QUEEN And Queens also?

MELBOURNE Queens not always, Ma'am: that is where their special value comes in. Queen Elizabeth knew how to lose her temper for political reasons, with excellent effect.

THE QUEEN I don't like Queen Elizabeth. I never did. She was so deceitful.

MELBOURNE She had to be, Ma'am; had she not been, she would have been assassinated more times than once.

THE QUEEN You can't be assassinated more than once, Lord Melbourne.

MELBOURNE *She* could have been, Ma'am. She was a cat with nine lives. I am sometimes inclined to think that she really was assassinated eight times, and concealed it from history while continuing to live out her ninth.

THE QUEEN She put to death my ancestress Mary Stuart. And most wrong of her it was.

MELBOURNE She did, Ma'am; it was a neck-and-neck race which head had to go; and she got in first.

THE QUEEN Yes, but all the same the Stuarts got in afterwards.

MELBOURNE They did, Ma'am; and a nice troublesome lot they were.

THE QUEEN (*correctively*) I am a Stuart, Lord Melbourne.

MELBOURNE You are, indeed, Ma'am; and now you are making yourself troublesome too — in the right quarter. (*He chuckles.*) As a matter of fact I'd heard all about it, before I came to see your Majesty. Sir Robert Peel told me himself.

THE QUEEN I don't like Sir Robert Peel, Lord Melbourne.

MELBOURNE There's no reason why your Majesty should.

THE QUEEN But isn't it better to have a Prime Minister one can like?

MELBOURNE Perhaps it is, Ma'am. Your Majesty will have to cultivate a taste in Prime Ministers before things are over: a taste which will have to vary.

THE QUEEN I don't want to do that — yet.

MELBOURNE And that unfortunately is where your Majesty and your Majesty's faithful Commons differ. They want you to like someone else — not me.

THE QUEEN Well, that I shall decide for myself.

MELBOURNE Quite right, Ma'am. Decide well, and don't let me or anyone else interfere.

THE QUEEN If I had my wish, Lord Melbourne, I wouldn't make any change at all. Never. So long as you have my confidence, isn't that enough?

MELBOURNE Not under the British Constitution, Ma'am.

THE QUEEN But is there any law against it? *I* don't know of any.

MELBOURNE Only the unwritten law, Ma'am. The law of the British Constitution is not written on tables of stone; but on the fleshly tablets of the heart of an occasionally rebellious people. That's where we've had trouble with our Kings in the past, and shall have it again, I don't doubt. When it's the letter versus the spirit — and when the letter's not written down — the spirit generally wins. Yes; confidence or no confidence, Ministers have to go, and Ministers have to come.

THE QUEEN If I were to marry one of my Prime Ministers, then they couldn't change him, however much they wanted to. Suppose I did that!

MELBOURNE If that suggestion, Ma'am, is personally addressed, I feel bound to say that neither the British Constitution nor my own would stand it.

THE QUEEN (*laughing*) Oh, my dear Lord Melbourne, did you really think I meant that?

MELBOURNE No, Ma'am, no; I wouldn't be such a fool. It was only a joke — in rather bad taste, I'm afraid. And now, Ma'am, as this is perhaps the last time that I am here in my official capacity, may I ask what your Majesty has finally decided to do?

THE QUEEN I am not going to part from one of my Ladies — *not one*. Is there any reason why I should? I never talk to them about politics.

MELBOURNE About politics, no, Ma'am. But what about persons? It might influence your Majesty, if you heard one of them saying all the things that they might say, about *me* — in the past, you know.

THE QUEEN I shouldn't allow it, Lord Melbourne. Not for one moment.

MELBOURNE Very good of your Majesty to say so. But some of your present Ladies, being of my Party, don't like Sir Robert Peel any more than you do. And Sir Robert Peel knows it. That's what he's afraid of.

THE QUEEN Then it is very weak and foolish of him to have any such idea; and shows a bad conscience, I think. I am very careful how I form my judgment about anybody; and if Sir Robert Peel deserves my confidence, I shall give it him, even if I don't quite like him. In public affairs I don't allow personal feelings to influence me in the slightest degree. (*At this* LORD MELBOURNE *gives a surprised cough.*) But he must understand once and for all that though I am very young and inexperienced as yet, I do mean to be Queen.

MELBOURNE H'm; yes, quite so. And if I may be allowed to say so, your Majesty already is — every inch — a Queen.

THE QUEEN Your saying it, Lord Melbourne, makes me hope that it is true.

MELBOURNE And that, Ma'am, suggests to my mind — a riddle.

THE QUEEN   A riddle?

MELBOURNE   Which I have just made, but to which I don't know the answer.

THE QUEEN   But a riddle must have an answer.

MELBOURNE   Then perhaps your Majesty can answer it. The riddle is this — if every inch is a Queen, what is a foot?

THE QUEEN   I don't understand?

MELBOURNE   There are twelve inches in a foot. If every inch is a Queen, how much is the foot, when the Queen puts the foot down? H'm?

THE QUEEN   Are you making fun of me, Lord Melbourne?

MELBOURNE   No, Ma'am; not at all. I am only wondering. This United Kingdom of Great Britain and Ireland is not an Empire *yet*; but under your Majesty's foot it may become one. But as an old man, speaking to a very young sovereign, whom he loves almost like a daughter — may I just say — Go slow; only one foot at a time. That will be enough.

THE QUEEN   Dear Lord Melbourne, whenever I am in any doubt, I shall always come to you for advice.

MELBOURNE   When you have a change of Ministry, Ma'am, that will not always be advisable — or even possible.

THE QUEEN   But when I ask for advice, will you not give it me?

MELBOURNE   Within limits, Ma'am. Under Party government your Majesty must not receive advice from the other side on matters of politics.

THE QUEEN   But surely, my Privy Council contains members of all Parties. And if so, have I not the right to consult them whenever I wish?

MELBOURNE   Yes, Ma'am; in theory you have. But your Majesty's Privy Council is only called into consultation when there is nothing to consult about — or nothing controversial. When you came to the throne; when you marry; and when you die, are the only usual occasions for the summoning of your Majesty's Privy Council. You have already had *one*. I hope soon that you will have another. The third one your Majesty need not begin to think about for many long years. Indeed, there is no occasion for you ever to think about it, as it will be called without your ...

(*A* GENTLEMAN *enters:* LORD MELBOURNE *stops short.*)

GENTLEMAN   May it please your Majesty, Sir Robert Peel begs audience of your Majesty.

MELBOURNE (*in an undertone to the Queen*) That means I must go. Meeting here would be awkward.

THE QUEEN   Will you say to Sir Robert Peel that I will see him presently.

(*The* GENTLEMAN *bows and retires.*)

Oh, dear! I do wish you could stay to advise me. This is going to be a most unpleasant business. But I don't mean to give way — *not one inch!*

MELBOURNE   No, Ma'am, no; you don't look like it. But if you ask for my advice, let me say again — only one foot at a time; and a short foot would be the better. Well, now you've got to turn me out.

THE QUEEN (*rising*) Good-bye, dear Lord Melbourne, good-bye. But this is *not* going to be the last time. Some day I shall send for you again. It may be very soon.

MELBOURNE   Well, Ma'am, that will be for you to decide. Your Majesty's humble and most grateful servant. God bless you, my dear.

(*He kisses* THE QUEEN'S *hand and bows himself out.* THE QUEEN *stands quite still for a few moments, then rings.* LEHZEN *enters.*)

THE QUEEN   Oh, Lehzen dear, I don't want you again yet. Will you say that I am now ready to see Sir Robert Peel?

(LEHZEN *goes.* THE QUEEN *moves into position in front of the chair in which presently she will seat herself. She stands facing the door; it opens. A* GENTLEMAN *makes formal announcement, and* SIR ROBERT PEEL *comes stiffly into the room, halts, and bows.* THE QUEEN'S *acknowledgement is cold, and as slight as good manners allow.*)

THE QUEEN   Sir Robert Peel, you wished to see me?

SIR ROBERT   I am here at your Majesty's command.

THE QUEEN I did not send for you.

SIR ROBERT Your Majesty's gracious communication which I have just received, made immediate attendance necessary.

THE QUEEN Yes?

SIR ROBERT I regret to have to inform your Majesty, that under the conditions laid down by your Majesty in that communication, I am unable to form a Ministry.

THE QUEEN You mean, if I do not let you take all my Ladies away from me — as you propose?

SIR ROBERT I have stated to your Majesty the reasons which obliged me to say that with a change of Ministry a change in the composition of your Majesty's Court is also necessary. All my colleagues, whom since receiving your Majesty's communication I have again consulted, agree. I fear, Ma'am (and with very deep regret) that I have nothing further to add.

THE QUEEN Then, Sir Robert Peel, neither have I.

(SIR ROBERT PEEL *makes a stiff bow.*)

SIR ROBERT That is your Majesty's final decision?

THE QUEEN That, Sir Robert Peel, is my final decision.

SIR ROBERT I thank your Majesty for having so clearly and with so little delay made your Majesty's good pleasure known; and I now beg permission to relinquish the task of forming a Ministry capable of receiving your Majesty's confidence, in which task I have so unfortunately failed.

THE QUEEN You have my permission, Sir Robert Peel. I thank you for your attendance. Good-bye.

(*She rises, but does not offer him her hand. He bows himself out. She stands rather frightened at what she has done, but triumphant, and with a quiver of pride in her voice she speaks:*)

Now I really am — a Queen!

(*The door opens. With avid interrogation in her eye,* LEHZEN *enters.*) Lehzen, send word to Lord Melbourne at once, that *he is to come back.*

LEHZEN (*rapturously*). Ah! so.

WOMAN PROPOSES

15th October 1839

15th October 1839

In a sitting-room at Windsor Castle PRINCE ALBERT *of Saxe-Coburg Gotha stands looking rather sadly out of the window. The outside prospect is beautiful; but some other prospect seems to depress him. Still very young, he has already a full-grown conscience, which at times becomes too much for him.*

The door opens, his brother, PRINCE ERNEST, *enters, shuts the door, and stands looking at him. After a pause he speaks: his English is good, but he has a foreign accent.*

ERNEST Well, Albert?

ALBERT (*not turning*) Jawohl, mein Bruder?

ERNEST We must speak English.

ALBERT (*turning*) Why?

ERNEST For practice. One of us — you or I — will have to always.

ALBERT (*sighing*) I suppose!

ERNEST (*guardedly*) Which of us, do you 'suppose', it is going to be?

ALBERT That is not for me to say. The decision will not be ours.

ERNEST But we shall have to say *something* — one of us — presently.

ALBERT Yes, presently. And only one answer will be possible.

ERNEST You mean it must be 'yes'?

ALBERT Since it cannot possibly be 'no'.

ERNEST Then — you do not wish — ?

ALBERT I have given up 'wishing', Brother. Wishes might hinder.

ERNEST You don't seem very happy about it . . . No?

ALBERT This foreign land terrifies me. Look!

(He indicates the landscape.)

ERNEST Rather beautiful, don't you think?

ALBERT Beautiful? Yes, but all the same it means exile — to live in it.

ERNEST But then — to be almost a King!

ALBERT No! The English people will never allow a foreigner — you or me — to be King: nor anything like one.

ERNEST We are hardly more foreigners than are some of their own Royalty. We speak as good English.

ALBERT But we were not *born* in England.

ERNEST What real difference does that make to a man — where he was born?

ALBERT Real? None. But — to the English — *all* the difference. Has it never struck you, Ernest, that the English are a very romantic nation?

ERNEST Rather materialistic, I should say.

ALBERT Yes, but very romantic over their material — some of it. Their history — their wars — their royal successions — their revolutions. I have been reading English history lately. It is all a romance. Their lost battles? Where are they? Except for one or two — they do not exist.

ERNEST What about their lost countries — France, and America?

ALBERT They don't know they have lost them — till it is such old history that it means to them — nothing. For three hundred years after they had been driven out, their Kings still called themselves Kings of France. That is true, Ernest. Don't laugh!

ERNEST Of France? Yet don't like foreigners, you say?

ALBERT Oh, they like *ruling* them. They do that as a favour. Here you or I will only be — a puppet, kept to breed by. If it is *you*, are you going to resign yourself to that — willingly?

ERNEST If it is to be *me*, you say? It is time that I speak, Albert. It *must* be me. Did not Papa tell you?

ALBERT Tell me? No! What?

ERNEST Oh, well: perhaps he found it more difficult to tell — you. I do not know. But this is quite sure. He wishes it shall be *me*.

ALBERT *You?*

ERNEST Are you sorry?

ALBERT (*resentfully*) Then — why did he make me come?

ERNEST (*with a touch of sarcasm*) Oh, she has to choose, she has to choose! But she has to choose — *me*.

ALBERT Why?

ERNEST It is Papa's wish. He says — that there are family reasons.

ALBERT Why did he not tell *me* so?

ERNEST I do not know, Albert; I do not know. But you were always our Mamma's favourite. So, perhaps, that is why I am his.

(*Some new thought seems to have come to* ERNEST. *He looks at* ALBERT *curiously.*)

ALBERT What was their quarrel about, Ernest?

ERNEST It was more than a quarrel. I am thinking. (*Evidently he is.*) . . . Do you remember our Mamma at all, Albert?

ALBERT Oh, yes. I remember her, just once, very well. She was crying. She took me into her arms and cried, and cried, till I cried too.

ERNEST You were very young when she — went away from us . . . I wonder . . . (*ponderingly*).

ALBERT She used to write me letters.

ERNEST Ah! She never wrote one to me!

ALBERT They came secretly, by hand. I was to let nobody know.

ERNEST Did you answer those letters?

ALBERT Yes.

ERNEST Secretly?

ALBERT Yes.

ERNEST So you never told *me*.

ALBERT I was not to do so, lest it should be found out.

ERNEST Though I was your Brother? Oh, yes! You were always more to her than I. She wanted to take you with her — did you know? *Me* — she did not want.

ALBERT When she went to live in Paris — alone, you mean?

ERNEST (*scoffingly*) Oh! not alone . . . (*Suddenly a thought strikes him.*) Ah! So *that* is it? Now I understand! . . . Yes . . . Listen, Albert . . . *It has got to be me!* You are my Brother, but you are not the son of my Father. I have just come to be sure of it.

ALBERT I am not — ?

(*He stands dumbfounded.*)

ERNEST (*with more emphasis*) *You are not the son of my Father.* And *that* is why he says now it must be *me* . . . Forgive me, Albert! You are very dear to me. But you must obey my Father.

ALBERT If what you tell me is true, why should I obey — *your* Father?

ERNEST Oh, well, Albert, because — whatever you are *not* — he is still your Reigning Prince. You owe him loyal duty and obedience, like all the rest.

ALBERT No!

ERNEST No?

ALBERT (*touched in his pride*) He did not tell *me*! Had he wished for my obedience, he should have told *me*, not *you*.

ERNEST The explanation would have been rather difficult.

ALBERT No doubt. That he did not choose to explain — removes the difficulty — so far as it concerns *me*.

ERNEST (*startled*) What, then, do you mean to do, Albert?

ALBERT If she asks me, I shall accept.

ERNEST Then she shall *not* ask you! Albert, we have the same Mother, and your honour is mine, and this shall never be known. But I must see that my Father's wishes are obeyed. I shall have you sent home.

ALBERT Sent home!

ERNEST Yes, at once. You shall be ordered to return. I shall send word to-day.

ALBERT   And what if I refuse to go?

ERNEST   My dear Albert, we are not English, we are German. If the Duke, my Father, your Sovereign Prince, sends for you to return, you *will* return. You know that perfectly well.

(ALBERT *looks at him in silence for a while; then turns slowly away*.)

I am not taking away from your happiness, Albert. You will be happier than I.

ALBERT   Happiness is not everything.

ERNEST   Almost.

ALBERT   Live for it, and you lose it! To be happy has never been my thought — about life. I have not aimed for that.

ERNEST   No? What, then?

ALBERT   To do something that shall be worth doing.

ERNEST   Just now you said — to be a 'puppet'. I save you from *that*.

ALBERT   (*coldly*) I would rather save myself.

ERNEST   Ah! So you have ambition?

ALBERT   Ambition? . . . I wonder . . . Is it ambitious to give oneself — up?

ERNEST   No, Brother; but you will not have to give yourself up. Only, in this, do as you are told.

ALBERT   As *you* tell me?

ERNEST   As your Reigning Prince tells you. As you will be told — very soon.

ALBERT   Well, about that — we shall see!

ERNEST   *Yes*, Albert.

(*Hearing a step, they turn.* VICTORIA *has entered. She has already taken in something of a situation which she is not to understand. And since she is to be denied its explanation, she intends to terminate it.*)

VICTORIA   What are you two looking so serious about?

ERNEST   The rain.

VICTORIA Oh, but it will clear presently; then we will go for a ride in the Park.

ERNEST Oh, that will be very nice, to be sure!

VICTORIA I hope you are going to enjoy your stay, Cousin.

ERNEST Very much. I shall find it most delightful.

VICTORIA And you too, Albert?

ALBERT You are very kind, dear Cousin. How could I help enjoying myself while I am with you?

VICTORIA Albert, that is the first pretty speech you have ever made me!

ALBERT I am sorry, Cousin.

VICTORIA Oh, but I like it!

ALBERT I mean — that it should be only the first.

VICTORIA Well, so long as it's not the last, I don't mind.

ERNEST The rain is clearing. It has stopped. Shall we go out now?

VICTORIA (*correctively*) Cousin Ernest, I have made all necessary arrangements. We shall go out when we do go out — and not before. Besides — have you practised your music yet? At home, I was told, you practise every day.

ERNEST But here one cannot find the time.

VICTORIA Go, and do it now; and there will be time.

ERNEST I tried one of the pianos the day we arrived, Cousin. It was not in very good tune.

VICTORIA But that doesn't matter. You will be alone. No one will hear you.

ERNEST Generally, when we practise, Albert and I practise together.

VICTORIA Duets, you mean? Oh, but if the piano is out of tune, duets would be dreadful. Go and practise by yourself, Ernest; and Albert shall practise by *him*self, another time.

ERNEST Is it a command, Cousin?

VICTORIA My dear Ernest, I wouldn't think of commanding you.

But I do want you to be quite at home here; and as you *always* practise at home, I want you to practise here, and now. We shall not start our ride for an hour. That gives you just time; so do go — now.

> (COUSIN ERNEST *is not pleased; but the little creature is so born to rule that she gets her way.*)

ERNEST   Very well, Cousin ... Albert, *remember!*

> (*He goes out, with a jerk of the head toward* ALBERT, *which conveys a meaning.*)

VICTORIA   How strangely Ernest spoke to you, then! Is anything the matter?

ALBERT (*with reserve*) Oh, no; nothing serious.

VICTORIA   You haven't been quarrelling, I hope?

ALBERT   We never quarrel.

VICTORIA   I think it would be very hard to quarrel with *you*, Albert. *I* couldn't.

ALBERT   Please, don't ever try!

VICTORIA   Some people are able to quarrel without trying.

ALBERT   Yes.

> (*A pause.*)

VICTORIA   I suppose they like it.

ALBERT   Yes, I suppose so.

> (*A pause.*)

VICTORIA   Won't you sit down, Albert?

> (*He takes a distant seat.*)

Why don't you sit nearer? Talking then is so much easier.

> (*He comes towards her.*)

ALBERT   You are very kind, Cousin, ever since we came: to both of us, I mean.

VICTORIA   I am very fond of — Ernest.

ALBERT   Yes, so am I.

> (*He sits down.*)

VICTORIA   You've always been together, haven't you?

ALBERT   We've never been apart yet.

VICTORIA   How very nice that has been — for both.

(*A pause.*)

Would it be a great trial to you, if you had to live away from him?

ALBERT   Of course, the parting would be a trial. But one would get used to it — as to other things — if it had to be.

VICTORIA   My life has been so different from yours. I have never had anyone always with me like that — one of my own age. All my life I have been so much alone, except, of course, with Mamma. I don't know what it can be like — to have a brother.

ALBERT   One gets very fond of a brother.

VICTORIA   Yes; but one can get fonder of someone else — can one not?

ALBERT   It happens, sometimes.

(*A pause.*)

VICTORIA   Albert! What are you doing?

ALBERT   I was listening to Ernest, practising. I can just hear him; it is Beethoven.

VICTORIA   Don't listen to Ernest! You must listen to me!

ALBERT   I beg your pardon, Cousin; I was listening. Please don't think I am inattentive.

VICTORIA (*after a long pause*) Albert . . . I have something to say to you.

ALBERT   Yes . . . what is it, Cousin?

VICTORIA   In my position, it is I who have to say it — unfortunately. Ordinarily it is not what a woman would wish to say herself. She would rather — *he* said it.

ALBERT   Is there anything you wish me to say — that I can say?

VICTORIA (*tremulously*) To hear you say you *can* love me, is all I can hope — yet. If you could say that you already *do* love me, that would be — almost like Heaven.

ALBERT   I do . . . love you, Cousin.

VICTORIA Enough to marry me?

ALBERT More than enough to marry you. For people in our position often marry without any love at all.

VICTORIA I couldn't do that — Albert.

ALBERT Nor could I — Victoria.

VICTORIA Then you will marry me?

ALBERT If it is still your wish — when you know me — I will, very gratefully and humbly, accept this dear hand that you offer me.

VICTORIA When I know you?

ALBERT Yes; for I, too, have something to say. A few minutes ago, I did not know about myself what I know now. Even now I have no proof. Yet something tells me that it is true.

VICTORIA Don't tell me — if it is anything I shouldn't wish to know, Albert.

ALBERT But I must. My brother Ernest and I had the same mother; but not the same father.

VICTORIA I don't understand.

ALBERT I am sorry you should have to . . . My Mother and my Father (Ernest's Father) separated — after I was born. They did not love each other . . . My Mother must have loved someone else.

VICTORIA While she was married? (*His head makes silent assent.*) Before you were born — or after?

ALBERT Before.

VICTORIA Who?

ALBERT I don't know. So neither do I know who *I* am. Perhaps I shall never know. Yet there must still be someone who could tell me — more than I have been able to tell you . . . Shall I — ? Do you wish me to go now? I had to tell you this.

VICTORIA Yes . . . of course.

ALBERT Then now — you wish me to go?

VICTORIA No . . . No . . . I wish you to stay. It makes no difference to *me* . . . And besides, who knows?

ALBERT Somebody must know. Ernest knows.

VICTORIA   Ernest?

ALBERT   It was he who told me. And his Father knows.

VICTORIA   But his Father sent you here — let you come.

ALBERT   Yes. But he hoped it would be Ernest.

VICTORIA   How very silly of him!

ALBERT   Why?

VICTORIA   How could it possibly be Ernest, after I had seen you?
. . . Oh, Albert! Albert! What does it matter? It is not your Father
that I shall marry: it is you!

(*And as she speaks they are in each other's arms. Her passionate
abandonment awakens response, though of a more restrained nature.*)

ALBERT   My very dear Cousin! My sweet Wife that is to be.

VICTORIA   Aren't you going to kiss me?

ALBERT   If I may. (*The kiss is given.*)

VICTORIA   Again, please! . . . Again!

ALBERT   I pray God you do not ever have to repent of this.

VICTORIA   Repent? How could I repent! It is not in my nature,
Albert. Besides, there isn't going to be time. We must be married
quite soon. Everybody expects it.

ALBERT   Expects it? They don't know!

VICTORIA   Expects me to marry, I mean. I had to choose
*some*body. But I wasn't going to choose *any*body.

ALBERT   Not even Ernest?

VICTORIA   Oh, I liked Ernest very much, from the first . . . I do
still.

ALBERT   (*with a touch of humour*) Is that why you sent him to
practise? . . . He *knew*.

VICTORIA   That this was going to happen?

ALBERT   No; he did not know *that*.

VICTORIA   What, then?

ALBERT   That you were going to ask me.

VICTORIA   Well, then, what else could he suppose *would* happen?

ALBERT   He expected me to say no.

VICTORIA   (*almost affronted*) But you couldn't have said 'No' to a Queen — could you, Albert?

ALBERT   No, dear; one couldn't say 'No' to a Queen.

VICTORIA   But did you want to?

ALBERT   No, Dearest One. All it means is that Ernest will be disappointed.

VICTORIA   Oh, I see. Poor Ernest! . . . Well, we must both try to be very nice and kind to him . . . And now it is quite time that we went for our ride.

ALBERT   Isn't Ernest to come, too?

VICTORIA   Why, yes, of course!

ALBERT   Then won't you send and say he may stop practising? This hasn't taken an hour, you know.

(*Enter* ERNEST.)

VICTORIA   Nor has he, either; for here he is. Are you ready to come riding, Ernest?

ERNEST   Quite, if you are, Cousin.

VICTORIA   Oh, yes, we are quite ready *now*. Everything has been settled. Tell him, Albert.

ALBERT   Ernest . . . You told me to remember . . . I *forgot*.

(ERNEST *has only to look at them: and the awful situation is explained. It will also have to be explained eslewhere. For when* VICTORIA *says that a thing is settled: it is settled — for good.*)

ENTER PRINCE

1840

In the same room in which she made her proposal of marriage, THE QUEEN *sits waiting, radiantly happy, and expectant; and when one of her* GENTLEMEN *opens the door to announce,* 'HIS ROYAL HIGHNESS, PRINCE ALBERT OF SAXE-COBURG GOTHA', *she springs eagerly to her feet.* THE PRINCE *enters; the door closes; and — for her, at any rate — ceremony is over. But the* PRINCE *remains a little stiff.*

VICTORIA   Good morning, Albert!

ALBERT   Good morning, Victoria.

VICTORIA   A kiss, please!

ALBERT (*conscientiously*)   Three, if you prefer.

VICTORIA (*as she kisses him*)   I would prefer so many — more than we have time for, Dearest! . . . But now we have to talk business.

ALBERT (*stiffly*)   Oh, yes; business.

VICTORIA   The time being now so short for getting everything settled — as it must be settled.

ALBERT (*coldly*)   I thought that you had settled everything for me already — before I came.

VICTORIA   Almost; not quite. You see, Albert, you were not altogether pleased with what I wrote to you in my letters. Talking things over is so much better and easier; because then I can explain. And I do so want you to be quite satisfied with everything I have arranged for you, and to understand that I was right.

ALBERT   I will do my best, Victoria, to be satisfied with all that you say is necessary.

VICTORIA   I am quite sure you will, Albert dear, now that we are together, so that I can make everything plain . . . Here is the list of all the things I want to speak about.

(*She seats herself.*)

ALBERT   Oh, yes.

VICTORIA   Please sit down, Albert! I can't have you standing before me, when we are *alone*.

ALBERT   Not even when I am receiving orders?

VICTORIA   You mustn't call explanations 'orders', Dearest! The only Order I have given you is my Order of the Garter, which I sent to you on the day when our betrothal was made public.

ALBERT   That was a great honour — very gratifying.

VICTORIA   What is the matter, Albert?

ALBERT   Nothing. You give me everything that it is right for me to have.

VICTORIA   Yes; I *like* giving it.

ALBERT   I am sure you do.

VICTORIA   Of course there are some things which must wait; and others which — for you — would not be suitable. Uncle Leopold wanted you to be made a Peer. But Lord Melbourne and I don't think it will do. A Peer, being a member of the House of Lords, has a voice in the government of the Country; and of course, in your case, that will be quite out of the question.

ALBERT   So? I see.

VICTORIA   It is so important for everyone to realize that, though you are my Consort, you will have nothing to do with politics.

ALBERT   Am I not to take an interest in your politics?

VICTORIA   Oh, yes; you may take an interest, Albert — I would like you to. But I shall not discuss them with you, as I do with my Ministers, or ask your opinion about them. That would not be right.

ALBERT   I see.

VICTORIA   It is the duty of my Ministers to advise me on all affairs of State; and then — when I have heard them — either I give my consent, or I advise them differently. But they must never think that the advice I give them comes from anyone but myself.

ALBERT   But you read, Victoria, books and newspapers; and you get some ideas from them, which help you to decide.

VICTORIA   Oh, yes, sometimes. But books and newspapers are different; they are quite impersonal.

ALBERT   They are all written by persons.

VICTORIA   Yes; but, in reading, one forgets that.

ALBERT   Then some day I will write a book for you, Victoria; so that you may forget it is *me*.

VICTORIA   Indeed, no, Albert! You couldn't write a book, and put your name to it. That would *never* do!

ALBERT   Anonymously, my Dear; so that you need not know.

VICTORIA   I hope, Albert, you will *never* do anything that I am not to *know*!

ALBERT   But you are going to do many things that *I* am not to know.

VICTORIA   Yes; but that is quite different. I am the reigning sovereign . . . but you will be only —

ALBERT   Yes? Only what?

VICTORIA   My own dear darling Husband: the only person I shall ever love more than I have loved anyone yet!

ALBERT   That is just between ourselves, Victoria — we two alone. But what am I to be in public? Where do I find myself then?

VICTORIA   *That* I was going to explain, Albert. Though I have quite decided that you cannot be a Peer, I shall make an Order in Council that you are to take precedence of all other members of my Family. To that my two Uncles — the Duke of Cambridge and the Duke of Sussex — have quite agreed; for, of course, I had to ask them first.

ALBERT   Of course.

VICTORIA   To make it quite pleasant, I mean. But I should have done it in any case; since you are my first consideration; and *that* everybody will have to understand — even my Uncle Ernest, who may be a little difficult about it.

ALBERT   Being himself a King, you mean?

VICTORIA   Yes. But, when he comes here, the King of Hanover

D

is not to think himself more important than the Prince, my Consort. I shall not allow it! If he means to, he must stay away.

ALBERT Decide that as you like, Victoria.

VICTORIA I have quite decided . . . And now for the next thing that I have here on my list . . . It is about our Honeymoon. Of course, it was very natural and dear of you, Albert, to wish that we should remain alone together for a longer time; but that is impossible. Two or three days are all that I can spare. When Parliament is sitting, I have to be consulted every day by my Ministers. Also I must have my Court about me: I cannot be alone.

ALBERT But for a Bride to appear in public after only the second day — will not that be rather embarrassing?

VICTORIA Oh, no, Albert; for a Queen, not at all. We have to accustom ourselves to living in public. It is expected of us: people like it.

ALBERT And you like it, also?

VICTORIA (*feeling that she is being criticized*) I like to do what is *right*, Albert; when I am sure — as I am now.

ALBERT (*nerving himself to speak*) Are you sure, Victoria, that you are 'right' to marry me?

VICTORIA Albert!

ALBERT It is going to be difficult to be — all that you wish.

VICTORIA But you are that already, Dearest! How can you think of such a thing? I have not told you before, how many others were offered me to choose from. But I could only choose *you*.

ALBERT That was very kind of you.

VICTORIA Though there was one whom all my Uncles would have much preferred.

ALBERT Indeed? Who was that?

VICTORIA My cousin, George of Cambridge. They thought that would be so much better than what they call a 'foreign marriage'. But I didn't wish it: nor, I think, did he. He came to see me again the other day — for the first time since the announcement:

very kind and civil, but not at all embellished in his appearance, and evidently quite happy to be clear of me.

ALBERT   A foreign marriage, they call it?

VICTORIA   Yes; though already you speak English as well as he does. It is only your moustache that makes you look different.

ALBERT   To cut *that* off will be quite easy — if you wish me to.

VICTORIA   Oh, no! I couldn't bear for you to do that!

ALBERT   But if it would make me more popular . . . Have you read this?

(*He puts a printed leaflet into her hand.*)

VICTORIA (*as she begins reading it*)   How did you get this, Albert?[1]

ALBERT   Quite a number of it was kindly sent to me by the post.

VICTORIA   But how abominable! How dare anybody write about you and *Me* like that?

ALBERT   Your English public, that you so like, is just a little difficult to please, that is all . . . it does not like foreigners.

VICTORIA   No; but they will not go on thinking of you as a foreigner, after I have married you.

ALBERT   No?

VICTORIA   That would be impossible!

ALBERT   It is not going to be easy for me to become English all at once — just by marrying you, Victoria.

VICTORIA   No; but all the arrangements I am making for you will help, I am sure. For instance, about the Gentlemen of your Household, whom I have chosen for you — you said you wished to choose them yourself. But that is impossible, Albert.

ALBERT   Why?

[1] The verses which the Prince has given her to read are from a broadsheet, hawked in the streets of London at the time of the Royal Marriage, and run as follows:
'His Royal Mistress, mournful and depressed,
Pined in his absence, whom she valued best —
Missed the hoarse whispers of his German tongue,
And the moustache above his lip that hung:
That dear moustache which caused her first to *feel*,
And filled her bosom with pre-nuptial zeal.'

VICTORIA   How can you choose them for yourself, when you know nobody? At present they are all strangers.

ALBERT   Yes. So I would like to have for my Secretary someone that I know, and can trust.

VICTORIA   But he *must* be an Englishman, Albert. You cannot possibly have a foreigner for your Private Secretary.

ALBERT   Why not? Is not your own Private Secretary, the Baronesss Lehzen, a foreigner?

VICTORIA   Oh, but that's different. Lehzen was my Governess. She has been with me all my life.

ALBERT   That was before you became Queen.

VICTORIA   Yes; but I could never let that prevent me from choosing my own Private Secretary.

ALBERT   No? But it is to prevent me now, when I become your Husband.

VICTORIA   Yes, Albert; that is quite different.

ALBERT   I am to be given to strangers.

VICTORIA   They won't remain strangers. I shall take the greatest care to find for you someone whom you will really like and trust.

ALBERT   I would prefer to do that for myself.

VICTORIA   I have already told you that is impossible, Albert. Please do not say it again!

(THE PRINCE *rises quickly; then, restraining himself, he moves slowly to the window.* THE QUEEN *consults her list.*)

Now, I wonder, is that all?

ALBERT (*turning*)   Is there anything else that I am to learn this morning?

VICTORIA (*anxiously*)   Has all this talking tired you?

ALBERT   Oh, no! I am not 'tired'. I am feeling too much alive! I would like to open this window. May I?

VICTORIA   Oh, Albert, on such a cold day: do you think it wise?

ALBERT   I do not know, Victoria. I only know that I would like to open it, for a little breath of fresh air.

(*Before* THE QUEEN *can answer, one of her* GENTLEMEN *enters to make announcement.*)

GENTLEMAN If it please — your Majesty's Ministers are in attendance.

VICTORIA Oh, Albert dear, now I must go, then. I do hope you will be able to amuse yourself. There is the Library, you know.

ALBERT I think that my friend, Baron Stockmar, will be waiting to see me.

VICTORIA Oh, yes. Then see him at once; and when I come back, we will go out together.

(*The* GENTLEMAN *has gone; but as she moves to the door it opens and closes again behind her.* THE PRINCE *sinks down into a seat in deep dejection, and is so sitting, when the door is discreetly opened, and* BARON STOCKMAR *enters. He stands for a moment looking at* THE PRINCE *with kindly understanding, then speaks.*)

STOCKMAR Does your Highness's servant intrude?

ALBERT Come in, Baron.

(*He rises, and moves despondently away.*)

STOCKMAR They informed me that your Highness was now ready to receive me.

ALBERT I am at liberty for a short time, Baron. Yes? Was there something you wished to speak to me about?

STOCKMAR A good many things, if there is time. But — pardon! — your Royal Highness does not seem in very good spirit to-day.

ALBERT Indeed, I have been merrier!

STOCKMAR Shakespeare.

ALBERT Yes; I have been reading Shakespeare a good deal lately — in English.

STOCKMAR And how does your Highness find him?

ALBERT I find him — like the English people — rather hard to understand.

STOCKMAR Your Highness has not been in the country very long. Just at first, the people — like their language — are a little difficult. And so — your position also.

ALBERT   Difficult! Impossible! Baron, it is now a question whether I can — go on!

STOCKMAR (*in consternation*)   Oh! Your Highness! but that is incredible! You cannot break off from marriage with a Queen!

ALBERT   What does he become, who marries a Queen?

STOCKMAR   That — depends.

ALBERT   On what?

STOCKMAR   On who means to be master.

ALBERT   There you have it! She is that already; her great position gives it her.

STOCKMAR   No doubt . . . till she gives it to *you*.

ALBERT   She will never do that — willingly!

STOCKMAR   Oh, yes: . . . she will . . . she will.

ALBERT   But how is it possible? Why should she?

STOCKMAR   She loves you — very much.

ALBERT   Too much! but not as I would wish to be loved. I am not to belong to myself any more.

STOCKMAR   Patience, patience! It will come in time.

ALBERT   And what — meanwhile? Have you thought enough about that?

STOCKMAR   Yes . . . yes . . . For my beloved Prince there is going to be a hard time . . . But he will win.

ALBERT   But, Baron, how can I — fight for myself against one who — so loving, and so generous — is giving me *every*thing, as the world sees it?

STOCKMAR   Will your Highness listen to one who, in his life, has had much experience: not indeed just alone with himself, but from watching others? . . . This little Queen — still so young, so pleased, and proud of herself, as she is now: of her position, her importance, her power — as she thinks. It will not go on. Her Ministers flatter her, making things easy for her — and for themselves. Presently she will have to change her Ministers for others whom she does not so much like, or so much trust. Then it will be *your* turn. She will come to you — for help . . . And, besides (THE BARON *is now smiling*) — have you ever looked at yourself, enough to know how handsome you are? No, do not laugh! Look at yourself, my Prince! look! (*He leads* THE PRINCE *up to a mirror.*) Some day — it may be quite soon — she will become a mother — of *your* children. Then, my Prince, if she still loves you, you will not be her Puppet, nor her Plaything any more. You will be *King*.

ALBERT King?

STOCKMAR Oh! The title does not matter; that is nothing! You have a head of your own, my Prince, that you know and can use — well. And if you keep your head *now*, you are not going to have it cut off — not by her, nor by anybody. No! . . . By your Highness's leave, now I go . . . I have said what I came to say.

(*Whereupon, he bows himself out.* THE PRINCE *returns to the mirror, and stands looking at himself. And if he does not see there a full prophecy of what is to be, at least he sees nothing to make him despair.*)

MORNING GLORY

11th February 1840

A bell has just sounded. Into THE PRINCE'S *dressing-room at Windsor, where two candles are already burning, comes an elderly Valet. With deft movement, and the utmost correctitude of deportment, he places hot water, razors, soap, shaving-brush, and towel. He then proceeds to lay out in orderly sequence* THE PRINCE'S *clothing for the day; then goes to the window, draws back the curtains, raises the blind, and puts out the candles. The sun is already well up, for the hour is late. Having done all, he stands to attention, and waits. A door opens;* PRINCE ALBERT *enters, in a fine brocaded dressing-gown, and a silk night-cap of rather Eastern design, in which he looks well.*

ALBERT That will do. I will shave myself this morning. When I want you, I will ring.

(The Valet makes a short bow, and retires. THE PRINCE *goes to the glass, throws off his night-cap, and, taking up a comb, passes it through the long locks of his rather disordered hair. He then uncords his dressing-gown, sits down, and removing his fur-edged slippers, draws on a pair of pantaloons. He rises, resumes his slippers, and advances to the dressing-table. Opening the collar of his night-shirt, he prepares to shave himself, and is already applying the lather, when there comes a light tabbering on the door by which he has just entered. He turns a little surprised; the door opens: it is* THE QUEEN. *At first we only see her head, in a pretty frilled night-cap, with the strings hanging loose; but presently she is all there, wearing a rose-coloured dressing-gown, and over it a white Cashmere shawl with long fringes. She looks very happy and charming.*

THE QUEEN Albert, may I come in?

ALBERT Yes, Dearest, if you wish to.

(She gazes in pleased astonishment at a spectacle she has never seen before: the solid foam of shaving-soap on a human countenance is something quite new to her.)

THE QUEEN What *are* you doing?

ALBERT Shaving.

THE QUEEN Oh! How exciting! May I stay, and watch you?

ALBERT If it would interest you, Weibchen.

THE QUEEN But, of course! to see you shaving is wonderful! Something I never thought of.

ALBERT Oh? Did you think one did not have to shave at all?

THE QUEEN I never thought about it — till now . . . You see, Albert, I have never seen a man shave himself before.

ALBERT No, I suppose not.

THE QUEEN How often do you have to do it? Once a week?

ALBERT Every day.

THE QUEEN Every day! But how absurd! It can't grow as fast as all that.

ALBERT Oh, yes, it does.

THE QUEEN How very troublesome! Why, I only cut my *nails* once a week.

ALBERT Nails can wait longer; beards won't.

THE QUEEN I wouldn't like you to have a beard, Albert!

ALBERT Nor would I. That's why I am taking it off now.

(*Having sufficiently lathered, he now begins to shave.*)

THE QUEEN How strange it looks! . . . and how interesting! — fascinating! . . . Is it dangerous?

ALBERT Not if you don't talk to me —

THE QUEEN (*a little startled*) Oh!

ALBERT — not just while I am stroking myself.

THE QUEEN Stroking yourself! Oh, Albert, you are funny!

ALBERT Is that not the right word? Ought I to have said 'wiping myself' — or what?

THE QUEEN Really, I'm not sure, Albert. It's a part of the English language, which — from not having to know — I've not been taught.

ALBERT Ah, Vicky! It is nice to hear you say that! Then you, too, do not know the English language quite like a native. For that — if it were not for the soup — I would kiss you.

THE QUEEN   The soup?

ALBERT   This, I mean.

THE QUEEN   Oh! not 'soup', Albert darling. *Soap!*

ALBERT   Ah! Soap, then.

THE QUEEN   But I don't mind the soap, Albert — *your* soap — if you would like to.

ALBERT   Very well, then; now I will.

(*Having wiped his lips, he kisses her, and then goes on with his shaving.*)

THE QUEEN   Let me see what you do it with.

(*He gives her a razor; she takes it, and examines the edge.*)

Oh! how sharp it is!

ALBERT   Yes, it does have to be sharp — always.

THE QUEEN   Does it hurt?

ALBERT   No.

THE QUEEN   Do you ever cut yourself?

ALBERT   No; not when I am alone. I had a valet once, that used to shave me, before I knew how for myself. One day, he cut me, rather badly. After that, I had to learn; and for a long time, shaved only myself.

THE QUEEN   And what happened to him?

ALBERT   Oh, he had his head cut off, I suppose . . . I did not inquire. I sent him out of the room, and told him never to come back. And oh, how he ran!

(*He laughs.*)

THE QUEEN   And then?

ALBERT   Then the Court Physician came running in a terrible fright, for the man having told him. He thought to find me bleeding to death.

THE QUEEN   To death? Why?

ALBERT   Because, my Dear, my brother Ernest — and his Father — once so nearly did. But that did not happen to *me* . . . I am not that way, you see. What I told you makes the difference.

THE QUEEN   Oh, Albert! Then that 'difference' has, perhaps, saved your life?

ALBERT   Possibly.

THE QUEEN   Then, how thankful I really ought to be.

ALBERT   To my Mother, and my Father, you mean?

THE QUEEN   Yes . . . Albert, suppose you had died before we got married, *could* I have married anyone else?

ALBERT   Of course, Dearest. You had to marry someone. You could not disappoint your people by not giving them an heir to the Throne.

THE QUEEN   Oh, Albert! Shall I? Will that really happen?

ALBERT   We will hope so, Dearest — in time.

THE QUEEN   In time? I hope it will be very soon. Oh, isn't it wonderful? We really are — married now, aren't we?

ALBERT (*covertly amused*)   Yes, Weibchen, I think so.

THE QUEEN   Yesterday seems almost like another world — so different. All the crowds, and the cheering, and the firing, and the bells: and thousands and thousands of people all looking at us, as if we belonged to them: as, of course, in a way, we do . . . And now we are all by ourselves — all alone — just we two.

ALBERT   Yes, all alone — just we two. Shall I be able to make you happy, — you think? . . . You *are* happy?

THE QUEEN   Happy? So happy, I can't — I can't tell you, Albert! . . . And to think that this will go on, and on, for years and years . . . It's like Heaven!

ALBERT   No, Vicky, not just like this — that is not possible . . . That is not human nature.

THE QUEEN   But I shall never love you less than I do now, Albert.

ALBERT   No, Dearest, perhaps not. But you will be less excited about it — less romantic, perhaps. I shall have become less strange to you. We love each other, but we are still both rather strangers. We have to learn each other's characters — and ways. That will take time. . . .

(*She shakes her head fondly, confident that she knows him already by heart.*)

ALBERT Oh, yes . . . You have come to see me shave to-day — for the first time. That pleases — that excites you. But it will not always excite you as much as to-day. You will not come, I think, to see me shave every day — for the next twenty years.

THE QUEEN Why not?

ALBERT Because, Dearest, you will have too much else to do. Also you will know so well what it looks like, which to-day you see only the first time. So, that it should become less of a spectacle, is only reasonable.

THE QUEEN I don't want to be reasonable with *you*, Albert!

ALBERT But you *will* want — in time, I hope, Vicky. So shall I. You have a great life of duties to perform, in which I am to share. Is that not so?

THE QUEEN We can't share everything, Albert. Some things I shall have to do alone — affairs of State, in which it would not be right for you to concern yourself.

ALBERT (*a little sharply*) So?

THE QUEEN Yes. You must take great care, Dearest. The English are jealous; and to them you are still a foreigner.

ALBERT And — to *you*?

THE QUEEN To me you are everything — life, happiness, peace, and comfort! When I am with you, I shall want to forget every-thing — except our love.

(*It is a prospect over which, as she flings herself into his arms, she looks more happy than he does. All at once, from the Terrace outside, comes a burst of music. With the happy excitement of a child, she draws him to the window, and points.*)

Hark! Look! That is the Band of my Royal Life Guards. I gave orders for it to be here this morning an hour earlier — so that we might hear it before we came down . . . I thought you would like it.

ALBERT   Oh, yes; it is very good music.

THE QUEEN   What is it they are playing?

ALBERT   You do not know?

THE QUEEN   No. I only said that some suitable pieces were to be chosen — it being such a special occasion. What is it?

ALBERT   That, my Vicky, is Mendelssohn's *Wedding March*, from his new setting to Shakespeare.

THE QUEEN   Mendelssohn! Oh, I'm glad. He is one of the world's greatest composers, is he not? . . . No, I have never heard it before. But now it is going to be my favourite piece.

ALBERT   You could not choose better. But you will not want to hear it every day, Weibchen.

THE QUEEN   Perhaps not quite every day.

ALBERT   Any more than you will want to see me shave — every day.

THE QUEEN   Now you are laughing at me.

ALBERT   Just a little, Dearest; because you — and I, are both to-day so young.

THE QUEEN   And so happy! Look how the sun is shining!

(*She goes and stands in the window.*)

ALBERT   Ah, do not stand so near to that window, Vicky!

THE QUEEN   Why not?

ALBERT   The people might see you.

THE QUEEN   Well, but why shouldn't they? It would please them.

ALBERT   (*uncomfortably*)   Yes: too much . . . That is why I say — don't!

THE QUEEN   Albert, darling, we have got to appear in public again almost at once. It's no use being shy. And why should we, when I'm so proud of having got you?

ALBERT   (*rescuing modesty with common sense*)   I want my breakfast,

Vicky! Please to go and get yourself ready — quick. I am going to ring now for my dresser to come.

THE QUEEN (*revelling in wifely submission*) Order me to go, Albert! . . . *Order* me!

ALBERT (*playing up*) *Go*, woman! He says to you, *Go!*

(*Gazing at him adoringly, she drops a deep mocking curtsy, and retires. He stands looking fondly after her: then, with a sigh, turns, and rings the bell. His Valet enters. The Band plays on.* THE PRINCE *proceeds to dress himself with formal correctness for the very difficult new life which now awaits him.*)

THE BELL

1840

In the small private apartment at Windsor which PRINCE ALBERT *has prepared for the quiet retirement of their leisure hours,* THE QUEEN *and* THE PRINCE *stand looking round upon all the new arrangements, including pictures and furniture, imported from* THE PRINCE'S *home in Germany.*

ALBERT   So here now we are at home; and there shall be nobody to disturb us. And this is where we shall come whenever we wish to be alone together — when you have the time . . . You like it?

THE QUEEN   Oh, Albert, how can I help liking it? For this is *you*.

ALBERT   Yes: this is me. Here are my books which I have brought from Rosenau: some day I shall read you all of them. No, not quite all, Vicky: but those that you choose. And this my own piano, on which I learned at home. That too I have brought; and I shall play on it to you; and you sing to me.

THE QUEEN   Yes, Albert.

ALBERT   And sometimes, Vicky, you will sing to me in German — to please me.

THE QUEEN   When we are here, Albert, I will do anything you like — anything. I promise.

ALBERT   Then now give me a kiss — one . . . (*correctively*). Vicky, I said 'one'.

THE QUEEN   Aren't three better?

ALBERT (*playfully*) Yes: as a rule — but when I said 'one' I meant one. It was to see if you really could be obedient to me — just for once. I find you cannot.

THE QUEEN   You should have begun with something — less difficult. It's very hard to kiss you — only once.

ALBERT (*fondly*) I forgive you, Vicky.

THE QUEEN   And now what else? Show me!

ALBERT Well, here is the portrait of myself and my brother Ernest, when we were boys together; and this is of my Mother whom I have not seen since I was only five years old.

THE QUEEN She was beautiful, Albert.

ALBERT Yes; and she died . . . And this, Vicky, is the portrait that you gave me of yourself — before I came to belong to you. So you see: in your great Castle of Windsor, this is my own little home, to which you come with me — to be away from everyone — sometimes . . . Shall we sit down?

THE QUEEN Yes . . . but, Albert dearest, there is just one thing more I *would* like.

ALBERT What is it?

THE QUEEN I would like the fire to be lighted; for I'm feeling rather cold.

ALBERT Oh, Vicky: but I had one lighted: it has gone out. (*He goes and looks.*) No, not quite: but the servant has not come to look after it. That is the whole matter. There are so many of them that they all forget to do anything.

THE QUEEN Perhaps, Albert, it was because they were told that *no one* was to come here but ourselves.

ALBERT Ah yes: perhaps . . . But is there no coal? . . . No!

THE QUEEN Then, I suppose we must ring.

ALBERT Yes. (*He goes to ring.*) But Vicky, there is no bell.

THE QUEEN No bell?

ALBERT No. Here, in Windsor, is a room that has not a bell. And I did not find that out!

THE QUEEN Then — what are we going to do, Albert?

ALBERT I do not know . . . How, at Windsor, do you make a servant to come, if you have not a bell?

THE QUEEN I don't know, Albert. Perhaps there is one waiting somewhere outside.

(*He goes to look.*)

ALBERT No . . . Do you think, if I clap my hands, someone will come? They did that in the middle ages; so perhaps at Windsor it is the same.

THE QUEEN You might try, Albert. Though I think it would sound a little strange — not quite proper, I mean.

ALBERT But we must do *something*. The fire is going out, and you are feeling the cold.

THE QUEEN Yes, I suppose we must.

ALBERT I will try. (*He goes out and claps.*) No . . . there was an echo, that was all. I think, Vicky, I must go to one of the rooms where there *is* a bell: I must ring it, and must say that in here the fire is expecting itself to go out.

THE QUEEN Yes: I'm afraid that is the only thing to do.

(*He goes:* THE QUEEN *sits waiting. Presently he returns.*)

ALBERT Oh: but this is much better. I have just met Stockmar. Of him we make an exception. He may come in, may he not? Come in, Baron, come in!

(BARON STOCKMAR *enters, and bows to* THE QUEEN.)

See here, my dear Baron, we are in a difficulty. Our fire has gone out, and there is no bell; and we do not know what to do about it . . . What are we to do?

STOCKMAR If your Royal Highness will leave it to me — that is all you *have* to do. I have her Majesty's permission?

THE QUEEN Oh yes, please; for with no bell we feel quite helpless.

(THE BARON *goes on his errand.*)

ALBERT What a useful man — that Baron. He never loses himself to do anything. He has his head on — all round.

THE QUEEN I think, Albert, that when the servant does come, the fire will need a good deal of attending to. Wouldn't it be as well if we did not just have to sit and watch? Hadn't we better be doing something?

ALBERT That is a good idea, Vicky. Very well: then now let us get out some music, so as to disengage our attention. You shall choose something, and then I shall play to you while the fire is having itself seen to.

THE QUEEN Oh yes, that will do nicely . . . Oh, Albert, isn't it funny?

ALBERT Funny? Why? I do not think it is funny not to have a bell.

THE QUEEN Not even a fire-bell, to keep us from being frozen to death.

ALBERT Hush, here comes the man.

(THE BARON *enters, followed by a* FOOTMAN *with scuttle, firelighters, and bellows.*)

STOCKMAR (*covertly amused*) Your Majesty is served.

ALBERT Ah, yes. Will you stay, Baron? Her Majesty and I are going to have some music. Shall we sing, my dear: or shall I only play?

THE QUEEN I would rather hear you play.

ALBERT What would you like — this? Mendelssohn's *Spinning Wheel.*

(*He plays:* THE QUEEN *sits at his side watching. The* FOOTMAN *makes up the fire and blows it into a flame. The* BARON *stands at musical attention. When the fire is well alight, the* FOOTMAN *gathers up his materials, bows to the back of Royalty, and retires.*)

ALBERT (*looking round as the door closes.*) Ah, that is better! Thank you, Baron, for your assistance. To-morrow we will have a bell.

(*The* BARON *bows himself out.* THE QUEEN *has gone toward the fire, and stands facing it. She calls him to her without turning.*)

THE QUEEN Albert . . . (*He goes toward her.*) I have something to tell you.

ALBERT Yes . . . What is it?

(*She takes his hand and draws him to sit beside her: then, gazing at him fondly, counts on the fingers of one hand, her lips shaping the numbers without being heard. At the eighth she gives a confirming nod.*)

ALBERT (*embracing her*) Oh, Vicky, liebes, kleines Frauchen!

THE QUEEN It must be a boy, Albert.

ALBERT We will hope so.

THE QUEEN Oh, but it *must* be!

ALBERT Since you say so — I suppose it will. And — when that happens — oh, how the bells will ring!

THE QUEEN Yes: how the bells will ring!

ALBERT And not only here; but all over the country they will ring. And when Sunday comes, there will be sermons about it in all the churches; and their text — shall I tell you, Vicky, what their text will be?

THE QUEEN What? How do you know?

ALBERT Because it cannot be anything else. 'Unto us a child is born, unto us a son is given; and the government shall be upon his shoulder.' But not yet, Vicky, no, not yet. Not for a long, long time — we will *hope*.

(*They embrace.*)

THE FIRST-BORN

1840

In the ante-room of the Royal private apartments, the HEAD-NURSE *is in attendance, with other Nurses at call. Within half-drawn portières, folding doors lead to the inner chamber where only yesterday took place the happy event — not quite so happy as had been hoped — for which the whole nation had been waiting expectantly. At the ante-room door comes a discreet knock. The* HEAD-NURSE *sails importantly across, while the door is opened by one of her underlings. One of the Prince's* GENTLEMEN *presents himself; he is allowed to enter.*

GENTLEMAN His Royal Highness has sent me to inquire how is Her Majesty this morning?

HEAD-NURSE Doing very nicely, Sir. Her Majesty has had a good night and is well rested. Her Majesty is still asleep.

GENTLEMAN The doctor informed His Royal Highness that he would, perhaps, be able to see Her Majesty for a few minutes to-day, if you would be good enough to send word what time would be best.

HEAD-NURSE When Her Majesty has wakened and had her breakfast, His Royal Highness shall be informed. But he is not to stay, tell him, more than five minutes. Her Majesty mustn't be excited.

GENTLEMAN (*stiffly*) I will tell His Royal Highness what you say.

HEAD-NURSE (*as one accustomed to have her orders obeyed*) Ah! Mind you do!

(*The* GENTLEMAN *moves towards the door, then pauses.*)

GENTLEMAN And Her Royal Highness, the Princess — how is *she*?

HEAD-NURSE (*proudly*) Well, Sir, for a one-day old — and I've seen hundreds of 'em — I say she can't be beaten.

GENTLEMAN Very satisfactory, I'm sure. Quite healthy?

HEAD-NURSE Healthy! You should have heard her! Ah! She's

got a will of her own already — like her mother, *I* say; and I ought to know, for I came to Kensington Palace as Under-Nurse when Her Majesty was the one herself. And a nice handful she was!

GENTLEMAN   Dear me! Very interesting . . . (*Then ingratiatingly.*) Nurse, would it be asking too much — would you allow *me* just to see the little Princess for a moment — only for a moment!

HEAD-NURSE   *You*, Sir? No, Sir; certainly not, Sir! Not till His Royal Highness himself has seen her is anyone else going to. Not if *I* know it.

GENTLEMAN   I humbly beg pardon of your Majesty.

HEAD-NURSE   Granted!

GENTLEMAN   Have I your Majesty's leave to retire?

HEAD-NURSE   Go along with you!

(*The* GENTLEMAN *proceeds to back out of the room; a performance which is lost on the* HEAD-NURSE, *who abruptly turns her back on him. From the inner room enters the* UNDER-NURSE; *stepping cautiously she speaks in a whisper.*)

UNDER-NURSE   Her Majesty is waking up. At least I think so.

HEAD-NURSE   Then go along and get Her Majesty's breakfast, quick and sharp.

(*The* UNDER-NURSE *goes. The* HEAD-NURSE *enters the inner room, and draws back the bed-curtains.*)

HEAD-NURSE   Is your Majesty awake?

THE QUEEN   Yes, Nurse, I'm awake. At least I'm going to be. What time is it?

HEAD-NURSE   Six o'clock, your Majesty.

THE QUEEN   Morning?

HEAD-NURSE   Yes, your Majesty; it's morning now. Your Majesty has had six hours' good sleep; and you'll have another, after your Majesty has had her breakfast.

THE QUEEN   I don't think I want any breakfast — not yet.

HEAD-NURSE   No, your Majesty; but your breakfast wants *you*.

THE QUEEN   Not till I have seen the Prince, I mean.

HEAD-NURSE Your Majesty can't see His Royal Highness the Prince till you've had your breakfast. No! It's Doctor's orders.

THE QUEEN Then let me have it at once.

HEAD-NURSE It'll be here in a minute, your Majesty: I've sent for it.

(UNDER-NURSE *enters with tray*.)

Ah! here it is. Bring it in, Nurse. Put it down.

(*The tray is deposited, the* HEAD-NURSE *proceeds to officiate*.)

THE QUEEN What's that?

HEAD-NURSE That's what we call a feeding-cup, your Majesty. It's the same one Her Royal Highness, the Duchess, had when your Majesty was born. Yes, the same one.

THE QUEEN Oh? How interesting. It's the first time I've ever used one.

HEAD-NURSE Ah! and it'll not be the last — let's hope. Now your Majesty has only got to lie still. Don't move. I'll give it you.

THE QUEEN While I'm taking it, will you send word to the Prince — to come and see me?

HEAD-NURSE Word's been sent. His Royal Highness will be here as soon as we are ready for him. Now then — this is going to do us good — your Majesty . . . Now a little more . . . And a little more . . . And now just to finish it . . . Oh, yes, you can, you can, if you *try* . . . There! . . . And good and gracious you've done it . . . Does your Majesty hear the bells ringing?

THE QUEEN What are they ringing for?

HEAD-NURSE What for? Why, for the Princess, to be sure.

THE QUEEN The Princess? Ah, yes, of course. (*She sighs*) Oh, I do so want to see the Prince!

(*The* HEAD-NURSE *goes out into the ante-room where the* UNDER-NURSE *is waiting*.)

HEAD-NURSE Go, and say that His Royal Highness can come now. (*Then returning to the bed-side*) There! Now I've sent word. His Royal Highness will be here in another minute.

THE QUEEN Tidy me, Nurse. Tidy me! How do I look?

HEAD-NURSE (*as she does the tidying*) Your Majesty's looking very nice indeed. Just a little pale; but that's to be expected.

THE QUEEN Let me look at myself . . . (THE NURSE *holds up a hand-mirror*) Oh, Nurse, I look dreadful!

HEAD-NURSE You don't, Marm. You look sweet — and like a *mother*.

THE QUEEN How's Baby?

HEAD-NURSE Oh, she's all right. Your Majesty needn't worry about *her*. She's having her twenty-four hours' sleep, and having it well.

THE QUEEN Twenty-four hours' sleep? Impossible.

HEAD-NURSE No, your Majesty; it's what babies always have to do when they first come . . . to get over the shock.

THE QUEEN The shock of what?

HEAD-NURSE Of being born, your Majesty. It's hard treatment they get sometimes, poor wee things!

THE QUEEN Did *she* have very hard treatment?

HEAD-NURSE No: your Majesty treated her beautifully, like as if you'd been the mother of twelve.

THE QUEEN Oh!

HEAD-NURSE Now you must lie still, and not talk till His Royal Highness the Prince comes.

THE QUEEN When he does come, Nurse, you must go.

HEAD-NURSE (*Horrified*) *Go!* Your Majesty?

THE QUEEN Yes; I wish to see him alone.

HEAD-NURSE But I *mustn't* go, your Majesty. It's Doctor's orders.

THE QUEEN This is the Queen's orders. You will do as I tell you.

HEAD-NURSE I've never done such a thing before; but if your Majesty really means it.

THE QUEEN I really mean it, Nurse.

HEAD-NURSE (*Hearing the outer door open*) Well, here His Royal Highness is, then.

(*She bustles forward to meet* PRINCE ALBERT *as he enters, shown in by the* UNDER-NURSE.)

PRINCE ALBERT Mrs. Nurse, how long may I stay?

HEAD-NURSE (*Her stature restored to her*) Only five minutes, your Royal Highness, *please*.

PRINCE ALBERT Very well.

(*He looks at his watch, and goes forward to the inner room. The* HEAD-NURSE *drives out the* UNDER-NURSE *with a look; then takes up her stand within the screen which shuts off the outer door. Thus, out of sight and hearing, she obeys the orders.*)

PRINCE ALBERT Weibchen! . . . Liebes, kleines Frauchen! Wie geht es Dir?

(*He bends over and kisses her.*)

VICTORIA Oh, Albert darling, have I disappointed you?

ALBERT Disappointed me? But how? Why, Weibchen?

VICTORIA That it wasn't a boy.

ALBERT You wished it to be a boy?

VICTORIA Albert! Of course. How could one have wished anything else — for an heir to the throne. The heir to a throne *must* be a boy — if possible.

ALBERT Well, Vicky, I do not know that that has *always* to be. For if you had been your bruder instead of yourself — *this* would not have happened.

VICTORIA 'This?'

ALBERT I mean that I should not have then married you.

VICTORIA Then you are not disappointed?

ALBERT Oh, there is plenty of time, Vicky, you may yet be a mother of twelve.

VICTORIA That is what Nurse said.

ALBERT Oh? Did she? Well, let us hope that she was right.

VICTORIA No, Albert, I don't want to have twelve — not quite. You see it would be such an interruption to my being Queen.

ALBERT   Yes: I suppose. But while that was so, I could be looking after things for you perhaps. No?

VICTORIA   No . . . No, Albert, that would never do. My people wouldn't like it.

ALBERT   (*sadly*) So.

VICTORIA   No. Two or three will be quite enough, I think. Perhaps I wouldn't mind four . . . in time. So you really don't mind? Oh, how good you are to me! I was so afraid I hadn't quite done my duty.

ALBERT   Well, Vicky, if it is anyone's fault, it is my fault too.

VICTORIA   Oh! No, Albert, no! the father has nothing to do with whether it is a boy or a girl.

ALBERT   Indeed? You seem to be very learned in the subject, Vicky. You surprise me. I thought it was something nobody knew anything about.

VICTORIA   Oh, yes. I am quite sure of it. I have thought so much about it, you see — lately. So I *know*.

ALBERT   Well, if it is all your doing that it is a girl, let us hope that it will be good like its mother.

VICTORIA   But it won't be clever like its father; a girl can't be. That is not possible.

ALBERT   Perhaps not — as a rule. But being clever is not everything. (*Then sadly*) And if one cannot use one's cleverness, what use to have it?

VICTORIA   What do you mean, Albert, 'cannot use'?

ALBERT   Oh, nothing, nothing! — not that matters just now. Besides (*looking at his watch*) it is time I went. Nurse told me I was only to be here five minutes.

VICTORIA   Nurse told you!

ALBERT   Yes; and she was quite right. It was Doctor's orders. And when Doctors order, Kings and Queens must obey . . . So now, for a little, good-bye.

(*He kisses her.*)

VICTORIA   Again! (*they kiss*) Again. . . .

ALBERT   No, no! not again. You must not so excite yourself . . .
Good-bye.

(*Going out he meets the* HEAD-NURSE *at the door.*)

Have I been more than my five minutes, Nurse? No? . . . But it
was a little hard to obey . . . And now, if you will let me, I would
like to look at Her Royal Highness, the Princess.

HEAD-NURSE   She is in here, your Royal Highness — asleep.

ALBERT   Ah! then we must be careful that we shall not wake her.
You think it will be quite safe?

HEAD-NURSE   Quite safe, if your Royal Highness will allow me to
go in first. This way.

ALBERT (*half returning*) Oh, Vicky! What a thing to be a father!
Das ist wundervoll!

(*The* HEAD-NURSE *goes in. He tip-toes after her.*)

VICTORIA   Oh! he's pleased! really pleased! Well, Dearest, if you
want twelve you shall have them. Anything — *anything*, to please
you. But oh, I do wish it had been a boy — a boy!

(*From the next·room comes the loud screeching of a baby; the
Princess Royal has woken, with a will of her own, which nothing is
ever going to take from her.*)

THE COURT CIRCLE

(*A Conversation Piece*) 1841

The Ladies of the Court have come up from dinner, followed by the Gentlemen. They stand about in groups, talking; but their tones are subdued, for they are awaiting the entry of THE QUEEN *and* PRINCE ALBERT, *and to be caught talking then would be like talking in church. One of the Ladies goes to a glass to rearrange her head-dress; another Lady is plunging vainly among her flounces for a missing handkerchief.*

1ST LADY Oh! my dear. I've lost my handkerchief. Can you lend me one?

2ND LADY Impossible! I've a cold myself; as I always have now — with the Queen so fond of draughts.

(*A Gentleman has picked up the missing handkerchief, and presents it with a bow.*)

1ST LADY Oh! *thank* you! I'm saved!

(*She buries her nose joyfully in the restored article.*)

THE DOWAGER LADY SEWARD Oh, dear! This standing about! I do hope I shall be sent to play whist with the Duchess to-night.

3RD LADY But you don't like whist, Mama.

DOWAGER I like it better than standing; though playing against the Duchess one always loses, because you mayn't tell her when she revokes — which she often does . . . And when she loses she gets cross and quarrels with everyone. There! I shall sit down till they come.

(*She does so.*)

3RD LADY Mind they don't see you, Mama.

DOWAGER I shall keep my eye on the door.

(*And you see her keeping her eye on it. Meanwhile* GREVILLE [*of the Memoirs*] *has strolled up to two of the Gentlemen of the Court who stand talking together.*)

1ST GENTLEMAN Good evening, Greville. Rather a dull dinner, don't you think?

GREVILLE Much as usual — the conversation.

1ST GENTLEMAN A bit longer, though; and the cooking not very good.

GREVILLE It's not the cooking so much as the service. It's generally luke-warm by the time it gets to me. Being only a commoner, I don't get served till last.

2ND GENTLEMAN They don't give you much wine, do they? — not now.

1ST GENTLEMAN D'you want more of it? If, as one of his new activities, the Prince is his own taster — he doesn't know what good wine is, *I* say.

GREVILLE Oh, I think he does. But drinking is not encouraged now — as it used to be. That's why we have to come up with the Ladies.

2ND GENTLEMAN I hear that His Royal Highness, the Duke of Sussex, is going to look in this evening.

1ST GENTLEMAN Oh . . . Invited?

GREVILLE I think not. He seldom is now, you know.

2ND GENTLEMAN His Lady Cecilia is going to be made a Duchess, I'm told.

1ST GENTLEMAN Yes: of Inverness, his second title. I suppose he's coming to return thanks.

GREVILLE Rather absurd making her a Duchess — Inverness being only an Earldom.

2ND GENTLEMAN Yes; but it's very nice and handsome of Her Majesty — shows respect for her old uncle.

GREVILLE The only respectable one left: Hanover not counting.

(*They laugh, for the morals of Ernest, Duke of Cumberland, and King of Hanover are a byword.*)

DOWAGER Oh! Here they come!

(*She pulls herself up from her chair. Hastily the Ladies and Gentlemen form themselves into a half-circle and stand at Court-attention.*)

Attendants have thrown open the doors: THE QUEEN *enters, accompanied by* PRINCE ALBERT, *and* THE DUCHESS OF KENT.)

THE QUEEN Go and sit down, Mama dear. Who would you like to have at your whist-table this evening?

THE DUCHESS Oh, I do not mind, my dear. Anybody you like. (*Then, in a whisper*) But not that old Lady Seward: she always looks so cross when I win from her anything.

THE QUEEN Albert, will you send two of the Gentlemen?
(THE DUCHESS, *pausing on her way to speak to one or two Ladies of the Court, goes over to her whist-corner, where others presently join her, and they sit down to play. Meanwhile* THE QUEEN *and* PRINCE ALBERT *have begun their nightly round.* THE QUEEN *starts with one of the Ladies,* THE PRINCE *with one of the Gentlemen. And as most of what they say is a mere formal routine, it does not much matter if, as they speak together, we do not always hear what each is saying.*)

THE QUEEN Good evening, Lady Normanby. I hope you are quite well.

LADY NORMANBY I thank your Majesty; I am — very well indeed. And your Majesty is quite well also?

THE QUEEN Oh, yes, I am *quite* well. I always am. And now will you be good enough to go and join the Duchess for whist, Lady Normanby?

LADY NORMANBY With pleasure, your Majesty.

(THE QUEEN *moves on to the next,* LADY NORMANBY *makes her a curtsy, and goes.*)

DOWAGER (*to daughter*) Oh, dear! There goes *my* chance. So stand I must!

(*Meanwhile* PRINCE ALBERT *has made a similar start. He picks out his two Gentlemen: and as he goes up to them they bow.*)

THE PRINCE Ah, good evening, Gentlemen. It has been a fine day, has it not?

1ST GENTLEMAN It has indeed, your Highness.

2ND GENTLEMAN A very fine day, your Highness.

E

THE PRINCE Her Royal Highness, the Duchess, requires two Gentlemen to make up her whist-party. Will you be good enough? (*They bow*) Thank you.

> (THE PRINCE *moves up one. The two Gentlemen make their parting bows, and go across to the whist-table. And now* THE QUEEN *has started on conversation number two; with* THE PRINCE *following sedately at her heels. Thus, by good timing, they are able, with just a passing word and a bow, to pick up alternatives.*)

THE QUEEN Good evening, Lady Charlotte. I am glad you have got back from your holiday. I hope you have enjoyed it.

LADY CHARLOTTE Very much, your Majesty.

THE QUEEN But you were not at dinner this evening.

LADY CHARLOTTE No, your Majesty; I was unfortunately late in arriving.

THE QUEEN You have dined somewhere, I hope?

LADY CHARLOTTE Oh, yes, your Majesty.

THE QUEEN After your long journey, it would be so necessary.

LADY CHARLOTTE I thank your Majesty, I had all that I needed.

THE QUEEN And to-morrow you will be in attendance again?

LADY CHARLOTTE Yes, your Majesty.

> (THE QUEEN *moves on, and passes with a bow and a smile the one who stands next in the circle.*)

THE QUEEN Good evening, Lord Trevors. I think the Prince wants to have a word with you.

THE PRINCE (*following on*) How do you do, Lord Trevors, so you are back from abroad at last. You have been away a long time.

LORD TREVORS For three months, Sir.

THE PRINCE And how did you find Europe?

LORD TREVORS Still a little uncertain, your Highness, whether she belongs to the eighteenth or the nineteenth century.

THE PRINCE That is true of England also.

LORD TREVORS But surely less so, your Highness, than of most countries.

THE PRINCE   I am not so sure of that as you seem to be. What you are accustomed to, I see freshly. Windsor is not eighteenth century: it is fifteenth, sixteenth, and seventeenth. I am going to require your assistance, as Lord Steward of the Castle, to make Windsor more of the nineteenth century than it is at present.

LORD TREVORS   I shall be most honoured, your Highness.

THE PRINCE . About that I shall see you to-morrow.

(THE QUEEN *has now come to* MR. GREVILLE. THE PRINCE *passes on, and enters into conversation with* THE DOWAGER LADY SEWARD *and her daughter.*)

Good evening, Lady Seward, I hope that I see you well.

LADY SEWARD   Quite well, I thank your Highness.

THE PRINCE   And your daughter, she is well also? She has recovered from those measles that she had?

LADY SEWARD   Oh yes: quite recovered now, your Highness thank you.

THE QUEEN   Good evening, Mr. Greville. Have you been riding to-day?

GREVILLE   No, Ma'am, I have not.

THE QUEEN   It was a fine day.

GREVILLE   Yes, Ma'am, a very fine day.

THE QUEEN   It was rather cold, though.

GREVILLE   It *was* rather cold, Ma'am.

THE QUEEN   Your sister, Lady Francis Egerton, rides, I think, doesn't she?

GREVILLE   She does ride sometimes, Ma'am.

(*There is a short pause; then* GREVILLE *himself takes up the running.*)

Has your Majesty been riding to-day?

THE QUEEN   Oh, yes, a very long ride.

GREVILLE   Has your Majesty got a nice horse?

THE QUEEN   Oh, a very nice horse.

(THE QUEEN *smiles, inclines her head, and passes on, leaving* MR. GREVILLE *with his deep bow still unfinished.*)

THE PRINCE (*coming to the next upon his round*) Lord FitzWilliam, will you come and play chess with me?

LORD FITZWILLIAM Most honoured and delighted, Sir.

THE PRINCE (*as they move off to the chess-table*) I must give you your revenge. Last week I beat you.

(THE QUEEN *comes to* THE DOWAGER LADY SEWARD *and her daughter.*)

THE QUEEN You look tired, Lady Seward.

LADY SEWARD I am rather tired, your Majesty.

THE QUEEN I am sorry I can't ask you to sit down — not here — unless it were to play whist. But I'm told that you don't like whist.

LADY SEWARD Oh, but I do, your Majesty. Only I play so badly that I nearly always lose.

THE QUEEN That is a pity: it makes playing rather depressing, doesn't it?

LADY SEWARD It does rather, Ma'am.

THE QUEEN (*to the daughter*) And do you, also, sometimes play whist; as well as music?

(*Before the question can be answered one of the Queen's Gentlemen has come in, and is now waiting to catch the Royal eye, and receive permission to speak.*)

THE QUEEN Yes?

GENTLEMAN His Royal Highness, the Duke of Sussex, is here, your Majesty.

THE QUEEN Oh?

(*She turns in some doubt and looks towards* PRINCE ALBERT, *who has now sat down and started his game of chess. But no time is given her;* THE DUKE *himself enters, without waiting for further announcement.*)

SUSSEX Ah! Victoria, my dear; you didn't expect to see me, did you?

THE QUEEN No, Uncle Augustus: we asked you last week, you know.

SUSSEX Yes; and last week, I couldn't come — a touch of gout; so I've come now instead.

THE QUEEN   But, my dear Uncle, we have already dined.

SUSSEX   Oh, yes, and I've dined too: that's all right.

(Evidently he has; he sways as he stands, and his words are not quite as clear as they ought to be.)

I wanted to thank you, my dear, for what you've promised to do for Lady Cecilia.

THE QUEEN   Oh, yes, but we won't talk of that now — please.

(But apparently he will talk of it.)

SUSSEX   She's delighted; so am I. It should have been done long ago; but your Uncle George wouldn't, nor would your Uncle William, damn him! ... And now *you've* done the right thing. Much obliged to you.

THE QUEEN   Uncle Augustus, please, not *now*. Besides — I have not done it *yet*.

(At the warning thus conveyed, THE DUKE opens flabbergasted eyes. Can she mean ...? But while he stands mumbling for the word, there comes interruption. At the whist-table the voice of THE DUCHESS is raised in sudden excitement, and presently becomes tempestuous.)

THE DUCHESS   Oh, but you have revoked! You take my trick? No!

LADY NORMANBY   Pardon me, Ma'am, indeed I have *not* revoked.

THE QUEEN   Excuse me, dear Uncle. I must go to Mama.

THE DUCHESS   But there — the last trick: you did not play a trump. No, you did *not*. See!

(She turns up the cards, and points.)

LADY NORMANBY   I beg pardon, your Royal Highness; but that was not *my* card. It was your Royal Highness who forgot to play a trump.

THE DUCHESS   You can say it was I that revoked? Oh, how can I play with such people! *(Then, diverting her wrath to her own partner)* And with a partner who does not know how to play!

THE QUEEN *(intervening)*   Mama dear, I'm afraid you are not enjoying the game: would you not like to leave off!

THE DUCHESS   No, no!

THE QUEEN Then perhaps you would prefer a change of partners?

THE DUCHESS (*emphatically*) Yes, I would!

THE QUEEN Then, Gentlemen — will you please change places? And, Lady Normanby, when you have finished the rubber, would you mind if I ask Lady Seward to take your place?

LADY NORMANBY Anything that pleases your Majesty.

THE DUCHESS No! I do not want her.

THE QUEEN I think it will be better, Mama. I will go and tell her.

(*Meanwhile* THE DUKE *is talking to* LADY SEWARD)

THE DUKE Well, Lady Seward, and how are you? I was told you were out of town — having measles, all of you?

LADY SEWARD Oh, no, sir; only one of us — my daughter, who has now quite recovered.

THE DUKE (*to the daughter*) What *you*? Keep your distance, then! Keep your distance! With measles one can never be sure. And I've never had 'em. I think I'd better be off. (*So saying, he moves away.*)

THE QUEEN (*going across to* LADY SEWARD) Lady Seward, will you come and take Lady Normanby's place at the whist-table, as soon as this rubber is over?

LADY SEWARD Oh, delighted, your Majesty.

(*They go across to the whist-party.*)

(*Ever since* THE DUKE's *arrival,* THE PRINCE *has been regarding him with a disapproving eye. He now signals one of his Gentlemen to come and speak to him.*)

THE PRINCE Will you go and ask His Royal Highness if he will be pleased to sit down?

(THE DUKE, *with a slightly swaying motion, is now making towards a group of the Gentlemen in Attendance, who stand staidly talking in the hushed voices which Court etiquette requires. But* THE DUKE's *voice is by no means hushed.*)

THE DUKE Ah, good evening, Gentlemen; good evening.

(*The Gentlemen turn and make the formal bows required by Royalty.*)

GENTLEMAN   The Prince has charged me to say that he hopes your Royal Highness will be pleased to sit down.

THE DUKE   Sit down? Of course I shall sit down, when I want to sit down. (*Then, mumbling to himself as he goes*) Shouldn't wait till His Paper Highness gave me permission. No!

> (*Insinuatingly the Prince's Gentleman has manœuvred him to a chair which is half-screened from the Royal Presence.*)

GENTLEMAN   I think your Royal Highness will find this chair a comfortable one.

THE DUKE (*a little tetchy at being thus looked after*)   All right, all right! (*He turns, and looks back before seating himself.*) Here, Munro, come and talk to me, I've something to tell you.

> (LORD MUNRO *leaves the group and goes across to* THE DUKE.)

THE QUEEN   Lady Normanby, if Mama can now spare you, will you come and look through this portfolio of drawings with me? They are by Landseer; studies of dogs and horses, most beautifully done.

LADY NORMANBY (*rising*)   Indeed, Ma'am, I shall be charmed — delighted.

> (*And now we hear* THE DUKE *getting into the thread of his narrative.*)

THE DUKE   Yes: well, you know who I mean — needn't name names. She used to be a circus-rider, you know; rode beautifully, but no one was supposed to know it. Well, here was he up to his eyes in debt; and his horse not much in the running. But she says that if he'll let her dress up as a jockey (with a boy's name, you know) she'll win it for him. Long and short of it was he did let her, and she did win it. Then they found out and wanted to disqualify. Don't know what damned rule there was against a woman being a jockey; did you ever hear of one?

MUNRO   No, sir, I never did.

THE DUKE   But for that race apparently there was. Well, there was going to be an awful row about it, but it was hushed up. No more's going to be heard of it — not by the public, at any rate. But I'm telling you. And I know it's true because now he's paying some of his debts. (*He breaks into loud chuckles.*) As for *her* — in another year I shouldn't wonder, she'll be back at the Circus, making money for both of 'em.

(*Once more* THE PRINCE *signals to his Gentleman.*)

THE PRINCE   Will you go, please, and inform His Royal Highness that his carriage is waiting.

THE QUEEN (*as she turns over the portfolio*) And isn't that beautiful? So like life: you can almost see him wagging his tail. I do think Mr. Landseer is a great artist.

LADY NORMANBY   He is indeed, Ma'am.

(*The Gentleman has had to wait while* THE DUKE *is finishing his last bout of laughter, before delivering his message.*)

GENTLEMAN   The Prince requests me to inform your Royal Highness that your Royal Highness's carriage is waiting.

THE DUKE   Waiting? Well, damn it! Let it wait! You hear that, Munro? You hear that?

MUNRO   I did hear it, Sir.

THE DUKE   Damned impudence, I call that. I've more than a mind to go and ask the Queen what she thinks of it.

MUNRO   I wouldn't, if I were you, Sir.

THE DUKE   You wouldn't? Well, anyway, I shall write to her.

(THE PRINCE, *seeing that* THE DUKE *makes no sign of going, by a slight gesture of the head summons the Gentleman to report to him.*)

THE PRINCE   What did he say?

GENTLEMAN   He said, Sir, 'Damn it: let it wait.'

THE PRINCE   You will please to go and inform His Royal Highness that his carriage is still waiting, and is not to be kept waiting.

GENTLEMAN (*stiffly obedient*) Yes, Sir.

(THE DUKE *meanwhile has cocked an eye in* THE PRINCE'S *direction. He watches the Gentleman as he returns diffidently to the charge.*)

GENTLEMAN   I beg pardon, Sir. I am to inform your Royal Highness —

(*He is allowed to say no more.* THE DUKE *stumbles to his feet, puffing with rage.*)

THE DUKE Get out of my way! Don't want to hear another word. I'm going. (*Then, turning to* LORD MUNRO) So this is the way he thinks he can treat me, is it? We'll see.

(*Still rather uncertain on his feet, he passes defiantly in front of* THE PRINCE, *who on a half-rise, bows acknowledgment of his departure, and in a tone more frigid than silence says 'Good night, Sir.'* THE DUKE *glares, but does not respond.* THE QUEEN, *meanwhile, who all along has been uncomfortably aware of things, now looks up apprehensively, and a little distressed.*)

THE DUKE Good night, Victoria. Your old Uncle's carriage is waiting.

THE QUEEN Good night, Uncle.

(*He has gone. She turns and looks at* THE PRINCE, *who imperturbably resumes his game.*)

THE PRINCE Check.

THE QUEEN Mama, are you winning?

THE DUCHESS No; I am not winning — anything.

THE QUEEN Miss Seward, did you remember to bring your music?

MISS SEWARD Yes, Ma'am.

THE QUEEN Then will you go into the music-room and sing something?

MISS SEWARD Is there anything your Majesty would like me to sing?

THE QUEEN No, sing just what you like. Something soothing would be nice.

(MISS SEWARD *curtsies and goes into the next room, the folding doors of which stand open.*)

LORD MUNRO (*in an undertone to* GREVILLE) Well, what do you think of that?

GREVILLE I'm rather grateful to the old boy. It has made the evening a little less dull.

(*And now* MISS SEWARD, *out of a rather small repertory, has made her selection. The songs of Mrs. Norton, though popular, are barred*

on account of that lady's matrimonial troubles; and 'Shepherds tell me'
[with its inquiries about 'Flora'] has also, during the last year, fallen
into disfavour. But as a harmless though quite unnecessary soporific
what the young lady has now chosen could not be bettered: sweetly
and softly through the open door come the strains of music — voice
with piano accompaniment.)

MISS SEWARD

Peaceful slumbering on the ocean,
Seamen fear no danger nigh;
The winds and waves in gentle motion
Soothe them with their lullaby.
Lullaby, Lullaby,
Lullaby, Lullaby,
Soothe them with their lullaby.

(As the music begins the Gentlemen stop talking. They have to
appear attentive, but they are bored. Two of the younger ones relieve
their boredom by furtive by-play, from a soundless mouthing of the
words, they pass gradually into a subdued representation of seamen
slumbering. From this they are roused by the voice of THE DUCHESS.)

THE DUCHESS *(throwing down her cards)* I have no luck to-night!
The cards are all wrong. And this *(indicating the music)* is making
me so sleepy. *(Then, in a whisper to* THE QUEEN) Victoria, my dear,
do you mind if I go to bed?

(But Victoria does mind)

THE QUEEN We shall all go to bed at eleven, Mama. Please wait.
(The song, with its long drawn 'Lullabies', goes on. A symbolic
fading of light falls over the stage. At the whist-table somebody deals;
THE QUEEN *continues to turn over the portfolio of Landseer drawings;*
THE PRINCE *continues to play chess. The Gentlemen of the Court,*
now that even conversation is denied them, continue to stand, and
yawn. MISS SEWARD *continues to soothe them with her lullabies.*
The clock has not yet struck the blessed hour of eleven, when the
curtain slowly closes.)

LEADING-STRINGS

1841

THE QUEEN (*it is still in the early days of her marriage*) *sits writing in one of the private apartments at Windsor. She looks at the clock which has just struck, and speaks to a Lady-in-Waiting, who stands at attention in the background.*

THE QUEEN Will you, please, go and send the Prince to me? It is ten o'clock; he ought to be here.

(*The Lady curtsies and goes.* THE QUEEN *takes up a small framed portrait: gazes upon it fondly: and resumes her writing. A stage-minute later (that is to say, ten seconds)* PRINCE ALBERT *enters: he carries a small nosegay, which he deposits with courtly grace in front of her. She lays down her pen, and, taking up the flowers to smell,* **says,** *correctively but not severely:*)

Ah! I was wondering when these would come.

ALBERT (*still very foreign in his pronunciation*) You did not think that I had forgotten?

THE QUEEN No, I only thought you were a little late; as you *are*.

ALBERT Just one minute. I do not yet quite know, to realize, how long at Windsor, it shall take to get from one place to another.

THE QUEEN It is all very grand and large, is it not? But that is what we — in our position — have to put up with.

ALBERT Would it not be rather nice to make one corner of it our own?

THE QUEEN How do you mean — our own? It is *all* ours.

ALBERT More private: where no one can come but ourselves. I mean — during the day.

THE QUEEN But we are quite private enough here, are we not?

ALBERT No. At any moment someone comes and knocks; one of your Ladies, or Secretaries. I mean a room — a suite all private to itself — where, when you have seen your Ministers, and all the rest, we can go in together, and not be disturbed by anyone: where it is known that — except on something emergent — no one shall come.

THE QUEEN   Yes. Ah! yes.

ALBERT   Where, by ourselves, you could sing to me, and I could play to you, and read to you.

THE QUEEN   Yes, Albert, that is just what I should love. I will have it all arranged for.

ALBERT   Will you not let me do it — my own way?

THE QUEEN   You think I shall not do it as you wish, Albert?

ALBERT   Not so at all. But this I would just like to do — myself. At present it seems there is so little I *may* do.

THE QUEEN   But you do a great deal, Dearest, everything that I *want* you to do.

ALBERT   (*sadly*)   Yes. And that is all.

THE QUEEN   Is that not enough? . . . What is the matter?

ALBERT   I could wish that you wanted me to do a little more, Vicky — in my own way.

THE QUEEN   But what else *can* you do?

ALBERT   Who knows — till you have let me try? There are so many things here that want doing badly.

THE QUEEN   What sort of things?

ALBERT   Almost everything. The service — the ménage here is more than one hundred years old. We are still in the Middle Ages — almost.

THE QUEEN   But that is so interesting!

ALBERT   And so wasteful.

THE QUEEN   Wasteful? Why?

ALBERT   I will give you just an instance. The other day, for curiosity, I asked to be told the scale on which things for the commissariat are ordered — daily, weekly, monthly; the meat, the wine, and all the rest of it. My Dear, it is more like the provisioning of an army than of a single establishment.

THE QUEEN   But this is Windsor.

ALBERT It is a dozen Windsors — the Windsors of four Reigns at least all rolled into one. One of the things I discovered was that anything once ordered always goes on being ordered. The thing is sent in and paid for, but it is not used.

THE QUEEN Then where does it go?

ALBERT Where? You may well ask.

THE QUEEN Then I shall look into it at once, and have it altered.

ALBERT Why not let *me* do it?

THE QUEEN You, Albert? But you do not understand our English ways.

ALBERT But it is I who have discovered it.

THE QUEEN Yes. How did you? Did you go into the kitchens, Albert?

ALBERT No; and I did not disguise myself either. I went to the Controller's office, to the desk of the Head Accountant, and asked if I might see the books. I was told no, impossible. I went and took them down from the shelf, and looked at them myself. I have been doing that now for a week.

THE QUEEN Behind my back; without asking me?

ALBERT Behind your back, Weibchen. And now, to your face, I tell it. Here you are, the Queen of England, and being cheated by your own servants. Let me give you just one or two instances. You have in your stables twice so many horses than you can use. Who uses them? They have become the perquisite of your head-stableman. He hires them out.

THE QUEEN My horses hired! How improper! How abominable!

ALBERT Yes.

THE QUEEN And how dishonest!

ALBERT They do not think so. Custom has sanctioned it. They are quite open about it, when it is found out; and when you alter it, as it should be altered, they will consider themselves defrauded.

THE QUEEN Then they shall! But how extraordinary that such a thing should ever have been allowed!

ALBERT I will give you one other instance — very funny. I found there was in the provision list, every month, forty pounds' weight of tallow candles. It surprised me to find that tallow candles were used here at all. I inquired; they were not. The tallow candles just come in to be looked at, and go out again. They are one of the kitchen perquisities.

THE QUEEN (*scandalized*) Really!

ALBERT And how did they come in the first place? Thirty years ago, old King George, your Grandpapa, had a cold in his nose; and tallows were ordered for it. In those days that was the cure. So the tallow has been on order ever since, though the nose that it was ordered to soothe has been twenty-one years in the grave.

THE QUEEN But forty pounds, Albert!

ALBERT Yes, my Dear, for the nose of a King — forty pounds; anything less than that would not have looked well in the accounts.

THE QUEEN And you have found all this out, Albert, by yourself?

ALBERT Yes. With a lot of black faces looking on — while I did so.

THE QUEEN I think you should have come to me first, before doing so.

ALBERT Why?

THE QUEEN For permission; that you might have my authority.

ALBERT No, Vicky, I am not going to ask your permission for everything.

THE QUEEN Do you mean that?

ALBERT Very much so, I mean it.

THE QUEEN Albert, is this going to be the first time that you disobey me?

ALBERT Perhaps it should have come earlier. It will not be the last.

THE QUEEN Albert! You forget yourself!

ALBERT I think, sometimes, that *you* forget *me*: that I am not your lover only, for you to play with and fondle. I am your husband too.

THE QUEEN And am not I — a good wife?

ALBERT   You are all that is kind; and I am grateful. But am I always to be a stranger in this country of yours?

THE QUEEN   Oh, do not say that; you hurt me! But it takes time. You see, Albert dear, you are so good — so serious about things — that you find it difficult to understand people — *other* people, I mean, who are different.

ALBERT   Goodness should not prevent understanding, Vicky.

THE QUEEN   But it does, Dearest! It makes you judge people too strictly.

ALBERT   But do I?

THE QUEEN   Of course you do! And in a way, I like it — because it shows me *you*. But sometimes it is rather inconvenient, you know.

ALBERT   For instance?

THE QUEEN   Well, don't you remember, the other night, when Uncle Augustus came in after dinner, having dined elsewhere. And of course, he *had* dined as usual; and so — almost at once — you sent one of your gentlemen, with your compliments, to tell him that his carriage was waiting.

ALBERT   How did you know?

THE QUEEN   He wrote to me the next day: such an explosive letter, saying such things about you, that I couldn't possibly let you read it . . . So you see, Dear —

ALBERT   Do you wish that I had let him stay?

THE QUEEN   I wish that you had left it to me, Albert; for I had already decided what to do.

ALBERT   And what had you decided?

THE QUEEN   I was going to bring the Court to an end by retiring early. Then all would have gone off quite naturally, and no one would have noticed. It would have been better, Dearest.

ALBERT   And suppose the incident had been repeated?

THE QUEEN   Well, Albert, after all he is an old man; and we can't expect to alter him now.

ALBERT   But we do expect your Court to alter, from what it has been, do we not? From what I have heard, there is already a great difference.

THE QUEEN Oh, yes; and it is nearly all your doing, Albert. And I would not have it otherwise, except for my Uncle, for whom we must make allowance.

ALBERT Even your Uncles should be made to respect you.

THE QUEEN But they do, I am sure.

ALBERT It was not respectful for him to come as he came the other night.

THE QUEEN It would not have been, had he quite realized — had he known —

ALBERT How drunk he was?

THE QUEEN Albert, he *is* my Uncle. Please don't use such a common expression about one of *us*.

ALBERT Is it too common — that word — said in English? Forgive me; I will say it in German.

THE QUEEN No, Albert. I wish you to talk English still, till you are more used to it.

(*He moves away from her, controlling himself by an effort. She goes after him.*)

Of course, Dearest, I love to hear you speak your own language, *sometimes*. It is so much more yourself. But till you know it better, you must, please, still speak English. And it is the same about English ways and customs — you must get to know them better, and be more like the rest of us.

ALBERT You wish me to become English?

THE QUEEN Why, of course. *I* am English; so my Husband must be English, too.

ALBERT For that one should have begun earlier.

THE QUEEN I married you as soon as ever I could, Albert.

ALBERT Ah! Weibchen! So long as you do not repent of it.

THE QUEEN You are happy, Albert?

ALBERT I will be more than happy, so long as — serving you — I am able to make a life worth living. But you must let me serve you — not feel myself useless.

THE QUEEN Useless!

ALBERT   Sometimes I feel that I am put — not quite in the corner, but on the shelf, just a little.

THE QUEEN   Who does that?

ALBERT   You, my Dear.

THE QUEEN   But I — I worship you, Albert.

ALBERT   Too much! Let me come down to earth a little, now and then. Give my hands and brain something to do, so that I may be able to respect myself. Am I only your plaything? Your —

THE QUEEN   Albert!

ALBERT   All day you work for hours with Ministers and Secretaries. And while they are with you, I may not come in. At the end of it I see you worn out from doing it all alone; but I may not help you. You do not even speak! Sometimes there are things that are still doubtful — how to decide; and I may not advise you. You do not ask me, or tell me anything!

THE QUEEN   But Albert! Albert! You do not understand! The English are so jealous; they don't know you as I know you. They still look upon you as a foreigner, and are suspicious, for fear I should let you — advise me.

ALBERT   Am I *never* to help, or advise you — never? From your life's work am I always to be shut out?

THE QUEEN   But you do help me — so much!

ALBERT   Let me help you *now*.

THE QUEEN   How?

ALBERT   Let me see some of those papers that you spend so long over. I could read them for you, and make a few notes. That would save you time.

THE QUEEN   Oh, but I must see everything *myself*. That is what I am here for.

ALBERT   Do you suppose your Ministers show you everything?

THE QUEEN   Why, of course!

ALBERT   Impossible. Government is not as simple as all that. They themselves have to rely upon others for much that has to be done; even in things for which they are responsible. Cannot you rely upon me . . . a little?

THE QUEEN Albert, Dearest, you distress me! In every way that is possible, I do already rely on you; and always, in everything that I have had to decide *for* you, I have only done it for your good.

ALBERT Yes, you even chose my secretary for me.

THE QUEEN Why of course, Albert! How could *you* know — coming here a stranger — who would be the best?

ALBERT (*continuing*) Who reports to you — regularly, I believe.

THE QUEEN Surely you don't mind my knowing?

ALBERT I would prefer to tell you myself what I do. In future I mean to.

THE QUEEN Why, of course. I always wish to hear everything.

ALBERT Yes. The other day I made an engagement. You cancelled it.

THE QUEEN Yes, Albert. I had very good reason for doing so.

ALBERT No doubt. You did not speak to me about it.

THE QUEEN But that was to spare your feelings.

ALBERT But my secretary knew. When I questioned him why one engagement entered into my diary for this week had been struck out, he said he had done so under instruction.

THE QUEEN Yes, Albert.

ALBERT From *you*.

THE QUEEN You were going to dine, he told me, with a foreign Minister. It would have been in the papers. My Government did not wish that, just now, any member of the Royal Family should pay him such a compliment.

ALBERT You see, I am told nothing of your relations with foreign countries. I see only what appears in the newspapers . . . Not only do you not give me your confidence, but you have me watched. To-morrow I am going to choose another secretary — for myself.

THE QUEEN Albert, you are making a great mistake!

ALBERT Repairing one. I ought to have done this before.

THE QUEEN You are not to do it, Albert . . . I say you are not to.

ALBERT   Then, for the present, I leave you.

(*He turns to go.*)

THE QUEEN   Where are you going?

ALBERT   In here, to my own room, to write my letters — alone.

(*He goes in, and closes the door. We hear the key turn in the lock.* THE QUEEN *also hears it, and starts to her feet. Very angry, but a little frightened, she pauses, then advances resolutely to the door, and tries it. The door does not yield. She beats upon it violently with her hand, pauses, then beats again.*)

THE QUEEN   Open the door! Albert, open the door!

ALBERT (*from within*)   Who is that speaking?

THE QUEEN   Her Majesty, the Queen!

ALBERT   Her Majesty, the Queen, must wait.

(THE QUEEN *stands, hardly believing her ears. She stands for a long time. Her eyes turn to the door questioning it about this unbelievable situation, which (for such a thing has never happened before) she cannot yet understand. For a moment, foolish, fiery resolution takes hold of her: she crosses the room and lays her hand upon the bell-rope. Ye Gods! What is her little Majesty going to do now? But fundamental common sense comes to her rescue; and with common sense comes, also, understanding. Timidly now, biting her lips, trying to keep back the tears, she crosses again, and stands irresolutely at the door. In a very different way now, her hand advances, she knocks softly, pauses, and knocks again. And as she listens the beloved voice speaks again from within.*)

ALBERT   Who is there?

(*There is a pause. The tears come rushing; her voice trembles as she speaks.*)

THE QUEEN   Your Wife, Albert! Your poor, unhappy little Wife!

(*The door opens.* ALBERT *appears. She flings herself into his arms.*) Oh, Albert! Albert! Albert!

ALBERT   Hush, hush, Weibchen! Don't cry! Don't cry! It's all right.

(*But she does cry. How long does not matter, for it is doing her good.*)

'A GOOD LESSON!'

1842

It is ten o'clock, and a bright morning. In THE PRINCE'S *writing-room at Buckingham Palace,* MR. ANSON, *his Private Secretary, stands by the table, sorting correspondence; opened letters he places in one heap, unopened in another. The door opens; one of* THE QUEEN'S GENTLE-MEN *enters.*

GENTLEMAN Her Majesty wishes to know whether the Prince has yet returned?

ANSON (*in a quiet, matter-of-fact tone*) No . . . At least, so far as I know, he has not.

GENTLEMAN (*hesitating*) Oh? . . . Do you know, Mr. Anson, where the Prince *is*?

ANSON (*with studied nonchalance*) Now? . . . No, I don't.

GENTLEMAN (*with embarrassment*) You know, I suppose, that His Highness did not return to the Palace, last night?

ANSON (*as before*) From the Royal Academy Dinner? Oh indeed . . . didn't he?

GENTLEMAN (*making a plunge*) Did he *go*, Mr. Anson?

ANSON Oh, yes, I think so. The papers *say* that he did. Here is his speech, fully reported, in this morning's *Times*; and a very good one, too.

GENTLEMAN Very strange, Mr. Anson!

ANSON Not at all. His speeches generally are.

GENTLEMAN I meant — his not returning.

ANSON (*coldly*) Hadn't you better report to Her Majesty that His Highness has *not* yet returned? That, I believe, was all you were sent to find out.

GENTLEMAN (*stiffly*) Certainly. I will.

> (*He goes.* ANSON *continues sorting the letters. There comes a knock at the door; and permission given — in comes* THE PRINCE'S *Valet,* MR. RICHARDS.)

RICHARDS I beg pardon, Sir. I heard you were alone: so I came to see you, Sir.

ANSON Yes? What is it, Richards?

RICHARDS His Royal Highness, Sir . . . He hasn't sent for me this morning, Sir: and didn't last night, either. He doesn't seem to have been in his dressing-room at all, Sir: not since I dressed him last night, for the Dinner.

ANSON Oh, it's all right, Richards. His Royal Highness was unexpectedly called elsewhere, at a late hour last night, so did not return.

RICHARDS (*reassured*) Oh, very good, Sir.

ANSON I expect His Royal Highness to be back before long. So you be ready for him.

RICHARDS Yes, Sir. Very good, Sir.

(*He goes.* ANSON, *left to himself, can no longer conceal his anxiety.*)

ANSON But is it 'all right', I wonder? . . . God!

(*Nervously he snatches up the paper, then throws it down again. He moves restlessly to the window, and back again. The door opens; in comes* PRINCE ALBERT, *looking very calm and collected.*)

ALBERT (*quietly*) Good morning, Anson.

ANSON Good morning, Sir.

ALBERT Is there any news this morning? — anything special?

ANSON In the papers, Sir? A full report of the Academy Banquet. (*He takes up* The Times, *and offers it.*) Did that go off well, Sir?

ALBERT (*not taking it*) Very well.

ANSON I was just reading your Highness's speech.

ALBERT Yes, Anson; of which you wrote for me the notes.

ANSON At your Highness's dictation.

ALBERT Well, I did not make it too long, I hope?

ANSON It reads very well, Sir. And it seems to have been well received.

ALBERT   Yes; it was altogether a very well managed affair. And I found the company quite interesting. We were talking of the decorations for the walls of the new Houses of Parliament; and I was proposing that there should be a Competition and a Fine Arts Commission to decide it. They thought it was a good idea.

ANSON   Well, Sir, if a Competition will produce the right artists, it certainly will be. But we have not had much practice of mural art in this country, Sir, I'm afraid; we don't run to it.

ALBERT   We must begin, then, and try.

ANSON   Yes, Sir.

ALBERT   That was Sir Francis Chantrey's objection. But when I said to him — 'How would it do, then, to employ foreign Artists?' he said that if they came, their heads would be broken; and that — old as he was — he would himself lend a hand for the purpose.

ANSON   Indeed, Sir?

ALBERT   Yes, indeed! So you see! . . .

(THE PRINCE *seats himself at his writing-table.*)

ALBERT   Letters?

ANSON (*handing some*) These, Sir, I think, are all that your Highness need see for the present.

ALBERT   Thank you.

(THE QUEEN'S GENTLEMAN *again enters.*)

GENTLEMAN   Her Majesty sent me to inquire if your Royal Highness was disengaged?

ALBERT   Oh, yes. Tell Her Majesty I am quite free, if she wishes to see me.

(*The* GENTLEMAN *bows, and retires.* THE PRINCE *continues to look over his correspondence.*)

Now you may go, Anson. Take all those letters, and leave me these.

(ANSON *retires.* THE PRINCE *goes on opening his correspondence. A minute passes; suddenly the door is flung open, and* THE QUEEN *makes a flamboyant entry.*)

THE QUEEN   Albert! Where have you been?

ALBERT To Windsor, Victoria.

THE QUEEN Windsor? Impossible! Why did you not come back, last night?

ALBERT I did not come back last night, Victoria, because of the way in which you sent for me.

THE QUEEN I told you before you went, that I wished you to be back by half-past ten at the latest.

ALBERT Yes.

THE QUEEN At half-past ten you had not come; so I sent for you.

ALBERT Yes, I received from you this note. (*He produces it.*) . . . 'Albert, it is quite time you were back. Please to come at once!'

THE QUEEN Yes; I wrote it; I sent it; and my orders were that it should be put into your hand by the Messenger to whom I gave it.

ALBERT It was put into my hand. I sent back word to say that I had received it.

THE QUEEN Yes; but you did not come!

ALBERT I did not come, because I was not then ready to come.

THE QUEEN Albert! when you go anywhere without *me* (as you *had* to do on this occasion), I do not expect you to be late.

ALBERT No. But when I do go without you, you must leave it for me to decide, myself, when I shall return.

THE QUEEN But this time I had already told you my wishes, and had decided *for* you . . . I sent again.

ALBERT Yes. At eleven o'clock, I received this. (*He produces it.*) 'Albert, I order you to return at once! V.R.'

THE QUEEN And still you did not!

ALBERT I did not.

THE QUEEN So you disobeyed your Queen!

ALBERT (*serenely*) Yes, my Dear; I disobeyed my Queen. Send me to the Tower for it, and cut off my head.

THE QUEEN I do not regard this as a subject for amusement and jest, Albert.

ALBERT No? Then it is lucky that *I* do. For if neither of us thought it amusing, we might have quite a serious quarrel about it. But now — as it is only you who do not think it amusing — the quarrel will not be so serious.

THE QUEEN Albert, what did you do, after I had ordered you to return? Where did you spend the night?

ALBERT At Windsor, as I have told you.

THE QUEEN I don't believe it!

ALBERT Don't you?

(*Quietly he turns back to his letters.*)

THE QUEEN Albert, I will not be treated like this! Please to remember that, though I am your Wife, I am also your Queen.

ALBERT (*kindly*) Sit down, my Dear, sit down! there is nothing to stand up about . . . Last night there was; so I had to. But now I am ready to sit here and talk it over, quite reasonably and comfortably: just you and me, Weibchen — with the Queen left out . . . Please! (*With a gesture he gets her seated.*) Listen to me, my Dear. When you married me, you made a promise that was strange for a Queen to make: but you made it . . . To love, honour, and obey. And because it was so strange — so unlikely — I have never once told you to obey me — except for fun, when you wished it. Now, my Dear, as I have not expected *you* to obey *me* in anything — so there are some things in which you must not expect *me* to obey *you*.

THE QUEEN When you do things for me in public — officially, that is to say — then I *do* expect you to obey me.

ALBERT When I do things for you in public, my Dear, I obey you by doing them. But you must trust me to do them in my own way —

THE QUEEN No, Albert.

ALBERT — not to interfere with me, while I am doing them, as you did last night. That is why, when I started back — after having received your 'orders' — I told the Coachman to drive — not to Buckingham Palace, but to Windsor.

THE QUEEN The Coachman! You told him that! What must he have thought?

ALBERT   I will tell you what he thought . . . At first he thought it was very strange. But when we got to Windsor, he thought that he knew the reason.

THE QUEEN   Why, only then?

ALBERT   It was rather late: almost half-past one. But when we got there, there were lights, and music, and dancing.

THE QUEEN   Music! . . . Dancing! . . . *In* the Castle?

ALBERT   In the Castle . . . Behind our backs — so sure that we should be away — the servants were having a fancy-dress ball.

THE QUEEN (*her anger quite diverted*) What an improper liberty! Most extraordinary! And how fortunate that you should have caught them!

ALBERT   Yes; a curious coincidence, was it not? So, of course, the Coachman thought that I had got wind of the affair, and had come there to catch them at it.

THE QUEEN   Where were they dancing, Albert?

ALBERT   In the great Hall.

THE QUEEN   And in fancy-dress, you say?

ALBERT   Yes. Two of them had dressed up to look like you and me.

THE QUEEN   Albert! Did you see who they were?

ALBERT   No. They ran too quick! I went in, and stood . . . They were all very much surprised to see me.

THE QUEEN   Indeed, I should think so! . . . What happened then?

ALBERT   First, the dancing all stopped; then all the music . . . I stood there and looked at them. It was very funny: I tried not to laugh.

THE QUEEN   I hope you did not, Albert!

ALBERT   No; I composed myself to look as though I was very angry.

THE QUEEN   I hope you did. And then, what did you do?

ALBERT   I told them that they might go on for just five minutes more; but that it was not to happen again.

THE QUEEN   No, indeed!

ALBERT   And it will not, I am sure.

THE QUEEN   Did you get any explanation, as to why they had *dared* to do such a thing?

ALBERT   Oh, yes; it was explained. You see, they were to have had a ball soon after Christmas; but on the very date the Court had to go into mourning; so it was put off, and forgotten. And as they had got all the dresses, they were naturally disappointed.

THE QUEEN   But, Albert, that such a thing *could* happen without our knowing — well, it means that such a lot of other things may be happening too.

ALBERT   Yes; I am afraid so . . . I think, my Dear, that you had better make me your Manager of Windsor — factotum, you call it? They will not like it, because I have too much of a head for business; but it will be good for them. And for you, a great saving of unnecessary expense.

THE QUEEN   Yes; and if I do it at once, everybody will understand *why*.

ALBERT   It was a good thing, Vicky, was it not, that I was brought up rather poor?

THE QUEEN   So was I.

ALBERT   Yes? But you had not to manage much for yourself, had you? What for are you smiling at?

THE QUEEN   The servants, Albert! It *was* funny! I'm so glad you went; for now they will all be thinking how clever it was of you to find out! And what a good lesson it was for them, to be sure!

ALBERT   Yes, my Dear, a good lesson . . . But Weibchen, you have not kissed me 'Good Morning' yet . . . Please!

> (*And he says it so simply and sweetly, that, quite forgetting now what she first came about, she kisses him with true wifely affection, very fondly and contentedly.*)

UNDER FIRE

30th May 1842

In a room of Buckingham Palace overlooking the Park, PRINCE ALBERT
*moves impatiently to the window, and back again. He looks at his
watch; a slight sound of annoyance escapes him. The door opens; his
Private Secretary enters.*

ALBERT (*stiffly*) Mr. Anson, you are late.

ANSON I am sorry, Sir. I was just coming, when the Chief
Inspector of Police sent word that he wished to see me.

ALBERT (*sharply*) Has he news?

ANSON None, Sir. They can't trace the man. So he very
urgently begs that Her Majesty shall not drive out to-day.

ALBERT But that is nonsense! If Her Majesty does not drive in
the Park as usual, the man will suspect that we know. So we shall
not catch him.

ANSON It is a great risk, Sir.

ALBERT It is a risk. It has to be taken. It will be a greater risk
if we leave him to choose his own time later, when the Police will
not be so ready for him as they are to-day.

ANSON He will choose his own time in any case, Sir.

ALBERT Yes; but now it will be the earliest possible. Yesterday
when his pistol missed fire, he did not know that he was seen by
anyone. Her Majesty herself was looking the other way.

ANSON That was very fortunate, Sir.

ALBERT Perhaps . . . Why?

ANSON Had Her Majesty shown any alarm, it would have told
him.

ALBERT Her Majesty would have shown no alarm. You may be
quite sure of that. When I told Her Majesty afterwards, what had
happened, she was not alarmed at all; only rather surprised that one
of her subjects should have done anything so wicked and foolish.

ANSON Ah, yes, Sir; that is, indeed, how it might well —

ALBERT (*continuing*) Nor is Her Majesty alarmed now. It was her own decision, not mine, that we should go out to-day. When I told her that the man was sure to make another attempt, she said that he had better make it at once then, and get it over.

ANSON That was very courageous of Her Majesty.

ALBERT And very sensible. Sense is sometimes more valuable than courage — and much rarer where Kings are concerned. It is so here. I have no doubt that this afternoon the man will try again. It is better that he should try again, when we expect it, than at some later time when we do not. And that, Mr. Anson, is why — if the Inspector is so stupid that he must have it explained — that is why Her Majesty drives out again to-day, at her usual time. You will go and tell him that at once. (*He moves to the window.*) Out there are the people, waiting to see Her Majesty start. Tell him that we shall be punctual.

ANSON I will, your Highness . . . I hope —

ALBERT (*cutting him short*) We *all* hope, Mr. Anson. It is the only sensible thing to do. Ah, here is Her Majesty.

(THE QUEEN *enters in bonnet and shawl.* MR. ANSON *stands aside for her to pass, then bows himself out. A little nervous, but very self-controlled,* THE QUEEN *advances towards* THE PRINCE.)

ALBERT (*approvingly*) You are very punctual, my Dear.

THE QUEEN Yes; we mustn't be late to-day.

ALBERT You look very well — very charming! That bonnet suits you.

THE QUEEN Kiss me, Albert.

ALBERT (*as he does so*) You make a very good Queen, my Dear.

THE QUEEN With you to help me.

ALBERT Even by yourself, I think, you would not do so badly.

THE QUEEN That will never happen, Albert. I couldn't live without you.

ALBERT You can do very unexpected things, my Dear. You never expected that you would have to do anything like this. But you are going to. It is having to do it that makes it possible.

THE QUEEN Doing it with you, Dearest, I *like* doing it.

ALBERT So do I. It makes our life mean so much more to us . . .
Look at all those friendly people, waiting for you to smile on them
. . . Rather amusing, is it not? — that none of them knows in the
least — what *we* know.

THE QUEEN (*tremulously*) Albert, this must be rather like going
into battle.

ALBERT Just a little, my Dear. But we have to do it in cold blood,
without any excitement. That makes it rather more difficult,
perhaps.

THE QUEEN Oh, but it excites me very much, Albert. For this is
really to be a Queen. And with you I feel quite safe that I can
behave like one.

ALBERT Yes; so do I, Weibchen; so do I.

(*The door opens; a* COURT USHER *enters to make formal announcement.*)

USHER May it please: your Majesty's Ladies are in attendance.

THE QUEEN Oh, yes . . . Tell them to come in.

(THE USHER *retires.* THE QUEEN *turns quickly to* THE PRINCE.)

Albert, I didn't say anything to them before; I thought it was
better not. But *they* mustn't come with us to-day; it wouldn't be
safe.

ALBERT You are quite right, my Dear. It would be, for them, an
unnecessary risk. We must go alone.

(*The two Ladies-in-Waiting enter, dressed for going out. They
make their curtsies, and stand to receive orders.*)

THE QUEEN Lady Muriel, Lady Grace, I do not require either of
you this afternoon. I and the Prince are going out alone.

(*The two Ladies receive this information with perfect correctness; but
there is a suspicion of offended coldness in* LADY MURIEL'S *tone as she
speaks.*)

LADY MURIEL And your Majesty will not require us again —
later?

THE QUEEN No; not this afternoon. You can wait till we have gone. And then I shall not require your further attendance till this evening . . . And now, Albert, I am quite ready to start . . . I wonder if it is going to rain?

ALBERT   I think not. Just now it looked quite promising.

(*And so, talking of the weather, they go out, to give Fate and its Fool their opportunity for ending the Victorian Era before it has earned its name.*

And now the two Ladies-in-Waiting are alone; and, defrauded of her afternoon ride with Royalty, before admiring crowds (for which, with bonnet and shawl, she has so elaborately prepared herself), LADY MURIEL *breaks out.*)

LADY MURIEL   Well! I do think that's too bad! Here have we been kept waiting all for nothing; and if I'd known, I could have got off for the whole afternoon, as I very much wanted to do. I do call that inconsiderate of her!

LADY GRACE   It's what she is, my dear. I suppose she can't help it. It's being a Queen. When you are so important yourself, you can't think much about other people. Oh, it's happened before; and it'll happen again! It's what we are here for.

LADY MURIEL   Oh, there! I've torn my glove. Dear, dear! My own fault, I suppose, taking it off in a temper.

LADY GRACE (*at the window*)   Now, they're off. There they go! . . . No cheering this afternoon; the crowd isn't big enough. It always takes a certain number to cheer; — haven't you noticed? . . . But we bow, all the same. Oh, how he does take his hat off! — So like a foreigner! He'll never learn to be English.

LADY MURIEL   Which way are they going?

LADY GRACE   Which way? Why, there's only one way to the Park that I know of, my dear: up Constitution Hill.

LADY MURIEL   If they are only going to the Park, isn't it rather strange that they should choose to go alone? The Prince so insists on the Queen being properly attended. It's my belief they've been quarrelling about something; and she wants to have it out with him.

LADY GRACE   But she can't do that in the Park, with people staring at them.

LADY MURIEL Oh, *can't* she? She can say anything she wants to say, without moving a muscle of her face! She can whip you with a word, while she's smiling to someone else across the room. It's happened to me; so I know. She'll be able to say *all* she intends to say while they are driving in the Park. Yes; he's going to catch it about something.

LADY GRACE But does he ever 'catch' it?

LADY MURIEL My dear! She adores him, as we all know; but she can be jealous. And when she *is* jealous, she lets him know — you may depend on it.

LADY GRACE Well, of course, he *is* dangerously handsome. It's a wonder we don't all fall in love with him: but we don't.

LADY MURIEL Oh, he could be much more dangerous, if he chose, my dear. But it isn't manners that makes the man with him — it's morals.

LADY GRACE I suppose that's why he's so stiff when he talks to us. Oh, I've seen her watching him. I've been told that once, in the very early days, he gave one of her Ladies a present. There was a frightful row. He never did it again!

LADY MURIEL Perhaps it was something more than a present.

LADY GRACE Oh, my dear, I don't think you ought to say that!

LADY MURIEL I know I oughtn't! And that's why it's such a relief to say it! He's so good, he irritates me. Everything so proper! Life here is just a row of 'oughts', all standing to attention — rules, rules, rules! I wonder he puts up with it.

LADY GRACE I think it's just as much his doing as hers. It's the way he was brought up: he doesn't know how to be natural.

LADY MURIEL Just as well, perhaps . . . I don't believe he loves her a little bit.

LADY GRACE But he *must*!

LADY MURIEL Why?

LADY GRACE Well, he's stiff; but he's got a heart. And not to love one who loves him so terribly well, would be heartless.

LADY MURIEL She only loves him selfishly .

F

LADY GRACE No, my dear, not selfishly — jealously, perhaps. But she knows how much he's her superior; and a selfish person wouldn't . . . What's that?

LADY MURIEL I didn't hear anything.

LADY GRACE It sounded like a shot.

(*But to neither of them does a chance shot seem a matter of importance; so talk goes on.*)

LADY MURIEL Well, my dear, I suppose we've been wasting time in a very ignoble conversation — running down our betters, which, after all, we have to admit they are . . . What are you going to do?

LADY GRACE I don't know: it's too late to go anywhere now. But I don't want to stay here and watch them come back.

LADY MURIEL Isn't it funny how people *do*? Look, there's the crowd still waiting. They've seen them once; but they want to see them again. And I believe that sometimes it's the same people who come day after day — day after day.

LADY GRACE Oh, well, Royalty are one of the sights of London. Country Cousins expect to see them; and if you read your Court Circular, they can always be seen *here* at the stated hours.

LADY MURIEL My dear! What are all those people running for? Look! Constitution Hill is full of them! What can have happened?

LADY GRACE Has there been an accident?

LADY MURIEL No, no! Not an accident. They are cheering, waving, shouting! And here come mounted police — such a lot of them.

LADY GRACE They are coming back! They are coming back!

LADY MURIEL Who?

LADY GRACE The Queen! Something exciting must have happened! Has there been a declaration of war?

LADY MURIEL There's no one just now to declare war against, that I know of.

LADY GRACE Well, they must have done something very popular, anyhow. Look! The crowd's quite crazy.

(*And then in bursts another of the Ladies-in-Waiting, panting, and flapping her hands with excitement.*)

LADY-IN-WAITING She's been shot at! She's been shot at!

LADY MURIEL AND LADY GRACE Who?

LADY-IN-WAITING The Queen!

LADY MURIEL AND LADY GRACE Where? When?

LADY-IN-WAITING Just now; on Constitution Hill.

LADY GRACE (*highly excited*) I heard it!

LADY MURIEL } Was she hurt?

LADY GRACE   } Who did it?

LADY-IN-WAITING No; not hurt. A man — a madman, they think.

LADY GRACE Caught? Was he caught?

LADY-IN-WAITING Yes; they were expecting it. He'd tried to do it before — yesterday.

LADY MURIEL How do you know?

LADY-IN-WAITING I don't know. It mayn't be true. But everybody says so.

LADY GRACE Look! now they're coming in. The police are pushing the crowd back — such a lot of them on duty, they *must* have known.

LADY MURIEL Oh! Then — *She* must have known too!

LADY-IN-WAITING Yes; I suppose so.

LADY MURIEL (*catching hold of* LADY GRACE) Then that was *why*! Oh, my dear! She *knew*! — went, knowing that she was going to be shot at — *so didn't take us!* Oh! what a worm I feel myself now!

LADY GRACE (*sharing the feeling*) Yes, dear.

LADY MURIEL I want to run away, and hide; I'm so ashamed of myself!

LADY GRACE You can't go! They are coming.

(*The door opens;* THE QUEEN *enters, followed by* PRINCE ALBERT. *The Ladies curtsy with an emotional reverence which makes the formality almost beautiful.*)

LADY MURIEL Oh! your Majesty!

THE QUEEN Lady Muriel, why are you here still? Didn't I tell you that I should not want you again till this evening? Now go at once.

LADY MURIEL Oh, your Majesty! before I go, may I — may I — kiss your Majesty's hand?

THE QUEEN Why, certainly, if you wish to. Now don't cry: don't be silly! It's all over.

LADY MURIEL Oh, I'm so sorry, Ma'am: so sorry! So ashamed of myself!

THE QUEEN Ashamed? Why?

LADY MURIEL When your Majesty said we were not to come out with you this afternoon, I was foolishly cross: I didn't understand.

THE QUEEN Of course not. It was not necessary that you should. But now you *do*. So that will help you to know better — another time.

ALBERT (*turning sharply*) Another time!

THE QUEEN Go, please, Lady Muriel. I don't want you any more now.

(*And* LADY MURIEL *curtsies herself out after the others who have already gone.*)

Why, yes, Albert: there *may* come another time. Why not?

ALBERT (*taking her in his arms*) Oh, my Dear, my Dear! And you can say that *now* — as if you did not mind if it *should* come again! Is that really true?

THE QUEEN Yes, Albert: it was wonderful! For, with you, I felt — so safe . . . Didn't you?

ALBERT No, Weibchen. I was afraid!

THE QUEEN Afraid?

ALBERT I was afraid that — if he missed *one* of us, it might be *me* that he missed. Ah, no, no, no! do not talk of another time! I could not bear it — another time!

THE QUEEN (*startled*) Oh, Albert, had I thought for a moment that it might be *you* — I *couldn't* have gone! But that *that* could happen I didn't think!

ALBERT What a very good thing it was, then, my Dear, that you did *not* think. Queens must not think too much about others — only about themselves!

(*And having made that little joke, very much to his own satisfaction, he kisses her.*)

THE QUEEN Dearest! Have I pleased you?

ALBERT Very much. You have more than *pleased* me. You have behaved — like a Queen!

THE QUEEN Then now I must go and take off my things. Oh, dear! what a lot of letters I shall have to write *now*! To Uncle Leopold, and to everybody! How it will interest them! 'Just think!' I can hear them say, 'Poor Vicky's been shot at!'

(*And out she goes, very conscious that, having been shot at, she has something worth writing about.*)

A FALL FROM POWER

1842

In her private room at Windsor, THE QUEEN *sits at her usual occupation when alone, writing her diary. The door opens, and in the manner of one demanding, rather than soliciting permission for an audience, the* BARONESS LEHZEN *enters, and speaks. Her accent is decidedly German.*

LEHZEN Your Majesty?

THE QUEEN Yes?

LEHZEN May I come in?

THE QUEEN (*laying down her pen*) Of course.

LEHZEN Your Majesty is disengaged — not too occupied? The Prince is not with you?

THE QUEEN As you see, Lehzen dear, I am quite alone. What is the matter?

LEHZEN I have to tell your Majesty — this cannot go on!

THE QUEEN What cannot?

LEHZEN Either I am your Majesty's Private Secretary, or I am not. Which is it to be?

THE QUEEN But, of course, you are my Secretary. Who said you were not?

LEHZEN I have only the facts, your Majesty. They speak for themselves — though nothing has been *said*.

THE QUEEN Please, explain, Lehzen.

LEHZEN Yesterday I wrote five letters, for your Majesty — to sign. To-day they come back to me unsigned. I am told that the Prince has written them for you — instead of me.

THE QUEEN Not all of them.

LEHZEN *Three* of them. So what I have done is of no use; and I am put in the waste-paper basket — *so!*

(*She makes a descriptive gesture.*)

167

THE QUEEN I am sorry, Lehzen. It happened that after I told you to write them, the Prince and I talked them over together; and when we had decided what to say, and how it should be said, he proposed writing them himself.

LEHZEN *He!* Ha, yes! So it was his doing, not yours.

THE QUEEN (*composedly*) I ought to have told you: I forgot. I'm sorry.

LEHZEN (*still unappeased*) This is not the only time.

THE QUEEN No? . . . When?

LEHZEN Every day. You do not now send on to me all the letters you wish to be written.

THE QUEEN No: some I still write myself; some the Prince writes for me. Isn't that quite natural? Often it is so much more convenient.

LEHZEN It did not use to be so. Till two years ago I did *everything*.

THE QUEEN Two years ago I was not married, Lehzen, and had nobody but you to help me.

LEHZEN Did your Majesty marry just to have a new Secretary and so — to get rid of me?

THE QUEEN Lehzen, you hurt me! How can you think such a thing? Haven't you always been with me? — all my life, almost.

LEHZEN Yes. You were to me as my own child! I taught you everything.

THE QUEEN Almost.

LEHZEN And when you became Queen, I was not to go . . . You did not wish to lose me, you said — ever!

THE QUEEN I hope I never shall, Lehzen.

LEHZEN (*vehemently*) But this cannot go on! If I am not your Majesty's Private Secretary — if my work is interfered with, and done by another — what am I left to be?

(LEHZEN *has so 'let herself go' that when, at this moment,* PRINCE ALBERT *enters, it is quite evident to his observant eye that something unusual is happening.*)

ALBERT   What is the matter?

THE QUEEN   It was my fault, Albert. I forgot, yesterday, that I had given directions to Lehzen about those letters which you wrote for me. And now — in consequence —

(*She pauses.*)

ALBERT   Yes?

THE QUEEN   Well, Lehzen feels that what she wrote is not wanted — after all.

ALBERT   Of course not.

THE QUEEN   But you see, Dearest, I ought to have told her.

ALBERT   Why? If, by mistake, the letters were not sent twice over — does it matter?

LEHZEN   Your Highness, as I am Her Majesty's Private Secretary by appointment, I would wish not to have my duties interfered with!

ALBERT   They will not be, I am quite sure, Baroness — certainly not by me. But your duties do not require you to undertake more of Her Majesty's private correspondence than Her Majesty chooses to entrust to you.

LEHZEN   Her Majesty had given me those letters to answer *myself.*

THE QUEEN   Yes, Lehzen; but I have already explained.

LEHZEN (*with humble dignity*)   Your Majesty's explanation — permit me to say — does not quite satisfy me.

ALBERT   I am afraid it will have to, Baroness. A small mistake was made, which is not likely to occur again. In future it will be arranged that before *any* private letters are passed on for you to answer, Her Majesty and I will look through them together, and will reserve those which we wish to deal with ourselves.

LEHZEN   Do I understand that your Majesty approves of that arrangement?

THE QUEEN   Yes, Lehzen; I think it will be quite a good thing. It will save you from a lot of unnecessary trouble. I fear that I often give you more to do than you can easily find time for.

LEHZEN (*with offended dignity*) I have not complained, your Majesty, of having too much to do.

THE QUEEN No, Lehzen; it's all the other way. You do too much, without complaining.

LEHZEN If your Majesty thinks I am no longer equal to the duties which I undertook — so willingly, I would be glad if your Majesty would inform me.

ALBERT Her Majesty will, I am sure. And I think, Baroness, that, for the present, that will do; if, as it seems, Her Majesty no longer requires you.

THE QUEEN No, that is all . . . You may go, Lehzen.

LEHZEN Then your Majesty has nothing more to say to me? . . . And when, may it please your Majesty, am I to know whether I am still to be —

(THE PRINCE *crosses to the door, and opens it with stiff politeness.*)

ALBERT Baroness.

(*Rigid with rage,* THE BARONESS, *forgetting even to curtsy herself out, sweeps from the room.*)

THE QUEEN (*compunctious, and a little distressed*) Oh, Albert! It's so difficult!

ALBERT Not at all, my Dear . . . That woman must go.

THE QUEEN Go? How can she? She has been with me so long — as long as I can remember.

ALBERT Yes: when you were a child, she was your Governess, was she not?

THE QUEEN Yes.

ALBERT You must not have a Governess now, my Dear; it does not do. And that is what she does not understand.

THE QUEEN But to send her away, Albert — so faithful and devoted as she has been, seems too cruel! She loves me.

ALBERT Yes; and because she loves *you* she hates *me*. I do not mind her hating me; she is only one of many. But she must not prevent me from being useful to you. And that is what she would like.

THE QUEEN Oh, Albert — twenty years she has been with me. If I send her away, what will she do with herself?

(THE PRINCE *walks slowly to the window, and stands looking out. He turns, and comes towards her.*)

ALBERT Weibchen, there is something I want to say to you.

THE QUEEN Yes?

ALBERT Rather difficult.

THE QUEEN Why should it be difficult for you to tell me anything?

ALBERT Because, Dearest, when you make up your mind, you are then a little *hard*.

THE QUEEN '*Hard?*' . . . But not to *you*.

ALBERT To change, I mean.

THE QUEEN Perhaps . . . sometimes.

ALBERT (*seating himself*) You know, Vicky, that my Mother was not true to her own husband — went away, and left him.

THE QUEEN Yes.

ALBERT But I have always loved her: nor, in my own mind, did I ever really blame her.

THE QUEEN I know. But why do you tell me this — again?

ALBERT Vicky . . . Have you yet forgiven your own Mother, for something much less than what mine did?

THE QUEEN Less? It was the same thing, Albert.

ALBERT Oh, no, Vicky: she was a widow; she had no friends; she was lonely . . . *Have* you forgiven her?

THE QUEEN Why do you ask me this, Albert?

ALBERT Because she writes to me, and is lonely. She loves you still . . . Do you not love her?

THE QUEEN Yes, Albert, of course I love her.

ALBERT But you see her so seldom: never alone. You have always one of your Ladies with you. I go to see her; and you do not . . . Why not now? There may once have been a reason. But *he* is no longer there.

THE QUEEN Oh, Albert!

ALBERT Shall I tell you why you do not go?

THE QUEEN Why?

ALBERT Lehzen is why . . . Lehzen! . . . It was she who was jealous of your Mamma, as she was also jealous of me. I am not afraid of Lehzen — for myself; but is it right, Weibchen, that she should have decided it for you — and be doing it still — how you should treat your own Mother?

THE QUEEN You think I have been — *hard*, Albert?

ALBERT A little: but also weak, to let anyone else make you be hard to *her*.

THE QUEEN Weak, you say? Oh, I don't know what to think!

ALBERT Oh, yes . . . you do . . . you *do*!

(THE QUEEN *sits for a moment undecided. But now, with the truth put before her, she is too honest to deceive herself.*)

THE QUEEN Yes . . . you are quite right . . . It's true . . . It *was* Lehzen.

ALBERT I was sure of it, my Dear. Your Mamma and the Baroness are too like each other; they love you too much in the same way — jealously. But your Mamma has accepted *me*, very kindly, very generously. Lehzen never will.

THE QUEEN And you don't like Lehzen?

ALBERT No . . . But only because I think she is bad for you.

THE QUEEN Then that must settle it, Albert. Yes; she shall go . . . Poor Lehzen! Poor Lehzen!

(*She bursts into tears.* THE PRINCE *rises, and laying his hand fondly on her head, strokes it.*)

ALBERT Poor Vicky! . . . Poor little Vicky! . . . And to have only *me* instead!

(*She flings herself into his arms.*)

THE QUEEN Oh, Albert, Albert, Dearest! Promise, promise never to leave me! Promise to let *me* die first!

ALBERT That is not for me to decide, Vicky . . . But I do not think I shall live to be very old.

THE QUEEN But why not?

ALBERT I am not so fond of life as you, my Dear . . . If I were
ever very ill, I should not make a great fight for myself. No.

VICTORIA But that would be very wrong — very selfish of you,
Dearest!

ALBERT So? . . . Yes? . . . Why?

VICTORIA Think of me! Think of *me*!

ALBERT Ah, yes, Weibchen! I will try always to think of you —
only of you!

THE INTRUDER

1845

From the brilliantly-lighted drawing-room (Buckingham Palace has three, and this is the smallest of them) the Royal Presence has just been withdrawn. Backs are bent to the disappearing train, which is all that we see. Then, as the door closes, the GENTLEMEN *straighten their backs, the* LADIES *rise from their curtsies. In obvious relief from the tension of Court etiquette, faces and limbs find relaxation, the* GENTLEMEN *cough, draw breath, heave sighs of relief; the* LADIES *yawn politely behind their fans. A* DOWAGER-LADY *totters to a sofa, and sinks into it, half-fainting.*

DOWAGER   Oh! my poor legs! What has become of them?

LADY-IN-WAITING   Don't say 'legs', Mamma! The Gentlemen! (*She indicates that they are listening.*) Feet!

DOWAGER   Feet? I haven't any left! All this standing! . . . and after dinner, too! To people of my age — it's cruel! Why does the Queen allow it?

LADY-IN-WAITING   The Prince insists on it, Mamma.

DOWAGER (*sighing*)   Yes, I know . . . I know!

LADY-IN-WAITING   Come to bed, Mamma, dear!

(*She raises her Mother, and leads her towards the door.*)

DOWAGER (*drawing back*)   Wait! Take care! We mustn't overtake them. The Queen doesn't like it.

LADY-IN-WAITING   It's all right, Mamma. They are letting us out now.

(*For now the doors are opening again, an indication that the way is clear, and that the Court is now free to go to bed, if it likes. The* GENTLEMEN *stand back, and bow for the* LADIES *to pass first, and the* LADIES *curtsy themselves out.*)

FIRST GENTLEMAN   Did you hear what happened to-night?

SECOND GENTLEMAN   Happened?

FIRST GENTLEMAN To Lady Peel, I mean?

SECOND GENTLEMAN What about her?

FIRST GENTLEMAN Well, you know that she is — expecting, quite soon. The Queen told her that, when the Prince came in, she might remain seated; and that two of her ladies should stand in front of her, so that the Prince shouldn't see.

SECOND GENTLEMAN Very kind of her . . . very considerate.

FIRST GENTLEMAN Yes, but he did see her; and word went to her that she was to stand.

SECOND GENTLEMAN How very like him! What a drill-master he would have made!

FIRST GENTLEMAN Well, of course . . . German, you know, German. It's the mediaeval idea. He can't get rid of it.

SECOND GENTLEMAN And yet, in other things — so alive and up-to-date!

FIRST GENTLEMAN Yes. He looks into everything — cupboards, even, so I'm told.

SECOND GENTLEMAN Eh?

(*A respectfully hovering Attendant catches his eye; he perceives that they are the last. He takes his companion's arm.*)

Come, we must be going. It's Buckingham Palace's bed-time.

FIRST GENTLEMAN It's early yet. Will you come down to my Club with me?

SECOND GENTLEMAN Thanks. Delighted.

(*They go out.*)

(*And, now, with due ceremony, a transformation scene takes place. The* ATTENDANT *crosses to a side-door, opens it, and calls: 'All out.' Through it enter, first a* SERGEANT STEWARD *of the Palace service, then a troop of Attendants, carrying dust-sheets and extinguishers. They proceed to cover the sofas and chairs for the night, and to put out the wax-candles. On the sofa, where the* DOWAGER *has sat, an* ATTENDANT *finds a fallen bracelet.*)

FIRST ATTENDANT (*to* SECOND) Hey! Here's something been left.

SERGEANT STEWARD (*sharply*). No talking, there!

FIRST ATTENDANT No, Sir. But this, Sir. Somebody's left it behind them!

(*He brings the bracelet.*)

SERGEANT STEWARD (*taking it*) You could have found that without speaking. In future, remember!

FIRST ATTENDANT Yes, Sir.

(*The Attendants pass on into the next room. The last candles are put out. In the next room we see the same process beginning. The* SERGEANT STEWARD *takes a last look to see that all is right, and goes, closing the door. A clock is heard striking the hour. It finishes. A side-door opens, through it comes a dim light; dark against it, a queer figure creeps stealthily in. He halts, strikes a match, and stands looking vacantly round him. He has a youthful face, with a half-witted expression. The match burns on; he fumbles in his pocket, pulls out a candle-end, which he lights, then drops the burnt-out match on to the floor.*)

INTRUDER Here I am, then! And nobody's seen me. My! What a place to burn down! And won't it be in all the papers?

(*Roaming the room, he goes to the window, and takes hold of the curtain-cord; he pulls it; the curtains open, revealing moonlight through blind.*)

INTRUDER (*startled*) Lord! Look at that, now! And I hardly touched it!

(*He crosses to the main door, opens it, peeps, and is about to pass through, but draws back, closing it again.*)

INTRUDER Someone coming!

(*He stoops, lifts a dust-sheet, and creeps under the sofa. Slowly the door opens,* PRINCE ALBERT *appears, carrying a candle. He enters, leaving the door wide, and begins to inspect the room. Behind him, secretively inquisitive, perhaps a little suspicious, enters* THE QUEEN; *her evening toilette covered by a large cream-white shawl with long fringes. She stands looking at him; he turns, and sees her.*)

THE QUEEN Albert, Dearest, what are you doing here?

ALBERT What are *you* doing here, my Dear?

THE QUEEN (*with a touch of fond reproach*) You went . . . I missed you.

ALBERT I came, Weibchen, to see whether my orders had been carried out.

THE QUEEN Your orders?

ALBERT Yes.

THE QUEEN You did not tell me of them.

ALBERT It was not necessary.

THE QUEEN But I would like to know, Albert.

ALBERT Very well. I found that it was the custom here to leave all the candles burning, and nothing covered for the night.

THE QUEEN The candles — burning?

ALBERT Yes, till they were all burnt out.

THE QUEEN Most extraordinary!

ALBERT Not at all, my Dear. Just the sort of thing that I would now expect.

THE QUEEN How did you find out?

ALBERT As I find out everything, my Dear. First by personal inspection, then by inquiry.

THE QUEEN The candles left burning — every night? How wasteful!

ALBERT Yes. And the reason? What, do you suppose, the reason was?

THE QUEEN Just carelessness, I suppose.

ALBERT Oh, no! Quite the reverse. It was by strict orders. During the Regency of your Uncle George, orders had been given that no servants were to enter, or be seen anywhere near the royal apartments, after midnight.

THE QUEEN After midnight?

ALBERT The Regent's late hours — and what he did with them — were not to be disturbed by any intruder.

THE QUEEN I see.

ALBERT   And so — leaving the candles to burn out has become a
palace tradition.

THE QUEEN   And when did you find that out, Albert?

ALBERT   A few days ago.

THE QUEEN   How?

ALBERT   After we had gone to bed, I came down again.

THE QUEEN   How was it I didn't miss you?

ALBERT   I came down, my Love, from my dressing-room . . .
before coming to you.

THE QUEEN   I see. And you said nothing.

ALBERT   I never do say anything, my Dear, which might worry
you, that I can avoid saying.

THE QUEEN   How thoughtful you are, Albert, always!

ALBERT   There is so much here that needs to be thought about.
In the past, things have been much neglected.

THE QUEEN   I hope all this care is not going to age you, Albert.
You are so beautiful! But often I see you looking tired.

ALBERT   No, no. I like it. It interests me.

THE QUEEN   Because you are so good and conscientious in
everything you do. You were born to rule, Albert!

ALBERT   Ah! Weibchen, if I had not your love and your trust,
I could do nothing. Everyone here is jealous of me.

THE QUEEN   Yes, I know! And it makes me so angry, Albert!
One day, I mean that you shall be made King.

ALBERT   King?

THE QUEEN   Yes, Not Prince, or Prince *Consort*: *King* Consort —
as you really are.

ALBERT   Why cause trouble, my Dear? For it will cause trouble.
What's in a name?

THE QUEEN   My love, Dearest; in that name, all my love for you.
   (*To this fond outburst the* PRINCE *does not respond. He is looking at
      something,* THE QUEEN, *perceiving his attention riveted, asks:*)
What are you looking at?

ALBERT   A match! There is a burnt match lying on the floor.
How did it come there?

(*He looks round sharply and inquisitorially.*)

And those curtains have been drawn open. Someone must have
been in.

(*He gets no further. From under the sofa comes a sound.*)

THE QUEEN   Hush! What is that? (*She points.*) Somebody is
there!

ALBERT   Stand away, Dearest!

(*He goes to the sofa, and lifts the dust-sheet.*)

Who is that under there? . . . Who are you? . . . Come out! . . .

(*Compelled by the stronger will, the* INTRUDER *emerges, and rises
slowly to his feet.*)

THE QUEEN   Oh, take care, Albert! Take care! He may be
going to shoot you.

ALBERT   How did you get in here?

(*The* INTRUDER *turns slowly, and points.*)

INTRUDER   Through yon door.

ALBERT   How did you get in at all?

INTRUDER   I come through the stables.

ALBERT   And then?

INTRUDER   Through the kitchen.

ALBERT   When?

INTRUDER   After they'd done cooking the dinner . . . when they
was all busy washing-up.

ALBERT   What did you come for?

(*There is a pause. The* INTRUDER *stares round, but does not answer.*)

I ask you — what did you come for?

INTRUDER   Just to see.

ALBERT   To see what?

INTRUDER   To see if I could see where the Queen lived, and
what it was all like.

ALBERT Yes?

INTRUDER So as I could tell people.

ALBERT Did no one see you come in?

INTRUDER They may ha' done. No one didn't stop me.

ALBERT And when you had come, and seen — what did you intend doing? . . . Now, I mean, when everything is locked up?

INTRUDER I was just going to open a winder, and get out.

ALBERT Did you mean to steal anything?

INTRUDER No, Sir. But I thought as how I'd set fire to it, perhaps.

ALBERT Set fire? . . . Why?

INTRUDER So as to see it in the papers, to-morrer.

THE QUEEN (*whispering*) He's mad, Albert! He's mad!

ALBERT (*quietly*) Very likely. Go and ring the bell; and then go yourself — at once.

THE QUEEN (*after looking round for it*) There is no bell, Albert.

ALBERT Then go, go quickly!

THE QUEEN No, Albert; I am not going to leave you.

   (*So, for the present, the position has to remain unaltered.*)

ALBERT Which door did you say you came in at?

INTRUDER (*pointing*) There . . . That one.

ALBERT Then go through it again, at once.

   (*The* INTRUDER *obeys, meek as a lamb. The* PRINCE, *following him up, closes the door behind him.*)

ALBERT No bell; but there is a key. (*He turns it.*) Now, Weibchen, do you feel that I am safe enough for you to leave me?

THE QUEEN Oh, Albert! How brave, how brave you are!

ALBERT Only sensible, my Dear. Now go quickly, and send somebody at once.

   (*She goes. Left alone, the* PRINCE *pauses, then goes to the door, unlocks it, opens it, and calls:*)

You ... fellow! Are you there? What are you doing? (*He looks in.*) Ah! gone ... gone ... Yes, of course.

 (*As he turns away the* SERGEANT STEWARD *enters, panting, by the main door.*)

SERGEANT STEWARD Oh, your Royal Highness! I pray pardon! What has happened? ... Her Majesty has sent me.

ALBERT (*sharply*) Who are you, Sir? What do you call yourself?

SERGEANT STEWARD Your Royal Highness, I am the Sergeant Steward.

ALBERT That means, I suppose, that you have the safety of the Palace in your keeping?

SERGEANT STEWARD Yes, your Highness. Yes.

ALBERT Of the Royal Family, also?

SERGEANT STEWARD That is so, your Royal Highness ... at least ...

ALBERT Then it may interest you to know that there is, at present, somewhere in the Palace, a lunatic at large, who was able to walk in here without anyone preventing; and whom I myself, and Her Majesty, found hiding under that sofa —

SERGEANT STEWARD (*horrified*) Oh! your Highness!

ALBERT — intending, so he told me, to set fire to the Palace; so that he might 'see it to-morrow in the papers'.

SERGEANT STEWARD And, where, your Royal Highness ... where has he gone now?

ALBERT Where he is now hiding himself I do not know. He went through that door. You had better go after him ... I say, you had better go after him.

SERGEANT STEWARD (*quailing*) But, your Royal Highness, he may be armed.

ALBERT He may be ... quite likely. But he didn't shoot *me*; so perhaps he will not shoot *you*. But you must go and see.

 (*The* SERGEANT STEWARD *moves irresolutely toward the door.*)

Oh, before you go, draw those curtains again!

(*The* SERGEANT STEWARD *does so.*)

And pick up that match!

(*The match is picked up.*)

It ought not to have been there. Now go and see where that man is.

SERGEANT STEWARD (*in abject supplication*) Your Royal Highness! . . .

ALBERT I order you to go and see!

(*As a lamb to the slaughter, the* SERGEANT STEWARD *goes.*)

And don't leave the door open!

(*The door is shut.* THE QUEEN *enters, still anxious.*)

THE QUEEN Albert, why are you laughing?

ALBERT I have told that man to go and see if he will get shot; and he does not like it . . . If he does get shot, his widow must have a pension. If he does not get shot, you will have to dismiss him for his incompetence.

(*Suddenly, in the distance, an alarm bell rings, and through the main doors come running in single file six Royal Footmen armed with shovels and pokers. Without perceiving the Royal Couple, they dash through in pursuit of whatever danger is ahead of them.*)

ALBERT Really, my Dear, this place *has* become a lunatic asylum. No wonder *he* found his way into it! . . . Come, let us go back to bed.

QUEEN But I shan't *sleep*, Dearest! After all this!

ALBERT (*fondly*) Oh, yes . . . you *will* — you will. Come, Weibchen.

(*He kisses her; and they go out hand-in-hand.*)

THE ROSE AND THE THORN

1846

THE QUEEN *is holding her Court at Windsor. A Footman opens the folding-doors of a small ante-chamber; and from its softly illumined interior one sees across the broad corridor, through looped curtains, the large music-room (where presently performance is to take place) brilliantly lighted. Under its crystal chandeliers, the Ladies and Gentlemen of the Court are beginning to gather. The small room has in it little furniture: away from the wall, on one side of the door, stands a small settee; on the other, a grand-piano. On the same side, lower down, is a smaller door. Into the room come four musicians, carrying their instruments: their conductor, the future* SIR JOHN OAKLEY — *now only* 'MR.' — *leading them.*

OAKLEY We must come in here, for a moment. Her Majesty does not allow any tuning-up to be done in her presence.

(*He opens the piano, and strikes notes and chords for the musicians to tune by.*)

So . . . You are all ready? Come, then!

(*They go out, leaving the folding-doors open, and cross the corridor to the music-room. A little later, the doors of the music-room are closed, and one hears from within, very softly, the performance beginning.*
And now two Ladies of the Court enter: the one a very beautiful DUCHESS *of middle age, the Queen's Mistress of the Robes; the other her cousin,* LADY JANE, *small, young: and pretty.* THE DUCHESS, *leading the way, lays down on the settee a richly embroidered shawl, and a feather fan. Meanwhile the younger lady is speaking:*)

LADY JANE But, your Grace, it's so difficult!

DUCHESS My dear, Court life *is* difficult. Its difficulties are the larger part of its duties.

LADY JANE   But to be suspected — and for nothing — is so humiliating!

DUCHESS   Yes, my dear; high positions, when they are not the highest, involve humiliation for all of us. Do you think *I* never feel humiliated?

LADY JANE   You! Your Grace?

DUCHESS   When I am sent out of the room, as if I were a servant, I feel it.

LADY JANE   But you do it so grandly — with such an air!

DUCHESS   Yes, that is how one covers the humiliation. After all, Court life is mainly made up of formalities; and being sent out of the room is one of them. Ministers are dismissed, and so are we. Even Lord Palmerston had a narrow escape the other day.

LADY JANE   Lord Palmerston!

DUCHESS   Yes, and quite right, too!

LADY JANE (*who has gone to the mirror, to rearrange the flowers in her hair*) What for?

DUCHESS   Well, it wasn't the Queen who told me, or I shouldn't repeat it. He told me himself — cross, but half-laughing. He wanted the Prince out of the room, while he discussed Foreign Affairs with her. And, to avoid it, he sent off some despatches without first submitting them. So there was trouble.

LADY JANE   I should think so!

DUCHESS   Yes, my dear; anyone who touches the Prince, touches a bomb, which goes off. She's the bomb: *He* isn't.

LADY JANE (*reverting to her grievance*) But I haven't touched him!

DUCHESS   No; but you've looked at him. That's enough.

LADY JANE   But, your Grace, he's there to be looked at! And how can one help admiring him, when he's so handsome?

DUCHESS   You needn't help it; but you mustn't be admired in return.

LADY JANE   Oh, why doesn't she only have *plain* women about her?

DUCHESS Even that wouldn't always meet the difficulty. Plain women have often a way with them. And it wants something more than mere looks to attract *him*.

LADY JANE (*with a touch of spite*) He isn't a bit in love with *her*!

DUCHESS No; but he's very fond of her. The Prince is — what is so rarely found amongst Royalty — the domestic man; and he's not only domestic, he's conjugal.

LADY JANE Then why is she so jealous of him?

DUCHESS My dear, she can't help it: she's possessive, and she's in love with him.

LADY JANE But *I'm* not!

DUCHESS Of course not, my dear. I know you wouldn't take such a liberty.

LADY JANE I wish she'd send me away! If this goes on, I shall ask to resign my appointment.

DUCHESS No, no, my dear! Don't do anything so out of character. 'Hold your ground!' is the motto of our family. Hold it! . . . What, exactly, happened to-day?

LADY JANE We were out riding in the Park; and the Prince came and rode beside me, just for a moment. My reins had got caught and he was putting them straight for me. And the Queen pushed her horse right in between us; and she said, 'Lady Jane, if you don't know how to ride properly, you had better not come out with us!' And the Prince said, 'Lady Jane rides very nicely and well.' Oh, you should have seen the Queen's look then! And it's true; I *do* ride nicely — better than she does; and she knows it!

DUCHESS And was that all that happened?

LADY JANE All that happened to *me*. But the Prince left the Queen, and went straight off, and rode with one of his Gentlemen. And then the Queen suddenly turned round, and we all had to ride back to the Castle. And of course everybody knew that something was the matter, for we hadn't gone half our usual round. And now, I believe, she has put Lady Maud to spy on me.

DUCHESS Oh, I don't think that's likely, my dear. The Queen wouldn't say anything to anyone — she's too proud.

LADY JANE Well, she *is* spying anyway — hoping perhaps to tell tales presently. If I catch her, I'll slap her face!

DUCHESS My dear, I think I'd better arrange for you to take a little holiday — change of air. You shall see your doctor, and he will advise it. But don't give up your post. If the Queen proposes to dismiss you, I shall say something. She won't dismiss *me*.

LADY JANE No; but perhaps she will send you out of the room.

DUCHESS Perhaps she will, my dear. She has done it before; and I have continued the conversation the next day, with the Prince there to help me.

LADY JANE To help you?

DUCHESS Oh, yes; she's always much more easy to reason with when he's there.

LADY JANE He has such beautiful manners to everyone, hasn't he?

DUCHESS He is a very good corrective; and she knows it. I'm very fond of her; but she needs managing; and he is the only person who can do it.

LADY JANE He didn't manage her this morning!

DUCHESS He didn't try . . . You wait!

LADY JANE Oh, dear! I don't know that I *can* wait. Everybody knows I'm in disgrace; so they won't speak to me.

DUCHESS Now be brave, my dear, be brave! The unfortunate thing has happened, and now it's over. You keep under my wing; and you shan't look as if you've been sent to Coventry by anyone . . . There's the music coming to an end. We must go back, or she will be missing us.

(*Forgetting her shawl and fan, she goes towards the door of the music-room, followed by* LADY JANE. *At that moment the doors open, from within comes a polite murmur of applause. The Musicians come out, carrying their instruments, and pass down the corridor. Behind them comes* MR. OAKLEY, *in the doorway he turns and bows. He, also, is retiring, when one of* THE QUEEN'S GENTLEMEN *comes after him.*)

GENTLEMAN Her Majesty wishes to speak to you, Mr. Oakley.

(THE QUEEN *appears in the doorway. She is followed by* PRINCE ALBERT, *who, with stiff formality, crosses the corridor, and enters the ante-room, while* THE QUEEN *stays to speak to* MR. OAKLEY.)

THE QUEEN That was very beautiful, Mr. Oakley. Thank you. It was your own composition, I believe?

OAKLEY It was, your Majesty.

THE QUEEN We should very much like to hear another piece presently.

OAKLEY Most honoured, your Majesty.

(*Leaving* MR. OAKLEY *to receive the congratulations of other members of his audience,* THE QUEEN *follows* THE PRINCE *into the ante-room.*)

THE QUEEN Albert, why are you so cold to me?

ALBERT It is a cold day, my Dear. And this morning we did not take enough exercise.

THE QUEEN You did not come to me afterwards. I have hardly seen you since — except with others.

ALBERT (*stiffly*) No; that is so.

THE QUEEN Albert, have I offended you?

ALBERT My Dear, you must not try to give me riding lessons — before others.

(*He moves away.*)

THE QUEEN I want to speak to you, Albert.

(*Paying no attention, he returns to the corridor, and seeing* MR. OAKLEY, *pauses to speak to him. The other members of the Court draw back respectfully. Meanwhile* THE QUEEN, *after standing for a few moments, angry and undecided, turns and goes quickly past them. At the music-room door she stops to exchange words with some of her Ladies. Meanwhile* THE PRINCE *is speaking.*)

ALBERT Ah, Mr. Oakley, I have some news that I hope will please you. We are expecting to have the great Mendelssohn with us again soon. He is coming to England in the Spring.

OAKLEY That is great news indeed, Sir. Will he also be coming to Windsor?

ALBERT We hope so. We have invited him to come.

OAKLEY For all who love music, as does your Royal Highness, it will be a great occasion.

ALBERT It will, indeed.

(*Dismissing* MR. OAKLEY *with a courteous gesture,* THE PRINCE *turns towards the music-room; but at sight of* THE QUEEN *standing in the doorway, he re-enters the ante-room, where* THE DUCHESS, *followed by* LADY JANE, *has returned to pick up her fan and shawl. Just as* LADY JANE *is entering, a rose falls from her hair.* THE PRINCE, *with courtly grace, stoops and picks it up for her.*)

ALBERT Lady Jane, here is something that you have dropped.

(*He presents the flower.*)

LADY JANE (*nervously*) Oh, your Highness, I am sorry! — sorry to have given your Highness the trouble!

ALBERT (*gallantly*) No trouble . . . a pleasure. . . . It is a colour that suits you.

(*Meanwhile* THE DUCHESS *has moved to the door, and is looking back with an amused smile, when* THE QUEEN, *pushing past her, comes swiftly into the room. Trembling with rage, she advances upon* LADY JANE, *and snatches the flower from her hand. With an instinct for the emergency,* THE DUCHESS *closes the folding-doors: such a scene must have no spectators.*)

LADY JANE (*with tremulous courage*) Your Majesty must pardon me: that flower is mine.

THE QUEEN How dare you speak to me! Go! Go, instantly!

(LADY JANE, *her head very erect, makes a swift, deep curtsy, and goes out of the room. Meanwhile* THE DUCHESS *is speaking to* THE PRINCE.)

DUCHESS (*urgently*). I beg your Royal Highness to allow me to explain. I saw just what happened.

(THE PRINCE *hesitates for a moment, then turns abruptly, and goes out of the room by the other door. There is a pause.* THE QUEEN *stands crushing the flower in her hand.*)

THE QUEEN Go and tell the Prince to come back! I wish to speak to him.

DUCHESS Will your Majesty —

THE QUEEN At once! Do as I tell you!

DUCHESS Yes, Ma'am, yes; in a moment. But first I beg your Majesty to allow me to speak — to explain.

THE QUEEN There is nothing to explain.

DUCHESS But there is! There is! I saw everything.

THE QUEEN So did I. I saw the Prince give her this flower — this rose. Do you mean to deny it?

DUCHESS No, your Majesty, no; he did not give it her. She had dropped it.

THE QUEEN (*suspiciously*) Dropped it? Ah, yes!

DUCHESS No, Ma'am; quite by accident. It fell out of her hair. The Prince only picked it up and returned it to her.

THE QUEEN You saw that, you say? You know that — for certain?

DUCHESS I assure your Majesty it was so.

THE QUEEN Do you know, also, what happened this morning?

DUCHESS I do, Ma'am. My Cousin has told me everything.

THE QUEEN Did she try to explain it?

DUCHESS There was hardly anything to explain, Ma'am. It might have happened to anyone.

THE QUEEN Then why did she tell you about it?

DUCHESS She was very much upset at the way your Majesty had taken what was a mere accident.

THE QUEEN It may have been an accident: I don't know. What has happened now is much more serious.

DUCHESS *Very* much more serious, your Majesty.

(THE QUEEN *looks at her in surprise:* THE DUCHESS *does not flinch. There is a pause.*)

THE QUEEN (*defensively*) It was all so sudden — so unexpected. One hadn't time to think.

DUCHESS   That is so. Your Majesty gave yourself no time — to think.

THE QUEEN   I was too hasty, you mean?

DUCHESS   Does your Majesty wish me to say more than I have said?

THE QUEEN   I only wish you to tell me the honest truth.

DUCHESS   I will, Ma'am ... At least, I will try. But the truth is sometimes difficult.

THE QUEEN   It should not be.

DUCHESS   Not even when it is — to a Queen, Ma'am?

THE QUEEN   A Queen may need it sometimes, far more than others.

DUCHESS   If she knows that she needs it, Ma'am, she is already on the side of truth.

THE QUEEN   I do know it — I do! ... Tell me! — is it possible that I have been unjust?

DUCHESS   It is possible, your Majesty.

THE QUEEN   I did not intend to be.

DUCHESS   No one, who knows your Majesty, would think that for a moment.

THE QUEEN   Thank you, dear Duchess, for saying that! In my position, I would wish never to be unjust to anyone ... Will you — will you ask your Cousin — Lady Jane — to come and speak to me?

DUCHESS   (*hesitating*) I am not sure, Ma'am, that she will come — now.

THE QUEEN   Will you say 'please' for me?

DUCHESS   If I can say it, Ma'am, as you have said it — (*Her voice breaks; she kisses* THE QUEEN'S *hand, and goes.*)

(THE QUEEN, *left to herself, sits rigid — facing an ordeal which, for her, is of an almost unbelievable character. Nevertheless, she faces it. Presently the door opens, and* LADY JANE *enters. She halts at the door, and curtsies: the word 'please', which has brought her, has been left unexplained, and the expression of her face does not make things easier for* THE QUEEN.)

G

THE QUEEN Lady Jane ... I have sent for you to say ... I am sorry ... Forgive me ... I was quite wrong.

(LADY JANE *curtsies deeply, but does not speak. Slowly* THE QUEEN *reaches out her hand.* LADY JANE *goes quickly forward, kisses it, and bursts into tears.*)

THE QUEEN I am sorry, so sorry to have upset you. You had better go to bed now, and rest ... And, Lady Jane, if you would like — only if you would like — to go away for a little, for a change — pray do so. I'm not asking you to go; but should you at all wish to do so, you have my permission.

LADY JANE I thank your Majesty for so kindly suggesting it.

THE QUEEN Then that shall be arranged ... And now will you tell the Prince — I mean, will you ask someone to tell the Prince that I wish to see him?

(LADY JANE *makes her final curtsy, and goes.* THE QUEEN *sits with bowed head, motionless: time passes.* THE PRINCE *does not come. Her head sinks lower; she is shaken by sobs. Then, very quietly, the door opens, and* THE PRINCE *enters. He comes gently towards her, stands at her side, and reaching down his hand, begins softly to stroke her hair. Neither of them makes any attempt to speak, or any further move. Presently, leaving her, he goes to the piano, seats himself, and begins playing. It has to be something very simple and familiar — otherwise she might miss its meaning. He plays a few bars; then, in a low undertone, sings words which she already knows by heart.*)

ALBERT 　　　　　　Drink to me only with thine eyes,
　　　　　　　　And I will pledge with mine;
　　　　　　　　Or leave a kiss but in the cup,
　　　　　　　　　And I'll not ask for wine.
　　　　　　　　The thirst that from the soul doth rise,
　　　　　　　　　Doth ask a drink divine:
　　　　　　　　But might I of Jove's nectar sup,
　　　　　　　　　I would not change for thine.

(*As the first verse draws to its close,* THE QUEEN *rises, crosses slowly, and stands behind him. As he begins the second verse, timidly she lays a hand upon his shoulder; and when the verse is half-way through, she lets her head fall upon his, and is so standing, with her cheek resting against the beautiful hair, which is already beginning to grow thin, when the verse ends.)*

> I sent thee late a rosy wreath,
>   Not so much honouring thee,
> As giving it a hope that there
>   It could not withered be.
> But thou thereon didst only breathe,
>   And sent'st it back to me:
> Since when it grows and smells, I swear,
>   Not of itself, but thee.

(The song ends. What happens then — who knows? As the last chords are played, the curtain falls slowly, but neither of them has moved.)

AIMS AND OBJECTS

1849

In his private apartment at Buckingham Palace, PRINCE ALBERT *sits writing; his back is to the door.* THE QUEEN *enters, and moving softly across the room, stands behind him. Very fondly she feasts her eyes on the top of his head, which is growing prematurely bald. He continues to write, unconscious of her presence.*

THE QUEEN   Albert, leave off writing! I want to talk to you.

ALBERT (*laying down his pen*)   Yes, Weibchen; what is it?

THE QUEEN   Albert . . . You *do* love me, don't you?

ALBERT   My Dear, have you any doubt?

THE QUEEN   No; but say it!

ALBERT (*kindly, but without fervour*)   I love you.

THE QUEEN   Say it again, *and* again!

ALBERT   Certainly, my Dear, if you wish . . . I love you . . . I love you . . . I love you . . . Isn't that enough?

THE QUEEN   I was waiting to see how long you would be able to go on.

ALBERT   Saying what is so unnecessary?

THE QUEEN   Not unnecessary to me, Albert. For I shall never be quite sure that it will always be so.

ALBERT   Why not?

THE QUEEN   Because you are so much above me — in everything but rank. And *that* I am not allowed to alter. Every time I speak about making you King Consort, my Ministers won't hear of it.

ALBERT   Does it matter?

THE QUEEN   You know it matters, Albert. It means that to them you are still only just a foreign Prince, who has come to marry me and give me children.

ALBERT   We must be patient, my Dear.

THE QUEEN   Patient! Have we not been patient for ten years?

I am sick of being patient! I would like to go and tell them that, if they do not make you Prince, or King Consort, I shall resign! . . . That would make them do it, Albert!

ALBERT   Yes, Frauchen, perhaps. But you must not do it.

THE QUEEN   Why not, when I love you so much; when you are everything to me, and so much wiser, that I know it is really you that ought to be King?

ALBERT   Because, Dearest, when I came here — when I accepted what you offered me — you were not able to offer me *that*: and I knew it. What they do not want now, I knew that they would never want. I accepted — not only the greatness of the honour, but its limitations. Therefore, Dearest — that is why.

THE QUEEN   But, Albert, so much has happened since then. My children are your children; some day Bertie will be King. How *can* they still go on thinking of you as a foreigner, after all that?

ALBERT   But they will, Weibchen; and nothing that we can do will change them — nothing!

THE QUEEN   And yet, Albert, now that you are always with me when I see my Ministers — advising, directing, deciding — they must know that it is your reign as much as mine. Yet still they will not let you even be Prince Consort[1] — only Prince Albert! And you — you seem not to mind!

ALBERT   Now that surprises me. Have I acted my part so well? I suppose I ought to be glad.

THE QUEEN   You *do* mind?

ALBERT   I mind very much. I have your love, your trust; but here I am still in exile: and shall be — to the day of my death.

THE QUEEN   Oh, don't say it, Dearest: don't say it! You mustn't die — before I do.

ALBERT   But I shall, Weibchen: only — not yet. And listen! Here is something that shall a little console you. When that happens, they will no longer have to be suspicious, or afraid of me. They will not trouble to think of me as a foreigner when I am dead. Only till then . . . But no, no, you must not look so sad!

[1] The title of Prince Consort was not granted him till 1857.

Here is something more practical and important, which concerns us now. I have some plans to show you. See!

(*He takes up, and spreads out for inspection some large sheets of paper.*)

THE QUEEN   What are these, Albert?

ALBERT   The designs for the building of the Great Exhibition, which the Royal Commission has accepted — if you agree. Mr. Joseph Paxton, the architect, has had a wonderful idea for it — quite new. It is to be all of glass.

THE QUEEN   Of glass, Albert? But won't it break?

ALBERT   Not if it is put into a frame — a metal frame, like a window. But this will be *all* window: not a solid wall anywhere. Look well at it; for this, perhaps, is what modern architecture is going to be.

THE QUEEN   Oh, how beautiful, and how wonderful! All glass! How it will light up when the sun shines on it.

ALBERT   Yes . . . If all goes well it may become the symbol of your reign, my Dear; and of England leading the World to peace.

THE QUEEN   And when it does, then it will be your doing, Albert. (*Then, as she examines the design*) Oh, yes; I am beginning to see it now; it will be far more beautiful than St. Paul's Cathedral, I'm sure — glass being so much more beautiful than stone. And so original!

ALBERT   Yes; and so suitable for the purpose. That is what makes it so beautiful. And it will not take so long to build, either.

THE QUEEN   Where is it going to be?

ALBERT   In Hyde Park, if you will agree. To be in a Royal Park, it must first have your permission. You approve?

THE QUEEN   Of course! I think it is going to be the most wonderful building in the world, yes, and the most beautiful. And the Exhibition itself will be one of the most wonderful things in History; and the invention and planning of it all yours! I have always wanted this Country to be as great in the Arts as in Industry and Commerce; and now it is going to — thanks to you! Oh, if only my People could know what you are doing for them, how happy we should be!

ALBERT We will still be as happy as we can, Weibchen; and perhaps some day more shall come of it. And, talking about Art, my Dear, is it not time that you gave Mr. Edwin Landseer some kind of a title?

THE QUEEN (*doubtfully*) A title?

ALBERT Yes. He is a great painter — especially of dogs, which you are so fond of. And now that he has also done his great picture of the Duke's visit last year to the Field of Waterloo, would it not be well to make him a Baronet, or a Knight?

THE QUEEN Oh, not a Baronet, Albert! that would be too much. Mr. Landseer is not a man of any Family; he only comes from the people.

ALBERT Well, make him a Knight, then.

THE QUEEN I don't want to do anything unusual, Albert. Titles mustn't be made too cheap. Till now it is only Presidents of the Academy, or Painters by Royal Appointment, who have received titles; and I don't think Mr. Landseer will ever be President. Mr. Eastlake, I am told, is almost certain to be the next.

ALBERT But Mr. Landseer is quite as great an artist, my Dear, as any who have previously received titles. Sir Thomas Lawrence himself was only the son of a village innkeeper. So don't you think that you might?

THE QUEEN Why, yes; that does make a difference, of course; other artists of less merit having received the same honour.

ALBERT Then, do you not think, my Dear, that we might, at the same time, buy one of his pictures?

THE QUEEN Oh, yes; but not a large one; for I do not think we could find room for it.

ALBERT I think room could be found. And there was one at the Academy this year, which I remember you liked. May I buy it for you?

THE QUEEN Yes, Albert, if you liked it also. But remember, when we do a painter the great honour of buying one of his pictures, we only pay a certain price for it — thirty pounds, I think.

But General Grey is sure to know; he will tell you. Yes, I am almost sure that it is thirty pounds.

ALBERT Ah! a very good arrangement. Had I known that before, I might by now have made quite a collection for you of other artists — of Academicians, I mean.

THE QUEEN No, Albert, Dear, we mustn't make ourselves cheap; that would never do! You see, it is such an advantage to an artist to have a commission from *Us*. When we sat to Winterhalter, it got him quite a lot of other commissions. He stayed in England more than a year.

ALBERT Ah, very satisfactory — very improving to the English taste!

THE QUEEN So I don't think we ought to buy from more than one artist at a time. One in four or five years is quite enough, I think; except, of course, when we have to sit for our portraits. But Mr. Landseer is certainly my favourite painter — his subjects so appeal to me.

ALBERT Yes; what a pity we cannot sit to him as a family group of his favourite species — 'Queenie, Prince, and their six puppies'.

THE QUEEN (*rather shocked*) Oh, Albert, dear!

ALBERT I was only laughing, my Love. But, speaking of the family reminds me that I have something now much more serious to talk about. Our son, Bertie, is now eight years old.

THE QUEEN Oh, not yet, Darling!

ALBERT He will be in November; and it is quite time for his real education to begin. As some day he will have to be King, we must no longer think of him as a child.

THE QUEEN Isn't it too soon — too early?

ALBERT Had you not to be Queen rather sooner than you might have wished, my Dear? But for it you had been trained. We must not be afraid to face the fact that it might happen to him also. So for that we must be prepared.

THE QUEEN Oh, yes; of course you are right, Albert; for he has not yet learned nearly as much as I had done when I was his age.

ALBERT So have I found out. We must make a change; he must not have a Governess any more — he must have Tutors. He must learn history, and languages, and how to write and spell correctly in all of them; also about politics, and the making of the English Laws and Constitution.

THE QUEEN Yes, of course, that is most important.

ALBERT So I have, this week, been drawing up a scheme — a schedule — of the work he must do. To begin with — till he is ten — his lessons will be only six hours a day; when he is ten they must be eight.

THE QUEEN How many Tutors ought he to have, do you think, Albert?

ALBERT He must have an English Tutor, of course, so as not to have a foreign accent; also a French and a German master — three times a week each. He must learn also to dance well, and to draw just a little; and every day he must drill, and he must ride. Also he must be taught the art of conversation. His manners he will get, let us hope, from us. I do not think he need have a Chaplain yet — perhaps not till he is twelve; but he must have religious instruction every day. You see, my Dear, we have to make him a really good man, with a taste for serious things — what your English Kings have so seldom been. The only one in the last five reigns who was good at all, went mad. It was a pity. Your Uncle George was not at all what he ought to have been — not at all!

THE QUEEN Poor Uncle George! I can just remember him picking me up and kissing me; and I noticed how fat he was, and how he smelt of brandy. But he was quite nice and kind to me; so please don't say anything against him now he is dead.

ALBERT No; for it is not necessary. But I am glad, my Dear, that you did not wish to have any of your children named after *him*.

THE QUEEN But George is a very popular English name, Albert — St. George being our Patron Saint: you mustn't forget that.

ALBERT No; and some day perhaps — with our grandchildren — it will be safe for the name to be used again. But not yet. It will not be the name of the next King, at any rate.

THE QUEEN No; that will be 'Albert Edward'.

ALBERT Why not Edward the Seventh?

THE QUEEN Because, Albert, I intend that my People shall some day recognize what they owe to *you*; and *that* will do it.

ALBERT Then why not Albert alone?

THE QUEEN Oh, no, Dearest; that I could never allow! If he could be called 'Albert the Second' — yes! But Albert alone — just as if no other Albert had come first — would be an act of disrespect to you, not to be thought of!

ALBERT Perhaps it is a matter we shall not be allowed to decide, Weibchen.

THE QUEEN But I mean to! Oh, Albert, I do wish Bertie had Vicky's brains! She is going to be so clever; and I'm afraid he is *not* going to be.

ALBERT We must make his brain to grow like his body. It can be done; it is only a matter of proper education. That is why I have already drawn up this scheme, so as to begin in good time.

THE QUEEN (*who is now standing by the window*) Look, Albert! There he is, in the garden, playing with Vicky. How prettily he moves; and how fond they are of each other! Look!

(*She turns toward* THE PRINCE, *who now also looks out. Suddenly he taps angrily on the glass, then opens the window, and calls.*)

ALBERT Ah! Do not do that! Come in here, Bertie, at once!

THE QUEEN What did he do?

ALBERT What he must be taught not to do. You did not see?

THE QUEEN No.

ALBERT Ah, it is quite time that we began to give him a real education, and a real training in how to behave. He must learn discipline.

(*The door opens. Very timidly, fearful of the scolding which awaits him, the little* PRINCE OF WALES *creeps into the room, and stands holding the door.*)

ALBERT Come in! Come in! What were you doing?

THE PRINCE Only playing, Papa.

ALBERT Playing! I saw you throw a handful of gravel at your Sister.

PRINCE Only for fun. She didn't mind.

ALBERT You are not to do it! If the gravel had gone into her eye, it would have blinded her.

PRINCE (*his voice breaking*) I didn't throw it at her face, Papa!

ALBERT It might have hit her face.

PRINCE (*weeping*) But it didn't!

ALBERT Don't answer! Got up to your room!

(*The culprit retires, weeping.*)

ALBERT (*loudly*) And shut the door after you!

(*The door is shut.*)

THE QUEEN I'm afraid he's going to be difficult, Albert.

ALBERT Children always are difficult, till you make them understand what you mean them to be, and whom they have to obey . . . Patience, my Dear, patience! It will take time; and it will not always be easy, or pleasant. But it has to be done.

(*And on these excellent intentions the curtain falls, to rise again, some twelve years later — when the directing hand has been withdrawn — on a specimen of genial but faulty humanity, which — could he but have seen it — would have made 'ALBERT THE GOOD' turn in his grave.*)

THE 'GO-BETWEEN'

December 1851

MR. MACAULAY, *the eminent Historian, has not yet received the Peerage which is soon to descend on him. But the honour of a command call from* HER MAJESTY *has brought him to Windsor; and in the temporary absence of Prince Albert,* THE QUEEN *is doing her best to carry on an intellectual conversation with one who finds it difficult to make his conversation small, or other than informative. Apparently* MR. MACAULAY *has been talking on his pet subject — Constitutional Liberty, as exemplified by English History.*

THE QUEEN But when it gets to breaking the *law*, Mr. Macaulay, then liberty becomes licence!

MACAULAY It may, Ma'am, or it may not ... You can't make an omelet without breaking eggs, Ma'am.

THE QUEEN Eggs?

MACAULAY Yes, Ma'am; and then, if you find they are bad, you throw them away, and make your omelet without them. Sometimes the Law turns out to be a very bad egg indeed; and you have to get rid of it as quickly as possible.

THE QUEEN But can it ever be right for the people to rebel against their own Sovereign, Mr. Macaulay?

MACAULAY To a descendant of the House of Hanover, Ma'am, I think I may say 'yes'.

THE QUEEN But I am a *Stuart*, Mr. Macaulay.

MACAULAY Your Majesty is many things by ancestry and inheritance — not only Scottish, but Welsh also; Norman, Saxon, French, Danish, *and* German. The value of mixed blood is pre-eminently exemplified in your Majesty's ancestry and person.

THE QUEEN I don't like mixed blood, Mr. Macaulay.

MACAULAY Your Majesty does not like the phrase. But in the *fact* lie the very foundations of our history and of our race.

THE QUEEN Oh, indeed? Well, Mr. Macaulay, if you say so, I am not prepared to deny it. I wish the Prince were here; he could argue with you so much better than I can ... But take India — surely India is a case where the trouble all comes from mixed blood?

MACAULAY Not so much mixed blood, Ma'am, as mixed religion. Were all Indians of the same religion, the mixed blood would not matter.

THE QUEEN Ah, yes; Religion is the most important thing in the world, is it not?

MACAULAY It is, Ma'am; even politically nothing matters more.

THE QUEEN So sad that they should be able to believe such things — the Indians, I mean. If they could only become Church of England, or Presbyterian — I suppose, then, as you say, government would be quite easy.

MACAULAY If that miracle were to happen, Ma'am, India, as we know it now, would vanish off the face of the earth. What would take its place, I cannot imagine.

THE QUEEN Still, it would be a great improvement; the people would understand so much better that we only rule them for their own good. What a pity it is that Eastern races cannot accept a reasonable form of Religion like ours!

MACAULAY The East, Ma'am, has its own mind on that subject, which the West finds some difficulty in understanding. Similarly, the East has some difficulty in understanding how anyone can believe the things that *we* do.

THE QUEEN Really! now that surprises me! How very extraordinary! To me it seems all so simple, so unanswerable.

MACAULAY Yes, Ma'am. But your Majesty must not expect the Eastern mind to grasp so easily great truths, which to your Majesty seem self-evident.

THE QUEEN Ah, no. I suppose not ... And how is your *History* getting on, Mr. Macaulay?

MACAULAY Since your Majesty so graciously released me from the cares of office, very well indeed, Ma'am.

THE QUEEN I shall read it with great interest. And now, Mr. Macaulay —

(*She rises from her seat, and is about to give* MR. MACAULAY *his dismissal, when* PRINCE ALBERT *enters.*)

ALBERT Lord John Russell is waiting to see you, my Dear ... Ah, Mr. Macaulay, are you just going?

MACAULAY I am, Sir. I fear I have been here too long. One who no longer holds office has no right to keep Her Majesty's Prime Minister waiting.

THE QUEEN I have been very much interested, Mr. Macaulay, in all you have told me. I wish you could have been here, Albert. ... Good-bye. And I shall greatly look forward to reading your *History*.

MACAULAY If my industry needed any further incentive, your Majesty has now provided it. (*Then, as he bows himself out*) Your Majesty's servant ... Your Highness.

THE QUEEN Did Lord John tell you what he has come about?

ALBERT He has come in reply to your letter about that man, Pilgerstein.[1]

THE QUEEN But we must take care not to call him Pilgerstein to Lord John. I so nearly did, the other day. Did you say I would see him at once?

ALBERT I said he was to be shown in as soon as you were disengaged.

THE QUEEN You have ready all the notes you made, Albert?

ALBERT I have them with me. .

THE QUEEN Well, Albert, if I forget anything, will you please remind me? We must get this settled now, once and for all.

(*The door opens, a Gentleman of the Court announces,* 'LORD JOHN RUSSELL, *your Majesty*'. *And the Prime Minister bows himself briskly into the room.*)

THE QUEEN Good morning, Lord John. I am glad that you have been able to come so soon.

---

[1] Nickname given to Palmerston by Prince Albert.

RUSSELL Instantly upon receiving your Majesty's command.

THE QUEEN It is upon a very unpleasant subject that I have to speak to you this morning.

RUSSELL I rather feared so, your Majesty.

THE QUEEN Yes. After hearing from you yesterday that Lord Palmerston had told you almost nothing about the way in which he has been treating me, I felt that I must see you at once.

RUSSELL I am sorry, Ma'am, that there should have been any misunderstanding.

THE QUEEN It is hardly a misunderstanding, Lord John. It has happened too often. I am now obliged to regard it as wilful disobedience.

RUSSELL I am sure, Ma'am, that Lord Palmerston never so intended it.

THE QUEEN Then he has let his lack of intention become a habit, which I cannot allow!

RUSSELL Will your Majesty be good enough to give me the full particulars of what your Majesty has to complain of?

THE QUEEN I will ask the Prince to read you the Memorandum which he has made for me, dealing with the whole matter. We have gone into it together very thoroughly.

RUSSELL I am your Majesty's most attentive servant.

ALBERT (*producing the Memorandum*) I will begin first, Lord John Russell, by reminding you of the previous occasions on which Her Majesty has had to complain of Lord Palmerston's actions and inattentions. They cover a very considerable period.

RUSSELL I was under the impression, Sir, that those previous occurrences had already been discussed, and settled — satisfactorily.

ALBERT Not satisfactorily, Lord John, if there is any recurrence of the misconduct complained of.

RUSSELL Misconduct is a hard word, Sir.

ALBERT It is an accurate one . . . Three years ago, Her Majesty had to complain that Lord Palmerston had failed to keep her properly informed of the despatches sent from the Foreign Office on important matters of policy: that he had got into the habit of letting them go without first submitting them for Her Majesty's approval. Lord Palmerston explained that he did not always have time; but he was unable to give any instance when the lack of time was due, in any way, to Her Majesty being unwilling, or unable to receive him ... A few months later, Her Majesty spoke to you again, at some length, of her growing dissatisfaction with Lord Palmerston's very independent way of conducting Foreign Policy; also with the rather provocative tone in which so many of his despatches were written. With Her Majesty's criticisms, you expressed yourself as being generally in agreement, but you said that Lord Palmerston's Foreign Policy had the approval of the Cabinet, and also that he was a difficult and dangerous man for you to deal with, on account of his general popularity. So *that* matter was 'satisfactorily settled' by nothing being done.

RUSSELL   I ask pardon, Sir. Is this Her Majesty's Memorandum: or are these your Highness's own comments made upon it?

ALBERT   They are the comments, arising from the Memorandum, which Her Majesty has herself made to me. If I say anything of which Her Majesty does not approve, she will correct me ... On a later occasion, when it was found that Lord Palmerston had sent off to our Legation at St. Petersburg a very important despatch, without first submitting it, he endeavoured to escape criticism by describing it as a private letter, individually addressed to a Member of the Legation, though this 'private letter' had been placed in the records of the Foreign Office.

RUSSELL   I understood that Her Majesty accepted that explanation.

ALBERT   Her Majesty accepted that explanation in the sense that she could not tell Lord Palmerston that she did not believe him.

RUSSELL   I am sorry that Her Majesty should have been left in any doubt.

ALBERT   So am I. It placed Her Majesty in a very difficult position. That difficulty has come more often than once.

RUSSELL   That Her Majesty finds herself unable to *believe* — ?

ALBERT   That Her Majesty has found herself forced — or at least pressed — by her Prime Minister, to accept explanations which she did not think satisfactory.

RUSSELL (*stiffly*) I am not aware, Sir, that I have ever brought 'pressure' to bear upon Her Majesty, in offering my humble advice.

ALBERT Advice without pressure, on a difficult problem, Lord John, is rather like an engine without steam. I think I am not wrong in saying that Her Majesty is now putting pressure upon you — legitimate pressure. It is only of illegitimate pressure that Her Majesty would complain.

RUSSELL (*stiffly*) If your Highness would kindly specify any undue pressure of which I have been guilty, I should know better where I am.

ALBERT Shall we put it like this? — Is it legitimate to let a 'difficult and dangerous person' go on being dangerous because of his general popularity?

RUSSELL I believe I warned Her Majesty — and I think rightly — that Lord Palmerston was quite capable of destroying the Government; and, under certain circumstances, might not be unwilling to do so.

ALBERT The Government of which he was a member? What a *safe* sort of colleague to have to do with!

RUSSELL Cabinet Government has its difficulties, your Highness.

ALBERT We, also, find that. But while it *is* Cabinet Government, under a Reigning Sovereign, it is not right for any member of it — however popular — to go his own way, without first consulting those who have the right to be consulted.

RUSSELL I humbly submit, Sir, that while the Government, as a whole, still enjoys Her Majesty's confidence, and while that Government is not in disagreement over the main lines of the policy pursued by its individual members — it is the bounden duty of the Prime Minister (even if he has to compromise somewhat more than he would wish), to do all he can to keep that Government in being.

ALBERT That word 'compromise' has two meanings, Lord

John. I am afraid Her Majesty feels that the compromise you sometimes thought necessary, has compromised *her*.

RUSSELL If what I have done ever seems to take on so serious a complexion as *that*, my resignation is always at Her Majesty's disposal.

ALBERT It is not *your* resignation, Lord John, that Her Majesty thinks necessary. We all make mistakes. But a mistake wilfully made, and wilfully repeated — *that* cannot be tolerated.

RUSSELL If your Highness —

ALBERT Just a moment, Lord John. I will put you in possession of all the points that Her Majesty wishes you to consider: that factor of wilfully repeated disobedience being the most important . . . Last year, Lord Palmerston, without previous consultation, ordered the British Fleet to the Piraeus, to make a hostile demonstration against the Greek Government: an action which might have led to War.

RUSSELL Over that matter, Sir, Lord Palmerston was given a strong vote of confidence by the House of Commons.

ALBERT 'Without consultation', I said. In the House of Commons that point was carefully not raised — was not even mentioned. You, yourself, considered that three weeks' grace should have been allowed before what Lord Palmerston ordered to be done in twenty-four hours.

RUSSELL The result was successful, your Highness.

ALBERT The result would have been equally successful, and more conciliatory in its effect, had more time been granted. Lord Palmerston, when it suits him, can be as dilatory as he is sometimes hasty . . . Last year, over the Spanish question when he had again sent off a despatch without submitting it to Her Majesty, he was three weeks in answering her letter of complaint. It is conduct like that, which makes Her Majesty sometimes doubt whether Lord Palmerston is even a Gentleman.

RUSSELL (*uncomfortably*) I have to admit, Sir, that this is the first I have heard of so grave an omission in duty and courtesy toward Her Majesty. I think it must have been forgetfulness.

ALBERT We think not. But, in any case, manners though important (and, to one's Sovereign, a matter of loyal duty), are not the most important thing in politics: though, I fear, it is the tone of Lord Palmerston's notes to Foreign Chancellories, far more than his policy (which Her Majesty has often approved) that has drawn down upon this Country the hatred of all the Governments of Europe.

RUSSELL Over the Greek question, I must remind your Highness that the whole Government was prepared to take over the blame (if there was any), and offer resignation. And I communicated that fact to Her Majesty. As Her Majesty was not willing to accept our resignation, I could have hoped that the matter had been disposed of — finally.

ALBERT It would have been, Lord John — as would also those other matters — had there not been this persistent repetition of a course of action which you, yourself, have never attempted to defend — this sending off of despatches without consultation . . . And now we come to the present — to the gravest matter of all. We have been faced in France by the violent accomplishment of a *coup d'état*, which has shocked the moral sense of the whole Country. Pending a further decision, Her Majesty's Ambassador in Paris was instructed to maintain an attitude of strict aloofness, and by no word to express either approval, or acceptance, of what has taken place. Behind his back, and without a word of advice to Her Majesty, Lord Palmerston has written a letter of encouragement to the new Government; and Lord Normanby, our Ambassador, only hears of it by accident. Her Majesty now says that this cannot go on. And she wishes to know what you are prepared to do in the matter.

RUSSELL I must admit to your Majesty that Lord Palmerston's precipitate action on this occasion is greatly regretted by the whole, or at least by a large majority of your Majesty's Government. I have myself told Lord Palmerston that, in this matter, I shall be unable to excuse or defend him if your Majesty is determined to press the case against him. And having now been informed so fully of your Majesty's mind, I will see Lord Palmerston again, and represent to him how very gravely, in your Majesty's view, the matter stands.

THE QUEEN What you propose to do has my full approval.

RUSSELL If it is your Majesty's pleasure, I will do that at once; and I will, as soon as possible, come back and report to your Majesty the result of our interview.

THE QUEEN Please do so. And please understand, Lord John Russell, that *this* time there must be a result, which will admit of no further *pretence* of misunderstanding.

RUSSELL I will bear very carefully in mind your Majesty's command.

(*And so saying,* LORD JOHN RUSSELL *bows himself out.*)

ALBERT You did very well, my Dear.

THE QUEEN I hardly said anything.

ALBERT That is what I mean. Considering how strongly you feel in this matter, you showed great self-restraint . . . Exit Mr. Pilgerstein! — I *think*.

SCENE II

In a very comfortable arm-chair before the fire, in his room at the Foreign Office, LORD PALMERSTON *is taking his afternoon nap. His feet rest upon a cushioned stool, a silk handkerchief of bright pattern covers his face. A Foreign Office* ATTENDANT *enters, and with studied diffidence rouses him from sleep. With a jerk and a grunt, his Lordship sits up, the handkerchief falls from his face.*

ATTENDANT I beg pardon, my Lord, for disturbing your Lordship. Lord John Russell is here, and hopes that he may see your Lordship.

PALMERSTON Oh, yes; ask him to come up!

(*The* ATTENDANT *goes, while* LORD PALMERSTON *slowly picks himself up, yawns, clears his throat, gives a rub to his hair, and (taking his stand on the hearth-rug with his coat-tails over his arms) prepares to receive his Visitor.* LORD JOHN *enters with pursed lips, and a self-conscious expression of importance mingled with severity.*)

PALMERSTON Well, John?

RUSSELL It isn't well at all, Palmerston. I'm afraid that, this time, you've done it.

PALMERSTON Oh, you've been giving me away, have you?

RUSSELL You've given yourself away . . . I've warned you! . . . I've warned you!

PALMERSTON Yes; and I've warned *you*. You wouldn't take my warning; I wouldn't take yours. So far we are a match; but there it stops: same Government — opposite camps.

RUSSELL Opposite, eh?

PALMERSTON Yes, it's the battle of Constitutional Government I've been fighting: and not one of you had the guts to back me up!

RUSSELL I was under the impression that I had stood by you through a good many battles, at great personal inconvenience to myself.

PALMERSTON Bah! What would have been the good of all Wellington's battles, if he'd run away at Waterloo?

RUSSELL He wouldn't have won Waterloo, if he hadn't *waited*. That's been your mistake, Palmerston; it's your hunting instinct, I suppose: no sooner do you see a gate than you want to go over it. Now you've come a cropper.

PALMERSTON Oh, have I? Have you come to ask for my resignation?

RUSSELL (*temporizing*) I've come to talk about it. You'll have to make a big concession, this time, to avoid it; and you'll have to *stick* to it. You know, Pam, about this French business, you are all wrong.

PALMERSTON Am I? D'you suppose that *coup d'état* is not going to succeed?

RUSSELL I'm afraid it has succeeded.

PALMERSTON Quite so! Well, the only proper policy for this Country in Foreign Affairs is not to let anyone do a damned thing we don't want 'em to do, if we *can* help it: but to put a cheerful face on it, if we *can't*.

RUSSELL There's not much morality in that, Palmerston.

PALMERSTON It's damned Scriptural! Making friends of the Mammon of unrighteousness, and getting yourself into everlasting habitations as a reward. Isn't it better to be friendly with France, than be a skulking, sulking enemy? There's Russia looming ahead, my Boy; and we can't tackle her alone.

RUSSELL But why couldn't you have *waited*? Our attitude was perfectly correct: we didn't express any disapproval — officially.

PALMERSTON Papers did: Normanby did — privately.

RUSSELL He denies that.

PALMERSTON He can't prevent fools blabbing, if he talks to 'em. He was making mischief for us. I wanted to send that letter; I *meant* to send it. She wouldn't have let me — or *He* wouldn't! And that's my point. He's her legal husband; but he's not the legal husband of the British Constitution. And, by God! if I chose to stand up and fight him, and give all the facts, I could get a vote of censure passed on him in the House of Commons any day.

RUSSELL You couldn't.

PALMERSTON I'd have a damned good try, if it came to it! Or anyway, I could carry a counter-vote of confidence in myself; which would come to much the same thing.

RUSSELL If you tried that on *this* time, you'd get none of the Cabinet voting for you.

PALMERSTON Oh! Shouldn't I? . . . John, you are not a very good judge of character: you don't even understand mine.

RUSSELL Don't I?

PALMERSTON No. You think I'm a regular fire-eater. I'm not . . . I'm a peaceful, easy-going fellow: hate trouble — don't like giving trouble to others. I'm charitable in my judgments — fond of my fellow-men, so long as they aren't Germans . . . By God! if Albert had been on the front Opposition bench, he'd have got us out before now — *me*, anyway! Lord! how he hates me! . . . Oh, but the fellow's got a brain: and works like four cart-horses. He's made *me* work, you know! Again and again, I'd have to be out of my bed by ten o'clock in the morning, to write those damned despatches he thinks he's got to correct before the mail goes.

RUSSELL (*put wise*) So getting out of bed has sometimes been the trouble, has it?

PALMERSTON Well! can you wonder? One can't keep the hours of a Gentleman since he got the pull of things ... It's a pity, John! ... It's a pity! She's not the same woman she was — now. She's a deteriorated character.

RUSSELL Indeed! I should have said rather the reverse.

PALMERSTON Ah, you didn't go to Court as early as I did. In old Mel's day, she used to listen to jokes and stories she won't listen to now ... Mel used to tell 'em; so did I. And, i' gad! how she'd laugh at 'em! But after she got *him* — Lord! if I'd tried to tell one of my old stories then, she'd have ordered me out of the room!

RUSSELL Yes, Palmerston, but that isn't what I've come to talk about. This is serious, you know.

PALMERSTON Oh, is it? What did you say to them — or what did they say to you?

RUSSELL A good deal was said, first and last, up and down — more than I can remember. But the main point was this: that you'd done the same thing too many times for her to put up with it any more. And he had got it all down for her in black and white — dates and everything. There was no disputing the facts. I had to admit that you hadn't behaved as you should have done ... Over one complaint she made, you left her three weeks without an answer.

PALMERSTON Good Lord! I wish she'd leave *me* three weeks without an answer! It's the three answers a day I get from her sometimes, that drive me almost crazy! ... Look here, John! Do you, in your senses, think it possible for me to run the Foreign Office with him putting his nose into every despatch that goes out? ... Last year I signed and sent off twenty-eight thousand of 'em. Do they imagine that they can take on a job of that size, or anything like it? Ask 'em that!

RUSSELL Well, that certainly *is* a point.

PALMERSTON Of course it is! Why, there are thousands and thousands they don't ever set eyes on — and don't want to. But if just one happens to go, and they miss it — then I'm made to hear of it. Damned humbug!

RUSSELL   Well, well, but what am I to say, Palmerston?

PALMERSTON   Say what you damned well like! What should you like to say? What d'you *want* to say?

RUSSELL   I would like to say — if possible — that if owing to certain irregularities inadvertently committed — you have failed to give satisfaction in the discharge of your duties as Foreign Secretary, you once more express your sincere regret; and further, that if, upon my recommendation, it were Her Majesty's pleasure, you would be willing to accept a change of office.

PALMERSTON   Oh, indeed! What office?

RUSSELL   Lord Lieutenant of Ireland.

PALMERSTON   I'll be damned if I do!

RUSSELL   Then, my dear Palmerston, I have no alternative but to ask for your resignation.

PALMERSTON   Oh? . . . What does the Cabinet say to that?

RUSSELL   I have consulted seven members of the Cabinet. They all agree.

PALMERSTON (*calculating the situation as thus presented*) Seven — and yourself eight, eh? . . . So you've got a majority . . . Very well. Shall I write it now?

RUSSELL   Please.

(LORD PALMERSTON *sits down, and begins writing.*)

PALMERSTON   How do you spell 'resignation', John? It's a word I've never written before.

RUSSELL   You spell it with an 'R'.

PALMERSTON   H'm! Glad you've got some sense of humour left in you . . . There you are, my Lord John! (*He hands him the document.*) And, mind you, by making it a resignation, I'm doing the generous by both of you. By the Lord! if I made her dismiss me — what a hullabaloo there'd be in all the papers!

RUSSELL (*ingratiatingly*) I'm sure, my dear Pam, you would always wish to do what is best — not for yourself, but for the Country.

PALMERSTON (*not so sure, but unable to say so*) Oh? well . . . I suppose so! Is that correct enough for 'em? If it isn't, I'll write a more formal one later.

RUSSELL Thank you . . . I'm sorry, Palmerston.

PALMERSTON Not as sorry as you pretend to be. Are you going back to Windsor now?

RUSSELL I said I would return directly I'd seen you. I'm sorry I have not been more successful.

PALMERSTON I think you've been very successful . . . You've got what you wanted.

RUSSELL No, Palmerston. What I wanted — and offered — you refused.

PALMERSTON Ireland? You thought you'd send me to Ireland, eh? . . . I don't put my head into a sack with my eyes open. I'm not that sort. Well, be off with you to Windsor! Carry the glad news! You've finished with me — for the present . . . Who are you having instead?

RUSSELL A while back they suggested — Granville.

PALMERSTON Got it all arranged, had they? Oh, he'll do the pretty-pretty all right, if that's all you want! Well, God be with you! And my best respects to both of them.

RUSSELL Good-bye, Palmerston. I say again, I'm sorry.

PALMERSTON You aren't! But some day you will be.

(LORD JOHN *has gone out, and is closing the door, when* PALMERSTON *calls after him.*)

Hi! John, John!

(LORD JOHN *reopens the door.*)

RUSSELL Well?

PALMERSTON If she accepts my resignation (which I suppose she will) who d'you reckon is going to be next Prime Minister, after you? . . . I mean, when the Liberals come in again.

RUSSELL Really, I haven't thought.

PALMERSTON Oh? . . . Well, I'll tell you, then . . . It'll be *ME*.

RUSSELL You?

PALMERSTON Yes; *me*. And I shall make you my Foreign Secretary. With a bit of training, you'll make a very good one. You'll write the despatches; I'll come in and correct them . . . Easy enough correcting despatches, once someone else has written them.

RUSSELL (*with a wry smile*) Well, if that ever *should* happen, I might find life easier, working *under* you, than working *over* you!

PALMERSTON Oh? Think so?

RUSSELL *That* hasn't been easy, I can assure you! All the same, I'm sorry.

(*He nods good-bye; then goes quickly, closing the door.* PALMERSTON, *listening to his hurried departure, grunts an amused commentary.*)

PALMERSTON Trot away, little Man! You are an ass; but you are a clever one.

(*Then, as he goes to sit down again, he rings the bell. And while he is settling into his chair, the* ATTENDANT *enters.*)

PALMERSTON Oh, Peters, see that I'm not disturbed for the next twenty minutes or so. I want to finish my nap.

(*Pulling out the silk handkerchief, he lies back, and again covers his face.*)

SCENE III

We are again at Windsor. A Gentleman enters, and announces: 'LORD JOHN RUSSELL, *your Majesty'. And the Prime Minister, fresh from his not very comfortable interview with* LORD PALMER-STON, *re-enters.*

THE QUEEN You have been very expeditious, Lord John. We hardly expected you so soon.

RUSSELL I could wish, Ma'am, that my expedition had the accompaniment of more personal satisfaction over the result.

THE QUEEN (*anxiously*) Has Lord Palmerston not agreed, then, to what you told him he must do?

RUSSELL Not in the way, Ma'am, that would have given me most satisfaction. I had hoped (with your Majesty's gracious permission), to advise that his resignation should be effected by a change of office; and that your Majesty might be pleased to appoint him Lord Lieutenant of Ireland — that post being about to fall vacant. But Lord Palmerston would not hear of it.

THE QUEEN (*frigidly*) I think that, perhaps, Lord Palmerston was right. To be my representative in Ireland, is one of the highest honours in the gift of the Crown.

RUSSELL It is, Ma'am.

THE QUEEN (*rubbing it in*) What else would Lord Palmerston 'not hear of'?

RUSSELL I ask pardon, your Majesty: the phrase was an unfortunate one ... Lord Palmerston requests me to convey to your Majesty his humble duty, and his very deep regret that he should have seemed in any way inattentive to your Majesty's wishes and claims upon his service. He admits certain omissions complained of by your Majesty, as regards despatches sent out without their having first received the Royal sanction. But he submits — I was to put this before your Majesty — that, in the course of the year he has had (in the performance of his duties as Foreign Secretary), to send out no fewer than twenty-eight thousand despatches; and he questions whether your Majesty could possibly be expected to consider all of them with the attention that some of them may require.

ALBERT If Lord Palmerston has been able to give due consideration to twenty-eight thousand despatches in a year, so also can Her Majesty.

RUSSELL I would not, Sir, for a moment, question Her Majesty's willingness to do so. Those numbers were merely given as an illustration of the large amount of routine-work, which has to be dealt with by others. Lord Palmerston submits, therefore, that, in his omission to present certain despatches for your Majesty's consideration, he has merely made a mistake — not so much in principle, as in selection.

ALBERT (*caustically*) His selection has been sometimes rather unfortunate.

RUSSELL It has, your Highness: that I most fully admit.

THE QUEEN Then what does he propose now to do?

RUSSELL I have received from him, Ma'am — I have it here — his resignation of office, as your Majesty's Secretary of State for Foreign Affairs.

THE QUEEN (*correctively*) You mean, Lord John, that he asks my permission to resign. He cannot do *that*, without first obtaining my consent.

RUSSELL That is so, Ma'am, of course. What I hold now, was only written hurriedly. Lord Palmerston requested me to say that his more formal offer of resignation would be submitted later.

THE QUEEN That will be quite satisfactory. Thank you, Lord John. I am very glad that, at last, you have made him see reason.

RUSSELL On this occasion, he did not make any difficulty, Ma'am ... And his last words to me — *almost* his last words — spoken very feelingly: were a request that I would convey to your Majesty (and also to your Royal Highness) the expression of his most deep and dutiful respects.

(LORD JOHN *is distinctly pleased with himself over this manipulation of the farewell message:* 'respects' *is true — verbally; and* 'feelingly' *is also true — in a way*.)

THE QUEEN When you next see him, Lord John, will you please to thank him for that message. But do not let there be any delay in his sending of a properly-worded request for permission to resign.

RUSSELL I will not, Ma'am.

THE QUEEN There was one occasion, you know, when — having offered resignation — he withdrew it the next day.

RUSSELL He will not do so on this occasion, Ma'am, I am quite sure.

THE QUEEN Of course, Lord John, if you would like me to offer him a Peerage, so that he may go to the House of Lords, I am quite willing to do so.

RUSSELL I think, Ma'am, that he hopes to be able still to serve your Majesty, with more efficiency, in the House of Commons ... In the House of Lords, he might feel himself rather lost.

THE QUEEN Very well; that shall be as he wishes. (*She rises.*) I thank you very much, Lord John, for what you have done for me to-day. You have taken a great load off my mind. It was quite wearing me out.

RUSSELL Well, Ma'am, in that case — though my errand has been a sad one — I have some cause for satisfaction.

THE QUEEN You have, indeed. Good-bye!

RUSSELL (*as he bows himself out*) Your Majesty's most humble servant! ... Your Highness!

ALBERT (*returning his bow with stiff formality*) Good-bye, Mr. Prime Minister.

(*No sooner has the door closed, than* THE QUEEN, *almost clapping her hands, runs to* THE PRINCE.)

THE QUEEN Oh, Albert, Albert! I must write to Uncle Leopold at once! How delighted he will be to hear that Pilgerstein has resigned at last!

ALBERT (*with more reserve*) Oh, yes: he will be quite pleased, I am sure.

THE QUEEN And it was *your* doing! I couldn't have managed it without you.

ALBERT No?

THE QUEEN So, at last — *you have won!*

ALBERT Yes: I suppose so!

THE QUEEN Is anything the matter?

ALBERT I was only thinking of something the Duke of Wellington once said — that there was nothing so sad as a Victory, except a Defeat. Poor Pilgerstein! How he must be feeling it now!

(*But, as a matter of fact, Pilgerstein, having finished his afternoon nap, is as happy as anybody concerned; for now he sees plainly the Premiership waiting for him.*)

THE POPULAR VOICE

1853

In the room at Buckingham Palace where she receives her Ministers, THE QUEEN *is giving audience to* LORD ABERDEEN, *the Premier. War has not yet been declared on Russia (though it soon will be); and* LORD ABERDEEN *still hopes to avert it, while in the Country at large the war-fever is steadily rising and is making his position difficult.*

THE QUEEN Well, at any rate, I am thankful that Lord Palmerston is not now Foreign Minister. Had he been, he would already have plunged us into war with Russia, which we are still hoping to avoid.

ABERDEEN Your Majesty's observation is a very just one. But even as Home Secretary, Lord Palmerston has become a very troublesome, I might even say a dangerous, member of your Majesty's Government; and unfortunately he has a strong following both in the House and in the Country, which is violently in favour of war. Indeed, his popularity is now so great that it would be within his power (were he to resign) to overthrow the present Government and form another with himself as Prime Minister.

THE QUEEN He could not do that, Lord Aberdeen, unless *I* sent for him.

ABERDEEN No, Ma'am; of course not.

THE QUEEN Which I certainly should not do.

ABERDEEN Circumstances might make it unavoidable, Ma'am.

THE QUEEN Not under any circumstance. I have no confidence whatever in Lord Palmerston.

ABERDEEN Unfortunately, Ma'am, neither have I.

THE QUEEN Then why, Lord Aberdeen, have you proposed that he should be Minister in Attendance when we go down to Balmoral?

ABERDEEN I was sorry, indeed, Ma'am, to do so; especially as I was aware of your Majesty's reluctance to receive him in that capacity. But it is the very fact that he is dangerous and hostile to our efforts to preserve peace, which makes it necessary to give him no ground for legitimate complaint. As your Majesty's Home Secretary, he might naturally expect to have the honour of being called for Ministerial attendance — an honour which, so far, has not been accorded him; and were there any further delay he would probably resent it, and attribute it perhaps to ill-will and jealousy on *my* part. Whether he did this or not himself, the public and the press would not fail to do so, and would make it a ground for attacks more bitter and hostile than those which we have recently had to face, and to which, I have good reason to believe, he has himself given encouragement.

THE QUEEN How dishonourable!

ABERDEEN As he is still a member of the Cabinet, I merely state the case, Ma'am, without comment.

THE QUEEN How is it that he has made himself so popular?

ABERDEEN He has qualities, Ma'am, of a kind which appeal to the general public, and to the more extreme members of the Opposition. Your Majesty may not be aware of the amount of flattery which is offered to Lord Palmerston by the Tory party, with the hope of separating him altogether from the Government. They may yet succeed in their design. I fully admit, Ma'am, that my proposal may fail to produce any good effect; but if Lord Palmerston has any generous feeling, he will surely appreciate the personal compliment which Ministerial attendance on your Majesty at Balmoral will imply.

THE QUEEN I wish I could do it more sincerely, Lord Aberdeen. It is only upon your advice as Prime Minister that I give my consent.

ABERDEEN I am sorry, Ma'am; I am also grateful. I am still more sorry to have to inform your Majesty of certain most scandalous attacks which have of late been made upon His Royal Highness, the Prince, for his supposed influence on the policy of your Majesty's Government, in a direction contrary to the interests of this Country.

THE QUEEN (*sharply*) Who is making them?

ABERDEEN I can give no names, Ma'am; such attacks are made anonymously; but they are unfortunately receiving a wide and increasing circulation.

THE QUEEN In the newspapers, do you mean?

ABERDEEN Not, of course, in any of the respectable newspapers, Ma'am; but there are others.

THE QUEEN Can they not be prosecuted?

ABERDEEN They might be, Ma'am; but I hardly think that would be advisable. It would not be seemly for His Royal Highness (however well-justified) to bring an action for libel against these rabble of the press.

THE QUEEN Then can they not be suppressed?

ABERDEEN No, Ma'am, I'm afraid not; it would do more harm than good. The liberty of the press has become so much a fetish with the British people that only a very popular Government could safely venture on the suppression of anything but matter which had no popular support behind it.

THE QUEEN But has this?

ABERDEEN Yes, Ma'am, I fear it has.

THE QUEEN Then, Lord Aberdeen, what do you propose to do about it?

ABERDEEN I propose, Ma'am (if it be your Majesty's pleasure), that these base accusations shall forthwith be brought to the notice of Parliament, in order that their absolute groundlessness may be exposed beyond all further question. I have already consulted the Leaders of your Majesty's Opposition, and am assured of their full support and agreement. And I have no doubt, Ma'am, that we shall secure the unanimous voice of all parties both in the Lords and the Commons.

THE QUEEN Yes, Lord Aberdeen, you have my consent to that being done. And let it be done as soon as possible. Who, do you propose, shall speak for the Government?

ABERDEEN In the Lords, I myself shall have that honour. In the House of Commons the duty will fall naturally to the Leader of the House — that is, to Lord Palmerston.

THE QUEEN   Indeed? How interesting! And — you think he will?

ABERDEEN   He cannot well refuse, Ma'am. The matter is to come before the Cabinet to-day; and though we are not a very harmonious body just now, there can, in this case, be no possible disagreement. After all — however much we are politically divided — we are all, I hope, decent and honourable English gentlemen.

THE QUEEN (*acidly*)   But Lord Palmerston is not English, only Irish.

ABERDEEN   Even in Ireland, Ma'am, gentlemen are not unknown.

THE QUEEN.   Well, we shall be interested to read his speech — when he has made it.

ABERDEEN   I believe, Ma'am, that he will make an excellent one.

THE QUEEN   We hope so. And now tell me, please, exactly what *is* being said and written about the Prince?

ABERDEEN   To put it briefly, Ma'am, that in supporting the efforts of your Majesty's Government to avoid war, he is secretly working in the interests — not of this country, but of Russia. Some have even gone so far as to imply that, without the knowledge of your Majesty's advisers, he has been in treasonable correspondence with the Tzar.

THE QUEEN   How abominable!

ABERDEEN   Yes, Ma'am, indeed.

THE QUEEN   But does anyone believe it?

ABERDEEN   Some people are foolish enough to believe anything, Ma'am, that obtains as wide a circulation as this unfortunately has done.

THE QUEEN   And to think that it is still going on! Oh, Lord Aberdeen, the Prince mustn't know; he must never be told that such wicked things are being said of him. It would hurt, it would wound him too cruelly. Can you not somehow prevent it?

ABERDEEN   It may be difficult, Ma'am. He will necessarily see what is reported, when the matter is brought before Parliament. Of course he need not know — for we shall not even mention — the most scandalous of the rumours that have been put about; of which (as I hope your Majesty will agree) there is no need that your Majesty should be informed either.

THE QUEEN But indeed, I think it is your duty to tell me. I ought to know *everything* that is being said — however wicked and foolish it may be.

ABERDEEN Well, Ma'am, the most wicked happens also to be the most foolish — so I hope that your Majesty will not take it too seriously. The Prince is not mentioned by name; but he — with Another who is also left nameless — is stated to have been taken to the Tower on a charge of High Treason.

THE QUEEN Lord Aberdeen, has the country gone quite mad? Have people no common sense?

ABERDEEN Common sense, Ma'am, is the first casualty of war — even before it is declared. Then imagination, in people who previously had none, suddenly becomes rampant; it is a form of patriotism among the uneducated which has to be allowed for. Your Majesty should not let it disturb you.

THE QUEEN I cannot help being disturbed by what would so deeply affect the Prince, were he to hear of it.

ABERDEEN You said, Ma'am, that you did not wish the Prince to be told. I wondered, then, if he might not already have told your Majesty — something, himself.

THE QUEEN Pray, what might he have told me?

ABERDEEN That recently, when he rides in the Park, he has not been treated with proper respect. There have sometimes even been hostile demonstrations.

THE QUEEN No, he has told me nothing: so like him — knowing how it would hurt me! And only last week, writing to my uncle, King Leopold, I said, what I believed then to be true, that at last he was becoming popular. Oh, Lord Aberdeen, that he should be so treated! It makes me so ashamed of my people.

ABERDEEN It will pass, Ma'am, believe me. In public life one has to face unpopularity at times. I might say it is part of one's duty when political feeling runs riot, as it is doing just now.

THE QUEEN Yes; because they are all so ignorant! I wonder how many know that, before he died, the Duke of Wellington wished the Prince to succeed him as Commander-in-Chief. And Lord Derby actually made the offer.

ABERDEEN Which I was told, Ma'am, the Prince thought right to refuse.

THE QUEEN Yes, and for such good and noble reasons — because he did not wish to make himself prominent or give any occasion for jealousy that one who was not a born Englishman should hold such a position of power and authority. He is always so wise, so loyal, so considerate of the Country's best interests. And now *this*! It makes me so angry, I hardly know how to bear it.

ABERDEEN I am sure, Ma'am, that the unqualified condemnation which to-morrow will be voiced by both Houses of Parliament, will finally dispose of the matter.

THE QUEEN If it will, I am all the more sorry that the Prince should have to hear of it. But I suppose it is all that can be done . . . Of course, if we *do* have to declare war, the Government will have my fullest support (and his also) in giving Russia the lesson she seems to need.

ABERDEEN And when that is seen, Ma'am, the Prince will again share that measure of your Majesty's popularity which he so greatly deserves.

THE QUEEN Thank you, Lord Aberdeen, for saying so. I wish others knew it as well as you do. Am I advised now of all that you had to see me about?

ABERDEEN For the present, Ma'am, yes. I hope that this audience (which was not by appointment) has not occupied too much of your Majesty's time, or been otherwise inconvenient.

(*As an indication that the audience is over, the Queen rises.*)

THE QUEEN Indeed, no; for though usually I have the Prince with me, I am rather glad that he is now taking his morning ride. Good-bye, Lord Aberdeen; and I thank you for all the help and advice you have given me.

(THE QUEEN *gives him her hand. He bows over it, and retires. She rings. A* GENTLEMAN *of the Court enters.*)

Is General Grey in attendance?

GENTLEMAN He is, your Majesty.

THE QUEEN Ask him to come in.

(*The* GENTLEMAN *retires;* THE QUEEN *moves to the window. There is a clatter of horsehoofs below;* THE PRINCE *has returned from his ride. Presently* GENERAL GREY, *the Queen's Secretary, enters.*)

General Grey, I wish you to obtain for me at once copies of all the daily papers for the last week.

GREY Of *all*, Ma'am?

THE QUEEN Of course I don't mean *The Times* or *The Morning Post*, which I always see. I mean all the others.

GREY There are some, your Majesty, which are not of a very desirable character.

THE QUEEN It is those I particularly wish to see. (*Then, shrewdly, observing his embarrassment:*) Perhaps *you* have seen them already?

GREY I have, Ma'am; but I could hardly advise your Majesty to read them.

THE QUEEN (*stiffly*) I do not require that advice, General Grey. If you knew what was in them, I think it was your duty to take care that I *did* see them.

GREY I am sorry, Ma'am, if I have erred in the matter.

THE QUEEN Well, it is not too late — though it would have been better had they come to me sooner. But do not bring them to me till I am alone. The Prince has just returned, and I do not wish *him* to see them.

GREY That, Ma'am, I can well understand.

(*The door opens.* THE PRINCE *enters fresh from his morning ride.* GENERAL GREY *bows and stands aside; and a moment later, on an indication that his attendance is no longer required, retires.*)

THE QUEEN You are back early, Albert. Did you meet Lord Aberdeen as you came in just now?

ALBERT Yes; he seemed so much in a hurry that he did not wait to speak to me. And I had hoped that I had a little news for him.

THE QUEEN Indeed?

ALBERT And for you too, my dear. Have you heard that you and

I have been sent to the Tower for High Treason, and are going to have our heads cut off?

THE QUEEN   Oh, Albert, dearest, I did so hope you wouldn't hear of it.

ALBERT   Is it true, then? Are we really there? I thought it was only a joke.

THE QUEEN   A joke?

ALBERT   Yes, it was so funny.

THE QUEEN   How can such a shocking and wicked thing said about You and *Me* be funny, Albert? You have a strange sense of humour.

ALBERT   Yes; perhaps I have; German, not English. English jokes I do not always understand. But this — do you mean that it is serious?

THE QUEEN   Yes, Albert, very serious indeed. How did you come to know?

ALBERT   (*taking from his pocket a news-sheet*) This paper was pushed into the hand of my equerry while we were out riding in the Park. He passed it to me.

THE QUEEN   Read it, Albert.

(*He opens the paper, looks at it, and chuckles; then, apologetically to* THE QUEEN'S *look of disapproval:*)

ALBERT   I still think it is rather funny. We are not named, oh no; but there is no doubt who they mean it to be. Listen: 'We learn on what we believe to be good authority, that at a late hour last night two Personages of the highest rank' — ('Personages of the highest rank' can only be you and me, Vicky) — 'were secretly conveyed to the Tower, under a military guard, by order of the Government, and have there been lodged in safe custody to await their trial on a charge of High Treason for conspiring against the safety of the Realm.' There, Vicky, what do you think of that? (*He continues reading:*) 'This news, which it was not intended should at present be made public, will be received with the greatest satisfaction by all who have been aware of the danger to which our Country has lately and increasingly been exposed by the machinations of a certain powerful foreign influence behind the Throne.' That means me, Vicky.

THE QUEEN Oh, Albert, please don't read any more. I can't bear it. Lord Aberdeen has been here, and has told me all about it. He also told me, Albert, that lately (I believe he said 'daily'), people have been treating you publicly with disrespect. Is that true?

ALBERT Yes, perhaps; though I did not pay it much attention. Oh, yes; quite well-dressed people looked at me without taking off their hats; and others, who were less well-dressed, made noises at me. But you see, Vicky, with the English I have never been popular. The most popular thing I can do will be to die.

THE QUEEN Oh, don't say that, Albert!

ALBERT No, no, I don't mean that I am going to die — not yet. But as I know that I *could* make myself popular that way, it does not much matter to me that I am not . . . But tell me, what does Lord Aberdeen propose to do about it — about getting us back from the Tower, I mean, with our heads still on?

THE QUEEN Albert, do, please, be serious! . . . It has been arranged that to-morrow, the Leaders of all parties, the Government and the Opposition — are to speak in both Houses, and say how wicked and foolish and entirely without foundation all these stories have been, from first to last. And *that* will settle it.

ALBERT You think? I am not so sure. The English are so stupid.

THE QUEEN No, Albert, you mustn't say that! It isn't true. If the English people were stupid, they would never have succeeded as they have done, all over the world.

ALBERT Oh, but very clever people are often stupid — even when they are successful — in their way of doing it. There is Lord Palmerston; he has been very clever and successful in getting his way, but so stupid.

THE QUEEN Stupid?

ALBERT Yes. Why are we hated by all the other countries of Europe? Because he has so bullied and browbeaten every one of them in turn, when they did not do what he wished them to do. And because he has got his way, he thinks it does not matter. But it does — it does, Vicky. And he is the Popular Voice, because that is how the English like foreign countries — when they are small ones — to be treated.

THE QUEEN   About Lord Palmerston, of course, what you say is true, Albert. But this time he will be made to do the right thing. Lord Aberdeen has just told me that to-morrow in the House of Commons it is Lord Palmerston who will speak — for the Government.

ALBERT   A very good arrangement, my dear. For I think that it is Pilgerstein who has been behind all this; and that he would almost like that it should be true.

THE QUEEN   Lord Aberdeen assures me that he will make an excellent speech.

ALBERT   No doubt. Whatever he really thinks, Pilgerstein can always do that.

THE QUEEN   But he won't like making *this* one.

ALBERT   No; but he will have the consolation of knowing that what we tried for has failed, and that there is going to be war. And that means that before the war is over he will be Prime Minister.

THE QUEEN   No, Albert, never with *my* consent!

ALBERT   My dear, you cannot help it; he has the Popular Voice.

(*Prince Albert was quite right: two years later Palmerston became Prime Minister.*)

ROYAL FAVOUR

1859

Into one of the spacious apartments at Windsor Castle the morning sun streams through a high window. In the light of it, tempered by blinds, sits QUEEN VICTORIA. *One of her Ladies is now reading the regulation portion of the morning Scripture.*

LADY-IN-WAITING Proverbs, the twenty-sixth, Ma'am. . . . 'As snow in winter, and as rain in harvest, so honour is not seemly for fools. A whip for the horse, a bridle for the ass, and a rod for the fool's back. Answer not a fool according to his folly, lest thou also be like him. As the legs of the lame are unequal, so is a proverb in the mouth of fools. As he that bindeth a stone in a sling, so is he that giveth honour to a fool.'

(*The door opens, and* DR. STANLEY *is ceremoniously announced. Still young and pleasant-looking, not yet a Dean, he steps easily into the Royal Presence, and the obeisance he makes, though correct in form, is a friendly one. As he advances to bow over the hand graciously extended, he manages to give a glance of happy recognition to the Queen's Lady, who, when* THE QUEEN *rises, rises also. For this is* LADY AUGUSTA BRUCE, *destined presently to become his wife; and perhaps they already know it.*)

THE QUEEN Oh, good morning, Dr. Stanley. How very good of you to come, and so punctually! I wanted you to be here this morning.

STANLEY If in any way I can serve your Majesty, I shall be only too happy.

THE QUEEN You are always so kind. And here was Lady Augusta also looking forward to seeing you.

(*Thus graciously permitted,* DR. STANLEY *and* LADY AUGUSTA *press hands.*)

But to-day I did rather especially need you, for more reasons than one.

STANLEY Then I am specially fortunate, Ma'am. May I enquire? . . .

THE QUEEN Oh, yes. Do, please, sit down; both of you. You see, Dr. Stanley, I and the Prince have always felt that we ought — as far as we could — to encourage our distinguished men of literature. But there is always this difficulty. It is quite impossible to have at my Court, in the ordinary way, those with whom I cannot take the lead . . . intellectually, I mean, in conversation. I can, of course, make certain exceptions. Mr. Tennyson comes to see me sometimes; and though I have not read many of his poems myself, he reads them to me; so conversation becomes unnecessary.

STANLEY And does your Majesty enjoy the readings?

THE QUEEN Oh, yes; for even without understanding the poems, one can praise his reading of them. He has a beautiful voice; and he is so picturesque — so like a poet, is he not?

STANLEY He is indeed, Ma'am.

THE QUEEN Besides, he really is, I suppose, a great poet.

STANLEY A very great poet, Ma'am. I might even say that your Majesty is unusually fortunate in having such a poet for Laureate.

THE QUEEN I am so glad to hear you say so. There was just a question of offering the post to Lord Macaulay, whose *Lays of Ancient Rome* are certainly the finest poetry I know. But it was thought that would perhaps be too political an appointment. Mr. Tennyson, I understand, has no politics.

STANLEY None that I know of, Ma'am; or not so well as I know his poetry.

THE QUEEN No? Well, that is why Lord Macaulay was not chosen as I expected.

STANLEY The reason against it was sufficiently good, Ma'am. The alternative it led to was even better.

THE QUEEN Yes? Well, that was really settled for us by the Prime Minister. But often since, in other cases, it has been a great regret that one could not pay all the attention one would like — by commanding their attendance at Court — to those who, outside politics, have become eminent in literature.

STANLEY But at your Majesty's call, one meets certain eminent writers . . . Churchmen amongst others.

THE QUEEN Of course some of the Bishops have written books, I know. But it is as Bishops, not authors, that they come here. And of course, being Head of the Church, I feel myself their equal, though we don't talk theology. . . . Nor have we any difficulty about artists. Their minds are not remarkable in thought or conversation; they are quite quiet and modest, I mean — waiting until they are spoken to. Sir Edwin Landseer, for instance, is a great artist, one of the greatest of all ages; but when he talks, he is just like anyone else — quite modest and pleasant. And he does not mind his work being criticized; though, I believe, he knows more about dogs than I do.

STANLEY In that case, Ma'am, he must be a very great authority. Yet you don't feel any difficulty about him?

THE QUEEN Oh, no! About dogs, I don't mind. Books are different. If I am to meet an author, I feel I must have read one of his books, at least, and been able to understand it. And as I really have not time for doing so, that is one of the reasons why I cannot — except on very special occasions— have authors coming to my Court.

STANLEY And yet, Ma'am, I myself am an author.

THE QUEEN Oh, yes, Dr. Stanley; but you are not the kind of author I mean. Besides, on so many things we have the same opinions. But I really am dreadfully nervous this morning; for a really great writer — and a very famous one — is coming to see us. The Prince thought that we really ought to ask him.

STANLEY And may I be informed, Ma'am, who it is that your Majesty is about to honour in so very special a —

(*The interrogation is interrupted by the entry of the* PRINCE CONSORT. DR. STANLEY *rises, and bows low.*)

THE QUEEN Oh, here is the Prince. It must be nearly time, then.

ALBERT How do you do, Dr. Stanley. We are very pleased to see you. Has the Queen told you about the plans we are making, in which we shall need your assistance.

STANLEY Her Majesty did tell me that you were expecting somebody.

THE QUEEN (*interrupting*) Oh, no; I haven't told him anything yet, Albert, about *that*. I was leaving it till you came. Where is Bertie?

ALBERT   He is here, waiting within call. I told him not to come in yet.

THE QUEEN   It is about our son, the Prince of Wales, Dr. Stanley, that we wished to consult you.

ALBERT   Yes, my Dear; but this will hardly interest Lady Augusta, if Lady Augusta does not mind.

THE QUEEN   Oh, of course not. Lady Augusta, you may go; and take those letters with you.

> (LADY AUGUSTA, *who has stood since the* PRINCE'S *entry, curtsies, and retires.* DR. STANLEY *opens the door for her.*)

ALBERT   Yes, Dr. Stanley, the Prince is now eighteen — a difficult age.

STANLEY   Yes, Sir, as those who have lived through it know.

ALBERT   I lived through it without any difficulty, Dr. Stanley.

STANLEY   Then your Highness was a happy exception.

THE QUEEN   Of course he was, Dr. Stanley. (*Aside*) Albert, may not Dr. Stanley sit down?

ALBERT (*coldly*)   If you wish him to, my Dear.

THE QUEEN (*submissively*)   Oh, no.

> (*The* PRINCE CONSORT *seats himself.* DR. STANLEY *remains standing.*)

Well, it is about that . . . about the Prince, that we wished to have your advice, Dr. Stanley.

ALBERT   Your help, that is to say.

THE QUEEN   We think that perhaps next year he ought to go abroad, and see things for himself a little more. But we have to be so very careful whom he goes with.

STANLEY   Of course, Ma'am, naturally.

ALBERT   We have decided, Dr. Stanley, that it must be with someone not too old to take a share in his interests and pursuits, but at the same time one whom we can trust to exercise a certain amount of discipline and control — and, when necessary, to insist on securing obedience.

STANLEY A difficult task, Sir, when two are travelling abroad together — the two alone.

ALBERT A difficult task, as you say. It is for that reason that we ask you to undertake it.

STANLEY But, indeed, Sir, I —

ALBERT There is no one else in whom we can place such complete trust and confidence as yourself. You have the qualifications, and the gifts. Though so much his senior, the Prince will come to look upon you as his friend.

STANLEY I am very reluctant, Sir.

ALBERT That is understandable. You are probably aware that the Prince has already become a difficulty. He has now been at the University for his first term . . . It has been indicated to us that College life does not suit him, and that he had better leave as soon as other arrangements can be made. That is the position, Dr. Stanley, in which we come to you for help.

STANLEY Sir, I feel quite at a loss why I should have been chosen.

THE QUEEN Oh, surely, Dr. Stanley, you will not say no to *me*.

STANLEY If it is, indeed, your Majesty's fixed wish, then I can say no more.

ALBERT Ah, very good! That is settled, then.

(*The* PRINCE CONSORT *goes to the door, open it, and calls through*:)

Bertie! Are you there? You may come in.

(THE PRINCE OF WALES *enters. He stands, shy and sullen, and does not advance.*)

Come on in . . . and shut the door!

(*The* PRINCE *shuts it.*)

Don't stand there! Here is Dr. Stanley waiting for you to speak to him.

THE PRINCE OF WALES (*perfunctorily*) How do you do?

STANLEY How do *you* do, Sir? How did your Royal Highness like Cambridge?

PRINCE Hated it.

ALBERT Then you won't have to hate it much longer, Sir. Next year we are sending you abroad, and Dr. Stanley goes with you.

PRINCE I don't want to go abroad — with anybody.

ALBERT That is not for you to decide. We have decided it for you; and Dr. Stanley has most kindly consented to take charge of you. Now, what do you say to that?

PRINCE As I'm not to say anything, there's nothing for me to say.

THE QUEEN Bertie! Speaking to your Father like that!

PRINCE Well, what *am* I to say?

ALBERT You might, at least, say 'Thank you' to Dr. Stanley.

PRINCE (*sullenly*) Thank you.

STANLEY Oh ... pray, don't mention it!

(*There is a pause.*)

PRINCE Can I go now?

ALBERT No, Sir, you may *not* go. Wait here, and have your mind improved a little. We are expecting a visit from a very eminent man of letters; you will never have heard of him, of course. Well, stay and listen to him.

PRINCE I shan't understand a word he says.

ALBERT I dare say not. . . .

PRINCE (*sotto voce*) ... And shan't want to!

ALBERT (*following on*) But you can, at least, try. And, while in the presence of others, you might also try to look a little less of an injured martyr.

PRINCE Well, I can't pretend to look pleased, when I'm not.

(*A Gentleman of the Court enters, and, seeing* THE QUEEN *engaged in conversation with* DR. STANLEY, *goes and delivers his message to the* PRINCE CONSORT.)

THE QUEEN You must not mind, Dr. Stanley, if just at first there is this little unwillingness. Bertie so dislikes having to make up his mind about anything.

ALBERT   Yes, Her Majesty is ready to receive him.

(*The Gentleman bows and retires.*)

STANLEY   I must confess, Ma'am, that the unwillingness was shared by your most humble servant. I might even say that, in each case, our minds have been made up for us. So, naturally, there is at first a little difficulty in getting used to the prospect.

ALBERT   Our expected visitor is due, my Dear. I said that you would receive him as soon as he arrived.

THE QUEEN   Yes, I hope he will be punctual.

(*As she speaks, the clock on the mantelpiece strikes the hour.*)

STANLEY (*with a gesture towards the* PRINCE, *who stands moodily looking out of the window*)   Would it not be well, Ma'am, to begin our better acquaintance now? May I go and speak to him?

THE QUEEN   Oh, do, Dr. Stanley, do! It is very kind of you.

ALBERT   I think I hear him coming.

THE QUEEN   Oh, Albert, this is going to be very difficult. You must do all the talking, please.

ALBERT   We have Dr. Stanley to help us, my Dear. It will be all right.

(*The door opens; an* USHER *enters, followed by the much-expected Celebrity.*)

USHER   If it please your Majesty, Mr. Martin Tupper.

(MR. MARTIN TUPPER *bows himself in with more bows than the three which etiquette requires. He bows to everyone as long as time is left to him for bowing.*)

THE QUEEN (*rising*)   How do you do, Mr. Tupper?

ALBERT   How do you do?

(MR. TUPPER *reverentially touches the Royal hands, and says in a voice sonorous with emotion*)

TUPPER   So honoured, your Majesty! Your Royal Highness, so honoured!

THE QUEEN   We are so pleased to meet you, Mr. Tupper.

ALBERT   Having often heard of you . . . having also *read* you.

TUPPER   Ah, Sir, that is, indeed, for a writer, the reward of reward
— to be read!

ALBERT   Bertie, come and shake hands with Mr. Tupper. Mr
Tupper, this is my Son, the Prince of Wales.

PRINCE (*getting it over*)   How do you do?

TUPPER   How do *you* do, Sir? . . . Most honoured!

THE QUEEN   Dr. Stanley, you and Mr. Tupper already know each
other, I expect?

STANLEY (*bowing*)   I have not had the honour.

TUPPER   The honour is mine, Sir.

> (*There is a slight pause.* THE PRINCE OF WALES *draws furtively
> away. Presently he stands by the window and takes up a book
> turning its pages, merely to pass the time.*)

ALBERT   Mr. Tupper, I was reading one of your books to Her
Majesty, only last night.

THE QUEEN   Yes, and I enjoyed it — very much.

TUPPER   May I be allowed, Sir, to ask which?

ALBERT   Your *Proverbial Philosophy*, Mr. Tupper.

TUPPER   Ah! then your Majesty would, I am sure.

THE QUEEN   Yes; there are so many things in it with which I so
thoroughly agree.

TUPPER (*enthusiastically*)   Thousands and thousands of your
Majesty's loyal subjects have done the same, Ma'am. That book, I
am proud to tell your Majesty, has already gone into fifteen editions
— large ones.

ALBERT   How many editions, Mr. Tupper?

TUPPER   Fifteen, your Royal Highness.

ALBERT   Oh, I thought you said fifty. . . . I could have wished it
had been fifty.

TUPPER   It will be fifty, some day, your Royal Highness, I don't
doubt. The sales never diminish, Ma'am, never. That book, your
Majesty, brings me in a steady income every year.

THE QUEEN How very gratifying for you; and how satisfactory for the publishers.

TUPPER Satisfactory for the publishers, you say, Ma'am? Alas, still more satisfactory for the pirates!

THE QUEEN The pirates?

TUPPER (*with emotion*) Millions of my books, your Majesty — complete editions — have been stolen from me by American pirates across the sea. And they call it the Land of Liberty.

THE QUEEN American pirates! I did not think such things still existed. Most extraordinary!

STANLEY Mr. Tupper is speaking of book-pirates, your Majesty — a product of the American copyright laws. It involves not loss of life; only loss of property.

THE QUEEN Still, that is very wrong.

TUPPER Most wrong, your Majesty. My book, *Proverbial Philosophy*, has been translated into sixteen languages throughout the world. And in every country it has been honestly paid for, except in America. And they call themselves a civilized nation! Your Majesty must pardon me if I let my indignation carry me away.

THE QUEEN But what you say is so interesting, Mr. Tupper. And I can share your indignation over a thing like that. I can quite understand it.

TUPPER Your Majesty is very good to say so. It consoles me, nay more, it makes up for the monetary loss it has been to me, that I have your Majesty's kind sympathy.

(*There is a pause.*)

ALBERT How do you write your books, Mr. Tupper?

TUPPER How do I write them, Sir? — In what way?

ALBERT Precisely, 'In what way?' Do you write them slowly, with difficulty; or do they arise naturally and spontaneously to your mind, without effort?

TUPPER Oh, they come very quickly, your Royal Highness, very quickly indeed! I would not say without any effort of a kind — without strain. Emotional strain on the nervous system there must be, of course. But no delay in the actual expression — or the choice of words. They come entirely as they like. Sometimes I see them there on the paper before me, almost without having become aware that I had written them.

PRINCE (*sotto voce*) Good Lord! What an ass!

THE QUEEN How very interesting. Most extraordinary!

TUPPER Yes, your Majesty, I have to admit that it is extraordinary. But that is what being a writer of free, spontaneous verse — the form in which it comes to me — must necessarily mean.

ALBERT Indeed? Most interesting. . . . Well, I am sure you have given us a great deal to think about, Mr. Tupper. And if we had time for a longer conversation, we should learn more. Perhaps, on some other occasion.

(*This is a covert indication to* THE QUEEN *that the time for terminating the interview has arrived. She rises.*)

THE QUEEN Mr. Tupper, before you go, will you sign your book for us?

TUPPER Oh, your Majesty! let me not only sign it, but let me inscribe in it a few lines of impromptu verse, inspired by the occasion!

THE QUEEN Do . . . please! We should value it greatly. Where is the book, Albert?

ALBERT Why, there is Bertie reading it!

(*At that moment the* PRINCE *is cursorily reading it. As though detected in an act of guilt, he puts it down hurriedly.*)

ALBERT Bertie, let Mr. Tupper have his book for a moment. You will find pen and ink at that table, Mr. Tupper.

TUPPER I thank your Royal Highness. I shall not be a moment.

(*He goes across to the table, takes up the book, and opens it at the fly-leaf.*)

THE QUEEN (*seating herself again*) Would you like us to be silent, Mr. Tupper, while you are composing the lines?

TUPPER No, no! Oh, no, your Majesty! Pray do not think of it. When the Muse inspires me, I am so carried away that I hear nothing,

I assure you. Would your Majesty believe, now, that I wrote one of my best poems while a Punch-and-Judy show was performing under my very window?

PRINCE (*sotto voce*) *I* would!

THE QUEEN How extraordinary! And you were able to finish it, Mr. Tupper?

TUPPER I was, Ma'am.

PRINCE But you *did* hear it?

TUPPER Hear it? . . . Hear what, your Royal Highness?

PRINCE The Punch-and-Judy show.

TUPPER Oh, yes; I certainly heard it.

PRINCE Then, that time, you were not so inspired?

TUPPER Oh, I see what your Highness means. No, no. The Punch-and-Judy show took longer than the inspiration. I heard the beginning of it; and I heard the end of it: but not — not while I was composing. . . . May I sit down, your Majesty, while I am writing?

THE QUEEN Please do.

(*He sits down. . . . Inspiration descends on him.*)

ALBERT Bertie, you had better come away over here. You shouldn't talk so much.

(*The* PRINCE *moves away from the writing-table, but turns, and from a distance watches the process of composition which has now begun.*)

THE QUEEN (*speaking in a low voice*) Dr. Stanley, you will stay to lunch, will you not? Mr. Disraeli, the Minister-in-Attendance, will be here. You would like to meet him. He is so interesting, so amusing.

STANLEY Charmed, your Majesty, if I may, indeed, have the honour.

THE QUEEN Then do.

PRINCE (*imitating 'Punch'*) Judy! Judy!

THE QUEEN Bertie!

ALBERT If you can't behave yourself, you had better leave the room.

PRINCE Very well.

(*He moves to the door.*)

ALBERT Stay where you are! But you will take your lunch alone to-day, in your own room.

(MR. TUPPER *rises from his seat.*)

Ah, Mr. Tupper, have you done it all already?

(MR. TUPPER *bows, book in hand.*)

Then I am sure her Majesty would like to hear it.

TUPPER If Her Majesty will understand that it is only a very slight effort.

THE QUEEN Please!

TUPPER To England's Queen
  This book I give,
That here kept green
  It still may live.
From youth to age,
  Whene'er you need it,
Oh, Madam, turn the page,
  And read it.

THE QUEEN Oh, thank you!

TUPPER (*with a gesture*) Pardon, Ma'am . . . just two more lines.
  And should you ever
    Deign to quote it,
  Happy will be
    The Heart that wrote it.

(*He lays the book down.*)

THE QUEEN Very pretty indeed! Thank you, Mr. Tupper. (*She rises*) We looked forward very much to meeting you, and it has been a very, very great pleasure. . . . Good-bye.

ALBERT Good-bye, Mr. Tupper. We are glad to have had this opportunity of meeting you. Some day, I trust, we may meet again.

(*Over this last adieu,* MR. TUPPER *has been unable to voice his emotion. But at the door he turns, and bows.*)

TUPPER Your Majesty's most humble, and grateful servant.

(*The door, with liveried mechanism, opens to let him out, and closes again behind him.*)

THE QUEEN (*as she sits*)   How very pleasant he was, to be sure. And so well-informed.

STANLEY (*dryly*)   About his own writings? Yes, Ma'am.

THE QUEEN   He *must* be well-informed to be able to write them.

STANLEY (*assenting, in a non-committal tone*)   Oh, yes; I suppose so.

THE QUEEN   You have read his book, Dr. Stanley?

STANLEY   Ah, no. But I have been meaning to — now and then.

THE QUEEN   Oh, but you must! You would find things in it so useful in your sermons. Indeed they remind me of sermons a good deal . . . only put in such beautiful language.

STANLEY   Then I must, Ma'am — I must, indeed.

(*The door opens, and, with due announcement,* MR. DISRAELI *enters.*)

THE QUEEN (*rising to meet him*)   Oh, Mr. Disraeli, I am sorry you did not come a little sooner.

DISRAELI   I am always sorry, Ma'am, not to come sooner into so gracious a Presence. I am sorry when I have to leave it.

THE QUEEN   Ah, but I meant for quite a different reason, Mr. Disraeli. Had you come sooner you would have met a distinguished man of letters, like yourself.

DISRAELI   Like myself, Ma'am? To what other man of letters, in your Majesty's estimation, have I the honour of resemblance?

THE QUEEN   Oh, I only meant both being famous writers. . . . Mr. Martin Tupper.

DISRAELI (*becoming inscrutable*)   Ah? . . . Mr. Martin Tupper?

(*Meanwhile the* PRINCE CONSORT *has been at the writing-table, examining the newly autographed book with apparent interest. Thus, from a distance he has been able to acknowledge the entry of a Minister whom he dislikes, by a mere bow. Now he comes forward and joins in the conversation.*)

ALBERT   We understand that he has a great reputation.

DISRAELI   And a great circulation, Sir, to confirm it.

ALBERT You read his books, Mr. Disraeli?

DISRAELI I have not read them, Sir. It is an infirmity I have to confess, that, to read the works of men so greatly my superior in popular esteem, depresses me. I lose inspiration.

THE QUEEN That is a pity.

DISRAELI Yes, Ma'am, a great pity!

THE QUEEN But do you not read Shakespeare, Mr. Disraeli?

DISRAELI Oh, yes; I read Shakespeare, Ma'am. Shakespeare belongs to another age. He does not overshadow me, in popular esteem, in the same way as Mr. Martin Tupper. Of Shakespeare I have no jealousy . . . none.

THE QUEEN But you are jealous of Mr. Tupper?

DISRAELI Ah, Ma'am! do not probe, I beseech you, the dark and secret places of the human heart. What I feel about Mr. Tupper, with your Majesty's permission, I would rather not say.

THE QUEEN He has written some verses in his book for me; would you like to see them?

DISRAELI Any command of your Majesty's, I obey.

ALBERT Bertie, give Mr. Disraeli the book.

(DISRAELI *takes the book, and reads.* THE QUEEN *is watching his face; but his expression, made suitable at the beginning of the reading, does not change. He lays the book down.*)

THE QUEEN Very beautiful, don't you think?

DISRAELI Ah, Ma'am, could I write poetry like that, not another of my own poor works would I be able to publish.

(LADY AUGUSTA *re-enters.*)

THE QUEEN Dear Lady Augusta, come and talk to Dr. Stanley. You will sit together at luncheon, please. Albert, I want to speak to you for a moment.

(*They go to the window together; and with their backs to the others they stand talking.*)

PRINCE Mr. Disraeli, you didn't miss anything. . . . I'm glad he's gone.

DISRAELI So am I, Sir.

PRINCE An awful ass!

DISRAELI I feel bound to respect your Highness's judgment.

(*And now the colloquy of* THE QUEEN *and the* PRINCE CONSORT *is over.*)

ALBERT Don't you think, Mr. Disraeli, that, for the next Honours List, we might suggest to the Prime Minister, that he should submit Mr. Martin Tupper's name for inclusion?

DISRAELI Your Highness means in the next *Birthday* Honours, I presume?

ALBERT Why the Birthday Honours, specially?

DISRAELI The New Year's Honours being, as a rule, more political in character.

ALBERT Ah, yes, yes. Well, Mr. Tupper is *not* political — is he?

DISRAELI He has political views, Sir. And for that reason, I must regretfully suggest, that the submission of his name should be left — to the *next* Government.

THE QUEEN Oh, Mr. Disraeli, I am so sorry!

DISRAELI So am I, Ma'am. But I have to repeat that the inclusion of Mr. Tupper's name in *any* Honours List would be regarded by your Majesty's present advisers — as, politically, inexpedient.

ALBERT Now there, Mr. Disraeli, you have an instance of the difficulty in which we are always finding ourselves! Her Majesty is anxious to do honour to literature. And you see, immediately, something that has nothing whatever to do with literature arises and prevents.

DISRAELI How true, Sir! How very true! Something that has nothing whatever to do with literature, arises and prevents.

(*The door opens. A* FOOTMAN *appears.*)

FOOTMAN Your Majesty is served.

(*In due order, they go in to luncheon.* THE PRINCE OF WALES, *who is not to be of the company, stands back, and waits for* MR. DISRAELI *to pass him.*)

PRINCE Well stopped, Sir!

(MR. DISRAELI *bows his acknowledgment; he smiles, but says nothing.*

INTERVENTION

30th November 1861

On THE QUEEN's *writing-table a Government Despatch-box lies open.*
GENERAL GREY, THE QUEEN's *Private Secretary, stands reading to*
Her Majesty the despatch which Lord Russell, the Foreign Secretary,
has addressed to Lord Lyons, the British Ambassador at Washington,
on the seizure upon the High Seas, from the British ship Trent, *of*
the two Confederate officers, Slidell and Mason.

GREY (*reading*) The reparation which Her Majesty's Government
expect from the Government of the United States, and with which
they would be satisfied, would be:

1. The liberation of the four gentlemen captured, and their
   delivery to your Lordship with a view to their being again
   placed under British protection.

2. An apology for the insult offered to the British flag.

3. Should these terms not be offered by Mr. Seward, you will
   propose them to him. You are at liberty to read this
   dispatch. . . .

THE QUEEN Before you go on, General Grey, will you ring,
please.

(THE GENERAL *rings* . . . *One of* THE QUEEN's GENTLEMEN *enters.*)
Has His Royal Highness not returned from Sandhurst yet?

GENTLEMAN A few minutes ago, he had not, your Majesty.

THE QUEEN But it is so late! Was not the ceremony to have been
over by midday?

GENTLEMAN I believe so, your Majesty. It is possible that His
Royal Highness *may* have just returned.

THE QUEEN Please to go and see; and, if he has, bring back word
at once . . . General Grey, this looks very serious indeed! Is the
Messenger who brought it still waiting?

GENERAL GREY I am not sure, Ma'am.

THE QUEEN Will you please to find out? And if he has not gone, say that he is to wait . . . I do wish the Prince would come! It is so urgent; and with Lord Palmerston Prime Minister, one never knows what he may not do next, without waiting for *our* instructions.

GENERAL GREY Indeed no, Ma'am.

THE QUEEN At once, please!

(*As the* GENERAL *goes, the* GENTLEMAN *returns.*)

GENTLEMAN His Royal Highness has just returned, your Majesty. He has gone up to his room.

THE QUEEN Then go and ask His Royal Highness to come at once. Say that the matter is most urgent.

(*The* GENTLEMAN *goes.* THE QUEEN *takes up the despatch, and is re-reading it when* GENERAL GREY *returns.*)

GENERAL GREY The Messenger has gone, your Majesty.

THE QUEEN Without waiting!

GENERAL GREY He waited for an hour, Ma'am, I'm told.

THE QUEEN An hour! He should have waited all day, if necessary. Messengers from my other Ministers know that they have to wait. Why do not Foreign Office Messengers wait too? This is what is always happening: and then they pretend that the delay it causes is our fault, not theirs.

GENERAL GREY Cannot one of your Majesty's Messengers go, Ma'am — the matter being so urgent?

THE QUEEN Yes, he must. Tell one of them to be ready to start instantly.

(*As the* GENERAL *is going,* THE PRINCE CONSORT *enters. He looks haggard and tired.*)

THE QUEEN Oh, Albert, why did you wait to change? I have been so wanting you!

ALBERT My uniform was wet through, my Dear; and I was feeling very cold.

THE QUEEN (*taking his hand*) You are cold still, Dearest! your hand is like ice. Oh, why did you go in such weather, when I begged you not to?

ALBERT I had to, my Dear . . . What is the matter?

THE QUEEN It's about that trouble with America, for having taken the Confederate Envoys off one of our ships. And most wrong of them it was! This is the despatch Lord Russell is sending to our Ambassador in Washington about it. He wants it to go to-night.

ALBERT (*taking it*) Is the Messenger waiting?

THE QUEEN No; he's gone.

ALBERT (*sharply*) Gone? Ah! That is what one has now to expect, I suppose!

THE QUEEN Yes; it's that Pilgerstein again. Troublesome man!

ALBERT Yes; though this time it is Lord Russell that does it; that Go-between, who was always so apologetic and nice to us. Hah! But it is Pilgerstein — as you say — still. Oh, yes!

THE QUEEN Read it quickly, Albert. I want to know what you think about it.

(GENERAL GREY *re-enters.*)

GENERAL GREY I have given your Majesty's order. A Messenger is ready and waiting.

THE QUEEN Very well. And now that the Prince is here, General Grey, I shall no longer need you.

(*The* GENERAL *goes.* THE QUEEN *sits watching the* PRINCE CONSORT *as he reads. Not till he has finished it does he speak.*)

ALBERT This means War.

THE QUEEN Yes; I was afraid so. How foolish of them not to give in! For they must know they are in the wrong. And everything that Lord Russell says is true, is it not?

ALBERT (*deep in thought*) Quite . . . Quite . . . But — it won't do.

THE QUEEN But, Albert, as we are in the right, what else can we do?

ALBERT Alter a few words . . . Say it; but say it differently.

Often it is just the way a thing is said that decides whether it shall be peace or war. It is the same when two people quarrel. You and I, Weibchen, might often have quarrelled, had we said the same thing that we did say — differently . . . Russell? Oh, no: this is Pilgerstein, I think! He is the man that would *like* to have war with America. He has worked for it; and this is his opportunity — that we are in the right! . . . He shall not have it! War? Oh, yes; and this time we should win. But another time would come, and we should *not* win.

THE QUEEN But we could always beat America now, Albert.

ALBERT Ah, so? What if we were fighting someone else, Vicky; and America chose her time then? No; that is what these 'patriots' never think about . . . It is always — '*This* time, *this* time! We are *right*, and we shall do what we like!' What fools their patriotism makes clever men to be! And Pilgerstein the cleverest fool of them all! . . . And when he dies, they will say of this man — 'Oh, yes; he had his faults; but he always upheld the Honour of his Country.' And when they say 'Honour', they mean Pride. Again and again, he has been ready to sacrifice the Honour of his Country to its Pride. For Honour means that you are too proud to do wrong; but Pride means that you will not *own* that you have done wrong — at all. *That* is the difference.

THE QUEEN Then that applies to America, now.

ALBERT Yes. Here is America: she has done wrong, and she knows it . . . Invite her to reconsider — a mistake: something done by her agents without her instructions. She will think, and will behave reasonably . . . But say 'I order you!' and she will *not*.

THE QUEEN But, Albert, ought we to make it so easy for them as all that?

ALBERT Yes; because we should do just the same ourselves, if we were ordered. And we should call it 'Honour'. And for that Honour we should send thousands and thousands to die! What a wicked black thing Honour can become — when men make use of it — *so*!

THE QUEEN Then what are we going to do, Albert?

ALBERT　We are going to alter this, *now* . . . Sit down at once, and write! Say that this despatch is not to go, till he has heard from you . . . And your Messenger must go now, at once, and must see Lord Russell himself . . . This will take me more time; but you write your letter at once!

THE QUEEN　Yes, Albert, yes!

(THE QUEEN *seats herself at one writing-table. The* PRINCE CONSORT *goes to another.* THE QUEEN *begins to write, then rings, and continues writing. A* GENTLEMAN *enters, and stands waiting, while the letter is being finished.*)

THE QUEEN　Tell the Messenger to take this to Lord Russell, at the Foreign Office. He is to see him, and is to bring an answer.

(*The* GENTLEMAN *takes the letter, and goes.* THE QUEEN *goes across to the* PRINCE CONSORT. *She puts her hand on his shoulder, and leans over him.*)

ALBERT (*gently*)　Will you leave me alone, my Dear, while I do this? I shall try not to be long.

★

(*As the scene closes, the clock on the mantelpiece strikes four. When it opens again, some hours have passed. Candles are lighted.* THE PRINCE *is still at his desk, writing. He sits up; the pen falls from his hand.*)

ALBERT　That is done . . . *done!*

(*Slowly he reaches out, takes up a hand-bell, and rings. A* GENTLEMAN *enters.*)

Tell Her Majesty that I have finished . . . Ask Her Majesty to come.

(*The* GENTLEMAN *bows, and goes out.* THE PRINCE *tries to rise, sinks back into his seat: resting his hands on the table, he bends slowly forward; his head drops to the table.*)
(THE QUEEN *enters.*)

THE QUEEN　Albert, what is the matter? Are you ill?

ALBERT (*raising himself with difficulty*)　I have done. Read it! If you approve, send it!

(THE QUEEN *takes up the amended despatch and reads it. While she does so, the clock strikes seven.*)

THE QUEEN (*reading*) Yes ... Yes ... Yes ... I do — I do approve — every word.

ALBERT Then let it go — *now*!

(THE QUEEN *rings. She puts the paper into the Despatch-box, and locks it. A* GENTLEMAN *enters.*)

THE QUEEN See that this goes at once!

(*The* GENTLEMAN *goes.* THE PRINCE *has once more taken up his pen: he tries to write. The pen falls from his hand. He reaches out to* THE QUEEN, *with a gesture of helplessness.*)

ALBERT Take me to bed! ... Take me to bed, Weibchen! ... Ich bin so schwach. Ich habe kaum die Feder halten können!

(*Again he tries to rise, fails, and falls back into his chair.* THE QUEEN *throws her arms round him.*)

THE QUEEN Albert!

DEATH AND THE DOCTORS

14th December 1861

At Windsor: a large ante-room, plainly furnished, with side-entrances to right and left. In the centre are folding-doors. The subdued sound of a bell, ringing in the room to the left, is heard. Immediately the door opens; a Nurse enters, and advancing towards the folding-doors, taps softly, and waits. One half of the folding-door is opened: the HEAD NURSE *appears, and handing out certain sick-bed appliances, gives her orders in a quiet undertone.*

HEAD NURSE More hot water, Nurse; quick, please.

(As the Nurse goes on her errand, the HEAD NURSE *is about to close the door again, when, from within, comes the Queen's Physician* DR. JAMES CLARK. *She stands aside for him to pass. He comes out, and beckons her to follow him.)*

DR. CLARK The room wants airing; you must open a window. But you can't have it in there: open one of these, and then put open the doors.

(The HEAD NURSE *goes to the window, hitches back the half-drawn curtains, raises the lowered blind, and opens the window. Meanwhile the Doctor is on the point of departure, by way of the room used by the Nurses, when through the curtained entrance on the right* PRINCESS ALICE *enters.)*

PRINCESS ALICE Dr. Clark, don't go!

DR. CLARK *(excusingly)* Only for a moment, your Highness; just to wash my hands.

PRINCESS ALICE *(urgently)* Yes; but wait! I must speak to you before Mamma comes . . . How is Papa?

DR. CLARK Very much the same; the change we are hoping for hasn't come yet.

PRINCESS ALICE *(anxiously)* *Will* it?

DR. CLARK Oh, undoubtedly . . . undoubtedly . . . At least, we must hope so.

PRINCESS ALICE   Dr. Clark, Mamma does not know — does not in the least realize how ill Papa really is. She won't listen to any of us. She *must* be told! And it's only you who *can* tell her.

DR. CLARK   I assure your Highness that I have given Her Majesty my confidence as fully as she has given me hers — which is saying a great deal. When she asks me, I tell her everything — everything that I *know*. What I am not certain about, I don't say — to anyone.

PRINCESS ALICE   But have you told Mamma that he is dangerously ill?

DR. CLARK   'Dangerously' is a frightening word: therefore, I don't use it. (*Then to the* HEAD NURSE, *who has finished the opening of the window:*) Ah, yes, Nurse; that will do nicely. In a quarter of an hour, shut it again; but leave the door open.

(*The* HEAD NURSE *now goes and puts open the folding-doors; and through them we see the foot of the bed in which the Royal Patient is lying. She goes into the room, and passes out of sight. Meanwhile the* PRINCESS *and the* DOCTOR *are still talking.*)

PRINCESS ALICE   But, Dr. Clark, Papa's illness is of a very serious kind, is it not?

DR. CLARK   Very — very serious, your Highness: I would never suggest otherwise. But in this case, it is taking its normal course: normal — quite normal.

PRINCESS ALICE   But even if it goes on being normal, don't people sometimes — die of it?

DR. CLARK   That *has* happened, your Highness. But, in this case, we have no reason whatever for anticipating anything so unlikely — so disastrous. No, no! . . . And now, your Highness will excuse me, for I *must* go.

PRINCESS ALICE   May I go in now?

DR. CLARK   Oh, yes, yes, certainly! He will be waking presently. And when he does, Her Majesty wishes to be told, immediately.

PRINCESS ALICE (*meaningly*)   If you are not here to tell her, Dr. Clark, may I do so?

DR. CLARK (*turning sharply*)   Not that! Not that! I can't have my professional duties interfered with by anybody.

PRINCESS ALICE (*resignedly*) Very well, Doctor.

(*The* DOCTOR *has made his escape. The* PRINCESS *goes in, pauses at the foot of the bed, then passes round it, and out of sight. The Nurse returns, carrying a hot-water bottle. She stops at the door; the* HEAD NURSE *comes forward and takes it. Going to the foot of the bed, she effects the necessary exchange, and brings back the other to the waiting Nurse, who goes off with it. The* HEAD NURSE *is about to return to her Patient, when* THE QUEEN *enters.*)

THE QUEEN Who opened that window?

HEAD NURSE It was the Doctor's orders, your Majesty.

THE QUEEN What Doctor?

HEAD NURSE Dr. Clark, your Majesty.

THE QUEEN Oh! Then it may stay . . . Is Her Royal Highness, the Princess Alice, in there?

HEAD NURSE Yes, your Majesty.

THE QUEEN Ask her to come and speak to me.

(*The* HEAD NURSE *goes back into the room to give the message. The* PRINCESS *comes out.*)

THE QUEEN Is he awake yet?

PRINCESS ALICE Not yet, Mamma. But, just now, he seemed as if he were beginning to.

THE QUEEN Have those Doctors been?

PRINCESS ALICE No, Mamma dear, not yet.

THE QUEEN I do wish they would come, and get it over!

PRINCESS ALICE You will see them, Mamma, won't you?

THE QUEEN No; I don't wish to see either of them. Dr. Clark did not think it at all necessary for them to come; neither did I. But you all seemed so set on it!

PRINCESS ALICE Yes: we wished it very much. And I do wish you *would* see them, Mamma.

THE QUEEN I have said I will *not* see them . . . You may, if you like — if Dr. Clark has no objection.

HEAD NURSE (*coming in from the sick-room*) His Royal Highness is awake, your Majesty.

(*With a gesture indicating that* PRINCESS ALICE *must wait her turn,*
THE QUEEN *goes into the room. She goes round to the further side of
the bed. We see her reach out her hand, and a hand taking it.*)

THE QUEEN   Albert.

ALBERT (*heard, but not seen*) Weibchen! . . . Frauchen! . . . Liebes
Frauchen!

THE QUEEN   How are you, my Dearest? Better?

ALBERT   I don't . . . know . . . Sometimes . . . when one is better
. . . one feels worse.

THE QUEEN   But you are not feeling worse, my Darling, are you?

ALBERT   No? . . . I don't know . . . I don't know . . . Weibchen
. . . Kiss me! . . . Kiss me! . . . Again! . . . Once again! . . . That will
do . . . Frauchen; Kleines Frauchen!

(*And now, into the outer room, returns* DR. CLARK.)

PRINCESS ALICE   Papa is awake now, Doctor; Mamma is with
him.

DR. CLARK   Ah! I'm glad! That will do him more good than
anything . . . Always does . . . But I think Her Majesty wished to
speak to me . . . Would your Highness very kindly — ?

PRINCESS ALICE (*speaking through the open door*) Mamma, Dr.
Clark is here.

(THE QUEEN *comes out.*)

THE QUEEN   You may go in now, my Dear. Shut the door.

(*The* PRINCESS *goes in, closing the door behind her.*)

Dr. Clark, how do you find him this morning?

DR. CLARK   No change, Ma'am; no change. I'm disappointed
not to find the improvement that I was looking for. But there
has been no apparent loss of strength; and that's always to the good,
when one is fighting against time.

THE QUEEN   Just now he spoke to me — quite himself again. His
mind wasn't wandering, as it has been doing so much lately. That
is what I find so distressing — when he doesn't know me.

DR. CLARK   Ah, yes, Ma'am; that one can understand, of course.
To the feelings, very trying; but, medically speaking, it is quite a

normal symptom — quite normal. It need not add to your Majesty's anxiety in any degree whatever. Nothing unexpected has occurred — nothing, nothing.

THE QUEEN He *is* going to get well, isn't he?

DR. CLARK I have not a doubt, Ma'am: not a doubt.

THE QUEEN Nor have I, Dr. Clark. If I had, I couldn't bear it . . . But there are others here, who haven't my confidence and courage. I feel it: it's very trying! . . . Those Doctors! *I* didn't want them; but I had to give in — for the sake of others. I wish now that I had not . . . His knowing me, and speaking to me again, gives me such hope.

(*The clock of the Castle is heard striking three.*)

DR. CLARK Your Majesty is quite right to hope. There is no use in being anything *but* hopeful, and no reason not to be.

THE QUEEN That was three o'clock striking. Wasn't that the time the Doctors were to be here?

DR. CLARK It was, Ma'am.

THE QUEEN Then I think I'd better go! I don't wish to meet them. You quite understand, Dr. Clark, that it was no lack of confidence, on *my* part, which required these others to be called into consultation.

DR. CLARK I quite understand, Ma'am; and I appreciate greatly the confidence which your Majesty has placed in me.

THE QUEEN I hope they won't be here long.

DR. CLARK They will not be, Ma'am, I am sure. I shall not encourage it. The case, though serious, is quite a simple one.

THE QUEEN Very well; then now I will go.

(*As* THE QUEEN *goes out, the* HEAD NURSE *comes in to close the window. A* SERVANT *enters.*)

SERVANT Sir Henry Holland, and Dr. Watson, to see you, Sir.

DR. CLARK Oh, yes; let them come up: I'll see them here . . . Nurse, just see that nobody comes in while we are having our consultation. Go in now, and have everything ready. And, when I bring them in to see His Royal Highness, you will go out.

HEAD NURSE Yes, Sir.

(*She goes in, as the two Doctors make their appearance.*)

DR. CLARK Oh, good afternoon, good afternoon, Gentlemen! I'm sorry you should have been troubled: I don't think it was necessary — not at all necessary. Nor can I say that Her Majesty actually wished it. But in view of all the circumstances — the exalted position of my Patient, the public anxiety, and — and — things in general — others *did*. And so, Her Majesty ... Well, you are here; and I shall be willing — willing, after you have examined His Royal Highness — to hear anything you may have to say on the case.

SIR HENRY You have no doubt, I suppose, Dr. Clark, as to what the disease actually is?

DR. CLARK Oh, none, none! Gastric fever, just gastric fever — that's all.

DR. WATSON Nothing else? No complications?

DR. CLARK No, no; quite normal. But these three weeks of it, and all the responsibility have been a great strain to me. And Her Majesty is quite aware of it ... Well, will you come in? ... I've prepared His Royal Highness for your arrival; but he probably won't know you. It's only at intervals — just now and then — that his mind does not wander somewhat. I'll go in first, if you don't mind. A moment, just a moment.

(*So saying, he disappears into the room.*)

SIR HENRY Well? How does that little exhibition strike you?

DR. WATSON Oh, professional jealousy, I suppose. One must expect it.

SIR HENRY I don't mind his jealousy. It's his incompetence I'm afraid of. He's an old duffer, with a mind of yesterday.

DR. WATSON Court Physicians-in-Ordinary generally are, I'm afraid.

DR. CLARK (*returning*) Come in, Gentlemen.

(*They go in. The* HEAD NURSE *comes out, carrying a tray of medicine bottles and glasses. She sets this down, in order to close*) *the door. Then taking it up again, goes to the door on the left, and calls, 'Nurse'. The second Nurse answers the call.)*

HEAD NURSE Take these.

(As the tray is being handed over, PRINCESS ALICE *enters from the other side.)*

PRINCESS ALICE Have the Doctors come?

HEAD NURSE Yes, your Royal Highness, they've just gone in.

PRINCESS ALICE Will you, please, send word to Her Majesty, as soon as they have gone?

HEAD NURSE Yes, your Royal Highness; I will.

PRINCESS ALICE Nurse, how is he, do you think — really?

HEAD NURSE *(hesitating)* I don't know, your Royal Highness: I can't say . . . I oughtn't to say anything.

PRINCESS ALICE You are quite right, Nurse; I ought not to have asked you. Dr. Clark seems hopeful; but he does not tell one anything.

HEAD NURSE No, your Royal Highness.

PRINCESS ALICE Have you attended many cases like this?

HEAD NURSE Not quite like this, your Royal Highness. Patients are so different. Some take it one way, some another. I've never seen two cases quite alike.

PRINCESS ALICE But it is always a very — serious kind of illness, isn't it, Nurse?

HEAD NURSE Yes, your Royal Highness. But people do recover from it. There's always hope, if they can hold out long enough.

PRINCESS ALICE Is three weeks a long time?

HEAD NURSE Sometimes it's four, your Royal Highness: not often.

(At this moment another and a younger PRINCESS *tip-toes into sight. She comes from the improper direction of the Nurse's waiting-room. She is about fifteen.)*

PRINCESS ALICE *(reprovingly)* Nellie!

PRINCESS HELENA I *had* to come! Don't tell Mamma: she said I wasn't to . . . How is he?

PRINCESS ALICE   The Doctors are in there now, having a consultation.

PRINCESS HELENA   How many?

PRINCESS ALICE   Three.

PRINCESS HELENA   Who are they?

PRINCESS ALICE   I don't know — except, of course, Dr. Clark.

PRINCESS HELENA   Why had the others to come?

PRINCESS ALICE   Because it was so much better to have other opinions.

PRINCESS HELENA   Isn't Dr. Clark's good enough? . . . When are they going to let me see Papa?

PRINCESS ALICE   I don't know, Dear.

PRINCESS HELENA   I haven't seen him now — for ten days. I want to! . . . May I just look in?

PRINCESS ALICE   You can't now, possibly — not while the Doctors are there.

PRINCESS HELENA   I'll come again, then, when Mamma isn't here . . . You'll let me, won't you, Ally?

PRINCESS ALICE (*tenderly*)   Yes, my Dear, I'll let you.

PRINCESS HELENA   Oh, Ally, there's Mamma coming! I must run!

(*She bolts back by the way she came.* THE QUEEN *enters.*)

PRINCESS ALICE (*quietly*)   You had better go, Nurse, and wait in the other room.

(*The Nurse, with a curtsy to Her approaching Majesty, withdraws.*)

THE QUEEN   Haven't they gone? Haven't they gone yet?

PRINCESS ALICE   No, Mamma; they are still there.

THE QUEEN (*angrily*)   Why did they come? I didn't want them to come! But you all so insisted.

PRINCESS ALICE   Yes, Mamma: isn't it always right, in serious cases, to call other Doctors into consultation?

THE QUEEN I don't see why! I trust Dr. Clark more than any of them. Having attended us both for so long, of course he knows best what to do. If they differ from him, it only makes trouble; and if they agree, what more good does that do?

PRINCESS ALICE It should give Dr. Clark more confidence, Mamma dear.

THE QUEEN He has all *my* confidence; and that's all he needs.

PRINCESS ALICE (*hearing the bell ring in the Nurses' waiting-room*) I think they are coming, Mamma. Won't you wait and see them?

THE QUEEN No, I can't — I won't see them! I'll see Dr. Clark, after they've gone ... You are not to see them, either. Come!

(THE QUEEN *goes out, followed by* PRINCESS ALICE, *just as the* HEAD NURSE, *in answer to the bell, returns to take up her duty again. As she approaches the door, the Doctors come out.*)

DR. CLARK Well, Gentlemen, now that you have examined my Patient, if you wish to make any recommendations as to different, or further treatment, I am quite ready to hear them.

SIR HENRY I fear, Dr. Clark, that His Royal Highness's condition is more serious than you led us to suppose.

DR. CLARK I have always regarded his condition as serious — very serious, Sir Henry.

SIR HENRY Yes ... A question of degree.

DR. CLARK What degree of seriousness do you suggest, Sir Henry?

SIR HENRY I don't want to say there is no hope. But I'm very much afraid of what may happen in the next few hours, if there is not a change ... What do you say, Watson?

DR. WATSON I agree.

SIR HENRY I think, then, that Her Majesty ought to be told.

DR. CLARK Told what, Sir?

SIR HENRY What we have just told *you*, Dr. Clark.

DR. CLARK I cannot take that responsibility. It is highly important that His Royal Highness should not be subjected to any undue disturbance, or shock. If Her Majesty were told anything so alarming as what you propose — then, Gentlemen, undoubtedly the shock of it would communicate itself to my Patient also. Up till now, I consider that his strength has been largely sustained by the extraordinary courage and confidence in his recovery which Her Majesty has exhibited. From her it goes to him: deprive him of that sustaining force, and I cannot answer for the consequences.

SIR HENRY   Well, Dr. Clark, we have told you what we think. The matter is in your hands . . . Does Her Majesty wish to see us before we go?

DR. CLARK   I think not, Sir.

SIR HENRY   Perhaps that is as well — since we do not find ourselves in agreement.

DR. WATSON   Very much better; for if Her Majesty were to ask for my opinion, I should be bound to give it.

SIR HENRY   If you would like us to wait, Dr. Clark, within call — we will do so.

DR. CLARK   I thank you, but I think not. I understood from Her Majesty that she would not require a second consultation. This was only done to satisfy others.

DR. WATSON   If Her Majesty should ask you for a statement of our opinion of the case, Dr. Clark — what are you going to say?

DR. CLARK   I believe that Her Majesty will be quite satisfied with my own statement of the case, without further inquiry. She has honoured me, so far, with her confidence; and I do not expect now to find that it has been withdrawn.

SIR HENRY   Oh? . . . Then I think we had better say good afternoon, Dr. Clark . . . I wish I had *your* confidence.

DR. WATSON   Yes: sorry we could not be of more use . . . Too late, too late!

(*The Consultants part with frigid formality. As the two Doctors move towards the door by which they entered, gathering up each his hat and gloves as they go,* DR. CLARK *opens the inner door and beckons. The* HEAD NURSE *appears in time to see the intruders disappearing through the adjoining room.*)

DR. CLARK Nurse, just see there is somebody to show them out.

HEAD NURSE (*looking*) There is somebody, Sir.

DR. CLARK Oh, very well. Then, now send someone to tell Her Majesty that they have gone; but to say also, that, for the present, I think His Royal Highness had better not see anybody . . . I hope that, after this disturbance, he may sleep.

(*As the* HEAD NURSE *goes to perform her errand,* PRINCESS ALICE *is seen standing in the doorway.*)

PRINCESS ALICE I heard what you said, Dr. Clark. I will go and tell Mamma myself. And then — may I come back, and wait here?

DR. CLARK Oh, certainly, certainly. I am going myself now. I shall be back in about an hour.

PRINCESS ALICE (*anxiously*) You have no news for us? The Doctors said nothing that you can — ?

DR. CLARK Nothing, your Highness: nothing, that I did not know already . . . Nothing.

(*The Princess and the Doctor go out by opposite doors. The* HEAD NURSE *returns to the sick-room. Faintly, from a distance, come the sounds of the afternoon service in St. George's Chapel — the chanting of the Psalms. It is the 14th Evening of the month, and the 73rd Psalm is being sung. Presently the Princess returns; and, sitting down, she opens a Prayer Book and follows the words of the singing. Twilight begins to fall; time passes; it gets dark. Presently the Assistant Nurse, in answer to a bell from the sick-room, comes through, carrying a small shaded lamp. As she comes back, she sees* PRINCESS ALICE *seated at one of the windows.*)

NURSE Would not your Royal Highness like to have a reading-lamp?

PRINCESS ALICE No, Nurse: draw the curtains, and light the candles; that will do.

(*The Nurse carries out the order, then goes. The Princess sits waiting. An hour passes. . . .*

*

In the adjoining room the bell rings sharply. As the Nurse enters in

answer to the summons, the door of the sick-room opens, and the
HEAD NURSE *appears.*)

HEAD NURSE Call the Doctor! Quick!

(*The Nurse runs out.*)

PRINCESS ALICE (*springing up*) Is he worse?

HEAD NURSE Oh, will your Royal Highness please tell Her
Majesty to come!

(*The Princess goes hastily out:* DR. CLARK *arrives, and entering the
inner room, leaves the door half-open. A moment later* THE QUEEN
*comes hurrying in, followed by the Princess. As they enter, the
folding-doors are pushed back — the lower half of the bed can now
be seen. A sound of heavy breathing is heard: it becomes more and
more painful. The Nurse who has summoned the Doctor, now
stands inside the outer door, waiting. The* HEAD NURSE *comes out;
their eyes encounter; she shakes her head.*)

HEAD NURSE We are not to go in now: we are to wait here.

(*They stand motionless, listening: only the heavy breathing is heard:*
PRINCESS ALICE *comes hurriedly to the door.*)

PRINCESS ALICE Nurse, send word at once! Say that their Royal
Highnesses are to come — immediately.

(*The Nurse goes out.*)

HEAD NURSE Oh, your Royal Highness, has the Doctor *said*
anything?

PRINCESS ALICE Dr. Clark has just told us that there is no hope.

(*She goes back into the room, where, in the subdued light,* DR.
CLARK *is seen, passing across from the bed, and back again. The
laboured breathing grows slower, and fainter.*
*The Members of the Royal Family come in one by one. One sees
them, as they enter, pause, stand for a moment, then pass round the
bed, and kneel . . . The heavy breathing dies down — ceases. There
is a moment's silence, then from* THE QUEEN *comes a loud cry: and
his name . . . 'ALBERT!' There follows a sound of weeping: and* DR.
CLARK, *feeling that he is no longer needed, tiptoes softly out.*)

BEREAVEMENT

1861

In the deepest of widow's weeds, THE QUEEN *sits nursing a pet dog; and in the wistful gaze of the dumb beast she finds comfort, and a sympathy which she is less ready to accept when it is offered her by mere humans. She sits at her writing-table, having interrupted for a few moments the correspondence she is conducting on black-edged notepaper of the deepest dye.*

THE QUEEN Yes, you understand, don't you? — a little. No, you don't, you don't, Doggie! but you try to. That's the best you can do for me. It's all that anyone can do now. Nobody can really understand ... And now you must get down, dear; I must go on with my writing.

(She puts the dog gently down, and returns sadly to her correspondence. A GENTLEMAN USHER *enters, and stands waiting for permission to speak.)*

THE QUEEN *(after a pause)* Yes?

USHER Mrs. Gladstone, your Majesty.

THE QUEEN Oh, yes. Let her come in. And while she *is* here, I do not wish to see anyone.

(The USHER *bows, and goes.* THE QUEEN *takes up a portrait from the writing-table, and gazes at it fondly.)*

THE QUEEN Oh! Albert! Albert!

(The door opens; the USHER *enters, followed by* MRS. GLADSTONE.*)*

USHER Mrs. Gladstone, your Majesty.

THE QUEEN Dear Mrs. Gladstone, how good of you to come, so soon!

MRS. GLADSTONE Directly — when I got your Majesty's command. I was so grateful that your Majesty wished it.

THE QUEEN There are very few I wish to see, now, Mrs. Gladstone; but you were one. You have always been so kind to me.

MRS. GLADSTONE The kindness has been your Majesty's.

THE QUEEN You have come to see an unhappy woman, the joy of whose life is over.

MRS. GLADSTONE Oh, I understand how your Majesty must feel! And I won't talk about time making any difference. But memories will. Your Majesty will find a great comfort in memories — presently.

THE QUEEN They are a great pain to me. Almost more than I can bear.

MRS. GLADSTONE Yes, of course. But you would not be without them. They are already, Ma'am, are they not, the nearest to comfort — of anything?

THE QUEEN That is quite true, Mrs. Gladstone — quite true. Do, please, sit down! No; sit near me. . . . You also, at some time, must have known great sorrow.

MRS. GLADSTONE Yes, Ma'am; few of us can miss having it at some time in our lives.

THE QUEEN What has been your greatest sorrow, Mrs. Gladstone?

MRS. GLADSTONE My Sister, Ma'am, my only Sister. She was my closest and dearest friend.

THE QUEEN How long is it since you lost her?

MRS. GLADSTONE Four years, Ma'am.

THE QUEEN Does it seem long?

MRS. GLADSTONE No, Ma'am; she is still so much alive to me. At first she seemed dead — gone, utterly. She doesn't now. So much comes back; every day — new memories. Your Majesty will find that, too; I am sure.

THE QUEEN Thank you, Mrs. Gladstone; I hope so, too. But already I remember so much. I don't think there can be anything I have forgotten. As I read his diaries, and his dear letters, everything seems like yesterday.

MRS. GLADSTONE Yes: when we have loved much, time seems hardly to mean anything.

THE QUEEN You say the very thing I have been trying to say to myself, Mrs. Gladstone — and to believe. It's a comfort to hear someone else saying it. .... And, of course, now, *He* remembers everything too. So, in memory, we are together — still.

MRS. GLADSTONE Yes, Ma'am; and of one so really good as he was, what lovely and comforting memories you must have always with you.

THE QUEEN Yes, always; just as *he* was always with me. In all our married life, we were hardly ever apart; during twenty-two years only a few weeks. At first he was not with me so constantly — during the day, I mean. I had not found out then how much more he was fit to be King than I was to be Queen. And people were jealous and afraid — even my own Ministers — lest he should have too much influence over me. And, just at first, sometimes we differed, he and I; but he was always right — always right! And before long, I found that I could do nothing safely without him. And there he was, always at my side — helping, advising, directing, guiding — often saving me from making mistakes; and my Ministers also. As time went on, they also learned to listen to him, and wished him to be present in all our consultations; all except just a few — Lord Palmerston sometimes. But even he has written and spoken to me, very kindly and feelingly, about what we owed to his great wisdom and foresight. The very last thing he did has, perhaps, saved us from war with America. Will people ever know what this Country owes to him? He ought to have been King: he was — almost; for I decided nothing till he had advised me about it. And now he is gone — I am alone; and though people don't know it, a new reign has begun — a Queen without her King! Oh, what shall I do? What shall I do without him?

MRS. GLADSTONE Is it not possible, Ma'am — your Son, the Prince, now being of age — that he may be of some help to your Majesty?

THE QUEEN (*with some asperity*) No! Indeed, no, Mrs. Gladstone! He has not either his Father's mind, nor his Father's character. I cannot allow him to take any part, at present, in my responsible work of Government.

MRS. GLADSTONE But he must do so some day, your Majesty; and it is a work for which he will need training.

THE QUEEN I have to hope, Mrs. Gladstone, that it will not have to be yet — not till he is a good deal older, and more — settled. At present, he is far too much the man of pleasure, and amusement. He is devoted to me, of course; as I am also to him. But he makes me very anxious.

MRS. GLADSTONE I think he has a very kind heart, your Majesty. Wherever he goes, he attracts and wins people.

THE QUEEN Yes; and not always of the best kind. Attracting people is sometimes his great temptation, and he does not feel — no, he does not *feel* his Father's death as he ought to do. . . . Just think! Only a fortnight after, I found him — *smoking*! It was a great shock to me; his Father having always forbidden it. *He* never smoked — never felt the need of it. So why should Bertie?

MRS. GLADSTONE But so many more do so now, Ma'am. It has become very much more common.

THE QUEEN Yes, 'common'! that is the word for it. How much the world is changing — from what *He* would have wished! But *I* shall never change — anything.

MRS. GLADSTONE To be faithful in all one's thoughts and wishes, is a great help, Ma'am, is it not? It makes one feel nearer.

THE QUEEN Dear Mrs. Gladstone, you do say such nice things! I wish we could have talked longer; it would have done me good, I'm sure. But even now the affairs of my Government have to go on; and I as the head of it. And I believe that already I have an appointment, and that one of my Ministers is waiting to see me. So now I must say good-bye to you. Thank you for coming. You must come again — soon.

(*And as* MRS. GLADSTONE *curtsies over the hand offered her*, THE QUEEN *bends down and kisses her.*)

MRS. GLADSTONE Oh, yes, Ma'am, your Majesty has only to send for me. I wish — we all wish — that we could do anything that might be of use or comfort to your Majesty. But even love feels helpless sometimes.

THE QUEEN It is the only thing that can help now — that has helped me at all. . . . Good-bye!

(MRS. GLADSTONE *makes her last curtsy, and retires.* THE QUEEN

goes to the window, and stands looking out for a while; then, return-
ing to the writing-table, she rings a bell. The GENTLEMAN *enters.*

THE QUEEN If Lord Palmerston is here, I am now ready to see him.

USHER Lord Palmerston *is* here, your Majesty.

THE QUEEN Very well. Ask him to come in.

(*The* USHER *retires, and reappears, followed by* LORD PALMERSTON.)

USHER Lord Palmerston, your Majesty.

THE QUEEN Good morning, Lord Palmerston. You wrote that you wished to see me to-day, if possible.

LORD PALMERSTON I thank your Majesty for so graciously making the appointment. May I express the hope that your Majesty is now better?

THE QUEEN I am quite well, thank you, Lord Palmerston. You have come about something that requires my immediate attention, I believe?

LORD PALMERSTON I have, Ma'am, unfortunately. I would have been glad to have spared your Majesty, could it have allowed of postponement.

THE QUEEN Oh, no, please. I wish everything to go on as usual.

LORD PALMERSTON To-day, Ma'am, is the thirtieth of December; and the New Year's Honours still await your Majesty's approval and confirmation. To-morrow they must go to the Press, for next day's publication.

THE QUEEN Yes, of course. It would not do for there to be any delay in the usual announcements. . . . You have them with you?

LORD PALMERSTON I have, Ma'am. Lord Granville has com-municated to me your Majesty's wish that Mr. Dilke should be made a Baronet, and that Mr. Bowring should be made a Com-panion of the Bath. Both those things will be done accordingly. But there are also three other persons, whose names I have for some time wished to submit to your Majesty for the dignity of Baronet; and, if your Majesty should be graciously pleased to approve of them, the list would stand as follows: Mr. Dilke (THE QUEEN *bows her assent*), Mr. William Browne, of Liverpool.

THE QUEEN Who is he?

LORD PALMERSTON A very wealthy and distinguished merchant, Ma'am, who has lately made a magnificent present of a Public Library to his fellow-citizens. . . . Mr. Thomas David Lloyd, a well-known and respectable gentleman of high standing, in the County of Carnarvon; and Mr. Matthew Rich, to whom the Government is under great obligation for political services — he having vacated his seat for Richmond, Yorkshire, to enable your Majesty's Solicitor-General to be elected in his place.

THE QUEEN Have they all sufficient means, Lord Palmerston, to support the dignity in a becoming manner?

LORD PALMERSTON Oh, yes, your Majesty, they are all men of wealth — great wealth, most of them.

THE QUEEN Then WE approve.

LORD PALMERSTON I thank your Majesty.

THE QUEEN Is there anything else?

LORD PALMERSTON Nothing, Ma'am, that cannot conveniently wait for a later occasion.

THE QUEEN (*rising*) Very well, Lord Palmerston. Then, for the present, that will do.

LORD PALMERSTON May I, with your Majesty's gracious permission, be allowed, before I withdraw, to express a fervent hope that the intensity of your Majesty's grief may not lead your Majesty to neglect the preservation of your health, which is so necessary for the care and welfare of your Majesty's Children, and hardly less for that of your Majesty's devotedly attached and affectionate subjects, of whom, Ma'am, I am ever one.

THE QUEEN Thank you, Lord Palmerston. I am keeping quite well. Good-bye.

> (THE QUEEN *inclines her head, but does not offer her hand.* LORD PALMERSTON *bows and retires.* THE QUEEN *sits down again, and with her eyes fixed upon the portrait, speaks.*)

Oh, Albert! Albert! Albert! Why did you leave me? How can I bear to go on living, and doing all this — *alone*!

THE ANNIVERSARY

14th December 1862

The Prince Consort's dressing-room is seen in deep twilight; the blinds are half down; in the Castle Yard outside, the gas-standards are being lighted. The Castle clock strikes seven. No change has been made in the room since the Prince last left it. On an open bureau papers are still lying, on the dressing-table brushes, combs, and other articles of toilet. Beyond the dressing-table is a door leading to the Royal private apartments. On the wall hangs a portrait of the Queen in her youth. Opposite is the service door used by the servants.

There is the sound of a key turning in the lock, and MR. RICHARDS, the Prince's valet, enters, followed by another man-servant. MR. RICHARDS is now an old man, rather small and thin, and beginning to be frail. His companion is of larger size, middle-aged, and very correct in his deportment.

RICHARDS Come in. (*He closes the door softly*) James, this is the first time anyone has been in this room since last year — except me — and Her Majesty. She has one key, I've another. No one else comes in, so far as I know, unless it's with *Her*.

MAN-SERVANT Who does the dusting?

RICHARDS (*with a touch of awe*) I don't know. Perhaps *She* does it.

MAN-SERVANT The Queen!

RICHARDS It isn't the Queen comes in here; it's the Wife. No, not the Wife, the Widow. Aye! A year this very day. . . . Now you stand by, and watch while I show you what you've to do . . . every night.

(*He lights candles: draws blinds and curtains, goes to bureau, gets out clothes and lays them on couch.*)

RICHARDS See, this is how they go. Coat and vest there, these here; shoes . . . socks . . . and you put out a fresh shirt every night and change the studs and the links. Have you got that?

MAN-SERVANT Yes, I think.

279

RICHARDS   This is the last time I'll be doing it; so be sure you get it right. Her Majesty wished me to stay on for the year, so of course I did. Aye, I'd been with him twenty-one years, from the beginning to the end. I'd wanted to leave before, for I was feeling my age even then, but he wouldn't let me. 'You stay, Mr. Richards', he said (always called me 'Mr.'); 'it won't be for long.' *He* knew.

MAN-SERVANT   How did this start? — your having to do it after he was dead?

RICHARDS   It started after the doctors had been called in. The night he was taken bad, I'd already put his things out just as usual; next night I didn't. Two nights after that, the Queen herself sent for me. 'Richards', she said, 'why haven't you put out His Royal Highness's evening dress, as you always do?' 'I thought, your Majesty —' said I. 'You're *not* to think!' says she. 'His Royal Highness may recover any day. You will go on doing it, unless you receive His Royal Highness's orders not to' . . . I never did receive them — I laid them out again the day he died. He was dead when I did it, though I didn't know. The next day . . . well, I'd just left them. Evening of the day after, I was putting them away again, for good and all. Her Majesty came in from that door. *She* must have thought I was getting them *out*. 'You will do that always', she said, 'till further orders.' And went quick out again. So that's how it has been ever since. And now that I'm leaving, it's to be you. And you are to do it every night, till you receive other orders . . . which you never will.

MAN-SERVANT   My God! It's — it's like being in a grave.

RICHARDS   (*moving to the door*)   Yes.

MAN-SERVANT   Do we leave the candles?

RICHARDS   (*giving the word quiet weight*)   Yes. . . . To-morrow I give you this key. I keep it till I leave. You lock the door when you go out; and you don't let anyone else in.

> (*They go out; the locking of the door is heard. The clock chimes the quarter past. From the other door* THE QUEEN *enters, dressed in deep mourning. She comes forward, looks to see that the clothes are laid out, turns to the dressing-table and begins handling the things lying on it, one after another. She takes up a pair of hair-brushes,*

*looks at them fondly, shakes her head, and lays them down again.
Then she takes up a razor-case, opens it, considers it for a while;
this time her gesture indicates assent. She takes out one of the razors,
kisses it, and puts it away in the drawer of the looking-glass; then
closing the case, and keeping it still in her hand pulls the bell-rope
near by. Having rung, she stands facing the mirror, and does not
turn when the key sounds in the lock, and* RICHARDS *again enters
from the opposite door. Looking at his reflection in the glass, as he
halts at a distance, she speaks:)*

THE QUEEN Mr. Richards, before you go, I want to thank you for
your services — your faithful services to both of us.

(*From* MR. RICHARDS *comes a choked response, of which only the
words 'Your Majesty' become audible.*)

His Royal Highness, your master, had a great regard for you.

RICHARDS Oh, your Majesty! I loved him!

THE QUEEN I know . . . so I want to give you now something that
was his, and that you were accustomed to use in your attendance
upon him. I had meant, at first, to give you these hair-brushes; but
I couldn't let *them* go.

RICHARDS (*with emotion*) No, your Majesty.

THE QUEEN So here is his case of razors. I have kept *one*. Please take
all the rest. And now — you may go.

(*She hands him the case, still not looking at him. He takes it, and
backs respectfully to a distance. He goes out. The Queen flings herself down upon the outspread clothes.*)

THE QUEEN Oh, Albert, my King, my King! How can I live without you? Albert! Albert!

STABLE GOVERNMENT

1870

The ante-chamber to HER MAJESTY'S *writing-room at Balmoral is fear-somely furnished with trophies of the chase — mainly horns. These do not merely adorn the walls: they have also been adapted to form the legs of tables — and chairs, prickly as thorn-bushes, intended more to be looked at than sat on. It is ten o'clock in the morning, and* HER MAJESTY, *punctual to the stroke, is about to enter the sanctum where she works with her secretary, when* MR. JOHN BROWN, *making his own appointment for an audience, abruptly calls her to attention.*

BROWN   Did your Majesty remember to give that order I told ye about?

THE QUEEN   What order, Brown?

BROWN   Aboot the ponies — that they werrn't to be ridden by those that didn't know how to ride them?

THE QUEEN   Oh, yes, yes. I gave the order. It's not going to happen again.

BROWN   Ah, then I've got that off my mind. And don't ye go back on it, Ma'am.

THE QUEEN   Who was it, Brown, who didn't know how to ride?

BROWN   It wasna' one, Ma'am. 'Twas three.

THE QUEEN   Three?

BROWN   Ay; and the whole three of 'em here at Balmoral as thick as thieves.

THE QUEEN   Oh, you mustn't say *that*, Brown.

BROWN   No, Ma'am; only in a manner of speaking. But you know as well as I do, Ma'am, how 'tis ignorance that is catching. So when the three of them get together, each starts to go one worse than the other. And that's bad for the ponies.

THE QUEEN   But you haven't yet told me who they are, Brown.

BROWN   I've *not*, Ma'am. I thought, maybe, your Majesty would

283

prefer it to be *im*personal — seeing that there's two of 'em are what ye might call visitors. It's all sorts we get here; there's no keeping 'em out. It's sad for ye — being Queen — that ye have to be polite to so many as 'twould be better not to know 'em at all.

THE QUEEN I don't see how that matters to you, Brown. *You* don't have to know them.

BROWN Not socially, I don't, Ma'am; but I have to keep my eye on 'em. Eh, but it's not them; it's the ponies I'm minding about.

THE QUEEN Well, then you'd better tell me who they are.

BROWN Weel, then, first, Ma'am, there's Mr. Duckworth — or Canon do they call him?

THE QUEEN You surprise me. Doesn't *he* know how to ride?

BROWN He fancies he does, Ma'am; but fancying isn't knowing. All you can say for him is he doesn't fall off. But he would if the pony was na' so considerate of him. When she feels him coming loose, she waits for him. As for that German sculptor that's doing all the busts and the graven images ye're having put aboot the place — Mr. Bum as he calls himself — when he puts his own image and superscription over a pony . . .

THE QUEEN You mean Mr. Edgar Boehm, I suppose?

BROWN Maybe I do, Ma'am; but when he comes to Scotland he'd do better to leave his foreign pronunciation behind him. Mr. Bum, if he ever took riding lessons at all, took 'em, I wouldn't wonder, from watching Canon Duckworth, which is the catchingness of ignorance, as I've told ye.

THE QUEEN Brown, you're talking too much!

BROWN Well, Ma'am, if you don't want to hear any more, there's where I leave it.

THE QUEEN Who is the third?

BROWN He's the other German gentleman, that does all your letters for you.

THE QUEEN Not all, Brown; only some.

BROWN Aye, to be sure: he doesn't write any to me. Well Ma'am, he knows how to ride after a fashion. I'm not saying no to that. But it's not the kind of riding our ponies are accustomed to. They've been trained different. He got his riding in the German Army. Now a Hieland pony is not used to military drill; no, Ma'am. He goes his own way, and you've got to let him. And Mr. Stahl — that his name, Ma'am? . . .

THE QUEEN Yes.

BROWN Mr. Stahl thinks to make our ponies do military manœuvres by running up hills faster than God meant 'em. And being God's creatures, Ma'am (not German) that's all aboot it. And if you want to have all the ponies in your stables spavined, or broken-kneed, or broken-winded, or anything else bad for 'em that you might happen to wish — you let those three go riding 'em together, Ma'am. I'm only telling you.

(*At this moment one of the* QUEEN'S LADIES-IN-WAITING *enters, bound for secretarial duty, carrying a pile of letters.*)

LADY-IN-WAITING I beg pardon. Is your Majesty not yet ready for me?

THE QUEEN For my letters? Oh yes, go in; I'll be with you in a moment.

(*The* LADY-IN-WAITING *passes on into the Queen's writing-room.*)

Well, thank you very much, Brown, for all you've told me. As I say, I have already given orders; and it's not going to happen again.

BROWN Will your Majesty be out driving to-day?

THE QUEEN No, I don't think so. I've too much to do.

BROWN Then you'll not be wanting me again, maybe?

THE QUEEN No; but don't go off the premises, Brown.

BROWN I'll not, Ma'am. (*He goes out; then comes back to say:*) Here's your Majesty's Equerry, Colonel Ponsonby, wanting to speak with you. It's aboot the ponies, I shouldn't wonder.

THE QUEEN Ask him to come in.

(MR. BROWN *goes; his voice is heard conveying* THE QUEEN'S *instructions, and* COLONEL PONSONBY *enters.*)

THE QUEEN Good morning, Colonel Ponsonby.

PONSONBY I hope your Majesty will pardon me. I am sorry to have to trouble your Majesty.

THE QUEEN What is it?

PONSONBY Do I understand, Ma'am, that it is your Majesty's wish that certain persons are not to be allowed to have ponies from the stables when they ask for them?

THE QUEEN Not if they don't know how to ride them.

PONSONBY As to that, Ma'am, who is to be judge?

THE QUEEN *You* are, Colonel Ponsonby. I don't wish to name names; but I am told that three of my ponies have been taken out these three last days, and were not ridden properly. That is not to happen again.

PONSONBY Are they forbidden to ride at all, Ma'am?

THE QUEEN Oh, no; but someone must go with them to see that they ride properly. They are not to be trusted alone.

PONSONBY Hitherto they *have* ridden alone, Ma'am: the three together. It's going to be a little difficult.

THE QUEEN In what way?

PONSONBY I understand that your Majesty gave orders, but did not wish that they should be known as coming from your Majesty.

THE QUEEN No; why should I be brought into the matter? The Equerries have charge of the stables; and it is their duty to see that the ponies are not ridden by ignorant people. I engage people to do their duty, and not to expect me to do it for them.

PONSONBY It would be easier for them to do so, Ma'am, if it were known that they were carrying out your Majesty's orders.

THE QUEEN While they are in my employ, everybody ought to know that they *are* carrying out my orders. If they took orders from anybody else, they'd have to go. Who is it that is making all this trouble?

PONSONBY I wouldn't say that they are making trouble, Ma'am. But I hear that three gentlemen whom I would rather not name are very much aggrieved, because on going to the stables this morning they were not allowed to have any of the ponies.

THE QUEEN Did they go without first asking your permission?

PONSONBY They did, Ma'am.

THE QUEEN Isn't that against the rules?

PONSONBY It is, Ma'am.

THE QUEEN Very well, Colonel Ponsonby; then see that the rules are kept.

(*Re-enter* MR. BROWN.)

BROWN (*in a tone of grim satisfaction*) Ma'am! they're coming; they're wanting to see you: all three of them.

THE QUEEN I'm not going to see anyone. They mustn't come talking to *me*.

(*She goes in.* MR. BROWN *stands waiting; the* COLONEL *turns his back on him, and moves away. On turning again and seeing* MR. BROWN *still in position he gives him a cool word of dismissal.*)

PONSONBY I don't think you need stay, Mr. Brown.

(*And* MR. BROWN *goes.* COLONEL PONSONBY *walks to the window, and stands looking out, not seeming to be aware of the entry of the three gentlemen who now make their appearance, till he hears himself addressed. Of the three,* MR. HERMANN STAHL *is evidently the leading spirit: he is also much the most angry.* CANON DUCKWORTH *is polite and deprecating.* MR. EDGAR BOEHM *is merely humbly hurt. A little taken aback at seeing the man of whom he has come to complain standing in his way,* MR. STAHL *hesitates for a moment; then starts his attack.*)

STAHL Colonel Ponsonby, we are here wishing to see Her Majesty.

PONSONBY I'm afraid that is impossible, Mr. Stahl. Her Majesty is engaged, and is not to be disturbed.

STAHL Perhaps you know why we have come?

PONSONBY Possibly.

STAHL Then it may not be necessary that we should trouble Her Majesty at all. I will make my complaint first to you. (PONSONBY *bows attention.*) Then, if you satisfy me, no more need be said.

PONSONBY   I am all attention. Pray, what is your complaint?

STAHL   This morning, I and my two friends go to the stables to get ponies for our morning ride. They are refused to us.

PONSONBY   But, of course, it would have been contrary to orders for you to be allowed the ponies, without permission.

STAHL   Without whose permission?

PONSONBY   Without mine.

STAHL   Contrary to *your* orders, then, you mean?

PONSONBY   Contrary to orders, I said.

STAHL   And those orders are given by you?

PONSONBY   Those orders are given by me.

STAHL   And has the Queen told you to give those orders?

PONSONBY   Mr. Stahl, I am here in the Queen's service.

STAHL   Ah, you do not answer me! No. That is *no* answer.

PONSONBY   It is a sufficient answer. And it is the only answer to your inquiry that I can make to you.

STAHL   Then we shall see. If I cannot see the Queen, I shall write to her!

PONSONBY   Certainly. To that I have not the slightest objection.

STAHL   And if you had, it would make no difference. You are exceeding your orders, and you know it. It is an outrage! But here I give you this chance. You say it must be only with your permission that we are to be allowed ponies. Very well! I ask you for that permission — now.

PONSONBY   Not to-day, Mr. Stahl.

DUCKWORTH (*pleadingly*)   But, Colonel Ponsonby, is it not very unusual for permission to be thus refused?

PONSONBY   It is rather, Sir. I'm sorry.

DUCKWORTH   Then why — why do you do it?

PONSONBY   In the execution of my duty, Sir.

DUCKWORTH   But that explains nothing.

PONSONBY   No: duty cannot always be explained — unfortunately.

DUCKWORTH   I feel very much hurt.

BOEHM It is the first time that I have ever as a guest been refused a horse, anywhere.

PONSONBY A horse? Oh, I did not know that you ever rode a *horse*, Mr. Boehm. Would you like one?

BOEHM A horse? No, no, I do not. I only ride ponies.

PONSONBY To-day, unfortunately, the ponies are not available.

STAHL (*demandingly*) Why not?

PONSONBY They are having a rest, Mr. Stahl — after too much exercise.

DUCKWORTH But, Colonel Ponsonby, do you mean that — that I am never to be allowed to ride again?

PONSONBY If you will ride with me to-morrow, Canon Duckworth, I shall be delighted.

STAHL *I* shall not ride with you!

PONSONBY I did not suppose you would; nor did I offer it.

STAHL So it comes to this; that the order is only against *me*. Oh yes! I have seen the footmen riding — the footmen! I have seen it. Do you deny it?

PONSONBY No, Sir. Sometimes, when the ponies need exercise, the footmen do ride them. Some of them ride very well.

STAHL But *I* do not know how to ride, you mean? Let me tell you, Colonel Ponsonby, that I was trained to ride in the Cavalry of the German Army.

PONSONBY So I believe.

STAHL And it is only now that I have become a civilian, that you, because you are in the army, put upon me this insult!

PONSONBY We don't do that sort of thing in England, Mr. Stahl.

STAHL It is the last time that it shall be done to *me*. I shall write to Her Majesty now at once — for an explanation. (*Turning to* BOEHM *angrily*) Why do you not say something?

BOEHM (*despondently*) There is nothing to say. It is all very unfortunate. If I do not get my ride, I must go for a walk. It is necessary for my digestion.

K

STAHL You say you will go for a *walk?* You think? Then perhaps you would like *me* to go for a walk too. A walk! It is a fine day: so *we walk! we walk!*

(*Behind them the door opens.* THE QUEEN *enters followed by her Lady Secretary.*)

PONSONBY (*quietly*) Gentlemen, the Queen.

THE QUEEN Good morning, Gentlemen.

STAHL Oh, your Majesty, may I be permitted . . .

THE QUEEN No, Mr. Stahl. I shall not need you this morning for anything. I heard you proposing a walk. It's just the day for it, such a fine morning. Do go.

STAHL We were wishing to ride, your Majesty.

THE QUEEN Hadn't you better take a walk for a change? You've been riding so much lately; and sometimes the ponies need a rest. So go a walk. Colonel Ponsonby, I'm going over to the stables. Will you come with me?

PONSONBY With pleasure, your Majesty.

THE QUEEN Miss Somers, bring the bag of sugar for the ponies.

(THE QUEEN *goes out, followed by* COLONEL PONSONBY.)

BOEHM (*resignedly*) Are you coming, Canon Duckworth?

DUCKWORTH I shall be delighted. After all a walk *is* very good, very good for one; but one takes it so seldom. Mr. Stahl, you will not desert us, I hope? Walking, we change the subject.

STAHL (*after a fierce moment of indecision*) I will come!

(*He claps his hat violently on his head and follows.*)

(*Enter* MR. BROWN: *he crosses and stands looking after them through the window.*)

BROWN Eh! There they go, harmless for once—all three of 'em, doing the thing they better know how—walking. Ah, John Brown, ye know how to manage 'em all . . . men — *and* women.

EXTREMES MEET

1874

It is the afternoon of a certain day in the early 'seventies (the actual date can be verified by those whom dates interest), and in the drawing-room of the Deanery at Westminster, LADY AUGUSTA STANLEY *sits waiting, a little impatiently, while the* DEAN *(possibly for the soothing of his wife's nerves), makes a studied show of patience and quiet confidence by sitting lost in the book which he is reading, and pays no attention when* LADY AUGUSTA *gets up, and goes across to look at the clock.*

LADY AUGUSTA Five-minutes-to. I do hope he's not going to be late.

DEAN STANLEY He won't be, my dear.

LADY A. But I begged him so particularly to be *early*.

THE DEAN Then I am quite sure he will be. After all, five minutes *is* five minutes.

LADY A. Yes: but the Queen is always *so* punctual. And with Mr. Carlyle coming all the way from Chelsea in an omnibus, and having to change on the way, what is there to be sure about?

THE DEAN Only that he still has the frugal mind of a Scotsman, my dear — preferring omnibuses to cabs.

LADY A. I wish I'd sent James to bring him.

THE DEAN Unnecessary, as it happens: for here he comes.

(The door has opened; the BUTLER *announces* 'MR. CARLYLE', *and withdraws to make way for the expected visitor, a crumpled careworn figure, dressed almost ceremoniously for the occasion — since he is here to meet Royalty by special request — an honour for which, without wishing it, he has had to wait long.)*

LADY A. Oh, Mr. Carlyle, I'm so glad you have come. I was getting quite anxious.

CARLYLE You'd no reason to be, Ma'am. 'Tis yet four minutes to the hour; and four o'clock, you said.

LADY A.   Yes: but it would never have done for the Queen to
have come first: and she might have been early.

CARLYLE   Doesn't the Queen generally 'come first'?

THE DEAN   Not for appointments, my dear Carlyle. Queens
must not be kept waiting.

CARLYLE   Have ye a brush anywhere?

THE DEAN   A brush?

CARLYLE   Aye; out there at the back (I came in by the wrong way)
there was a dustman emptying his pans; and he's emptied some of it
over me.

LADY A.   Why, yes, he has indeed! Arthur, run and fetch a brush,
quick! (*The* DEAN *goes.*) Oh, Mr. Carlyle, how unfortunate!

CARLYLE   Eh, it's what we all come to: dust to dust, ashes to
ashes. 'Twas a good reminder, and me in my Sunday best, which
most go to meet God in, so as to be seen of men. I'm in it to meet
her gracious Majesty, the Queen; and first time of putting it on, 'tis
this that happens! (*Then, as the* DEAN *returns, and starts brushing his
back.*) Thank ye, thank ye. Aye, 'tis more than twenty years since
we last met — she and I. Maybe, she'll not remember me.

LADY A.   (*in disappointed surprise*) You have already met the
Queen, Mr. Carlyle?

CARLYLE   Aye. I took off my hat to her, and she bowed. That's
all there was to it. Kings and Queens have to do such a lot of
bowing, it means naething to them. But I remember it well. I
can even remember the hat I wore, and how I had a wonder —
was it good enough to take off to a Queen. But whether or no, she
bowed to it.

THE DEAN   (*having not-too-perfectly-finished the brushing*) That's
better.

CARLYLE   I thank you. But talking of hats, Lady Augusta, will
ye forgive me for asking what for are you wearing your own —
your bonnet, I mean, when ye're expecting so great a visitor?

LADY A.   Oh, one has to, Mr. Carlyle. Didn't you know?
When the Queen does one the honour of calling, one always puts

on one's bonnet, so as not to appear more at home in your own house than she. While she is in it, it becomes the Queen's.

CARLYLE   Ah! A very pretty bit of make-believe, that. Then have I got to keep my hat about me?

THE DEAN   No, Carlyle, that is not necessary. Men's headdresses being less noticeable than women's, we are let off.

LADY A.   Oh! here she is. And there's the clock striking, always so punctual. Arthur . . .

(*The* BUTLER *enters, and announces with ceremony:*)

BUTLER   If you please, my lady, Her Majesty the Queen is here.

LADY A.   You must excuse us, Mr. Carlyle: we have to go to the door to meet Her Majesty.

CARLYLE   Have I to come too?

LADY A.   No, no. You just stay here.

CARLYLE   And what have I to say when she speaks to me?

THE DEAN   (*genially*) Anything that comes into your head, my dear Carlyle.

(*They go out.* CARLYLE *is left alone to ponder the situation in which he finds himself.*)

CARLYLE   (*meditatively*) Aye, aye, so it's come to this, that here I am just for a show; and one of my own books set out to keep me company. (*He takes it up from the table, looks at it, and lays it down again.*) What a pair, the two of us! Eh, Jenny, my poor lass, how this would have made you laugh. And you liked laughing — at me, didn't you?

(*He has sat down, but rises again as the door opens.* THE QUEEN *enters, with the* DEAN *and his wife as following accompaniment. With a look of kindly interest, and a slight inclination of the head, she recognizes the presence of the old Celebrity she has come to meet, before presentation is actually made. The* DEAN *does it in correct form.*)

THE DEAN   May I present to your Majesty — Mr. Carlyle?

(*And thus formally made known to each other, the two exchange bows —* THE QUEEN *with her accustomed dignity,* MR. CARLYLE *a little stiffly, as one not well used to ceremony.*)

THE QUEEN   We are so pleased to meet you, Mr. Carlyle.

CARLYLE   Your Majesty does me great honour.

THE QUEEN   Lady Augusta was so kind as to say that she would arrange so that I might meet you here.

CARLYLE   It was from her that I heard of your Majesty's good wish.

THE QUEEN   I have long wished it, Mr. Carlyle; more especially since — since your great bereavement.

CARLYLE   That's kind of ye, Ma'am.

THE QUEEN   It was — (*she seats herself*) — it was nine years ago, was it not, that you lost your dear wife?

CARLYLE   Aye: lost my wife, and kept me life. Better had it been the other way.

THE QUEEN   Ah, yes: that is how I have always felt since I lost my dear husband, the Prince.

CARLYLE   There ye're wrong, Ma'am. Your people still wanted you for great service. But there's few now to be wanting me.

THE QUEEN   But your work, Mr. Carlyle.

CARLYLE   That's over and done now — such as it was.

THE QUEEN   You have finished writing — your histories?

CARLYLE   Aye; all but one.

THE QUEEN   What is that?

CARLYLE   'A poor thing, but mine own,' Ma'am, as they make Shakespeare say (though he never did). I'm writing it now.

THE QUEEN   Your own life, you mean? That must be very interesting.

CARLYLE   Very frightening, Ma'am. It's a fearsome thing to look into yourself and see the man you are, and the man you might have been.

THE QUEEN   Well, we do all fall short of what we would have wished to do in some things. As I know, only too well.

CARLYLE   You've been a good Queen, Ma'am.

THE QUEEN   I had a good teacher, Mr. Carlyle.

CARLYLE Aye, aye. But there's wisdom — rare in Kings — of knowing you can be taught. And now, with your Majesty's permission, I'll sit down. I'm an old man.

THE QUEEN (*generously covering this breach of etiquette*) Oh, yes; do sit down, all of you. (*They sit.*) . . . Have you yet read Mr. Theodore Martin's Life of the Prince Consort, Mr. Carlyle?

CARLYLE I have not, Ma'am.

THE QUEEN I think everyone should read it. Then my people would understand — better — what they have lost.

CARLYLE We all need better understanding, Ma'am, of what we've lost.

THE QUEEN I like to hear you say that, Mr. Carlyle. I've found it so true — myself . . . It was your dear wife you meant, was it not?

CARLYLE I meant everything, Ma'am, that one's let go, that one might have kept had one known better — to be more merciful.

THE QUEEN (*a little surprised*) Merciful, you say?

CARLYLE Yes, Ma'am; it's a thing some of us don't learn till it's too late: more especially with those we love — through not thinking.

THE QUEEN 'The quality of mercy is not strained,' Shakespeare says, does he not?

CARLYLE Aye; so he *says*. But it's a sore strain man puts on it when he least knows what he's doing. When we are thinking only of ourselves, we've small mercy for others.

THE QUEEN You have studied human nature, Mr. Carlyle; and no doubt you understand it better than I do, for I must confess that it often puzzles me.

CARLYLE It's the greatest puzzle that God has set for man in this world; and when we've solved it we shall have solved everything.

THE QUEEN Yes: I suppose it is the most difficult thing of all to understand and treat rightly — especially for those who rule, and hold power. It may sound unsuitable, but Kings do need to be humble.

CARLYLE Ye've said a wise thing, Ma'am, that some would find difficult to follow.

THE QUEEN Yes: to be a good King is very difficult. The Prince, my husband, was really a King by nature. To him I owed everything.

CARLYLE It's a great thing to know, Ma'am; and a great satisfaction the knowing of it must be.

THE QUEEN Yes, I am thankful that I do know it — that I have always known it, so well . . . But now about your writing, your histories, Mr. Carlyle: tell me, what is the last history that you have written?

CARLYLE The life of Frederick the Great, Ma'am — 'the Great' as they call him.

THE QUEEN But he was great, was he not?

CARLYLE Aye; with a lot of littleness added to it. And 'twas the littleness, maybe, that made half of his success for him. There's greater men that have died failures.

THE QUEEN Yes: Napoleon was a great man, was he not?

CARLYLE Aye, Napoleon: the man that didn't know where to stop. Had he known that, he might have conquered the world.

THE QUEEN (*with patriotic conviction*) Not *England*.

CARLYLE England, and Asia, and Africa, and America.

THE QUEEN Dear me! Most extraordinary that you should think that, Mr. Carlyle . . . But he *didn't*.

CARLYLE No, he didn't, Ma'am; but he'd got the idea of the United States of Europe — the same as they had over in America. But he made the mistake of thinking that France had got to be the head of it. Now, if he'd only had the sense to give up that notion, he'd have won; and Great Britain would have had to come in.

THE QUEEN Then I'm glad he didn't.

CARLYLE Well, Ma'am, there's no knowing what you might be glad of, fifty years from now.

THE QUEEN That won't be in *my* reign, Mr. Carlyle.

CARLYLE No, Ma'am; but it's well to think of your sons, and your sons' sons, and what may be happening in their day to this England and Scotland of ours.

THE QUEEN What do you think is likely to happen?

CARLYLE He'd be a great prophet, Ma'am — or a great fool, maybe — who'd think he could say what's likely to happen. There's only one thing we can be nigh sure of — whatever it's to be, it's likely to be bad.

THE QUEEN Why do you think that, Mr. Carlyle?

CARLYLE It's to no good end the way the world's going these days, Ma'am. So many working for a pittance so the rest can play; so many kept starving so that others can go stuffed. Money's a god that has no mercy; he lets none of 'em off; them as have not he breaks one way, and them as have he breaks another — and a worse.

THE QUEEN Yes; it's all very sad: but poverty seems to be a necessary condition, with so many people in the world. And you must have money, Mr. Carlyle.

CARLYLE Aye; if you've a good use for it, and do right work for it. You are a working-woman yourself, Ma'am; and it's work that's worth doing — done rightly. But if your Majesty was to put out of Court all them that didn't work, and were no good to anybody, there'd be more room, for ye to get to know some as would be better worth knowing, Ma'am.

THE QUEEN In the Highlands, Mr. Carlyle, I do know many quite poor people whom I regard as real friends; some of them with such good minds, and so interesting.

CARLYLE And a blessed change for ye, Ma'am, that must be — after London.

THE QUEEN Yes: I never have liked London. But I have to be here sometimes — far more than I wish to be. And you yourself live in London, Mr. Carlyle. Why do you?

CARLYLE So as to be near books that I cannot afford to buy for myself, Ma'am. With books, and their sellers, and their publishers, it's here I have to be, where all the folly and misery and sickness of the world are at their worst — and none, seemingly, that knows how to cure any of it. Yet so much doing that there's no peace to be had anywhere.

THE QUEEN Well, of course, there are a great many things being done, that one can't approve of — changes not only foolish but wrong. Still the country is prosperous.

CARLYLE Aye; prosperous — like to those Gadarene swine, Ma'am, which thought themselves properous, maybe, while they were all running down the hill: but the water was waiting for 'em at the bottom.

THE QUEEN But do you think England *is* going down hill, Mr. Carlyle?

THE DEAN (*tactfully intervening*) If Mr. Carlyle says Yes to that, Ma'am, your Majesty must remember that he has always taken the prophet Jeremiah as his model, believing that the best way of warning people against danger is to frighten them well beforehand. He has been frightening us for forty years, and as a consequence we have managed to survive the dangers he foresaw for us.

THE QUEEN I see. Well, Mr. Carlyle, I'm not going to let you frighten *me*. But even if we don't quite agree, I have found everything you say most interesting. You say things in such an interesting way that one cannot help being interested. And now, dear Lady Augusta, I'm afraid that I must go, though I should have liked to stay so much longer.

(*She rises. They all rise with her.*)

Good-bye, and thank you very much for asking Mr. Carlyle to come and meet me. Mr. Carlyle, meeting you has given me great pleasure.

CARLYLE Very honoured, your Majesty.

THE QUEEN And I hope it may not be the last time.

CARLYLE Eh, but it will be, Ma'am, I'm thinking: my ganging-about days are over. But I thank your Majesty for the wish, and for having given me this day to remember.

THE QUEEN I also shall remember it, I can assure you, Mr. Carlyle. Good-bye. (*She gives him her hand.*) No, Lady Augusta, please don't you come. You stay with Mr. Carlyle. Thank you, Dr. Stanley, if you will be so good.

(*And with the* DEAN *as escort, she goes out to her carriage;* LADY AUGUSTA *and* MR. CARLYLE *go to the window to watch her departure.*)

LADY A. Well, Mr. Carlyle?

CARLYLE   Aye, there she goes; a real Queen by the look of her: and a strange thing it must be to be a Queen, these days.

LADY A.   Tell me — how does she strike you?

CARLYLE   Oh, a very good, well-meaning woman. And no fool, either.

LADY A.   From you, Mr. Carlyle, that is high praise, I suppose?

CARLYLE   What else? I might say the same of you, and of a few others, maybe: but not so many as to make it common . . . I see here ye put out one of my books for her to know me by: a kind thought for both of us.

LADY A.   We always have it there, Mr. Carlyle.

CARLYLE   Did you see her look at it when she said 'histories' — helping her to make sure that I'd written any? And afraid she was lest I'd be asking whether she'd ever read one.

LADY A.   Oh, not afraid, Mr. Carlyle!

CARLYLE   Aye, for fear of having to hurt my feelings telling the truth — which it wouldn't have done. I'm no such fool. She learned to do what she'd had to do, without me helping her.

(*Re-enter* DEAN STANLEY.)

THE DEAN   Well, Carlyle, you'll be glad to hear you've made a very good impression on Her Majesty.

CARLYLE   Impression, eh?

THE DEAN   'What an interesting man!' was her first remark when we'd left the room. 'I'm so glad to have met him.'

CARLYLE   Ah; a straightforward statement, and true, maybe, but not so original that I've not heard it said before.

THE DEAN   And then, Her Majesty went on, 'Now that I have met him, I must really try to read one of his books. Which of them do you think I should be most likely to understand?'

CARLYLE   And what did you say to that?

THE DEAN   I said that, with time, I was sure Her Majesty would understand many of them; but that it would take more time than she could spare.

CARLYLE A canny answer, that was. So ye've headed her off. Understand? Who is there that does in all the world? Only John Ruskin, of all of ye, understands what I'm really after — not what's in my books, but in my heart. . . . What did she say then?

THE DEAN Well, nothing to *that*. What she *did* say was 'I'm sure he's a very good, well-meaning man. But,' she went on (she has a very quick eye, you know), 'he needs someone to look after him. His coat was very dusty.'

CARLYLE (*pointing an accusing finger*) Now whose fault was that?

THE DEAN Mine. I said so. I told Her Majesty exactly what had happened.

CARLYLE And what did she say?

THE DEAN She said, 'Oh? then that explains it.'

CARLYLE And couldn't have said truer. Lady Augusta, your servant. Good-bye. I thank you. If she's as wise and honest as I think her to be, she won't try.

LADY A. Won't try what?

CARLYLE Reading me. Mr. Dean, will you ask your man to call a cab for me? I came up by the omnibus; but I'll be going back in more style. After meeting high Majesty 'tis the least I can do to show my respect, and my sense of the great honour that's been done me. But the thought comes to me again — how Jenny would ha' laughed. . . . Good-bye to ye.

LADY A. Good-bye; and mind you get home safely.

(*He goes out, accompanied by the* DEAN.)

Yes: Jenny would have laughed. Poor man! How he misses her.

'THIS IS THE HEIR'

August 1875

THE QUEEN *is sitting in one of the tartan-clad apartments of Balmoral Castle, spending the first weeks of her Highland holiday in an environment which, by accentuation of her Majesty's historic sense of Stuart ancestry, relegates to a subsidiary position the regrettably intervening House of Hanover. Before her stands her devoted personal attendant,* MR. JOHN BROWN — *not yet made 'Esquire' by letters patent; but already a power behind the throne, cannily feeling his way to a position of influence and familiarity which, while amusing to mere onlookers, is deeply resented by some whom it more nearly concerns.*

THE QUEEN   Well, Brown? Has the carriage gone to the station to meet Mr. Disraeli?

BROWN   I believe it has, Ma'am; but ye'll no' have him here yet awhile: the train will be late.

THE QUEEN   Oh? Why?

BROWN   It always is, Ma'am; except when your Majesty comes by it.

THE QUEEN   What very bad management! I shall have to speak about it. When my Prime Minister comes to see me, he must be got here in proper time ... Oh, by the way, Brown, in the letter I had from him this morning he desired to send you his compliments.

BROWN   The same to him, Ma'am, from me, when ye've the opportunity for it.

THE QUEEN   Very well; and now, Brown, you must go, as I have to see the Prince before Mr. Disraeli arrives.

BROWN   Aye; he's waiting for ye, Ma'am, out there.

THE QUEEN   Then tell him to come in.

BROWN   He shall be told, Ma'am. Just now we're not on speaking terms.

THE QUEEN   Indeed? What is the matter?

BROWN It's just a little difference of opinion, Ma'am, about my position here. Being young, he hasna' got all the experience he should have, maybe. It'll blow over.

THE QUEEN Indeed, I hope so. I can't have members of my family quarrelling with you, Brown.

BROWN No, Ma'am, and we'll see that it shan't happen. So that's why, maybe, not speaking for a while is safer.

(*A* GENTLEMAN *in Attendance enters.*)

GENTLEMAN May it please your Majesty, His Royal Highness the Prince of Wales begs to inquire whether your Majesty is yet ready to receive him.

THE QUEEN Ask His Royal Highness to come.

(*The* GENTLEMAN *retires.*)

BROWN Then now I'll be going.

(THE QUEEN *gives him a friendly nod of dismissal, and very self-respectfully he takes himself off. Laying aside diary and letters* THE QUEEN *rises from her writing-table, and moves to an easy chair, in which she seats herself somewhat magisterially to await* THE PRINCE'S *arrival. Just now their relations are not quite comfortable; and though when he enters, she receives from him the conventional filial salute, she does not return it; nor does she tell him to sit down; and conscious that the omission is intentional,* THE PRINCE *remains standing.*)

THE PRINCE Good morning, Mama.

THE QUEEN Good morning, Bertie.

THE PRINCE How are you? Better?

THE QUEEN Much better than I was before we left London. But I have still far more to do than I have now really the strength for.

THE PRINCE I am always quite willing to help you, Mama, if you will let me.

THE QUEEN That, as you ought to know, is impossible. In all that I have to do, by myself, in matters of State, only your poor dear Father could have helped me . . . But now, Bertie, I have some very important things to say to you. And as Mr. Disraeli will be here presently, I had to see *you* first.

THE PRINCE (*dutifully*) Yes, Mama? (*An impressive pause follows.*)

THE QUEEN It is about your visit to India.

THE PRINCE Yes, Mama; what about it? I was told that you had arranged everything to your own satisfaction. But I was not consulted.

THE QUEEN There was no special reason why you should be, as regards all the State-arrangements. But there are certain personal matters about which it is necessary that I should speak to you — very seriously.

THE PRINCE I am all attention, Mama.

THE QUEEN Bertie, you have got to be very careful of your conduct while you are in India — more careful than I think you quite realize.

THE PRINCE In what way, Mama?

THE QUEEN In *all* ways — some which I would rather not name.

THE PRINCE How do you think that I shall not be careful?

THE QUEEN I can only judge by what I *know*.

THE PRINCE By what you have been *told*.

THE QUEEN I have no doubt that what I have been told — of some of your associations — is the *truth*. I wish it were not.

THE PRINCE (*stung to protest*) Why are you sending me to India, Mama — if you cannot *trust* me?

THE QUEEN Partly because I wish you to gain experience, for the position to which some day you will be called; and partly because you have not been behaving well *here*. A change will be good for you. You have got into a bad set, and you had better get out of it: all this fast living and pleasure-seeking, horse-racing, card-playing, betting and gambling — *and* other things besides! You are setting the nation a bad example, Bertie.

THE PRINCE One has to do something. You don't let me do anything.

THE QUEEN Don't let you do what? What don't I let you do?

THE PRINCE Anything useful; anything to train me for what I shall have to be some day.

THE QUEEN There's plenty you *could* do, if you had the mind for it.

THE PRINCE Being a show-piece, holding reviews, laying foundation-stones, opening hospitals, making speeches that are not mine. One doesn't need a mind for that sort of thing. If I went on doing that *all* the time (and I do a good lot of it) I should die of it. It would bore me stiff.

THE QUEEN Don't use slang, Bertie.

THE PRINCE Can't you realize that I must — live?

THE QUEEN There are ways and ways of living; you've chosen the wrong way. Well, in India, surely, you will find enough to interest you.

THE PRINCE Yes, I'm glad I'm going.

THE QUEEN And in letting you go, I am putting a great trust in you. Remember that!

THE PRINCE For the first time, Mama. Though it doesn't seem like it.

THE QUEEN You could have had it sooner had you deserved it. I had hoped that your terrible illness would have done something — but it hasn't, I'm afraid.

THE PRINCE Oh, yes, it has; it has made me feel ever so much older; but you still treat me like a child.

THE QUEEN I'm not treating you like a child now. I'm sending you to India, as my representative.

THE PRINCE Are you? That's one of the things I wanted to know. I've been told that Lord Northbrook takes the view that he, as Viceroy, will remain your representative, and that I shall only be there as his guest.

THE QUEEN Of course, he can't cease to be Viceroy, just because you come. You can't take over his duties. That is not to be thought of.

THE PRINCE Neither can he take over from *me*, that I am of Royal blood and the Heir Apparent. Is he to take precedence of me — in public, I wish to know?

THE QUEEN There need be no question of precedence. He will receive you just as I receive any monarch visiting this country. You will be a guest of honour. He will never walk in front of you, if that's what you are afraid of.

THE PRINCE And when presentations are made, will they be to him or to me?

THE QUEEN It has all been arranged, Bertie; there is no need for you to trouble yourself.

THE PRINCE No, Mama. You are mistaken. The arrangement has not yet been made — not to *my* satisfaction. I went to see Lord Salisbury yesterday; and he agrees with me that, while I am there, I should have precedence of everybody.

THE QUEEN You went to see Lord Salisbury! You had no right to do that without my permission.

THE PRINCE Whether I was right or not, I have done so.

THE QUEEN Lord Salisbury ought to have known better than to let you come without first consulting me.

THE PRINCE Very well; then you had better tell him to hand in his resignation.

THE QUEEN Don't talk nonsense, Bertie.

THE PRINCE I talk as I find things. What use is there to talk sense, if I am not allowed to use my own? You send me to India; you trust me, you say, with something that is very important; but you still pull all the strings — that I have to dance to. Well, do not be surprised if, at such a distance, some of the strings get broken. I might do something, Mama, that will surprise you.

THE QUEEN And what, pray, is that?

THE PRINCE Oh, well, it was just an idea for making myself more at home with the people of India. It was Lord Arthur Somerset who is going with me that said it — only for a joke, perhaps; but the idea rather pleased me. He said that if, for the time while I was there, I became a Mahommedan, or a Hindoo, or both — I should make myself very popular.

THE QUEEN What a shocking suggestion! Such things ought not to be said even in joke.

THE PRINCE Well, Mama, I do not see why. You are Queen of India, over more than three hundred million people; and when I have to be its King, would it not be a good thing for me to be of the same religion as most of my subjects? It is only like what you do here, you know, where by law you have to be of the Established Religion; south of the Tweed, you are Church of England, but when you go to Scotland, you seem to become a Presbyterian. And you would make yourself very popular in Ireland, Mama, if when you went there (which you never do) you became a Roman Catholic.

THE QUEEN Bertie, if you go on talking such wicked nonsense, I shall not let you go to India at all.

THE PRINCE It is too late to do that, Mama. You could not explain it to the papers, now that all the preparations have been made.

THE QUEEN Oh, yes, I could. If I were to fall ill, it would be quite impossible for you to go. You would have to remain in England — in case.

THE PRINCE You are not going to fall ill, Mama; and you know that you are much too fond of going about in all kinds of weather for the Court Circular to make it look possible — even to keep me from going to India . . . Mama dear, shall we not stop quarrelling? I will try to do everything that you wish me to do — even if I do a few other things to please myself now and then, in my spare time. You have kindly allowed me to take some of my own friends with me. For that I am grateful.

THE QUEEN Yes; but I don't think you have made a very good choice, Bertie. One of them, I am told, was very nearly concerned in a divorce-case. And I doubt whether any of them are regular churchgoers — even if they go at all. And that is one of the things that I very particularly wish you to be careful to do. It is so important for the people of India to see that we are a religious nation, and that we do observe Sunday as it ought to be observed (though not so well as they do here in Scotland). And there are two other things, Bertie. You must remember that the climate of India is very trying till people get accustomed to it — for which you will not have time. So do try to be *moderate* over your eating and drinking; and also to keep reasonable hours. Make a practice of going to bed at ten o'clock whenever it is possible.

THE PRINCE   Anything else, Mama?

THE QUEEN   Only that I shall expect you to write to me regularly once a week. Now don't forget, Bertie!

THE PRINCE   I shall not *forget* anything that you have told me, Mama. Whether I shall be able to do all, is another matter.

THE QUEEN   What is your difficulty?

THE PRINCE   I will remember to keep the English Sunday, Mama; that is, I will go to church in the morning; but I will not observe the Scotch Sabbath; we do not do that in England, and I cannot do it in India.

THE QUEEN   I did not ask you to do it, Bertie; you are making unnecessary difficulties.

THE PRINCE   And you, Mama, are making unnecessary rules, I think. Please do let me go to India as a grown-up man; and I promise that my visit shall be a success; but not if you make a child of me.

(*Enter* GENTLEMAN *in Attendance.*)

THE QUEEN   Yes, what is it?

GENTLEMAN   May it please your Majesty, Mr. Disraeli is in attendance.

THE QUEEN   Oh yes; let him come in.

(*The* GENTLEMAN *retires.*)

Now Bertie, you can go. I don't want you. Mr. Disraeli has come specially to consult me on all these matters that we have been talking about.

THE PRINCE   Is not that a reason why I should remain?

THE QUEEN   No, it is not at all necessary. Now go!

(*The* GENTLEMAN *in Attendance enters, followed by* MR. DISRAELI.)

GENTLEMAN   May it please your Majesty, Mr. Disraeli.

(*The* GENTLEMAN *withdraws.*)

THE QUEEN   Oh, how do you do, Mr. Disraeli? I am so glad that you have been able to come.

(MR. DISRAELI *bows low over the hand she offers him. A gesture from Her Majesty quickens* THE PRINCE'S *departure; but not before* MR. DISRAELI *has managed to insert a deferential bow to one for whom he has a high regard, and a good deal of sympathy.*)

DISRAELI I thank your Majesty for so graciously permitting an audience which was not by command.

THE QUEEN I am always ready, Mr. Disraeli, to receive my Prime Minister, when advice becomes necessary.

DISRAELI Indeed yes, Ma'am; I have good reason to be aware how graciously ready your Majesty is at all times to consider any advice that it may be my humble duty to offer. But now, Ma'am, it is not to advise but to be advised that I am here. It may be unconstitutional, but as your Majesty's First Minister, though old in years, I am still young in experience concerning matters of Court and State where your Majesty's judgment and experience are unrivalled. So, where I find difficulty, your Majesty finds none.

THE QUEEN Pray, what is *your* difficulty, Mr. Disraeli?

DISRAELI It is, Ma'am, over this matter of precedence, as between your Majesty's representative the Viceroy, who holds a symbolic office second to none, and one who by reason of his Royal blood and birth will represent your Majesty more intimately and personally, and whose appeal to the people of India will therefore necessarily be of a more moving and a more mystical character. Kingship is what the East best understands, and most reveres; and it is inevitable that when His Royal Highness sets foot in India, he will be to all its teeming millions not merely an envoy of the State, but an incarnation of that supreme personal Sovereignty to which, in distant time, he is the destined Heir.

We are faced therefore with a difficulty due to the outlook of an Eastern people, different from our own; and nothing must be done to diminish in the popular mind the splendour and prestige of the Prince's person, when as Heir to the throne, he comes to receive, on your Majesty's behalf, the homage of that vast Empire.

THE QUEEN But the Viceroy, while he *is* Viceroy, cannot possibly divest himself of his office, Mr. Disraeli. I could not allow that for a moment.

DISRAELI No, Ma'am. Of course not. And therefore, I would

suggest — or rather I would ask your Majesty to advise, whether it would not be well, after the Viceroy has received His Royal Highness on his arrival, for the Prince thereafter to make his Royal Progress entirely alone; and that the Viceroy himself should not be present at any of the State-functions where, with Indian Rulers about him, the Prince will hold his Court?

THE QUEEN   Yes, Mr. Disraeli, that will be a very good arrangement. I have already told the Prince that there will be no question of his ever appearing to come second.

DISRAELI   In that case, Ma'am, I have no further cause for anxiety. I might well have been assured that your Majesty's great experience would already have envisaged and solved the difficulty.

THE QUEEN   Yes, Mr. Disraeli; I think India is quite large enough for the Viceroy and the Prince both to be there without having to sit in each other's laps.

DISRAELI   How well and wittily — and kindly — your Majesty has administered the reproof which I feel I deserve.

THE QUEEN   Mr. Disraeli, I was far from intending any reproof. It was quite right, if you had any doubt, that you should come and consult me.

DISRAELI   Then, Ma'am, with your Majesty's gracious permission, may I now say further, something which I have deeply at heart, and which I trust will not be unwelcome — to a Mother's ear?

THE QUEEN   Anything you wish to say, I am ready to hear.

DISRAELI   Ma'am, the Prince, your son and heir, is about to do a great service to his country, and to this the greatest of its Imperial possessions, which may soon (if your Majesty so wills it) become an Empire not only in fact but in name. He has qualities, Ma'am, which will enable him to do that service with conspicuous success.

THE QUEEN   You really think so, Mr. Disraeli?

DISRAELI   I *know*; I am deeply sure of it ... I am conscious, Ma'am, that, in certain directions, the Prince has caused your Majesty disappointment.

THE QUEEN   Yes.

DISRAELI   Because — perhaps — of a somewhat delayed maturity of mind and purpose. He is still young, Ma'am; he has great grace of mind and attraction to people of all ranks alike; a valuable gift for one who is heir to a throne. He has also great ability which has not yet been tested. It is about to be tested, Ma'am. I am convinced that it will not be found wanting.

THE QUEEN   There is a great deal that he has yet to learn, and is not yet willing to learn — so it seems to me. He has no stability.

DISRAELI   May I beg your Majesty to give more weight to those other qualities which he does possess abundantly? I have had the privilege of late of conversations with him: he has done me the honour of confiding in me — his hopes and fears. He always speaks of your Majesty with affectionate devotion, and is deeply anxious that he may be allowed to do you and his country more service. And now the opportunity has come. A short while ago your Majesty confided to me a proposal of great moment — your royal wish to assume the title of Empress of India. As you know, Ma'am, I was doubtful at the time whether the assumption of a higher title of sovereignty over one part of your Majesty's dominions might not cause some jealousy here at home. We English are a loyal but a slow people; we cling to our traditions; I have always held that, at heart, we are a Conservative nation. Your Majesty would not wish to have that stability of political judgment disturbed by hasty improvisations and rash experiments, such as have recently been indulged in by politicians whom I will leave nameless.

THE QUEEN   No, indeed!

DISRAELI   Ma'am, the Prince's progress through India will draw upon you the eyes of the whole world. It is a great act of statesmanship, and will lead to great results. And one — to me, personally, the happiest — will be that it will enable me, as your Majesty's Prime Minister, to withdraw — not my opposition, but my demur, to the immediate fulfilment of your Majesty's wish to become Empress.

With the reality of Empire so splendidly demonstrated, I believe that your Majesty's assumption of the Imperial title will find acceptance in this country in a degree which it might not previously have secured. That, Ma'am, will be very largely due to the service which your son is about to render to his Queen and to his country. I am convinced, Ma'am, that from first to last he will prove himself worthy of the trust that you are about to place in him, and that you will no longer have to feel, Ma'am, a mother's disappointment.

THE QUEEN   It is not only a *mother's* disappointment that I feel, Mr. Disraeli. He is so — so totally unlike the dear Prince, his father.

DISRAELI   One cannot expect, Ma'am, replicas of that which was perfect.

THE QUEEN   No, no; of course not. And that is why my life is now such a lonely one. You see, I knew *him* so well — so perfectly.

DISRAELI   May I venture to suggest, Ma'am, that some of your trouble is because you know the Prince, your son — less well?

THE QUEEN   Yes, that is true. We don't understand each other. And that, perhaps, is my fault as well as his.

DISRAELI   By two such noble and generous natures, Ma'am, such a fault can surely be repaired.

THE QUEEN   I wish it could be.

DISRAELI   We authors, Ma'am, are readers of human character; and the more deeply we read, the more are we able to understand, to forgive, to make allowances. In that perfect work which has placed your Majesty in the forefront of living writers — admitting us to the daily intimacies of your royal family life — there are many tender and true readings of character, touched with such charity and understanding that as I read and re-read I am moved to something more than mere admiration. Ma'am, cannot your royal mind make similar allowances for the Prince your son? The measure of disappointment which your Majesty has experienced one can understand — one can sympathize. But there remains, believe me, Ma'am, something which you have yet to discover.

THE QUEEN   You mean that I *ought* to have discovered?

DISRAELI   Ah, Ma'am, I have dared greatly. May I hope to be forgiven?

THE QUEEN   There is nothing to forgive, Mr. Disraeli. I thank you deeply and sincerely for what you have said to me. I would like now to tell you that, as my Prime Minister, you have earned your Queen's trust; and you have made an anxious mother — happy.

DISRAELI   To have given happiness to such a Mother, to have earned the trust of such a Queen — what more can I wish? In the words of the aged Simeon, I can say truly 'Lord, now lettest thou thy servant depart in peace' . . . I shall not live to see the fulfilment of all that I hope and foresee for the Prince, your son and heir; nor could I wish it: the overwhelming shadow and bereavement — still far distant I trust — of the preceding event would be more than the heart of this old and faithful servant could bear without breaking. But believe me, Ma'am, that in all my political forecasts I have never made a more confident one than this — that he will perform his part worthily and well.

(THE QUEEN *rises from her chair.*)

THE QUEEN Thank you, Mr. Disraeli; you have said enough. I shall remember. I am grateful.

DISRAELI One last request, Ma'am, before I return to resume the burdens of my office: may I be permitted for a moment to speak with the Prince?

THE QUEEN I will send him to you. I have to go now for my morning ride; for I see Mr. Brown is there waiting for me with the pony. But, Mr. Disraeli, will you not stay at Balmoral for the night?

DISRAELI How kind, how gracious an offer! But that, I fear, Ma'am, is impossible. There is a meeting of the Cabinet to-morrow over which I shall have to preside.

THE QUEEN But that means you will have to travel all night.

DISRAELI It does, Ma'am.

THE QUEEN Oh, I'm sorry.

DISRAELI Ah, no, Ma'am, do not be. I am abundantly recompensed by the favour your Majesty has accorded me.

THE QUEEN Then now — good-bye. And remember that you are to be my next Minister in Attendance.

DISRAELI I had that already in mind, Ma'am, to ease this parting.

(THE QUEEN *gives him her hand.* DISRAELI *kisses it, bows her to the door, and remains reverentially bent till she has disappeared. Then straightening himself he moves to the window, and having watched*

her departure, adjusts himself decoratively to the short period of soli-
tude during which he has to await the arrival of THE PRINCE.
Presently the door opens, he turns; THE PRINCE *enters.*)

THE PRINCE   How do you do, Mr. Disraeli?

DISRAELI   How does your Royal Highness?

THE PRINCE   Oh, I'm all right — except when I'm all wrong.

DISRAELI   I begged leave to see your Royal Highness in order to
assure you that now there is going to be nothing wrong.

THE PRINCE   You mean — ?

DISRAELI   That your Royal Highness is about to have a smooth
passage to India; and that, by arrangement, so long as you are
there, the Viceroy will be kept — in his place.

THE PRINCE   Good! Mr. Disraeli, I think you must be a very
clever man.

DISRAELI   May I inquire why, at this particular moment, your
Royal Highness should think so?

THE PRINCE   Because just now when I met the Queen coming out,
she kissed me. It almost seemed as if you'd sent her to do it.

DISRAELI (*bowing his acknowledgments*)   Sir, I almost did.

(THE PRINCE *laughs.*)

THE QUEEN: GOD BLESS HER!

1877

A Scene from Home-Life in the Highlands

The august Lady is sitting in a garden-tent on the lawn of Balmoral Castle. Her parasol leans beside her. Writing-materials are on the table before her, and a small fan, for it is hot weather; also a dish of peaches. Sunlight suffuses the tent interior, softening the round contours of the face, and caressing pleasantly the small plump hand busy at letter-writing. The even flow of her penmanship is suddenly disturbed; picking up her parasol, she indulgently beats some unseen object, lying concealed against her skirts.

QUEEN No: don't scratch! Naughty! Naughty!

(She then picks up a hand-bell, rings it, and continues her writing. Presently a fine figure of a man in Highland costume appears in the tent-door. He waits awhile, then speaks in the strong Doric of his native wilds.)

MR. J. BROWN Was your Majesty wanting anything, or were you ringing only for the fun?

(To this brusque delivery Her Majesty responds with a cosy smile, for the special function of MR. JOHN BROWN is not to be a courtier; and, knowing what is expected of him, he lives up to it.)

QUEEN Bring another chair, Brown. And take Mop with you: he wants his walk.

MR. J. B. What kind of a chair are you wanting, Ma'am? Is it to put your feet on?

QUEEN No, no. It is to put a visitor on. Choose a nice one with a lean-back.

MR. J. B. With a lean back? Ho! Ye mean one that you can lean back in. What talk folk will bring with them from up south, to be sure! Yes, I'll get it for ye, Ma'am. Come, Mop, be a braw little wee mon, and tak' your walk!

(*And while his Royal Mistress resumes her writing, taking Mop by his 'lead', he prepares for departure.*)

Have ye seen the paper this morning yet? Ma'am.

(*The address of respect is thrown in by way of afterthought, or, as it were, reluctantly. Having to be in character, his way is to tread heavily on the border-line which divides familiarity from respect.*)

QUEEN   Not yet.

MR. J. B. (*departing*)   I'll bring it for ye, now.

QUEEN   You had better send it.

J. B. (*turning about*)   What did ye say? . . . Ma'am.

QUEEN   'Send it,' Brown, I said.   Mop mustn't be hurried. Take him round by the stables.

(*He goes: and* THE QUEEN, *with a soft, indulgent smile, that slowly flickers out as the labour of composition proceeds, resumes her writing.*)

(*Presently enters a liveried* FOOTMAN, *who stands at attention with the paper upon a salver. Touching the table at her side as an indication,* THE QUEEN *continues to write. With gingerly reverence the man lays down the paper and goes. Twice she looks at it before taking it up; then she unfolds it; then lays it down, and takes out her glasses; then begins reading. Evidently she comes on something she does not like; she pats the table impatiently, then exclaims:*)

Most extraordinary!

(*A wasp settles on the peaches.*)

And I wish one could kill all wicked pests as easily as you.

(*She makes a dab with the paper-knife, the wasp escapes.*)

Most extraordinary!

(*Relinquishing the pursuit of wasps, she resumes her reading.*)

(*In a little while* MR. JOHN BROWN *returns, both hands occupied. The chair he deposits by the tent-door, and hitches Mop's 'lead' to the back of that on which* THE QUEEN *is sitting. With the small beginnings of a smile she lowers the paper, and looks at him and his accompaniments.*)

QUEEN   Well, Brown? Oh, yes; that's quite a nice one. . . . I'm sure there's a wasps' nest somewhere; there are so many of them about.

J. B.   Eh, don't fash yourself! Wasps have a way of being aboot this time of year. It's the fruit they're after.

QUEEN   Yes: like Adam and Eve.

J. B.   That's just it, Ma'am.

QUEEN   You'd better take it away, Brown, or cover it; it's too tempting.

J. B.   (*removing the fruit*)   Ah! Now if God had only done that, maybe we'd still all be running aboot naked.

QUEEN   I'm glad He didn't, then.

J. B.   Ye're right, Ma'am.

QUEEN   The Fall made the human race decent, even if it did no good otherwise. Brown, I've dropped my glasses.

   (*He picks them up and returns them.*)

QUEEN   Thank you, Brown.

J. B.   So you're expecting a visitor, ye say?

QUEEN   Yes. You haven't seen Lord Beaconsfield yet, I suppose?

J. B.   Since he was to arrive off the train, you mean, Ma'am? No: he came early. He's in his room.

QUEEN   I hope they have given him a comfortable one.

J. B.   It's the one I used to have. There's a good spring-bed in it, and a kettle-ring for the whisky.

QUEEN   Oh, that's all right, then.

J. B.   Will he be staying for long, Ma'am?

QUEEN   Only for a week, I'm afraid. Why?

J. B.   It's about the shooting I was thinking: whether it was the deer or the grouse he'd want to be after.

QUEEN   I don't think Lord Beaconsfield is a sportsman.

J. B.   I know that, Ma'am, well enough. But there's many who are not sportsmen that think they've got to do it — when they come north of the Tweed.

QUEEN Lord Beaconsfield will not shoot, I'm sure. You remember him, Brown, being here before?

J. B. Last time was two years ago; he was no but Mr. Disraeli then. But he was the real thing, Ma'am: oh, a nice gentleman.

QUEEN He is always very nice to me.

J. B. I remember now, when he first came, he put a tip into ma hand. And when I let him know the liberty he had taken, 'Well, Mr. Brown,' he said, 'I've made a mistake, but I don't take it back again!'

QUEEN Very nice and sensible.

J. B. And indeed it was, Ma'am. Many a man would never have had the wit to leave well alone by just apologising for it. But there was an understandingness about him, that often you don't find. After that he always talked to me like an equal — just like yourself might do. But Lord, Ma'am, his ignorance, it was surprising!

QUEEN Most extraordinary you should think that, Brown!

J. B. Ah! You haven't talked to him as I have, Ma'am: only about politics, and poetry, and things like that — where, maybe, he knows a bit more than I do (though he didn't know his Burns so well as a man ought that thinks to make laws for Scotland!). But to hear him talking about natural facts, you'd think he was just inventing for to amuse himself! Do you know, Ma'am, he thought stags had white tails like rabbits, and that 'twas only when they wagged them so as to show, that you could shoot them? And he thought that you pulled a salmon out o' the water as soon as you'd hooked him. And he thought that a haggis was made of a sheep's head boiled in whisky. Oh, he's very innocent, Ma'am, if you get him where he's not expecting you.

QUEEN Well, Brown, there are some things you can teach him I don't doubt; and there are some things he can teach you. I'm sure he has taught me a great deal.

J. B. Ay? It's a credit to ye both, then.

QUEEN He lets me think for myself, Brown; and that's what so many of my Ministers would rather I didn't. They want me to be merely the receptacle of their own opinions. No, Brown, that's what we Stuarts are never going to do!

J. B.   Nor would I, Ma'am, if I were in your shoes. But believe me, you can do more, being a mere woman, so to speak, than many a king can do.

QUEEN   Yes; being a woman has its advantages, I know.

J. B.   For you can get round 'em, Ma'am; and you can put 'em off; and you can make it very awkward for them — very awkward — to have a difference of opinion with you.

QUEEN (*good-humouredly*)   You and I have had differences of opinion sometimes, Brown.

J. B.   True, Ma'am; that *has* happened; I've known it happen. And I've never regretted it, never! But the difference there is, Ma'am, that I'm not your Prime Minister. Had I been — you'd 'a been more stiff about giving in — naturally! Now there's Mr. Gladstone, Ma'am; I'm not denying he's a great man; but he's got too many ideas for my liking, far too many! I'm not against temperance any more than he is — put in its right place. But he's got that crazy notion of 'local option' in his mind; he's coming to it, gradually. And he doesn't think how giving 'local option' to them that don't take the wide view of things, may do harm to a locality. You must be wide in your views, else you do somebody an injustice.

QUEEN   Yes, Brown; and that is why I like being up in the hills, where the views *are* wide.

J. B.   I put it this way, Ma'am. You come to a locality, and you find you can't get served as you are accustomed to be served. Well! you don't go there again, and you tell others not to go; and so the place gets a bad name. I've a brother who keeps an inn down at Aberlochy on the coach route, and he tells me that more than half his customers come from outside the locality.

QUEEN   Of course; naturally!

J. B.   Well now, Ma'am, it'll be bad for the locality to have half the custom that comes to it turned away, because of local option! And believe me, Ma'am, that's what it will come to. People living in it won't see till the shoe pinches them; and by that time my brother, and others like him, will have been ruined in their business.

QUEEN   Local option is not going to come yet, Brown.

J. B. (*firmly*) No, Ma'am, not while I vote Conservative, it won't. But I was looking ahead; I was talking about Mr. Gladstone.

QUEEN   Mr. Gladstone has retired from politics. At least, he is not going to take office again.

J. B.   Don't you believe him, Ma'am. Mr. Gladstone is not a retiring character. He's in to-day's paper again — columns of him; have ye seen?

QUEEN   Yes; quite as much as I wish to see.

J. B.   And there's something in what he says, I don't deny.

QUEEN   There's a great deal in what he says I don't understand, and that I don't wish to.

J. B.   Now you never said a truer thing than that in your life, Ma'am! That's just how I find him. Oh, but he's a great man; and it's wonderful how he appreciates the Scot, and looks up to his opinion.

(*But this is a line of conversation in which his Royal Mistress declines to be interested. And she is helped, at that moment, by something which really does interest her.*)

QUEEN   Brown, how did you come to scratch your leg?

J. B.   'Twas not me, Ma'am; 'twas the stable-cat did that — just now while Mop was having his walk.

QUEEN   Poor dear Brown! Did she fly at you?

J. B.   Well, 'twas like this, Ma'am; first Mop went for her, then she went for him. And I tell ye she'd have scraped his eyes out if I'd left it to a finish.

QUEEN   Ferocious creature! She must be mad.

J. B.   Well, Ma'am, I don't know whether a cat-and-dog fight is a case of what God hath joined together; but it's the hard thing for man to put asunder! And that's the scraping I got for it, when I tried.

QUEEN   You must have it cauterized, Brown. I won't have you getting hydrophobia.

J. B.   You generally get that from dogs.

QUEEN   Oh, from cats too; any cat that a mad dog has bitten.

J. B.   They do say, Ma'am, that if a mad dog bites you — you have to die barking. So if it's a cat-bite I'm going to die of, you'll hear me mewing the day, maybe.

QUEEN   I don't like cats: I never did. Treacherous, deceitful creatures! Now a dog always looks up to you.

J. B.   Yes, Ma'am; they are tasteful, attractive animals; and that, maybe, is the reason. They give you a good conceit of yourself, dogs do. You never have to apologise to a dog. Do him an injury — you've only to say you forgive him, and he's friends again.

(*Accepting his views with a nodding smile, she resumes her pen, and spreads paper.*)

QUEEN   Now, Brown, I must get to work again. I have writing to do. See that I'm not disturbed.

J. B.   Then when were you wanting to see your visitor, Ma'am? There's his chair waiting.

QUEEN   Ah, yes, to be sure. But I didn't want to worry him too soon. What is the time?

J. B.   Nearly twelve, Ma'am.

QUEEN   Oh! then I think I may. Will you go and tell him: the Queen's compliments, and she would like to see him, now?

J. B.   I will go and tell him, Ma'am.

QUEEN   And then I shan't want you any more — till this afternoon.

J. B.   Then I'll just go across and take lunch at home, Ma'am.

QUEEN   Yes, do! That will be nice for you. And Brown, mind you have that leg seen to!

(MR. JOHN BROWN *has started to go, when his step is arrested.*)

J. B.   His Lordship is there in the garden, Ma'am, talking to the Princess.

QUEEN   What, before he has seen *me*? Go, and take him away from the Princess, and tell him to come here!

J. B. I will, Ma'am.

QUEEN And you had better take Mop with you. Now, dear Brown, do have your poor leg seen to, at once!

J. B. Indeed, and I will, Ma'am. Come, Mop, man! Come and tell his Lordship he's wanted.

(*Exit* MR. JOHN BROWN, *nicely accompanied by Mop.*)

(*Left to herself* THE QUEEN *administers a feminine touch or two to dress and cap and hair; then with dignified composure she resumes her writing, and continues to write even when the shadow of her favourite Minister crosses the entrance, and he stands hat in hand before her, flawlessly arrayed in a gay frock suit suggestive of the period when male attire was still not only a fashion, but an art.*

Despite, however, the studied correctness of his costume, face and deportment give signs of haggard fatigue; and when he bows it is the droop of a weary man, slow in the recovery. Just at the fitting moment for full acceptance of his silent salutation, the Royal Lady lays down her pen.)

QUEEN Oh, how do you do, my dear Lord Beaconsfield! Good morning; and welcome to Balmoral.

LORD B. (*as he kisses the hand extended to him*) That word from your Majesty brings all its charms to life! What a prospect of beauty I see around me!

QUEEN You arrived early? I hope you are sufficiently rested.

LORD B. Refreshed, Madam; rest will come later.

QUEEN You have had a long, tiring journey, I fear.

LORD B. It was long, Madam.

QUEEN I hope that you slept upon the train?

LORD B. I lay upon it, Ma'am. That is all I can say truly.

QUEEN Oh, I'm sorry!

LORD B. There were compensations, Ma'am. In my vigil I was able to look forward — to that which is now before me. The morning is beautiful! May I be permitted to inquire if your Majesty's health has benefited?

QUEEN I'm feeling 'bonnie', as we say in Scotland. Life out of doors suits me.

LORD B.   Ah! This tent light is charming! Then my eyes had not deceived me; your Majesty is already more than better. The tempered sunlight, so tender in its reflections, gives — an interior, one may say — of almost floral delicacy; making these canvas walls like the white petals of an enfolding flower.

QUEEN   Are you writing another of your novels, Lord Beaconsfield? That sounds like composition.

LORD B.   Believe me, Madam, only an impromptu.

QUEEN   Now, my dear Lord, pray sit down! I had that chair specially brought for you. Generally I sit here quite alone.

LORD B.   Such kind forethought, Madam, overwhelms me! Words are inadequate. I accept, gratefully, the repose you offer me.

   (*He sinks into the chair, and sits motionless and mute, in a weariness that is not the less genuine because it provides an effect. But from one seated in the Royal Presence much is expected; and so it is in a tone of sprightly expectancy that his Royal Mistress now prompts him to his task of entertaining her.*)

QUEEN   Well? And how is everything?

LORD B.   (*rousing himself with an effort*)   Oh! Pardon! Your Majesty would have me speak on politics, and affairs of State? I was rapt away for the moment.

QUEEN   Do not be in any hurry, dear Prime Minister.

LORD B.   Ah! That word from an indulgent Mistress spurs me freshly to my task. But, Madam, there is almost nothing to tell: politics, like the rest of us, have been taking holiday.

QUEEN   I thought that Mr. Gladstone has been speaking.

LORD B.   (*with an airy flourish of courtly disdain*)   Oh, yes! He has been — speaking.

QUEEN   In Edinburgh, quite lately.

LORD B.   And in more other places than I can count. Speaking — speaking — speaking. But I have to confess, Madam, that I have not read his speeches. They are composed for brains which can find more leisure than yours, Madam — or mine.

QUEEN   I have read some of them.

LORD B. Your Majesty does him great honour — and yourself some inconvenience, I fear. Those speeches, so great a strain to understand, or even to listen to — my hard duty for now some forty years — are a far greater strain to read.

QUEEN They annoy me intensely. I have no patience with him!

LORD B. Pardon me, Madam; if you have read *one* of his speeches, your patience has been extraordinary.

QUEEN Can't you stop it?

LORD B. Stop? — stop what, Madam? Niagara, the Flood? That which has no beginning, no limit, has also no end: till, by the operation of nature, it runs dry.

QUEEN But, surely, he should be stopped when he speaks on matters which may, any day, bring us into war!

LORD B. Then he would be stopped. When the British nation goes to war, Madam, it ceases to listen to reason. Then it is only the beating of its own great heart that it hears: to that goes the marching of its armies, with victory as the one goal. Then, Madam, above reason rises instinct. Against that he will be powerless.

QUEEN You think so?

LORD B. I am sure, Madam. If we are drawn into war, his opposition becomes futile. If we are not: well, if we are not, it will not be his doing that we escape that — dire necessity.

QUEEN But you *do* think it necessary, don't you?

(*To the Sovereign's impetuous eagerness, so creditable to her heart, he replies with the oracular solemnity by which caution can be sublimated.*)

LORD B. I hope it may not be, Madam. We must all say that — up till the last moment. It is the only thing we *can* say, to testify the pacifity of our intention when challenged by other Powers.

QUEEN (*touching the newspaper*) This morning's news isn't good, I'm afraid. The Russians are getting nearer to Constantinople.

LORD B. They will never enter it, Madam.

QUEEN No, they mustn't! We will not allow it.

LORD B. That, precisely, is the policy of your Majesty's Government. Russia knows that we shall not allow it; she knows that it will never be. Nevertheless, we may have to make a demonstration.

QUEEN Do you propose to summon Parliament?

LORD B. Not Parliament; no, Madam. Your Majesty's Fleet will be sufficient.

(*This lights a spark; and the royal mind darts into strategy.*)

QUEEN If I had my way, Lord Beaconsfield, my Fleet would be in the Baltic to-morrow; and before another week was over, Petersburg would be under bombardment.

LORD B. (*considerately providing this castle in the air with its necessary foundations*) And Cronstadt would have fallen.

QUEEN (*puzzled for a moment at this naming of a place which had not entered her calculations*) Cronstadt? Why Cronstadt?

LORD B. Merely preliminary, Madam. When that fortified suburb has crumbled — the rest will be easy.

QUEEN Yes! And what a good lesson it will teach them! The Crimea wasn't enough for them, I suppose.

LORD B. The Crimea! Ah, what memories — of heroism — that word evokes! 'Magnificent, but not war!'

QUEEN Oh! There is one thing, Lord Beaconsfield, on which I want your advice.

LORD B. Always at your Majesty's disposal.

QUEEN I wish to confer upon the Sultan of Turkey my Order of the Garter.

LORD B. Ah! how generous, how generous an instinct! How like you, Madam, to wish it!

QUEEN What I want to know is, whether, as Prime Minister, you have any objection?

LORD B. 'As Prime Minister.' How hard that makes it for me to answer! How willingly would I say 'None'! How reluctantly, on the contrary, I have to say, 'It had better wait.'

QUEEN Wait? Wait till when? I want to do it *now*.

LORD B. Yes, so do I. But can you risk, Madam, conferring that most illustrious symbol of honour, and chivalry, and power, on a defeated monarch? Your royal prestige, Ma'am, must be considered. Great and generous hearts need, more than most, to take prudence into their counsels.

QUEEN But do you think, Lord Beaconsfield, that the Turks are going to be beaten?

LORD B. The Turks *are* beaten, Madam. . . . But England will never be beaten. We shall dictate terms — moderating the demands of Russia; and under your Majesty's protection the throne of the Kaliphat will be safe — once more. That, Madam, is the key to our Eastern policy: a grateful Kaliphat, claiming allegiance from the whole Mohammedan world, bound to us by instincts of self-preservation — and we hold henceforth the gorgeous East in fee with redoubled security. His power may be a declining power; but ours remains. Some day, who knows? Egypt, possibly even Syria, Arabia, may be our destined reward.

(*Like a cat over a bowl of cream, England's Majesty sits lapping all this up. But, when he has done, her commentary is shrewd and to the point.*)

QUEEN The French won't like that!

LORD B. They won't, Madam, they won't. But has it ever been England's policy, Madam, to mind what the French don't like?

QUEEN (*with relish*) No, it never has been, has it? Ah! you are the true statesman, Lord Beaconsfield. Mr. Gladstone never talked to me like that.

LORD B. (*courteously surprised at what does not at all surprise him*) No? . . . You must have had interesting conversations with him, Madam, in the past.

QUEEN (*very emphatically*) I have never once had a conversation with Mr. Gladstone, in all my life, Lord Beaconsfield. He used to talk to me as if I were a public meeting — and one that agreed with him, too!

LORD B. Was there, then, any applause, Madam?

QUEEN No, indeed! I was too shy to say what I thought. I used to cough sometimes.

LORD B. Rather like coughing at a balloon, I fear. I have always admired his flights — regarded as a mere *tour de force* — so buoyant, so sustained, so incalculable! But, as they never touch earth to any serviceable end, that I could discover — of what use are they? Yet if there is one man who has helped me in my career — to whom, therefore, I should owe gratitude — it is he.

QUEEN Indeed? Now that does surprise me! Tell me, Lord Beaconsfield, how has he ever helped you?

LORD B. In our party system, Madam, we live by the mistakes of our opponents. The balance of the popular verdict swings ever this way and that, relegating us either to victory or defeat, to office or to opposition. Many times have I trodden the road to power, or passed from it again, over ruins the origin of which I could recognize either as my own work or that of another; and most of all has it been over the disappointments, the disaffections, the disgusts, the disillusionments — chiefly among his own party — which my great opponent has left me to profit by. I have gained experience from what he has been morally blind to; what he has lacked in understanding of human nature he has left for me to discover. Only to-day I learn that he has been in the habit of addressing — as you, Madam, so wittily phrased it — of addressing, 'as though she were a public meeting', that Royal Mistress, whom it has ever been my most difficult task not to address sometimes as the most charming, the most accomplished, and the most fascinating woman of the epoch which bears her name. (*He pauses, then resumes.*) How strange a fatality directs the fate of each one of us! How fortunate is he who knows the limits that destiny assigns to him: limits beyond which no word must be uttered.

(*His oratorical flight, so buoyant and sustained, having come to its calculated end, he drops deftly to earth, encountering directly for the first time the flattered smile with which the Queen has listened to him.*)

Madam, your kind silence reminds me, in the gentlest, the most considerate way possible, that I am not here to relieve the tedium of a life made lonely by a bereavement equal to your own, in conversation however beguiling, or in quest of a sympathy of which, I dare to say, I feel assured. For, in a sense, it is as to a public assembly, or rather as to a great institution, immemorially venerable and august that I have to address myself when, obedient to your summons, I come to be consulted as your Majesty's First Minister of State. If, therefore, your royal mind have any inquiries, any further commands to lay upon me, I am here, Madam, to give effect to them in so far as I can.

> (*This time he has really finished, but with so artful an abbreviation at the point where her interest has been roused that the Queen would fain have him go on. And so the conversation continues to flow along intimate channels.*)

QUEEN   No, dear Lord Beaconsfield, not to-day! Those official matters can wait. After you have said so much, and said it so beautifully, I would rather still talk with you as a friend. Of friends you and I have not many; those who make up our world, for the most part, we have to keep at a distance. But while I have many near relatives, children and descendants, I remember that you have none. So your case is the harder.

LORD B.   Ah, no, Madam, indeed! I have my children — descendants who will live after me, I trust — in those policies which, for the welfare of my beloved country, I confide to the care of a Sovereign whom I revere and love. . . . I am not unhappy in my life, Madam; far less in my fortune; only, as age creeps on, I find myself so lonely, so solitary, that sometimes I have doubt whether I am really alive, or whether the voice, with which now and then I seek to reassure myself, be not the voice of a dead man.

QUEEN   (*almost tearfully*)   No, no, my dear Lord Beaconsfield, you mustn't say that!

LORD B.   (*gallantly*)   I won't say anything, Madam, that you forbid, or that you dislike. You invited me to speak to you as a friend; so I have done, so I do. I apologize that I have allowed sadness, even for a moment, to trouble the harmony — the sweetness — of our conversation.

QUEEN   Pray, do not apologize! It has been a very great privilege; I beg that you will go on! Tell me — you spoke of bereavement — I wish you would tell me more — about your wife.

> (*The sudden request touches some latent chord; and it is with genuine emotion that he answers.*)

LORD B. Ah! My wife! To her I owed everything.

QUEEN She was devoted to you, wasn't she?

LORD B. I never read the depth of her devotion — till after her death. Then, Madam — this I have told to nobody but yourself — then I found among her papers — addressed 'to my dear husband' — a message, written only a few days before her death, with a hand shaken by that nerve-racking and fatal malady which she endured so patiently — begging me to marry again.

(THE QUEEN *is now really crying, and finds speech difficult.*)

QUEEN And you, you — ? Dear Lord Beaconsfield; did you mean — had you ever meant — ?

LORD B. I did not then, Madam; nor have I ever done so since. It is enough if I allow myself — to love.

QUEEN Oh, yes, yes; I understand — better than others would. For that has always been my own feeling.

LORD B. In the history of my race, Madam, there has been a great tradition of faithfulness between husbands and wives. For the hardness of our hearts, we are told, Moses permitted us to give a writing of divorcement. But we have seldom acted on it. In my youth I became a Christian; I married a Christian. But that was no reason for me to desert the nobler traditions of my race — for they are in the blood and in the heart. When my wife died I had no thought to marry again; and when I came upon that tender wish, still I had no thought for it; my mind would not change. Circumstances that have happened since have sealed irrecovably my resolution — never to marry again.

QUEEN Oh, I think that is so wise, so right, so noble of you!

(*The old Statesman rises, pauses, appears to hestitate, then in a voice charged with emotion says:*)

LORD B. Madam, will you permit me to kiss your hand!

(*The hand graciously given, and the kiss fervently implanted, he falls back once more to a respectful distance. But the emotional excitement of the interview has told upon him, and it is in a wavering voice of weariness that he now speaks.*)

You have been very forbearing with me, Madam, not to indicate

that I have outstayed either my welcome or your powers of endur-
ance. Yet so much conversation must necessarily have tired you.
May I then crave permission, Madam, to withdraw? For, to speak
truly, I do need some rest.

QUEEN   Yes, my dear friend, go and rest yourself! But before
you go, will you not wait, and take a glass of wine with me?

(*He bows, and she rings.*)

And there is just one other thing I wish to say before we part.

LORD B.   Speak, Madam, for thy servant heareth.

(*The other* SERVANT *is now also standing to attention, awaiting
orders.*)

QUEEN   Bring some wine.

(*The* ATTENDANT *goes.*)

That Order of the Garter which I had intended to confer upon
the Sultan — have you, as Prime Minister, any objection if I bestow
it nearer home, on one to whom personally — I cannot say more —
on yourself, I mean.

(*At that pronouncement of the royal favour the Minister stands,
exhausted of energy, in an attitude of drooping humility. The
eloquent silence is broken presently by* THE QUEEN.)

QUEEN   Dear Lord Beaconsfield, I want your answer.

LORD B.   Oh, Madam! What adequate answer can these poor
lips make to so magnificent an offer? Yet answer I must. We have
spoken together briefly to-day of our policies in the Near East.
Madam, let me come to you again when I have saved Constantinople, and secured once more upon a firm basis the peace of Europe.
Then ask me again whether I have any objection, and I will own —
'I have none!'

(*Re-enters* ATTENDANT. *He deposits a tray with decanter and
glasses, and retires again.*)

QUEEN   Very well, Lord Beaconsfield. And if you do not remind
me, I shall remind you. (*She points to the tray.*) Pray, help yourself!

(*He takes up the decanter.*)

LORD B.   I serve you, Madam?

QUEEN   Thank you.

(He fills the two glasses; presents hers to THE QUEEN, *and takes up his own.)*

LORD B.   May I propose for myself — a toast, Madam?

*(*THE QUEEN *sees what is coming, and bows graciously.)*

The Queen! God bless her!

(He drains the glass, then breaks it against the pole of the tent, and throws away the stem.)

An old custom, Madam, observed by loyal defenders of the House of Stuart, so that no lesser health might ever be drunk from the same glass. To my old hand came a sudden access of youthful enthusiasm — an ardour which I could not restrain. Your pardon, Madam!

QUEEN *(very gently)*   Go and lie down, Lord Beaconsfield; you need rest.

LORD B.   Adieu, Madam.

QUEEN   Draw your curtains, and sleep well!

(For a moment he stands gazing at her with a look of deep emotion; he tries to speak. Ordinary words seem to fail; he falters into poetry.)

> 'When pain and anguish wring the brow,
>   A ministering Angel, thou!'

(It has been beautifully said, they both feel. Silent and slow, with head reverentially bowed, he backs from the Presence.)

*(*THE QUEEN *sits and looks after the retreating figure, then at the broken fragments of glass. She takes up the hand-bell and rings. The* ATTENDANT *enters.)*

QUEEN   Pick up that broken glass.

(The ATTENDANT *collects it on the hand-tray which he carries.)*

Bring it to me! . . . Leave it!

(The ATTENDANT *deposits the tray before her, and goes. Gently* THE QUEEN *handles the broken pieces. Then in a voice of tearful emotion she speaks.)*

Such devotion! Most extraordinary! Oh! Albert! Albert!

(And in the sixteenth year of her widowhood and the fortieth of her reign, the Royal Lady bends her head over the fragments of broken glass, and weeps happy tears.)

LIFE IN THE HIGHLANDS

Over a low rise of rocky ground thick with heather, THE QUEEN, *having dismounted from her pony, is making her way slowly and with some difficulty, assisted by* JOHN BROWN, *whose strong push from behind is more helpful than a mere arm to lean on.* THE QUEEN·*walks with a stick. Under his arm* JOHN BROWN *carries a sketch-book. Down in a hollow to the right is a small cottage, with more roof than wall showing.*

BROWN Wumman, wumman, how stiff ye're getting to be!

THE QUEEN Well, Brown, that's only to be expected. I'm not so young as I was.

BROWN Ah, it isn't your years, Ma'am; it's the weight ye're putting on that does it. I'm only telling you.

THE QUEEN (*good-humouredly*) I can tell myself, Brown.

BROWN But you don't — not at the right time, anyway. Ye don't take enough exercise, Ma'am.

THE QUEEN I take as much as I've time for.

BROWN If you'd walk instead of just driving around ye'd do better. Sitting still in a carriage, or even riding aside a pony, is not the same thing. No, Ma'am.

THE QUEEN Riding suits me very much better than walking, Brown; it always has. But I'm afraid I shan't be able to ride much longer.

BROWN It'll be your ain fault, then. And when it happens don't say I haven't warned ye.

THE QUEEN Well, I've had enough exercise to-day at all events . . . (*She stops to look round.*) Brown, is this the place where I told you I wanted to come back and make a sketch, the last time we came here?

BROWN Ay; I put a mark in the ground for ye; and here it is.

(*He stoops, and pulls up a short piece of stick.*)

THE QUEEN Very thoughtful and sensible of you. Thank you, Brown. Yes; this is the view I was wanting. So now will you go to that cottage, and say the Queen's compliments, and may she borrow a chair and a small table?

BROWN   A small table?

THE QUEEN   Yes, a small table.

BROWN   How small, away from large, do you want it to be?

THE QUEEN   Just big enough for me to make my sketch on.

BROWN   Aye, and how big'll that have to be?

THE QUEEN   Why, of course, only just quite a small one. It can't be bigger than the sketch-book, can it? You have it there; give it me.

> (*He hands over the sketch-book.*)

And now the pencil-case, please.

> (*He brings it out of his pocket, and hands that over also. But though obedient in small things he still keeps command of the situation.*)

BROWN   Well, I'll see what I can do for ye. But I'll not have you be long. Else you'll be catching cold.

THE QUEEN   No, I shan't be long; and I'm not in the least likely to catch cold in this weather. So now go and get me the table — and the chair.

> (BROWN *goes, and presently returns with two tables, while* THE QUEEN *moves about, choosing her point of view.*)

Ah, yes, I think this will do, with that hill, and those trees in the distance.

> (*A* CHILD *comes carrying a chair; another follows. They both stand timorously at a distance.* JOHN BROWN *comes and takes the chair, and brings it to* THE QUEEN.)

THE QUEEN   (*to the child*)   Oh, thank you, my dear; and will you say thank you to your mother for me?

CHILD   To be sure and I will, your Majesty.

> (*They stand and stare while* JOHN BROWN *arranges the matter of the table.*)

BROWN   There, Ma'am. There's a choice for ye. Now which is it to be?

THE QUEEN I don't think either of them will do, Brown. This is too small, and that one is too large.

BROWN Too large for what?

THE QUEEN For me to make my sketch on.

BROWN You needna' cover the whole table with your sketch. And here we can't get tables made for you to order. So ye must just make that do.

THE QUEEN But isn't there another?

BROWN There's nae other that can be spared to ye. What the family Bible stands on canna' be moved for light doings of this sort.

THE QUEEN Oh, very well, then I must make this do.

BROWN As I told you; after so many words, you've got to the fact.

(BROWN *picks up the rejected table, and moving toward the cottage, calls to the boy:*)

Here, you!

(*The* BOY *comes, picks up the table, and carries it back to the cottage, followed by his sister.*)

THE QUEEN Brown, I don't think you are in a good temper to-day. What's the matter?

BROWN (*rich in his grievance*) It's what's always the matter. I carry out your orders only to get black looks for it, and be told I don't know how to behave myself.

THE QUEEN Who has been telling you that?

BROWN It was the Prince, Ma'am. He came up from Sandring-ham, as you know, specially for to see you: for the second time that was. But you'd told me you'd see nobody while you were having your afternoon nap. Well, he comes while you were having it, and I was by the door to keep any away that should come. Your ain orders. So I kept him away as I would anybody. Says he, very stand-offish, 'I wish to see Her Majesty the Queen!' Says I, your Mother's having her nap and you'll no' see her till she's through with it. Well, as you might expect, it didna' please His Royal Highness to be told that.

THE QUEEN No, Brown; and I really don't wonder. You should not have spoken to him like that.

BROWN It was in your Majesty's ain words, what I said to him. So for that, his equerry comes to me this morning to give me a piece of what he calls 'his mind'. I let him give it oot: said never a word, only looked at him. And he didn't like the way I looked at him, any more than I liked the way he took it upon himself to speak to me. Did the Prince say anything to you aboot it?

THE QUEEN No; though I could see that something had not pleased him. I have had to make it a rule now that if he has any complaints to make about you, he must make them through my Secretary. But you know, Brown, though I am the Prince's Mother, it would be better, more proper, when you speak to him about me, to say 'Her Majesty'.

BROWN Well, Ma'am, I'm as God made me; and I've never been presented at Court, so I haven't got Court ways with me; I can only speak as comes natural to me. You never trained me for a courtier, Ma'am, and you never will. I'm as God made me, so you'll have to put up with it.

(THE QUEEN *sits down to the table, opens her sketch-book, and begins sketching.* BROWN *goes and stands behind her.*)

THE QUEEN Don't watch me, Brown.

BROWN 'Twasna' you I was watching. 'Twas those birds over there. Are ye going to put them in before they fly away?

THE QUEEN I don't think it much matters whether I do or do not.

BROWN I would think, Ma'am, that when ye're sketching from nature, ye should put in what's there.

THE QUEEN I put in what I choose, Brown, and I leave *out* what I choose.

BROWN And ye call that honest, Ma'am?

THE QUEEN No, Brown; I call it common sense.

BROWN The Lord help ye!

(*Just for once* MR. JOHN BROWN *finds his remark ignored.*)

THE QUEEN What is the name of the woman you got the table from?

BROWN McIver, Ma'am.

THE QUEEN How many children has she?

BROWN I did not inquire, Ma'am. There was but those two within that I saw: just finishing their tea, they were.

THE QUEEN Go and tell them, if they have done, to come out and speak to me.

BROWN I will, Ma'am.

(*He goes to the door of the cottage and calls:*)

You, the two of you! Ye're wanted.

(*The two* CHILDREN *come to the door.*)

Boy, what's your name?

DONALD Donald McIver.

BROWN And what's hers?

MAGGIE I'm Maggie McIver.

BROWN Then you, Donald McIver, and you, Maggie McIver, come out both of you. The Queen wants to speak to you.

(*Shy, but eager, the* CHILDREN *follow* JOHN BROWN; *he conducts them to the Royal Presence.*)

There you have them, Ma'am.

(*Having done the introductions he moves away.*)

THE QUEEN Oh, yes. How do you do? (*To the girl*) What is your name, little one?

MAGGIE Maggie McIver, please your Majesty.

THE QUEEN (*to the boy*) And what is yours?

DONALD Donald McIver, please your Majesty.

THE QUEEN How old are you?

MAGGIE I'm ten, your Majesty.

THE QUEEN And you, Donald?

DONALD I'm ten, same as her, your Majesty.

THE QUEEN Then you are twins?

DONALD We was twins when we were born, your Majesty; but we arena' now; I'm grown the bigger.

THE QUEEN   Oh, yes, boys are always bigger than girls. But that doesn't alter your age. And do you both go to school?

DONALD *and* MAGGIE   Yes, your Majesty.

THE QUEEN   Where?

DONALD   Down below, at the schoolhouse.

THE QUEEN   Do you like going to school?

DONALD   I like better to be out of it.

THE QUEEN   Yes, I daresay. But some day you will be very glad that you did go; and so will you, Maggie.

(*To which* MAGGIE *gives a dutiful assent; but* DONALD, *more independent of mind, says nothing. All this time* THE QUEEN *has been sketching while she talks. Now she stops, searches in her reticule, and finds a penny, which she hands over to* DONALD.)

Well, Donald, thank you for bringing the chair. And here is something for you to share with Maggie.

DONALD   Thank you, your Majesty.

(*The* CHILDREN *stand hesitating.* THE QUEEN *turns and gives them a friendly nod of dismissal.*)

THE QUEEN   Well, now run back to your mother. And remember to say thank you for me for her having lent me the chair and the table.

(*The* CHILDREN *withdraw respectfully and return to the cottage.* THE QUEEN *goes on with her sketch.* JOHN BROWN *strolls back, and again stands behind her.*)

BROWN   It hasna' taken ye long.

THE QUEEN   Oh, no, I sketch very quickly.

BROWN   It's as well you do; it's coming on to rain.

THE QUEEN   Oh, not enough to matter. It won't hurt me; and if it rains enough to wet the sketch you must hold an umbrella over me.

(*This duty* JOHN BROWN *does not relish, so he proceeds firmly:*)

BROWN   It wasn'a you I was thinking of, Ma'am, nor the sketch, neither. Chairs and tables weren't made to stand oot in the rain.

THE QUEEN   A plain wooden chair and a table? How can it hurt them?

BROWN Maybe yes, and maybe no; but Mrs. McIver might be thinking that she didna' lend her furniture to stay out in the rain.

THE QUEEN (*closing her sketch-book*) Oh, very well, Brown. I see that you must have your way, so I won't sketch any more. You can take back the chair and the table. And remember to say thank you again to Mrs. McIver for her great kindness.

(BROWN *inverts the chair on top of the table, and carries them down to the cottage door.*)

BROWN Hi! you there! Take these back to your mother, and say the Queen thanks her for the use of them.

(*The two* CHILDREN *reappear. One takes the chair, the other the table, they go in.* THE QUEEN *is still putting away her pencils and fastening the band round her sketch-book when* JOHN BROWN *returns.*)

Now, Ma'am, I am ready if you are.

THE QUEEN I've not kept you waiting, Brown; but as I told you before, I think you are not in a very good temper to-day.

BROWN Will I put the peg in the ground for ye again?

THE QUEEN No; I've made as much of a sketch as I want to, thank you, Brown.

(*So saying, she gives* BROWN *the sketch-book and the pencils and moves away.* BROWN, *with a toss of the head, follows her. The* CHILDREN *come out, and at a respectful distance, stand staring, while off the scene* THE QUEEN *remounts her pony. As the pony starts down the hill, they start to follow.* MRS. MCIVER *comes to the door.*)

MRS. MCIVER What are ye doing there? Come back!

DONALD It's the Queen, Mither!

MRS. MCIVER And what if it *is* the Queen? Can ye no' let her alone? She doesna' come here to be stared and followed after. Ye wouldn't do it to any other lady, so ye'll no' do it to her. Come back in with you.

(*The* CHILDREN *go to the door.* MRS. MCIVER *spies the penny.*)

What have ye got there, Donald?

DONALD It's a bawbie the Queen gave me.

MRS. MCIVER What were ye meaning to do with it?

DONALD I was for buying sweeties with it, Mither, for the two of us.

MRS. MCIVER Ye'll do no such thing. Give it to me; I'll keep it for ye.

DONALD No, Mither. I would rather be spending it now.

MRS. MCIVER There's to be no spending of that, not if *I* know it. When ye're a grown man, ye're going to hang this bawbie on your watch-chain. Spend it, indeed! Have ye no reverence nor respect for a bawbie as the Queen gave ye!

MAGGIE (*whimpering*) But Mither, it's no' fair! He was to share it with *me*.

MRS. MCIVER Share it with you, was he? Well, here's a bawbie for the twa of ye. So her coming has cost me *that*. Eh, but it's a great honour the guid Queen has done us this day — what with the table and the chair, and this bawbie all put together. Come on in with you, and I'll give you another bawbie for celebrating the day.

HIS FAVOURITE FLOWER

1881

A Political Myth Exploded

LORD BEACONSFIELD *has not been at all well. He is sitting up in his room, and his doctor has come to see him for the third time in three days. This means that the malady is not yet seriously regarded: once a day is still sufficient. Nevertheless, he is a woeful wreck to look at; and the doctor looks at him with the greatest respect, and listens to his querulous plaint patiently. For that great dome of silence, his brain, repository of so many State-secrets, is still a redoubtable instrument: its wit and its magician's cunning have not yet lapsed into the dull inane of senile decay. Though fallen from power, after a bad beating at the polls, there is no knowing but that he may rise again, and hold once more in those tired old hands, shiny with rheumatic gout, and now twitching feebly under the discomfort of a superimposed malady, the reins of democratic and imperial power. The dark, cavernous eyes still wear their look of accumulated wisdom, a touch also of visionary fire. The sparse locks, dyed to a raven black, set off with their uncanny sheen the clay-like pallor of the face. He sits in a high-backed chair, wrapped in an oriental dressing-gown, his muffled feet resting on a large hot-water bottle; and the eminent physician, preparatory to taking a seat at his side, bends solicitously over him.*

DOCTOR   Well, my dear Lord, how are you to-day? Better? You look better.

BEACONSFIELD   Yes, I suppose I am better. But my sleep isn't what it ought to be. I have had a dream, Doctor; and it has upset me.

DOCTOR   A dream?

BEACONSFIELD   You wonder that I should mention it? Of course, I — I don't believe in dreams. Yet they indicate, sometimes — do they not? — certain disorders of the mind.

DOCTOR   Generally of the stomach.

343

BEACONSFIELD   Ah! The same thing, Doctor. There's no getting away from that in one's old age; when one has lived as well as I have.

DOCTOR   That is why I dieted you.

BEACONSFIELD   Oh, I have nothing on my conscience as to that. My housekeeper is a dragon. Her fidelity is of the kind that will even risk dismissal.

DOCTOR   An invaluable person, under the circumstances.

BEACONSFIELD   Yes; a nuisance, but indispensable. No, Doctor. This dream didn't come from the stomach. It seemed rather to emanate from that outer darkness which surrounds man's destiny. So real, so horribly real!

DOCTOR   Better, then, not to brood on it.

BEACONSFIELD   Ah! Could I explain it, then I might get rid of it. In the ancient religion of my race dreams found their interpretation. But have they any?

DOCTOR   Medical science is beginning to say 'Yes'; that in sleep the subconscious mind has its reactions.

BEACONSFIELD   Well, I wonder how my 'subconscious mind' got hold of primroses.

DOCTOR   Primroses? Did they form a feature in your dream?

BEACONSFIELD   A feature? No. The whole place was alive with them! As the victim of inebriety sees snakes, I saw primroses. They were everywhere: they fawned on me in wreaths and festoons; swarmed over me like parasites; flew at me like flies; till it seemed that the whole world had conspired to suffocate me under a sulphurous canopy of those detestable little atoms. Can you imagine the horror of it, Doctor, to a sane—a hitherto sane mind like mine?

DOCTOR   Oh! In a dream any figment may excite aversion.

BEACONSFIELD   This wasn't like a dream. It was rather the threat of some new disease, some brain malady about to descend on me: possibly delirium tremens. I have not been of abstemious habits, Doctor. Suppose — ?

DOCTOR   Impossible! Dismiss altogether that supposition from your mind!

BEACONSFIELD Well, Doctor, I hope — I hope you may be right. For I assure you that the horror I then conceived for those pale botanical specimens in their pestiferous and increscent abundance, exceeded what words can describe. I have felt spiritually devastated ever since, as though some vast calamity were about to fall not only on my own intellect, but on that of my country. Well, you shall hear.

(*He draws his trembling hands wearily over his face, and sits thinking a while.*)

With all the harsh abruptness of a soul launched into eternity by the jerk of the hangman's rope, so I found myself precipitated into the midst of this dream. I was standing on a pillory, set up in Parliament Square, facing the Abbey. I could see the hands of St. Margaret's clock pointing to half-past eleven; and away to the left the roof of Westminster Hall undergoing restoration. Details, Doctor, which gave a curious reality to a scene otherwise fantastic, unbelievable. There I stood in a pillory, raised up from earth; and a great crowd had gathered to look at me. I can only describe it as a primrose-crowd. The disease infected all, but not so badly as it did me. The yellow contagion spread everywhere; from all the streets around, the botanical deluge continued to flow in upon me. I felt a pressure at my back; a man had placed a ladder against it; he mounted and hung a large wreath of primroses about my neck. The sniggering crowd applauded the indignity. Having placed a smaller wreath upon my head, he descended . . . A mockery of a May Queen, there I stood!

DOCTOR (*laying a soothing hand on him*) A dream, my dear Lord, only a dream.

BEACONSFIELD Doctor, imagine my feelings! My sense of ridicule was keen; but keener my sense of the injustice — not to be allowed to know *why* the whole world was thus making mock of me. For this was in the nature of a public celebration, its malignity was organized and national; a new fifth of November had been sprung upon the calendar. Around me I saw the emblematic watchword of the great party I had once led to triumph: 'Imperium et Libertas', 'Peace with Honour', 'England shall reign where'er the sun', and other mottoes of a like kind; and on them also the floral disease had spread itself. The air grew thick and heavy with its sick-room odour. Doctor, I could have vomited.

DOCTOR   Yes, yes; a touch of biliousness, I don't doubt.

BEACONSFIELD   With a sudden flash of insight — 'This', I said to myself, 'is my Day of Judgment. Here I stand, judged by my fellow-countrymen, for the failures and shortcomings of my political career. The good intentions with which my path was strewn are now turned to my reproach. But why do they take this particular form? Why — why primroses?'

DOCTOR   'The primrose way' possibly?

BEACONSFIELD   Ah! That occurred to me. But has it, indeed, been a primrose way that I have trodden so long and so painfully? I think not. I cannot so accuse myself. But suppose the Day of Judgment which Fate reserves for us were fundamentally this: the appraisement of one's life and character — not by the all-seeing Eye of Heaven (before which I would bow) but by the vindictively unjust verdict of the people one has tried to serve — the judgment not of God, but of public opinion. That is a judgment of which all who strive for power must admit the relevancy!

DOCTOR   You distress yourself unnecessarily, dear Lord. Your reputation is safe from detraction now.

BEACONSFIELD   With urgency I set my mind to meet the charge. If I could understand the meaning of that yellow visitation, then I should no longer have to fear that I was going mad!

(*At this point the door is discreetly opened, and the* HOUSEKEEPER, *mild, benign, but inflexible, enters, carrying a cup and toast-rack upon a tray.*)

HOUSEKEEPER   I beg pardon, my Lord; but I think your Lordship ought to have your beef-tea now.

BEACONSFIELD   Yes, yes, Mrs. Manson; come in.

DOCTOR   Your are right, Mrs. Manson; he ought.

HOUSEKEEPER (*placing the tray on a small stand*)   Where will you have it, my Lord?

BEACONSFIELD   In my inside, Mrs. Manson — presently — he, he!

DOCTOR   Now, let me take your pulse . . . Yes, yes. Pretty good, you know.

(MRS. MANSON *stands respectfully at attention with interrogation in her eye.*)

BEACONSFIELD   Yes, you may bring me my cap now. (*Then to the* DOCTOR.) I generally sleep after this.

(MRS. MANSON *brings a large tasselled fez of brilliant colour, and adjusts it to his head while he drinks. She then goes to the door, takes a hot-water bottle from the hands of an unseen servant and effects the necessary changes. All this is done so unobtrusively that* BEACONSFIELD *resumes his theme without regarding her. When she has done she goes.*)

Ah! Where was I?

DOCTOR   If you 'could understand', you said.

BEACONSFIELD   Ah, yes; understand. Again a strange faculty of divination came upon me. I stood upon the international plane, amid a congress of Powers, and let my eye travel once more over the Alliances of Europe. I looked, Doctor, and truly I saw, then, surprising shifts and changes in the political and diplomatic fabric which I had helped to frame. Time, and kingdoms had passed. I saw, at home and abroad, the rise of new parties into power, strange coalitions, defections, alliances; old balances destroyed, new balances set up in their place. I saw frontiers annulled, treaties violated, worldproblems tumbling like clowns, standing on their heads and crying, 'Here we are again!' Power, after all, had solved nothing!

My eye travelled over that problem of the Near East, which, for some generations at least, we thought to have settled, to Vienna, Petersburg, Constantinople — and away farther East to Teheran and — that other place whose name I have forgotten. And, as I looked, a Recording Angel came, and cried to me in a voice strangely familiar, the voice of one of my most detested colleagues — trusted, I mean — 'You have put your money on the wrong horse!'

And I had, Doctor; if what I saw then was true — I had! Yes, if ever man blundered and fooled his countrymen into a false and fatal position — I was that man! It wasn't a question of right or wrong. In politics that doesn't really matter; you decide on a course, and you invent moral reasons for it afterwards. No, what I had done was much worse than any mere wrongdoing. All my political foresight and achievements were a gamble that had gone wrong; and for that my Day of Judgment had come, and I stood in the pillory, a peepshow for mockery. But why for their instrument of torture did they choose primroses? Oh, I can invent a reason! It was Moses Primrose, cheated of his horse with a gross of green spectacles cased in shagreen. But that was not the reason. For then came new insight and a fresh humiliation. As I looked more intently I saw that I was *not* being mocked; I was being worshipped, adulated, flattered; I had become a god — for party purposes perhaps — and this was my day, given in my honour for national celebration. And I saw, by the insight given me, that they were praising me *for having put their money on the wrong horse!* Year by year the celebration had gone on, until they had so got into the habit that they could not leave off! All my achievements, all my policies, all my statecraft were in the dust; but the worship of me had become a national habit — so foolish and meaningless, that nothing, nothing but some vast calamity — some great social upheaval, was ever going to stop it.

DOCTOR   My dear Lord, it is I who must stop it now. You mustn't go on.

BEACONSFIELD   I have done, Doctor. There I have given you the essentials of my dream; material depressing enough for the mind of an old man, enfeebled by indisposition, at the end of a long day's work. But I tell you, Doctor, that nothing therein which stands explainable fills me with such repulsion and aversion as that one thing which I cannot explain — why, why primroses?

DOCTOR   A remarkable dream, my Lord; rendered more vivid or, as you say, 'real' — by your present disturbed state of health. As to that part of it which you find so inexplicable, I can at least point toward where the explanation lies. It reduces itself to this: primroses had become associated for you — in a way which you have forgotten — with something you wished to avoid. And so they became the image or symbol of your aversion; and as such found a place in your dream.

(*So saying the* DOCTOR *rises and moves toward the window, where his attention suddenly becomes riveted.*)

BEACONSFIELD Perhaps, Doctor, perhaps, as you say, there is some such explanation. But I don't feel like that.

DOCTOR Why, here are primroses! This may be the clue? Where do they come from?

BEACONSFIELD Ah, those! Indeed, I had forgotten them. At least; no, I could not have done that.

DOCTOR There is a written card with them, I see.

BEACONSFIELD Her Gracious Majesty did me the great honour, hearing that I was ill, to send and inquire. Of course, since my removal from office, the opportunity of presenting my personal homage has not been what it used to be. That, I suppose, is as well.

DOCTOR And these are from Her Majesty?

BEACONSFIELD They came yesterday, brought by a special messenger, with a note written by her own hand, saying that she had picked them herself. To so great a condescension I made with all endeavour what return I could. I wrote — a difficult thing for me to do, Doctor, just now — presented my humble duty, my thanks; and said they were my favourite flower.

DOCTOR And were they?

BEACONSFIELD Of course, Doctor, under those circumstances any flower would have been. It just happened to be that.

DOCTOR Well, my lord, there, then, the matter is explained. You *had* primroses upon your mind. The difficulty, the pain even, of writing with your crippled hand, became associated with them. You would have much rather not had to write; and the disinclination, in an exaggerated form, got into your dream. Now that, I hope, mitigates for you the annoyance — the distress of mind.

BEACONSFIELD Yes, yes. It does, as you say, make it more understandable. Bring them to me, Doctor; let me look my enemy in the face.

(*The* DOCTOR *carries the bowl across and sets it beside him. Very feebly he reaches out a hand and takes some.*)

My favourite flower. He — he! My favourite flower.

(*Lassitude overtakes him — his head nods and droops as he speaks.*)

A primrose by the river's brim
A yellow primrose was to him,
    And it was nothing more.

Who was it wrote that? — Byron or Dr. Watts? My memory isn't what it used to be. No matter. It all goes into the account. My favourite flower!

'For I'm to be Queen of the May, mother, I'm to be Queen of the May!'

(*The* DOCTOR *takes up his hat, and tiptoes to the door.*)

Tell me, where is fancy bred,
Or in the heart or in the head?
How begot, how nourishèd?

(*He breaks, and lets the petals fall one by one.*)
(*The* DOCTOR *goes out.*)

Let us all ring fancy's knell;
I'll begin it — Ding-dong bell,
    Ding-dong, bell.

(*He goes to sleep.*)

RELIGIOUS DIFFICULTIES

1882

THE DEAN's *Study at Windsor is a comfortable room, lined with books. On the writing-table there is no parade of industry; and the chairs are beautifully easy for meditative minds to repose in. It is summer; the French windows are open, and one gets a glimpse of sunlit lawn, garden-path, and flower-border. From the garden comes the sound of tennis-players: 'Play!' is cried; 'Fault!' ... 'Another fault!' ... In through the open window steps a fair maiden, carrying a tennis-racquet of prehistoric design — a survival from the late 'Seventies', when lawn-tennis had barely begun, and the racquets were like egg-spoons. She is followed by a youth, not in flannels — for that is not yet the correct thing — he also carries a racquet.*

SHE This isn't the room! There are no strawberry-ices here.

HE Does it matter? Who wants a strawberry-ice? I want *you*! Come and sit down; and let's just talk!

SHE Nonsense! Don't be silly! This isn't the place, or the time for it. Come back at once! There's the Dean playing: and it's such fun watching him. We always try to make him win; but it's so difficult.

HE I don't care whether the Dean wins, or loses!

SHE (*slipping out again*) No; but *I* do.

(*She has gone; and he goes after her.*
Along the path outside stroll two Ladies with raised parasols, in quiet conversation. An inner door opens, and with elaborate respect an elderly MAN-SERVANT *bows into the room a Lady whose face everybody knows. But here, in such private surroundings, coming so unexpectedly, it takes a little time to recognize her. Only the wonderful way in which that figure of ample breadth, but diminutive stature, moves across the room assures us that it is* THE QUEEN *herself.*)

THE QUEEN What is going on here to-day?

MAN-SERVANT A garden-party, your Majesty.

THE QUEEN Then you must see the Dean alone, and tell him *privately* that I am here.

MAN-SERVANT Yes, your Majesty.

(And bowing to her back, he goes.)

THE QUEEN And before you go, you had better close that window.

(But the order has come too late to be attended to; and THE QUEEN, *finding herself alone, does not close it herself, but takes a seat a little away from it, with her face turned from the light. Thus, in her widow's weeds, she gives a sad finish to the quiet interior; and one of the guests, an* ELDERLY GENTLEMAN *in a white waistcoat, strolling past the window with his Wife, looks in, and sees her.)*

ELDERLY GENTLEMAN There's someone there, my dear — looking rather lonely, and out of it. Poor thing! I think I'll just go in, and speak to her.

(And in he goes, while his Wife strolls on. Very affable, and pleased with himself, he advances, rubbing his hands; and in a kind, ingratiating tone he opens conversation.)

I *think* I know the face?

(Does he? It gives him a haughty stare, then turns away, while his milk of human kindness continues its inappropriate flow.)

Such nice weather! So fortunate! All the young people enjoying themselves.

(And then the door opens, and THE DEAN *enters hurriedly.)*

THE DEAN Oh, your Majesty! I am so sorry to have kept your Majesty waiting!

THE QUEEN Mr. Dean, send that man away!

(But there is no need. Like a worm with a broken spine, the Intruder collapses out of the room, to spend the rest of that nice day in abject explanation of the appalling mistake he has made. And though he himself will take many days to recover from it, it gives the garden-party an added success; the Guests are enormously pleased to know that THE QUEEN *is there. Meanwhile* THE DEAN *is bestowing his sympathy where it is less needed.)*

THE DEAN   Really, your Majesty, I am most sorry! — *most* sorry! Very unfortunate!

THE QUEEN   Please do not apologize. It was my fault — not sending you word beforehand. I seem to have come on a wrong day.

THE DEAN   Oh, no, your Majesty, not at all! Quite the reverse. Your Majesty's arrival gave me a respite for which I am truly grateful. I had foolishly let myself be persuaded to a game of tennis: which — at my age —

THE QUEEN   Yes, indeed; very rash! *I* don't play tennis; I never did. Even croquet is now rather beyond me. You see, it doesn't do for the Queen always to be beaten; and when that happened, I left off.

THE DEAN   I am sure your Majesty's decision was a wise one.

THE QUEEN   Yes; but I can't always decide things as easily as that for myself. There are some things which I have to admit are quite beyond me.

THE DEAN   Indeed, Ma'am, I should hardly have thought so.

THE QUEEN   Oh, yes. And it is about something of that kind that I have come now. I want to consult you on a matter over which I am in real difficulty —

THE DEAN   I feel truly honoured, Ma'am.

THE QUEEN   It is on a matter of *faith*.

(*At once* THE DEAN'S *manner undergoes a spiritual change, the correct sort of change, which* (*as one having authority*) *he feels to be expected of him.*)

THE DEAN   Over any such matter as *that*, your Majesty has my deepest, my most earnest attention — and sympathy.

THE QUEEN   I think, then, you had better close the window —

THE DEAN   Ah, yes; I will, I will.

(*He does so.*)

THE QUEEN (*continuing*) — so that we can feel quite safe.

(*As a further proof of sympathetic feeling, he lets down the blind.*)

Thank you. That will do nicely.

(THE DEAN *is now all attention, in an atmosphere better suited to a consideration of religious difficulties than that afforded by an outlook on garden-party gaiety; and* THE QUEEN *begins.*)

THE QUEEN When I was in Scotland recently, I listened to a sermon from Dr. Donald Macleod, one of my Presbyterian Chaplains — with most of which I entirely agreed. But there was one part about which I felt a certain difficulty. He said that, as faithful Christians, we were bound to accept, without question, the story of Jonah and the Whale. Mr. Dean, is it really necessary that I should believe that Jonah *was* swallowed by a Whale?

THE DEAN (*ponderingly*) The question is a difficult one, Ma'am.

THE QUEEN Yes; that is why I ask it.

THE DEAN Difficult, I mean, to answer in a few words. There are, in fact — and that is what makes it difficult — *two* answers to the question.

THE QUEEN *Two* answers? It must be yes, *or* no.

THE DEAN It is yes, *and* no, Ma'am.

THE QUEEN That seems to me very puzzling, Mr. Dean.

THE DEAN I will endeavour to explain, Ma'am.

THE QUEEN Then do, please, sit down: for this may take a long time.

(THE DEAN *bows himself to a chair.*)

THE DEAN I was about to say, Ma'am, that we can have no doubt, since the story is given a very significant application in the New Testament —

THE QUEEN Yes; *that* was my trouble.

THE DEAN — that it was actually written under Divine inspiration, for our guidance and instruction. As an illustrative symbol of the great central Truth of our Christian Faith, it has a sanctity and a significance which cannot be denied. Nor, I think, ought we to say it could not *possibly* be also true literally, since with God all things *are* possible. And though, ordinarily speaking, there are biological difficulties, about which the scientists inform us — still, we must guard ourselves from saying that it was *impossible* for the Creator to 'provide' — for that is the word used — to provide a great fish fully capable of swallowing Jonah — had it been necessary.

THE QUEEN (*insistently*) But do you think that He *did*?

THE DEAN (*guardedly*) No, Ma'am, upon the whole, I do not think so.

THE QUEEN Neither do I!

THE DEAN But I also think He *could* have done so: which being granted — and we must faithfully grant it — then, I think, we are quite free to believe that the story was used by our Lord merely for its illustrative value:—Here was something which all His hearers knew and believed, on high Scriptural authority; and He used it to tell them of a greater wonder yet to come, about which we ourselves can have no doubt whatever. Theologically speaking, therefore, we must accept the story as both possible, and — in its doctrinal significance — *true*; though, biologically, we are free to think that God did *not* find it actually necessary for Jonah to be swallowed by a whale, or by any other form of fish.

THE QUEEN Then, to my mind, that settles it.

THE DEAN We have also to remember, Ma'am, that metaphor and other figures of speech are frequently used in Holy Scripture — in the Old and the New Testament alike. So I do not think that your Majesty's mind need be troubled over what may, after all, have only been a very striking example of poetical imagery, divinely chosen to enforce the great truth that with God all things are possible. Does that, Ma'am, meet your Majesty's difficulty; or does any other point still — ?

THE QUEEN No, Mr. Dean, you have now quite satisfied me; and I am so much obliged to you. It was, as you say, a very difficult question; and you have lifted a great weight off my mind ... I do not usually discuss matters of this kind with *anybody*. Even to my dear Husband, the Prince, I seldom mentioned them; for I was aware that in his great mind — too deep for my understanding — he held theological views with which he did not wish to trouble me — for fear we might not agree. He was so considerate always!

THE DEAN He was, indeed, Ma'am.

THE QUEEN Had he been here still, I should have asked *him*.

As it was, I first wrote to Sir Henry Ponsonby, who was away at the time, and whom, in smaller matters, I always find so helpful. It was he who advised me to come to you, as I have now done.

THE DEAN   I am very glad, and most honoured that your Majesty did so.

THE QUEEN   Yes; religion is sometimes very puzzling, is it not?

THE DEAN   It has that quality, Ma'am; but the difficulties have their value. We should not wish them altogether away.

THE QUEEN   Yet I always want to know more — about the next world, I mean.

THE DEAN   That, Ma'am, is understandable — especially under the shadow of such a bereavement as your own. Life is a great mystery.

THE QUEEN   But not so great a mystery as death.

THE DEAN   No, no. Of course to us, here and now, death necessarily seems a terrible and overwhelming event — because life seems to end *with* it. But when we have got beyond it, will it not surely look very different?

THE QUEEN   Yes, very different, no doubt: as one looks *down* a hill, after having come up it.

THE DEAN   Quite so; and therefore, as one looks back, smaller and less important. If one may compare small things to great — a visit to the dentist provides us with a similar comparison. When one goes to have a tooth out, the ordeal beforehand seems great; but when it *is* out, the ordeal is over.

THE QUEEN   Ah, yes! I have only had two teeth out in my life; and that was under gas; so I knew nothing about it.

THE DEAN   Your Majesty has, indeed, been fortunate.

THE QUEEN   And people, when they are dying, *are* generally unconscious, I believe?

THE DEAN   Yes, I suppose that is so. A merciful provision

THE QUEEN   The Prince was so, during his last hours.

THE DEAN   Ah, indeed? Yes.

THE QUEEN   And that, of course — the added sense of separation while still alive — was a great grief to me.

THE DEAN   But to him a blessing.

THE QUEEN   I wonder how long the unconsciousness lasts?

THE DEAN   After death, Ma'am?

THE QUEEN   Yes. Do we wake up suddenly; or do we sleep for a time?

THE DEAN   That, Ma'am, is one of the mysteries which it is not given us to know.

THE QUEEN   Still, I would *like* to know. The Roman Catholics don't seem to have any doubt about it. Why should *we?*

THE DEAN   The Roman Church, Ma'am, has always pretended to know more than we have any warrant for in Holy Scripture.

THE QUEEN   Oh, yes; of course, I know they are often in many ways superstitious. Still, one would like, about a thing of that sort, to have some assurance. And why shouldn't one? When one goes into the next world — not to meet those who are *waiting* for us, without waste of time, seems such a pity!

THE DEAN   It does, Ma'am, it does! To mere human understanding it must, indeed, seem so. Still, we are bound to believe that, in the other world, everything has been arranged for the best. Indeed, we *must* believe it.

THE QUEEN   (*reluctantly*)   Yes; I suppose so . . . Life in the next world, when we really get to it, will be very interesting.

THE DEAN   Very; very.

THE QUEEN   So much to see — and hear — and learn.

THE DEAN   Yes, indeed, Ma'am. Your Majesty has evidently thought deeply on these subjects.

THE QUEEN   I have. Since my beloved Husband was taken from me, naturally my thoughts have followed him a good deal.

THE DEAN   Ah, yes. Has your Majesty a great sense of — nearness, shall I say? As if death were something very slight and unreal?

THE QUEEN   No. It's the separation I feel. I always think of him as he *was*, here with me on earth: so handsome, so thoughtful, so affectionate, so attentive to all my wishes. And taken from me so soon! No one ever knew his true value, his greatness, his goodness, as I did.

THE DEAN That, Ma'am, is understandable. Who could? It was a terrible bereavement.

THE QUEEN It would be very disappointing to me to think that death was not going to end it.

THE DEAN Oh, but it will, Ma'am, of course!

THE QUEEN *At once*, I mean.

THE DEAN But however long the unconsciousness may last, it will *seem* at once. When we wake we shall surely be in the presence of those we love.

THE QUEEN But there will be others, too.

THE DEAN Undoubtedly.

THE QUEEN *Many* others — of all ages.

THE DEAN Yes: parents and children — the old and the young together.

THE QUEEN I meant — of other ages, in history.

THE DEAN Ah, yes; and how interesting! To meet all the great characters of history.

THE QUEEN Yes; the English Kings. I wonder how many of them will be there. Not all, I'm afraid.

THE DEAN It will be a very interesting encounter for your Majesty: quite an historic event.

THE QUEEN Yes. I wonder what I shall think of them. Some of them were not what they should have been. Still, they were all my ancestors, or my relatives — quite near relations, some of them.

THE DEAN But most of them rather distant.

THE QUEEN Yes, and sometimes distance has its advantages.

THE DEAN And its interest also. So the further back you go in history, the more interesting it will be — Julius Caesar.

THE QUEEN One hardly thinks of Julius Caesar as being in Heaven, does one?

THE DEAN   I suppose not, Ma'am. Still, let us hope!

THE QUEEN   Yes; hope is a Christian duty. But I haven't much of it in some directions.

THE DEAN   Still, Ma'am, however far back in history we go, there will always be the great characters of Holy Scripture. Of them, at least, one may be certain: *They* will be there.

THE QUEEN   Yes; that will be very interesting. Moses, and the Prophets; and Elijah — a most interesting character, especially in the way his life on earth ended. And Isaiah, who wrote so beautifully.

THE DEAN   Ah, yes; and the great Psalmist, David. To meet him will indeed be —

THE QUEEN   David? I hope not!

THE DEAN   (*astonished*) I beg pardon, your Majesty?

THE QUEEN   I said — 'I hope *not*'. I do not wish to meet King David anywhere.

THE DEAN   I really fail to know why your Majesty should —

THE QUEEN   He was not the sort of person I could ever wish to know. His conduct about Bathsheba . . .

THE DEAN   One has to make allowance, Ma'am, for the age in which people lived. Moral standards have changed.

THE QUEEN   He knew he was doing wrong, as well as I do.

THE DEAN   He also repented.

THE QUEEN   I'm not so sure about *that*!

THE DEAN   Oh, but surely!

THE QUEEN   There was Abishag, who came later. He wasn't married to Abishag.

THE DEAN   Well, Ma'am, then what about Solomon?

THE QUEEN   Solomon was a wise King, but he was foolish about women.

THE DEAN   Your Majesty is a shrewd judge of character.

THE QUEEN   I've had a good deal of experience, Mr. Dean: my Uncles — I don't mind telling you.

THE DEAN   Ah, yes, yes. But at your Majesty's Court things have become so different — thanks to your Majesty.

THE QUEEN   The Prince, my dear Husband, set such an example to everybody.

THE DEAN   Ah, yes. Indeed, indeed!

THE QUEEN (*rising*) Well, Mr. Dean, I have taken up quite enough of your valuable time; and now — I must go. But don't play any more tennis. At your age it is too risky.

THE DEAN   I will pay all attention to your Majesty's advice, for which I am duly grateful.

THE QUEEN   Yes; for that *is* a matter on which I can advise, as you on this matter have advised *me* — and have made it all so clear. But I shall go on hoping that it wasn't really a Whale.

THE DEAN   So, Ma'am, with due reservation, shall I.

THE QUEEN   For I do think Religion ought to be sensible, and not too hard to understand.

THE DEAN   I quite agree, Ma'am.

THE QUEEN   And in these days — what with Darwin, and Huxley, and people of that sort — it has become so difficult.

THE DEAN   It has indeed, Ma'am.

THE QUEEN   Well, good-bye, Mr. Dean. I hope nobody is about. I don't want to meet anyone.

THE DEAN   I think we shall find the way quite clear, Ma'am. Directly I heard your Majesty was here, I gave definite instructions . . . This way, Ma'am: this way!

(*And bowing her forward with courtly grace, he leads* THE QUEEN *out.*)

'WE ARE NOT AMUSED'

1885

In one of the apartments at Buckingham Palace, four LADIES *sit in attendance, waiting to be called. It is morning. Their Royal Mistress has not yet sent for them: it is before her accustomed hour; so, though they are all supposed to be doing something, they are not working very hard. Two of them, at a table by the window, are opening and sorting letters. The two others are at needle-work of an ornamental kind, which implies taste rather than usefulness. With fingers gracefully employed, they have minds free for conversation; and the two who are sorting the letters stop occasionally to listen.*

FIRST LADY But I really *couldn't* afford a new dress just then; so I had my pink satin altered, and re-trimmed with black lace.

SECOND LADY Very becoming, my dear!

FIRST LADY Yes. But, of course, *She* found out; so I was never able to wear it again. The first time I appeared in it, she looked me up and down, very disapprovingly. 'You seem very fond of that dress, Miss Somers,' she said, 'since you wear it so often.' 'I have worn it four times, your Majesty,' I replied. 'I have seen it *seven* times,' she said.

SECOND LADY Had she?

FIRST LADY Yes: seven was the exact number. Isn't she awful?

THIRD LADY Well, but really! How can she expect us always to have new dresses, on three hundred a year? I spend four hundred, at least.

FOURTH LADY I don't spend it, but I owe it.

SECOND LADY Still, as we do like being at Court, we must expect to pay for it.

FIRST LADY We should be more encouraged to pay for it, if she spent a little more on dress herself. This Widow-business is one of her saving ways.

SECOND LADY   Oh, my dear, I don't think you ought to say that!

FIRST LADY   But I do! And with all that old lace of hers, she can cover up any old rag; and you can't see whether it's old or new. Two of us once tried exchanging dresses — with alterations, of course. I took one of Lady Charlotte's; she took one of mine . . . The first time I ever wore it, the Queen said to me, 'Miss Somers, that dress doesn't suit you! You must get another.' And she said exactly the same to Lady Charlotte, when she saw her in mine . . . She *knew* what we'd done!

THIRD LADY   There's nothing she doesn't know, that she makes up her mind to know. She's got an eye like a gimlet.

FIRST LADY   And a memory like a pin-cushion! Everything that goes into it — sticks.

(*A* FIFTH LADY *enters in agitated excitement.*)

FIFTH LADY   Oh, my dears! I've just had such an escape!

SECOND LADY   What from?

FIFTH LADY   I almost met the Queen, coming out of her room — face to face!

SECOND LADY   But why shouldn't you meet her?

FIFTH LADY   Dear Innocence, when you've been here long enough to learn the ABC of Court Etiquette, and Queen's Whims, you'll know that to meet Her Gracious Majesty where you are not supposed to meet her — out of your proper place — is one of the unforgivable sins . . . I was carrying a vase of flowers — down the Queen's private corridor, of all places! It was rather full, so I had my eye on it.

THIRD LADY   The corridor?

FIFTH LADY   No; the vase . . . And all at once, I saw the Queen coming out of her room — with 'Mop'. I couldn't run; so I just dodged behind a window-curtain . . . Mop came trotting down the passage, and stopped to smell at me. Had he started barking, I should have been done for. Luckily I'd spilt some of the water; that distracted his attention. Then up comes the Queen. And there was Mop; and there was the water. So, of course, Mop was suspected of a small misbehaviour.

FIRST LADY   Oh, my dear! How thrilling!

FIFTH LADY   She was so near me, I could have touched her. Mop had run on: she called him back, in a tone that at once made him look guilty, poor lamb! (*And now, carried away by the interest of her story, she starts, in tone and gesture, to mimic Her Royal Mistress.*) 'Mop! Mop! Come here at once! What's this? . . . Who did that? . . . Now don't pretend, and look as if you didn't know! You are a very naughty, naughty, naughty, little dog. And you must be whipped for it.'

> (*The* LADIES, *who get so little in Court life to amuse them, go into squeals of laughter; and, in their paroxysms of mirth, do not perceive that the door is slowly opening.*)

LADIES   Oh! how perfectly lovely. How exactly like her!

> (THE QUEEN *enters; they all rise precipitately, and curtsy.* THE QUEEN *advances in measured silence, then speaks.*)

THE QUEEN   Like whom?

> (*There is an awful pause: nobody answers. With quiet precision,* THE QUEEN *repeats her question.*)

Like whom?

FIFTH LADY   I was only trying to give an imitation, your Majesty.

THE QUEEN   Yes. Of whom?

FIFTH LADY   I really couldn't say, Ma'am. Of no one in particular.

THE QUEEN   Oh? How do you give an imitation of 'no one in particular'?

FIFTH LADY   I mean, Ma'am, it was such a bad imitation.

THE QUEEN   I daresay. But — of whom? . . . I ask you — of *whom*?

FIFTH LADY (*wishing herself dead*)   Of your Majesty.

THE QUEEN   So I supposed. You will please to do it again.

FIFTH LADY   Oh, I *couldn't*, your Majesty!

THE QUEEN   And pray, why not?

FIFTH LADY   I did it so badly. It was silly of me. It wasn't really like, at all. It was only — Oh, I'm sure your Majesty will excuse me!

THE QUEEN As I trust that you would do nothing behind my back, Lady Jane, that you would be ashamed of doing to my face, I tell you to do it again.

FIFTH LADY I don't think I can, your Majesty!

THE QUEEN I daresay you don't; but *I* do.

FIFTH LADY (*bracing herself for the ordeal*) I do beg your Majesty to pardon me!

THE QUEEN When you have done it again; not before.

FIFTH LADY If your Majesty would only allow me to explain.

THE QUEEN I have no doubt, Lady Jane, that it will explain itself. . . . Now . . . begin!

> (*In a very lack-lustre way, the imitation is repeated — with modifications.* THE QUEEN *has seated herself. Mop, who has joined the company, stands looking on. He hears himself named, but cannot understand why: for here nothing has happened.*)

FIFTH LADY 'Mop! . . . Mop! . . . Where are you? You naughty, naughty, little dog! Who did that? . . .'

THE QUEEN What does '*that*' mean?

FIFTH LADY (*with feeble invention*) A torn curtain, your Majesty.

THE QUEEN Oh? Indeed? Mop is not in the habit of tearing curtains, Lady Jane, any more than I am.

FIFTH LADY No, your Majesty.

THE QUEEN *No.* . . . It was *not* a torn curtain — nothing of the kind. . . . *We are* NOT *amused.*

> (*She rises: and goes out.*)

FIRST LADY How awful! How very awful! She *knew*!

THIRD LADY Knew? Of course she knew! Why, it's only just happened.

FIFTH LADY Well, that settles it! After tea, I shall go and drown myself! *Then* she'll be sorry!

> (*The door re-opens;* THE QUEEN *again enters.*)

THE QUEEN Lady Jane, as you seem to have been a witness of

the incident, will you, please, take Mop, and whip him at once —
before he forgets? And then — *send* somebody!

FIFTH LADY (*tremulously*)   But it *wasn't* Mop, your Majesty!

(*But she is too late. Believing in Mop's guilt,* THE QUEEN *has
already gone.*)

FIRST LADY   Hadn't it better be?

FIFTH LADY (*miserably*)   Yes, I suppose so! For if I don't do it,
she'll find out. . . . Poor Mop! Come and be whipped!

(*She takes up the vicarious sacrifice in her arms, and goes out,
leaving the door open. And presently, from far down the passage,
we hear the mild yelpings of a small dog, who is being whipped —
not, perhaps, very severely. But the accompanying words —
'Naughty! Naughty!' are loudly given, so that — reaching* THE
QUEEN'S *ear — Her Majesty may be satisfied that her order has been
obeyed.*)

A DOMESTIC DIFFERENCE

Again we see THE QUEEN *seated in her garden-tent at Balmoral. She is now a good deal older than when we last saw her, pleasantly awaiting the arrival of her favourite Prime Minister, Lord Beacons-field. She is now waiting for somebody who pleases her less; but that other favourite,* MR. JOHN BROWN, *is still in attendance, ready as ever with instruction, admonition, and advice.* MR. BROWN *has just brought in 'the morning sherry', which he deposits on the table before her.*

BROWN Will your Majesty have it now?

THE QUEEN Not yet, Brown, it's too early. Has the Prince not yet arrived?

BROWN (*stiffly*) Yes, your Majesty, he has arrived.

THE QUEEN. Was the train very late?

BROWN No, Ma'am; 'twas as punctual as trains always are that have to bring Royalty.

THE QUEEN Then how long has he been here?

BROWN About an hour, Ma'am.

THE QUEEN Without coming to see me! Go and tell him to come at once. Say that I've been waiting for him.

BROWN I will, Ma'am.

(BROWN *braces himself with great self-satisfaction to go and deliver the message.* THE QUEEN *resumes her letter-writing; she has just finished, and closed the last, when a* SECRETARY *arrives to make inquiry.*)

SECRETARY Has your Majesty any letters ready for the morning mail?

THE QUEEN Yes; see that these go at once. They are important. And will you please tell the new Minister in Attendance — who is he?

SECRETARY Lord Kimberley, your Majesty.

THE QUEEN   Oh, yes; well, tell Lord Kimberley that I will see him at four o'clock this afternoon.

SECRETARY   I will, your Majesty.

(*The* SECRETARY *goes.* THE QUEEN *takes up a newspaper, but lays it down when, without being sent for, one of her daughters enters.*)

THE QUEEN   No, my dear, I don't want you here just now. I'm going to see Bertie.

THE PRINCESS   But mayn't I see him too, Mama dear?

THE QUEEN   No, not yet. I shall have to talk to him — very seriously, about a lot of things — things which — well, you had better not be here.

THE PRINCESS   I got a note from him just now.

THE QUEEN   Oh? What about?

THE PRINCESS   Just to say that he had arrived, and wanting to know whether you were alone.

THE QUEEN   Alone?

THE PRINCESS   Yes.

THE QUEEN   What did you say?

THE PRINCESS   I said I thought you still had Mr. John Brown with you.

THE QUEEN   You needn't have told him that or anything. What does it matter whom I have with me, when he knows I'm here — waiting for him?

THE PRINCESS   Shall I go and tell him, Mama?

THE QUEEN   No, I've sent Brown to tell him. So now run away, my dear.

(THE PRINCESS *goes;* THE QUEEN *again takes up the paper, but has hardly started when* MR. BROWN *returns. She looks up sharply over the top of her spectacles.*)

Yes? . . . Well?

BROWN   (*in a tone of 'duty done'*)   I've told him, your Majesty.

THE QUEEN   Very well; and when he comes, you can go.

BROWN   Aye; I'll go. But he didna' seem as if he was making a

great hurry aboot coming, Ma'am, though I told him in your Majesty's ain words that he was wanted.

THE QUEEN   Oh? What did he say to make you think that?

BROWN   As soon as I'd told him what I'd come for, he just sent me out of the room. 'Mr. Brown', says he, 'you can go'; which I did — finally.

THE QUEEN   What was he doing, Brown?

BROWN   He was sitting talking to Lord Kimberley, Ma'am; he was having a drink, and he was smoking — a cigar, a large one which he hadna' quite finished.

THE QUEEN   And what did you say? What *had* you said, I mean, when you gave my message?

BROWN   Nothing different from what your Majesty told me to say. 'Your Mother has sent me to tell you that you are to come and see her at once. She's been waiting.' At which, in a manner of speaking, he didna' seem to be pleased.

THE QUEEN   I daresay not. You know, Brown, he sometimes makes me very anxious.

BROWN   Aye, I'm anxious aboot him myself, Ma'am. He hasna' got them to advise him that would be best for him. Believe me, Ma'am, he's not a very good judge of character. If he were, maybe I could be of more use to him.

THE QUEEN   He's a long time coming.

BROWN   He's there down the garden, Ma'am — waiting.

THE QUEEN   Waiting? Go and tell him to come.

BROWN   He'll come, Ma'am, without telling, I wouldn't mind saying, when he's seen me go.

THE QUEEN   In that case, Brown, perhaps you had better.

BROWN   I will, Ma'am. I'll go up along the other way.

(*He starts to go, takes a look in* THE PRINCE'S *direction, then comes back to say:*

Aye; he's coming along *now*, Ma'am.

(*Exit* BROWN; *a minute later,* THE PRINCE *enters. Relations are evidently strained;* THE QUEEN'S *look is sufficient to indicate that the usual embrace of mother and son on first meeting is not to be expected.*)

THE PRINCE (*stiffly*) Good morning, Mama dear; I hope I see you well.

THE QUEEN (*sharply*) Bertie, why have you been so long coming?

THE PRINCE I should have come sooner, Mama, had you sent someone more suitable to tell me that you were ready to see me.

THE QUEEN What do you mean by 'more suitable'?

THE PRINCE I do not think it is suitable for you to send me orders by a mere lackey.

THE QUEEN Bertie, I will not allow you to speak to me like that!

THE PRINCE Then please, Mama, do not allow your lackey to speak to me as he did just now. Say to me what you like Mama; but do not make that man Brown your messenger.

THE QUEEN That man Brown, as you call him, is the best friend I have.

THE PRINCE It is very regrettable that it should be so. But however much he is *your* friend, Mama, you must not expect me to treat him as though he were mine.

THE QUEEN Bertie!

THE PRINCE Please listen, Mama! Do you know what that man said to me just now? 'Your Mother sends me to say that you are to come and see her at once. She's waiting.' He did not even trouble himself to say 'Your Royal Highness'.

THE QUEEN Well, of course that was a mistake; but it could only have been an accident. He just forgot.

THE PRINCE Yes, he forgot! I said 'To whom are you speaking?' And then he did say 'To your Royal Highness'; but only then.

THE QUEEN Yes? ... Well?

THE PRINCE I said 'Then now you can go.' He went; but even his manner of leaving the room was insolent.

THE QUEEN Bertie, you are always complaining about poor John Brown. He has a plain, straightforward way with him, which one has to allow for. He is a man I can trust.

THE PRINCE   You trust him too much, Mama. He takes liberties which he has no right to take. Even to you he is not properly respectful.

THE QUEEN   How is he not respectful?

THE PRINCE   Is it respectful for him to come to personal attendance upon you when he is the worse for drink?

THE QUEEN   I have never seen him the worse for drink, never!

THE PRINCE   Then you have shut your eyes, Mama, to what has been quite evident to others, for a long time, and is becoming more frequent.

THE QUEEN   I happen to have very good eyes, and I keep them open — as you have had good reason for knowing. But it isn't for you to pass on what malicious tattlers may have told you about poor John Brown, that I've sent for you now . . . Bertie, you must alter your manner of living.

THE PRINCE   In what way, Mama?

THE QUEEN   You are living a life of mere idleness and pleasure, and sometimes, I fear, dissipation: with — as I happen to know — certain very undesirable associates.

THE PRINCE   May I be told their names?

THE QUEEN   I am not going to name anybody.

THE PRINCE   But somebody must have named them to you, Mama. I think I have a right to be told who they are, and also who was your informant.

THE QUEEN   It is sufficient if I tell you this; you associate (amongst others of doubtful character) with one lady of title who, I am told, has become a rabid socialist; and also with divorced persons, including women.

THE PRINCE   In present-day society, Mama, that can no longer be avoided. And you yourself signed the law making divorce easier.

THE QUEEN   I have to sign a great many laws which I don't approve.

THE PRINCE   And I have to meet a great many people whom I would prefer not to meet; a necessary drawback to my having taken over so many of your social duties for you, Mama.

THE QUEEN My social duties?

THE PRINCE Yes, Mama, in addition to my own. And if you would have allowed me to help you also — in matters political — I should no doubt be living what you would regard as a more useful life, and not one which you mistakenly describe as a life of mere pleasure and idleness — and dissipation. Mama, I would be very grateful if you would let me help you — more.

THE QUEEN You can only help me, Bertie, when you behave so that I can trust you.

THE PRINCE Have you ever given me the opportunity of proving that I can be trusted?

THE QUEEN You must first change your habits, Bertie. Then perhaps —

THE PRINCE What habits do you mean, Mama?

THE QUEEN (*ignoring the question*) And also (it is painful for me to have to say this) show more respect to your dear Father's memory.

THE PRINCE In what way have I failed, Mama?

THE QUEEN Last year you did not come to Windsor on the anniversary of his death, though all the others did.

THE PRINCE I was under medical advice — not to go out.

THE QUEEN It was not the only time, Bertie.

THE PRINCE No; in winter one does sometimes catch cold.

THE QUEEN If it happens again I shall require a medical certificate.

THE PRINCE Meaning that you are prepared to accept the doctor's word, but not mine? I'm sorry, Mama.

THE QUEEN So am I.

THE PRINCE Then about that there is no more to be said. We disagree about many things, Mama; but often, in spite of differences, I obey you. May I ask you in return to do me one favour? When you have orders for me, will you please, in future, not send them by Mr. John Brown?

THE QUEEN I will send them by whoever I choose.

THE PRINCE Then, Mama, you may sometimes find that I am

less attentive to your wishes than you expect me to be. You have told me that I have undesirable associates, unsuitable for one in my position. I wish you could realize how unsuitable for one in your position is the familiarity which you permit from Mr. John Brown.

THE QUEEN   Bertie! Go — go instantly!

THE PRINCE   Very well, Mama. Good-bye; I shall return to Sandringham to-day.

THE QUEEN   You do not return to Sandringham till I say that you may. That is an order, and it is to be obeyed.

(*But* THE PRINCE *has already gone.* THE QUEEN *rings; an* ATTENDANT *enters.*)

Tell Mr. Brown that I want him — at once.

(MR. BROWN *has apparently not gone far; for he appears almost immediately.*)

BROWN   Was your Majesty wanting me?

THE QUEEN   Yes, Brown. Pour me out a glass of sherry — and take one yourself. And then, will you go and give instructions that *no* carriage is to go to the station to-day — whoever orders it.

BROWN   I will, Ma'am.

(*He pours out the two glasses of sherry. Presently the order is given. But* THE PRINCE, *too, has a will of his own; and finding the use of the Royal stables denied to him, he goes to the station in a hired conveyance — a proceeding which, when she hears of it, Her Majesty describes as 'Most extraordinarily improper'.*)

A VISIT TO BIRMINGHAM

1887

THE QUEEN *is receiving a visit from one of her daughters. The extra activities of her year of Jubilee have already begun to take up her time. But they have not yet lessened her vitality, or caused any depression of her spirits — quite the other way. In spite of her chronic ritual of widowhood, in which she has indulged for so many years, she is really rather enjoying herself; for the Nation has unanimously decided that, having reigned for fifty years, she has proved herself a good and a great Queen. And without any personal conceit, but under a sense of divine guidance, and firm belief that she has been true to the ideals instilled in her by the late Prince Consort, Her Majesty thankfully accepts the popular verdict.*

THE PRINCESS Well, Mama, so you have been to Birmingham. How did everything go?

THE QUEEN Beautifully. I never thought Birmingham would be so loyal, so enthusiastic. But it was — in spite of what used to be its bad politics. But that has all changed now. Mr. Joseph Chamberlain has become wiser in the last year or two; and yesterday he behaved very well, and never made a mistake, though I am told that until he became a Liberal Unionist he was still a Republican.

THE PRINCESS Your coming to Birmingham would quite cure him of *that*, I should think.

THE QUEEN Well, perhaps it did. Anyway he was as respectful as could possibly be, and spoke quite like a gentleman.

THE PRINCESS And you laid the stone for them? Did you do anything else?

THE QUEEN Yes; I did a great deal. There were addresses, which I had to answer; and presentations, *and* a public luncheon, which of course I didn't attend.

THE PRINCESS Oh, of course not, Mama.

THE QUEEN No; though I think they rather expected it. But I have always made that my rule — not to lunch in public *anywhere*.

THE PRINCESS But you have sometimes lunched at the Guildhall with the Lord Mayor of London, have you not, Mama?

THE QUEEN No, my dear; no, never. When Crowned Heads come to this country, we send them to a State luncheon with the Lord Mayor, but we don't go ourselves. On such occasions, they have to be in the place of honour; we couldn't *both* sit on the Lord Mayor's right hand; and as I couldn't sit anywhere else, I should be *de trop*.

THE PRINCESS Mama dear, you are wonderful! You seem to know exactly not only how everything ought to be done, but what has to be avoided.

THE QUEEN Well, of course, my dear, I have had long experience. But I always had a sort of instinct what *was* right on public occasions — better sometimes even than your dear Papa, who was so good at etiquette; and there were times when I had to hurt his feelings. I remember, at the opening of the Great Exhibition in 'fifty-one (which was all his own dear wonderful doing), he thought that he should walk by my side, with me on his arm. But I knew it wouldn't do. I, as Queen, had to walk alone; and he had to follow with Vicky and Bertie, holding their hands. He didn't like it: he said it made him look so like a nursemaid: and there was a picture of the ceremony, which he would not have hung at Windsor — though I had bought it from the artist, as being the right thing to do — wouldn't have it, just because of that. And when I opened Parliament it had to be the same; though, of course, we didn't take the children with us there, so it didn't matter. Ah, if he had lived till now, I don't think my dear people would have gone on being so jealous and suspicious of him. It was very wrong and foolish of them. Well, that is all over. But it is especially on these State occasions that I so miss him, with the feeling of being there all alone. Still, I did enjoy going to Birmingham. I hadn't been there for twenty-one years. Perhaps that was because of its politics, which is why I don't go to Ireland; but this year, I'm told I must. Mr. Chamberlain himself was Mayor then; now it was Mr. Martineau, a very handsome, well-behaved man . . . Of course, there were a few mistakes; one has to expect that where people are not accustomed to receiving Royalty. When the presentations were being

made (most of them quite permissible and proper) one, if you please, was the Birmingham Coroner. Well, I wasn't going to allow *that*! So, as he came forward I drew back, and gave him such a look! That ought to have been enough, but it wasn't. I told Mr. Martineau that I did not consider Coroners were presentable; and as he still stood there, waiting and bowing, someone pulled him away. Poor man, he did look so crestfallen! I was quite sorry for him at the time; though I heard afterwards that it was his own doing, he having insisted, thinking himself important enough. But it would never have done to allow such a precedent as that: a Coroner indeed!

THE PRINCESS What is a Coroner, Mama?

THE QUEEN Something medical, my dear. He has to do with dead bodies and post-mortems, and all that sort of thing. Not a Crown appointment at all, though it sounds like one — a mere public convenience, a sort of sanitary inspector; nothing more. And in these days when radicalism is so rampant, even leading to socialism, I shouldn't wonder — one mustn't let Royalty make itself too common.

(*A* GENTLEMAN *of the Court enters, and bows, awaiting permission to speak.*)

Yes?

GENTLEMAN Please, your Majesty, your Majesty's Home Secretary, Mr. Matthews, is in attendance to see your Majesty.

THE QUEEN Oh yes; let him come in. (*The* GENTLEMAN *withdraws.*) And as he is a Minister, you had better go, my dear. We may be talking politics.

(THE PRINCESS *goes out by another door, as* MR. MATTHEWS *is ushered into the Presence, and makes his bow.*)

Good morning, Mr. Matthews. You have come for an audience? Is there anything special?

MATTHEWS No, Ma'am; only it is my humble duty and happy privilege, to congratulate your Majesty on the great success of your visit to Birmingham. I am sure that, both politically and publicly, it has been most valuable.

THE QUEEN Well, Mr. Matthews, as you were responsible for

the arranging of it, I also must congratulate *you*. Everything went off most satisfactorily. Birmingham, whatever its past record, has now become a loyal city. And it was quite right that we should take the occasion of the opening of the new Law Courts for paying it this compliment.

MATTHEWS It has been greatly appreciated, Ma'am. And, as always follows when your Majesty or some member of your Majesty's Royal Family graciously performs any public ceremony for the benefit of the community, there has been a remarkable increase of loyalty and enthusiasm. Birmingham has benefited.

THE QUEEN Very satisfactory.

MATTHEWS I have here, Ma'am, a copy of the official report sent to the Home Office, which your Majesty may like to see.

THE QUEEN Thank you, I don't think that will be necessary. I am quite satisfied with what you have already told me. And now — that is all?

MATTHEWS There is one other matter, Ma'am, to which I would ask your Majesty to give consideration. I had the opportunity of speaking with Mr. Chamberlain yesterday, who, though he said that everybody was delighted with your Majesty's visit, did rather complain that while the town had made so lavish a display of decoration, there had hardly been enough show in response. He considered that there should have been more carriages in the procession, and a guard of the Household Cavalry.

THE QUEEN But my Household Cavalry never goes out of London, Mr. Matthews — at least not for occasions of *this* kind.

MATTHEWS I told him so, Ma'am: I also said how very much your Majesty preferred that things should be done simply. But he countered that by saying that simplicity was suitable to a Republic . . .

THE QUEEN To a Republic? Oh, indeed!

MATTHEWS . . . but that a Sovereign should make such visits in all possible State — that the Household Cavalry were paid for by the taxpayer, and therefore the people in the provinces had a right to see them.

THE QUEEN Ah! That's the business man speaking — always must have his money's worth. Anything else?

MATTHEWS With regard to London being the exception, Ma'am, he said that when your Majesty goes to perform any function in Edinburgh, a fine display of troops is always made there, generally of the Scots Guards.

THE QUEEN Yes: but then, Edinburgh is the capital of Scotland.

MATTHEWS I did so remind him, Ma'am: but Mr. Chamberlain seemed to think that Birmingham was quite as important as Edinburgh.

THE QUEEN Indeed! Then on that point we differ. Still there is some sense in what he says; for I do wish to give all my dear people satisfaction, this year especially when their personal devotion to me is being so wonderfully shown. So, if you think well, Mr. Matthews, you may let Mr. Chamberlain know that his suggestion is having my favourable consideration.

MATTHEWS I am greatly obliged, Ma'am; for just now it is rather important, politically, that Mr. Chamberlain should feel that any advice he offers is given consideration.

THE QUEEN Ah yes; to be sure. Well, I find him a much improved character. Even his manner is more respectful than when he first took office under Mr. Gladstone. It was then that I had to receive Radicals as Ministers for the first time — a very painful experience. Since then, unfortunately, I have become quite accustomed to it — though not liking it any better. Now, however, under Lord Salisbury, things are different . . . Well, have you anything else, Mr. Matthews, about which you wish to consult me?

MATTHEWS I think not, Ma'am.

THE QUEEN Then as you are here in your capacity of Home Secretary, I will take this opportunity of speaking to you about the Bill of which you have charge for the prevention of cruelty to animals, especially with reference to my poor dear friends the dogs. In that Bill, new powers are given to the police which, unless properly safeguarded, will be most dangerous, as I am sure you yourself must agree.

MATTHEWS As, for instance, Ma'am?

THE QUEEN The killing of dogs which are supposed to be mad. No dog should ever be killed by the police without a certificate from a veterinary surgeon.

MATTHEWS If the dog is at large, Ma'am, and a veterinary surgeon not available, delay might be dangerous.

THE QUEEN Of course, there may be such cases; but there must also be discrimination. Dogs at their masters' doors should be left alone and not molested. A faithful dog will often, under those circumstances, snap and snarl, or even bite, if interfered with by strangers.

MATTHEWS There would, of course, Ma'am, be no interference by the police unless the dog had shown previous symptoms.

THE QUEEN And of that who is to be judge? Fits are no proof. Many ignorant people think that if a dog foams at the mouth it must be mad. About that only a veterinary surgeon can decide. It distresses me to think that a dog which is merely having a fit can be legally beaten to death by a policeman's truncheon. Some provision against that *must* be made, or the Bill will not have my consent.

MATTHEWS I will do my best, Ma'am, to give effect to your Majesty's suggestion.

THE QUEEN It is more than a suggestion, Mr. Matthews, it is a *wish*.

(MR. MATTHEWS *bows submissively*.)

And there is another thing. Muzzles, except in the case of very *savage* dogs, should not be used; nor should dogs be run after and hunted to be caught.

MATTHEWS But a dangerous dog, Ma'am, must be caught — somehow: and if he runs away . . .

THE QUEEN Well, let him! Dogs are not dangerous if left to themselves.

MATTHEWS Sometimes, Ma'am.

THE QUEEN Only very exceptionally: yet this Bill seems to treat it as the rule, which I cannot allow. That point, however, I will not discuss further. It is very satisfactory to know that there *are* members of the House of Commons on whose humane principles I can thoroughly rely; and I trust that you will give careful consideration to any safeguarding amendments they may propose.

MATTHEWS I will, indeed, Ma'am.

THE QUEEN Then as regards slaughter-houses; they ought to be *large*, with proper provision of food and water up to the last, for any animals which have to be kept waiting. Slow killing should also be absolutely prohibited. It used to be done quite often to calves, geese, *and* pigs — though less now than formerly; and fish, too, merely for the sake of giving the flesh a better colour.

MATTHEWS Fish are not included in the Bill, Ma'am.

THE QUEEN I think that is a pity. Cruelty is far too common.

MATTHEWS It is, Ma'am.

THE QUEEN And ought to be put down. Habit makes people so thoughtless. Here in Windsor, where I live, I have already had my views made known to all the butchers; so I hope that Windsor sets a good example.

MATTHEWS I believe it does, Ma'am. Sir Henry Ponsonby himself informed me, when I was preparing the Bill, of your Majesty's concern about these matters. And I assure your Majesty that I will give every possible weight to your Majesty's wishes.

THE QUEEN Pray do, Mr. Matthews; for I consider this the most important — next to the prevention of Crime in Ireland — of all the Bills which will be before Parliament in the present session. And now (*she rises*), as I think I have said everything I wished to say, I will not detain you any longer. Good-bye, Mr. Matthews. We thank you for your attendance.

(*The* HOME SECRETARY, *restoring the Official Report to his pocket, makes the preliminary move for bowing himself out.*)

Mr. Matthews, you have dropped something.

MATTHEWS (*picking up the thing which he has dropped*) I am much obliged to your Majesty. Had I lost that it would have cost me something.

THE QUEEN What is it?

MATTHEWS Only my return railway ticket, Ma'am.

THE QUEEN Ticket? What is a ticket for?

MATTHEWS For railroad travelling, Ma'am.

THE QUEEN *I* never have a ticket, when I travel. I never heard of such a thing. The only tickets I ever heard of are 'tickets-of-leave' for criminals.

MATTHEWS Well, Ma'am, that is something we have to share with criminals. When we go by rail, a ticket-of-leave is necessary.

THE QUEEN Dear me! How humiliating!

MATTHEWS We don't feel it, Ma'am. We've got accustomed to it.

THE QUEEN I don't see why it should be necessary.

MATTHEWS It's to prevent people from cheating the company, Ma'am.

THE QUEEN *Would* they cheat?

MATTHEWS I'm afraid so. It does happen sometimes.

THE QUEEN Most extraordinary! And what would have happened, if you hadn't found that ticket?

MATTHEWS I should have had to pay over again, Ma'am.

THE QUEEN Dear me! How very inconvenient! Can't it be altered?

MATTHEWS I'm afraid not, Ma'am.

THE QUEEN People must so often be losing their tickets.

MATTHEWS If they are as careless as I was just now, Ma'am, I am afraid they do.

THE QUEEN Well, don't lose it again, Mr. Matthews. Though I do think that when my Ministers come to see *me*, they ought to travel free.

MATTHEWS That is a suggestion, Ma'am, which I am sure your Majesty's Ministers would welcome.

(THE QUEEN *bows as a signal that he may now take his departure.*) Your Majesty's most humble servant.

(*He bows himself out.* THE QUEEN *moves to her writing-table. She seats herself, takes up a hand-bell and rings. A* LADY *in Attendance enters.*)

N

THE QUEEN   Tell the Princess she may come back.

(*The* LADY *goes.* THE QUEEN *gets out her glasses, and makes preparations to begin writing.* THE PRINCESS *returns.*)

THE QUEEN   I don't much like that Mr. Matthews, my dear.

THE PRINCESS   No, Mama?

THE QUEEN   Such a careless man! He'd have lost his railway ticket if I hadn't saved it for him. (*Without noticing, she drops her glasses.*) I don't think he's going to make a good Home Secretary. No: I don't trust him. He hasn't a really kind heart — not for animals ... Pick up my glasses, my dear; they've dropped somewhere ... I shall have to keep a sharp eye on him to see that he treats the dear dogs as they should be treated. That Bill has got to be altered!

(*At that moment, a small yapping is heard at the door.*)

There's Tyrrie at the door: let him in!

(THE PRINCESS *goes to the door, opens it, and lets in* TYRRIE, *who runs up to* THE QUEEN.)

Well, Tyrrie; so they want to make you wear a muzzle, do they? No, Tyrrie; no; I won't allow it. I won't have any such nonsense here. No, no!

(TYRRIE *barks appreciation.*)

Note for the information of sceptical readers: The Queen's ignorance about railway tickets is a fact. Her refusal to have the Birmingham Coroner presented to her is also a fact. Her remarks about mad dogs, muzzles, and the feeding of animals 'up to the last' in slaughter-houses are given in almost her own words. But all the same, muzzles came in, till rabies went out; and all dogs had to wear them — except, of course, the Queen's.

THE BLUE RIBBON

1887

Monsieur Benjamin Constant's portrait of the Queen, sitting crowned and enthroned in a soft cascade of sunlight, is so well known that the fact of its back being now to the spectator hardly matters. MONSIEUR CONSTANT *has himself arranged it in the best light available; but the windows of Windsor Castle do not give quite the light that he would wish. Still, though the opportunity for favourable display is not all that the Artist could desire, the honour conferred by the Royal command more than compensates.* MONSIEUR CONSTANT, *ceremonially arrayed, flutters in front of his masterpiece, and the* COURT OFFICIAL *who has charge of him stands quietly looking on, admiring the gestures with which, almost as much as with words, the distinguished visitor conducts his conversation.*

COURT OFFICIAL I hope the light is as you wish, Monsieur?

CONSTANT The light? Oh, yes, as you cannot change the windows — it must do!

COURT OFFICIAL We can, if you like, Monsieur, have the windows closed, and the chandeliers lighted.

CONSTANT Ah, no, no, no, no, no! That might make my collars to look untrue. And my collars are very actually chosen.

(*The* COURT OFFICAL *realizes, after a moment, that it is his picture, not his clothes, that* MONSIEUR CONSTANT *is referring to. He turns to study it with the respect due to its vast size.*)

COURT OFFICIAL It is a remarkable picture, Monsieur Constant.

CONSTANT (*with proud humility*) Of so remarkable a Personage, it would be difficult *not*.

COURT OFFICIAL In Paris — it has been popular?

CONSTANT Popular? Ma foi! mais oui! It has struck the conscience of the whole Nation. They look: 'Ah! a Queen!' they say. 'Why have we not still Kings and Queens?' Our Government was quite glad that I brought it away to Bond Street — to relieve the political situation.

COURT OFFICIAL Dear me! And in Bond Street, also, it has been a great success?

CONSTANT Ah! If your Queen Victoria had not been popular before, this would have made her to be so!

COURT OFFICIAL You had no sittings from Her Majesty, Monsieur? But you must surely have come over to England to paint the Throne, and that background. The House of Lords, is it not?

CONSTANT Ah, yes; no! For that, photographs were sufficient. The rest — myself!

COURT OFFICIAL Indeed? And the light — the effect of light coming down from above — that is wonderful!

CONSTANT The light? Ah! yes, the light! Ah! that is my forte. That is where I excel in my imagination.

COURT OFFICIAL Remarkable!

(*And then the* COURT OFFICIAL *has a duty to perform, which must be done delicately.*)

Monsieur Constant, you have met Royalty before?

CONSTANT Ah, no! In Republican France, hélas! we do not have much opportunity for to meet Royalty.

COURT OFFICIAL I only asked because we have a certain etiquette — as to which I am sure you will find no difficulty. Our manners at Court are more like the French manners than the English.

CONSTANT More civilized, you would say?

COURT OFFICIAL Well, in your country you have more ceremony — more grace: so you will understand. . . . When Her Majesty enters, she will only bow to you. When she leaves she may give you her hand. If, then, she raises it slightly, you will kiss it — not otherwise. In conversing with Her Majesty, you will always say 'Your Majesty' or 'Ma'am' — pronounced so.

CONSTANT Ah! Parfaitement! 'Même' — toujours la même chose.

COURT OFFICIAL Her Majesty may ask you questions. You will avoid, as far as possible, asking any questions in return. For instance, you must not say 'Does your Majesty also paint?' If Her

Majesty wishes, she will inform you of the fact herself. If Her Majesty discusses Art with you — as she may do — do not insist too much upon your own opinion; allow Her Majesty to have the last word, and to have it early, in any matter on which you find that you differ.

CONSTANT Mais oui, Monsieur, parfaitement!

COURT OFFICIAL If anything Her Majesty says embarrasses you — I mean, if you feel embarrassed in stating your own view, then it will be always safe and correct for you to bow, saying nothing. And Her Majesty will herself change the conversation to some new subject.

CONSTANT That will be so? Ah!

COURT OFFICIAL I tell you this, Monsieur Constant, so that you may feel more at ease. Seeing Her Majesty constantly, to us it has become second nature. To those who only attend Court rarely, it is more difficult.

CONSTANT Monsieur, I am extremely obliged.

(*Another* COURT OFFICIAL *of lower grade now enters and indicates with a half-bow that he is there to know that all is ready, and to make announcement. You see the words 'Her Majesty' formed by his lips, but you do not hear them. He withdraws silently, closing the door.*)

COURT OFFICIAL Her Majesty will be here in a few moments.

CONSTANT Ah, then allow me!

(*Darting toward the picture, he draws a curtain across it.*)

COURT OFFICIAL But why are you covering the picture, Monsieur?

CONSTANT So that when Her Majesty stands just where she should stand to see it, then I open — so!

COURT OFFICIAL You must not expect Her Majesty to stand where you would wish, Monsieur. She will stand where she herself wishes.

CONSTANT But to see the picture from where it should be seen!

COURT OFFICIAL That Her Majesty will decide for herself, Monsieur.

CONSTANT Ah! Si? That is very English. Yes!

(*And now the door opens, and two Indian Attendants glide in, and stand motionless on either side. There is a pause; and then — small,*

short, stout, but with an amazing dignity which is almost grace, THE
QUEEN *enters. She moves forward, halts at a few paces from her
visitor (who meanwhile has been repeatedly bowing) and, as the*
COURT OFFICIAL *pronounces his name, she bows to him with that
marvellous mixture of distance and courtesy which turns her widow's
cap into a crown.)*

COURT OFFICIAL   Monsieur Benjamin Constant, your Majesty.

THE QUEEN   I am very pleased to meet you, Monsieur Constant.
You have come only recently from France?

CONSTANT   I have had that honour, your Majesty — that pleasure.

THE QUEEN   From Paris?

CONSTANT   It is from Paris I come, your Majesty.

THE QUEEN   It is your first visit to this country?

CONSTANT   It is, Madame, it is.

THE QUEEN   You live in Paris?

CONSTANT   I live always in Paris; I work in Paris, Madame.

THE QUEEN   It was very good of you to come, Monsieur. You
are going to show me your picture.

CONSTANT   Ah, yes! If your Majesty would condescend. Just
three steps more away.

THE QUEEN   But I always prefer to look at pictures closely, Monsieur, so as to see how they are done.

CONSTANT (*resignedly*) Ah, so!

THE QUEEN   One has to look closely before one can be sure that
they are good.

CONSTANT   Ah, but of this picture — a subject so illustrious — I
trust that your Majesty shall have no doubt.

(*He draws the curtain. There is a long pause.* THE QUEEN *looks at
the picture with calm, dignified detachment.*)

THE QUEEN   We are redder than that, Monsieur.

CONSTANT   Ah! but does your Majesty's gracious complexion
never vary — a leetle?

THE QUEEN   Never as much as that, Monsieur.

CONSTANT   Ah, c'est dommage!

THE QUEEN   A little more colour, Monsieur, could easily be added.

CONSTANT   But then, Madame, what will have to become of my collar-scheme — that is, my picture?

THE QUEEN   But this is a portrait, Monsieur, of *Me*.

CONSTANT   Yes, but of the imagination — all my own. I had no sittings from your Majesty.

THE QUEEN   Now that you have seen me, you will be able to correct it.

CONSTANT   Oh, but impossible!

(*The* COURT OFFICIAL *touches his arm, whereat he adds insinuatingly*) — unless your Majesty should graciously sit to me.

THE QUEEN   I have not sat for my portrait, Monsieur, for many years.

CONSTANT   But what a deprivation is not that, Madame, to artists, and to the whole world!

THE QUEEN   There is something else, Monsieur Constant, which you must correct.

CONSTANT   Comment?

THE QUEEN   The ribbon of the Garter — the blue; you have made it too light.

CONSTANT   But permit me to explain, Madame! The light shining on it — so bright from above — the texture, the silk, the reflection — they do all make it lighter than would look otherwise.

THE QUEEN   *It is too light*, Monsieur. I wear the Garter, so I know. Also, though you may not know it, I have practised painting myself. I had two masters to teach me — Sir John Hayter, and Mr. Cope; both excellent artists. They taught me to be true to nature.

CONSTANT   They painted your Majesty's portrait, ever?

THE QUEEN   No. When I was studying with them, I had my portrait painted — in a group with my whole family — by Winterhalter. I will give orders that you shall be shown it before you go. Winterhalter was a great painter, was he not?

CONSTANT Winterhalter? Oh, Winterhalter was everything that the public wished him to be. He had a great name in his day. Now he is dead.

THE QUEEN Yes; more than twelve years ago. I remember sending a wreath to his funeral, and also a letter to his widow. The Prince and I had a great regard for him. There are few artists to-day like him.

CONSTANT Very very few, Madame; or one never hears of them.

THE QUEEN No. . . . Your portrait of me has had a great success, Monsieur, I am told?

CONSTANT Un succès fou, Madame. That is the only word for it.

THE QUEEN In Bond Street.

CONSTANT There; yes, Madame.

THE QUEEN Have you other pictures on exhibition as well?

CONSTANT By myself, no, Madame — not in the same room. We are alone together.

THE QUEEN (*after a pause*) You mean, my picture is alone?

CONSTANT (*conscious that he stands corrected*) Yes, I do mean that, your Majesty — that only.

THE QUEEN I think it was very clever of you to do it without sittings. I wish I could have given you a sitting — just one. But I never sit now. And I hope, Monsieur, that you will at once make those two corrections: a little more red in the face, and to the ribbon more blue.

CONSTANT The red — oh, yes, Madame — if your Majesty orders it. But the blue — the blue, Madame, that — as the Artist — I must be allowed to —

THE QUEEN Good-bye, Monsieur Constant. It has been a great pleasure to meet you. Thank you very much for bringing the picture. As a picture, I like it. As a portrait, you will now be able, by those alterations, to make it better, I hope. Good-bye.

(*She offers him her hand. He bends and kisses it. She goes to the door, turns, bows, and retires, followed by her Attendants.*)

CONSTANT (*a little agitated*) Did I right — to kiss?

COURT OFFICIAL   I think so.

CONSTANT   Did she like the picture enough for me to kiss — you think?

COURT OFFICIAL   Oh, I think so, distinctly.

CONSTANT (*with an artist's grievance*)   Oh, but she did not understand! She did not understand!

COURT OFFICIAL   Her Majesty is accustomed to have her own opinion about things, Monsieur, and not to change it.

CONSTANT   Ah! So English!

COURT OFFICIAL   And now — we have Her Majesty's permission — would you like to see the Winterhalter?

CONSTANT   The Winterhalter? No! I know Winterhalter, and all about him, quite well. Eau sucré — that is what he is.

COURT OFFICIAL   Eau sacré. Holy water?

CONSTANT   Holy? No, I did not say 'holy'; not sacré — sucré: sugar — *and* water!

(*And then, once more, the* COURT OFFICIAL *of lower grade enters, and this time speaks audibly.*)

SECOND COURT OFFICIAL   Her Majesty requests that Monsieur Constant will wait a few moments. Her Majesty has something she wishes to send him.

(*Having delivered his message, the* COURT OFFICIAL *withdraws, leaving* MONSIEUR CONSTANT *in a twitter of excitement.*)

CONSTANT   Ah! but that is — that is — very unexpected! What will it be, you think? Some honour for me? Est-ce possible?

COURT OFFICIAL   Perhaps a souvenir, Monsieur. Probably a signed photograph.

CONSTANT (*his hopes dashed*)   Oh? . . . Well, so long as it is not a photograph of the Winterhalter, I do not mind . . . But — redder? How am I to make that a redder face, and not spoil the collar-harmony of my picture?

COURT OFFICIAL   Don't, Monsieur. Her Majesty will not see it again.

CONSTANT   Ah! Thank you; you are wise, and very kind.

(*Again the* SECOND COURT OFFICIAL *enters, bearing in his hand a small packet, which he presents to* MONSIEUR CONSTANT.)

CONSTANT (*his hopes rising again*) Oh, but this is not a photograph. No, it is too small. It is an honour, surely, an order that she send me! (*He opens the packet, while he speaks.*) Hey? What for is this small piece of blue ribbon?

COURT OFFICIAL There is a note pinned to it, I see.

CONSTANT Ah, yes! (*He unpins it, and reads.*) 'You see, Monsieur, I am right.' What this mean? — 'You see, Monsieur, I am right'?

COURT OFFICIAL (*after examination*) That is the ribbon of the Garter, Monsieur; the blue about which you and Her Majesty did not quite agree. You are to see, she says, that she was *right*.

CONSTANT Oh! Mais c'est incroyable! She do not understand!

COURT OFFICIAL No, Monsieur, perhaps not. But here we don't say so.

CONSTANT Ah! This is England! I must go back to France! Monsieur, I have to tell you she is no artist. Oh, but a great Queen! A wonderful person! Enfin! . . . This — I may keep?

(*He holds up the piece of blue ribbon.*)

COURT OFFICIAL Certainly, Monsieur.

CONSTANT (*his reward with him*) Ah! This blue ribbon — for me! Always! Merci!

(*And, with a flourish of satisfaction, he pockets the Souvenir, which will always give point and corroboration to his story whenever he tells it; as he will do frequently, until one day it reaches ears that were waiting for it: and so — finds its place here.*)

RULING POWERS

25th April 1888

The scene is laid in the Royal Palace at Charlottenberg, where, on her return from Italy, THE QUEEN *has come to pay a farewell visit to her dying son-in-law, the Emperor Frederick. Here, at her Majesty's request,* PRINCE BISMARCK, *the German Chancellor, comes to be received in private audience. Through folding-doors, thrown open by* ATTENDANTS *in gorgeous livery, a* GENTLEMAN *of the Palace ushers the* CHANCELLOR *into the apartment. He is followed by one of his Press Agents,* HERR BUSCH, *whose relations with the Chancellor are intimate, confidential, and peculiar.*

GENTLEMAN This way, your Excellency, this way. If your Excellency will be good enough to wait a moment, I will inform her Majesty of your Excellency's arrival.

BISMARCK (*brusquely*) How is the Emperor this morning?

GENTLEMAN Hardly so well as yesterday, I fear, Excellency. The expected improvement has not come as soon as had been hoped.

(BISMARCK *impatiently turns his back, the* GENTLEMAN *bows to it with profound respect, crosses the chamber, and goes out by another door.*)

BISMARCK (*angrily*) Improvement! There never will be! And they know it! ... How long will that Woman and her English Doctor go on keeping a dead man on the throne?

BUSCH Does your Excellency think that his Majesty himself knows —

BISMARCK That he's dying? Yes; but she won't let him say so. The last time I saw him, his look told me that. But she being there — nothing was said. She won't *let* it be said — knows it might be dangerous.

BUSCH Dangerous? Why, Excellency?

BISMARCK Why? Because, he being as he is, he had no right to the succession. There should have been a Regency: in which case *she* wouldn't have become Empress. That's what the game has been, and that's why she brought in her English Doctor to pretend the case was curable. And now it's the Mother — come to back her up — that I've got to deal with. Her sending for me means something; 'twasn't done out of mere politeness. The Daughter has been coaching her. There's been a lot of correspondence between them lately. And I know what about — that Battenberg marriage for one thing.

BUSCH   Does your Excellency think that is — possible?

BISMARCK   Some may think so.   My business is to make it impossible — which, perhaps, is why I'm here now.   I've no doubt she's got it all cut-and-dried, and is bringing the Parson with her in her travelling-bag, and the Bridegroom in her trunk; and means to pull off the marriage on the spot — before *He* dies, knowing quite well that Wilhelm wouldn't allow it.   Yes, they are having a race with death.   But it's I — not death — that's going to beat 'em . . . Tut, tut! How long is Her Britannic Majesty going to keep me waiting, I wonder?

BUSCH   It is hardly yet the hour that was named, Excellency.

BISMARCK   Oh? Come too soon, did I? I don't generally do that for people I've no wish to meet . . . Busch, I am not looking forward to this.   That old lady makes me feel nervous.

BUSCH (*protesting*)   Nervous, Excellency?

BISMARCK   Isn't it understandable? One can't be on equal terms with a Queen who's had fifty years of thinking that she and her damned country were always right, and everybody else wrong. Besides — women in politics are always a difficulty — if you can't be rid of them.   And this one has got half the Courts of Europe sitting in her lap — her own litter some of 'em.   One can't get rid of *her*.   No; she frightens me.

BUSCH   Your Excellency frightened? Impossible!

BISMARCK   So I should have said myself till I had to face the fact. The only woman who ever frightened me before was my own wife — over her childbearing.   That took the man out of me.   'Twas she who was the man then.

BUSCH   But Excellency, I am assured that, in spite of her great reputation, Queen Victoria is neither intellectual nor clever.

BISMARCK Intellectual? No; but she's intelligent. Clever? no; if she were I should know better how to deal with her: if it came to argument, I could beat her. But *will* she? What I'm afraid of is, of her getting me down where I shan't know what to do.

BUSCH Down?

BISMARCK Yes — to her own level.

BUSCH Your Excellency, then, being her superior.

BISMARCK Her superior? Of course I'm her superior in brain-power — any fool knows that. I am also, on my own reckoning, her superior both in weight and diplomacy (in Europe at any rate). But *she* doesn't know that. And even about that there's this to be said — *I* could fall from power — I may do yet — she won't. And there are big parts of the world where she counts more than I do — parts that some day will mean more than they do now. The British Empire has not come to its decay yet — no, not yet. . . . By the way, Busch, that was an excellent article you wrote the other day, showing up the dirty back-side of its African land-grabbing during the last fifty years.

BUSCH Which your Excellency immediately disowned as not representing your Excellency's view of the matter.

BISMARCK Of course: that's why I told you to write it — so that I could use it as I wanted. It told the truth, and she's read it. And now she's read that I don't agree with it, which isn't the truth. I *do*. So — just now — she's got some reason for being pleased with me; and that, for to-day's business, has its importance. Her gracious Majesty will be a little more graciously inclined toward the humble and obedient servant she means to make of me.

(*The* GENTLEMAN *of the Palace re-enters.*)

GENTLEMAN Her Majesty is now ready to receive your Excellency. Will your Excellency be pleased to come this way?

BISMARCK Wait for me, Busch. I shall want you when this is over.

(*Obsequiously attended by the* GENTLEMAN *of the Palace,* PRINCE BISMARCK *passes through a small ante-room, and then, through doors opened by the liveried* ATTENDANTS, *is bowed into the Presence.*

THE QUEEN, *alone and unattended, rises to meet him. The* GENTLE-
MAN *of the Palace, having announced the* STATE-CHANCELLOR *with
due formality, retires.*)

THE QUEEN Prince Bismarck, I am so glad to meet you.

BISMARCK I am greatly honoured that your Majesty should have
wished it.

THE QUEEN It has long been my wish; but there has never before
been the opportunity.

BISMARCK I did once have the honour of being in your Majesty's
presence, but without the honour of being presented.

THE QUEEN Indeed? Where, and when was that?

BISMARCK At Versailles, when your Majesty, during the Crimean
War, was paying a State-visit to your Majesty's ally, the Emperor
Louis Napoleon.

THE QUEEN How strange that we should have met there, of all
places. So much has happened since then that one could never have
expected, has it not?

BISMARCK It has, indeed, Ma'am.

THE QUEEN In which your Excellency has made history — to the
great advantage of your Country.

BISMARCK I would hope, Ma'am, of Europe also. It is a mistake
in the field of diplomacy to think of one's own country apart from
others.

THE QUEEN I am so glad to hear your Excellency say that. In
working for the welfare and security of my own Empire, that has
ever been *my* policy. I and my Government have always wished to
be in friendly relations with Germany — a wish, it has sometimes
seemed to me, that your Excellency has not entirely shared.

BISMARCK Indeed, your Majesty is mistaken. I admit that we
have had our differences; but they have never been acute, and never
dangerous. Why should they be? It is to Great Britain's interests —
in view of the somewhat suspicious drawing-together of France and
Russia — for the Central Powers of Europe to remain cordially
united. To which end we have to thank your Majesty for the good
service which you have recently rendered us.

THE QUEEN Indeed? I was not aware of it.

BISMARCK Does not your Majesty realize that the visits which you have just paid to Italy and Austria, and now to Germany, are not without political significance? Certain Powers, whose moves we have to watch carefully, have seen the Queen of England, like an officer going the round of his outposts to make sure that all is well — and finding that all *is* well in that pacific Alliance on which depends the peace and security, not only of Europe, but of your Majesty's Dominions throughout the world.

THE QUEEN If my visits have had that effect, I share your Excellency's satisfaction. But I did not know it.

BISMARCK That your Majesty was conferring the benefit unconsciously is but another instance of the formidable power which your Majesty is able to exercise in world politics.

THE QUEEN 'Formidable', do you say?

BISMARCK Yes, Ma'am, rare qualities are often formidable in quarters where they are not expected. The intimate human touch of friendly trust and confidence is not what politicians are used to — and for that reason, when wisely used — as your Majesty is able to use it — is formidable.

THE QUEEN Well, my dear Prince Bismarck, I hope *you* do not find me formidable.

BISMARCK I should, Ma'am, if I felt that I were undeserving of your confidence in my sincerity. But I do assure your Majesty that even should there arise in the future any matter of serious difference between us, I would far rather fail to please your Majesty than fail in sincerity over the statement of my reason for holding to a contrary opinion.

THE QUEEN Such an assurance from your Excellency makes what I have now to say less difficult.

BISMARCK I am at your Majesty's service, for anything that your Majesty may wish to say.

THE QUEEN Prince Bismarck, I wish to speak to you quite plainly.

BISMARCK The more plainly, your Majesty, the more I shall feel honoured.

THE QUEEN You and my daughter, the Kaiserin, do not get on well together. Why is that? I beg you to be quite frank with me.

BISMARCK To be frank, your Majesty — because, unfortunately, she spells Kaiserin 'Kaiser', and to be more frank, Ma'am, pronounces it in the English way.

THE QUEEN I hope your Excellency is not suggesting that English influence is brought to bear upon her where politics are concerned?

BISMARCK No, Ma'am; but her Imperial Majesty has an English mind.

THE QUEEN That can hardly be avoided, as she is English by birth.

BISMARCK The Prince her father, your Majesty, was a German. She seems to have found a difficulty in re-adopting her father's nationality.

THE QUEEN Your Excellency makes a grave charge.

. BISMARCK I fear so, your Majesty.

THE QUEEN Will you tell me where these difficulties occur?

BISMARCK I could hardly specify, your Majesty. They are so constantly occurring.

THE QUEEN But, for instance?

BISMARCK In this proposed marriage of her daughter the Princess Victoria to Prince Alexander of Battenberg — late of Bulgaria.

THE QUEEN That is a matter, your Excellency, about which I very specially wish to consult you.

BISMARCK Consultation, Ma'am, will be welcome. Hitherto I have *not* been consulted — only informed.

THE QUEEN You mean by my daughter, the Empress?

BISMARCK (*stiffly*) It is only through her Imperial Majesty that I am allowed to be informed at all. Since his return to this country I have never once seen the Emperor alone.

THE QUEEN That is certainly a mistake.

BISMARCK It is more than a mistake, Ma'am; it is a conspiracy.

THE QUEEN (*surprised*) Between whom?

BISMARCK Your Majesty bade me be frank: between the Empress and her English doctor.

THE QUEEN Surely conspiracy is hardly the word for it. A doctor has his duty to his patient. Your Excellency must remember that the Emperor is a dying man.

BISMARCK I have also to remember, Ma'am, that he was dying before he became Emperor. That fact, for constitutional reasons, should have been revealed, and a Regency been appointed.

THE QUEEN With what difference?

BISMARCK That, in the interim, there would have been no Emperor — and no Empress.

THE QUEEN That would have made my daughter's position very difficult.

BISMARCK It would, your Majesty.

THE QUEEN I hope you do not include *me* in any such 'conspiracy'.

BISMARCK I do not, Ma'am. Had I thought so, I should not have allowed myself the honour of this interview.

THE QUEEN Your saying so makes me the more glad that we have been able to meet. I may now tell you, Prince Bismarck, that I *have* seen the Emperor alone. I wished it, and so, I believe, did he.

BISMARCK Am I to have your Majesty's confidence on what then took place?

THE QUEEN Yes. I spoke to him about the marriage. I asked him whether he also wished it. He shook his head, and whispered — I could only just hear his poor voice — 'That is not for *me* to decide — now.'

BISMARCK Did your Majesty inform the Empress of what he had said?

THE QUEEN No; for I did not wish him to be again troubled. But I did tell her that, of course, the marriage could not now take place without the consent of her son, Prince Wilhelm, who will so soon, I fear, be in a position when it will be for him to decide.

BISMARCK That your Majesty so advised, affords me great relief. I am deeply grateful.

THE QUEEN I thought it right to say so. But why is your Excellency so much opposed to the marriage?

BISMARCK Because, Ma'am, as I said just now, one should not think of one's own country apart from others.

THE QUEEN In this case, what others?

BISMARCK Russia, your Majesty.

THE QUEEN What has Russia to do with it? Surely now that Russia has got her way and secured his abdication, Prince Alexander is free to marry where and whom he pleases?

BISMARCK Prince Alexander may be free to offer himself, but we are not so free to accept his offer.

THE QUEEN Pray, why not?

BISMARCK For the same reason, Ma'am, that your Majesty would not have allowed one of your daughters to marry the Prince Imperial after the abdication and exile of his father, the Emperor Louis Napoleon. Such a match your Majesty would have regarded as politically inadvisable. It would have roused the resentment and the suspicion of Germany.

THE QUEEN I do not think the two cases are parallel. The restoration of a Napoleon to the throne of France was still possible. There is no such possibility for the return of Prince Alexander to his Principality of Bulgaria.

BISMARCK I fear your Majesty underrates the suspicions of Russia. The Czar's attitude toward the Prince is one of personal antagonism. Germany cannot afford to share it, by allowing this marriage.

THE QUEEN But does your Excellency think that royal marriages have any longer the influence on international politics which they used to have?

BISMARCK There are marriages and marriages, your Majesty. Some do, some do not.

THE QUEEN The marriage of my son the Prince of Wales to a Danish princess did not prevent war between Germany and Denmark. Nor has the marriage of my second son the Duke of Edinburgh to the Czar's only daughter done anything to secure for us the friendship of Russia.

BISMARCK No, Ma'am, perhaps not; but the marriage of one of your Majesty's sons to a daughter of the Sultan of Turkey would most certainly have had a contrary and very disturbing effect.

THE QUEEN But that, your Excellency — marriage to a Mohammedan — would have been impossible.

BISMARCK It would have been very popular with a section of your Majesty's subjects in India. But I merely gave that as an illustration of the differing importance of royal marriages. The very fact that Prince Alexander has been deposed at the dictation of Russia would give political significance to so exalted a marriage, following so quickly after. Your Majesty may think I allow too much weight to the personal feelings of the Czar; but your Majesty's kingdom is an island, whereas Germany has frontiers which are more vulnerable; and the counsels of Autocracy tend to find expression not in the indicative or conditional mood, but in the imperative.

THE QUEEN There is much truth in what your Excellency says — as things are at present. But if it were postponed for a while, might not the marriage become more possible? It seems to me so sad that any union of affection — such a genuine love-match as this — should have to be broken by political considerations.

BISMARCK A love-match? On which side does your Majesty so regard it?

THE QUEEN Surely on both?

BISMARCK Well, Ma'am, it is of course possible (though not usual) for marital devotion to divide itself between two objects; it is less usual for a woman to be willing to share that devotion with another.

THE QUEEN What does your Excellency mean?

BISMARCK Is your Majesty not aware that Prince Alexander has had the consolation of very close union with a certain lady, an actress, for the last three or four years — and that it is still going on?

THE QUEEN Prince Bismarck, you amaze me! No, I never heard of it.

BISMARCK That hardly surprises me, your Majesty, even though I have every reason to believe that others *have*.

THE QUEEN   I feel hardly able to believe it of him.

BISMARCK   If your Majesty requires proof, it can certainly be forthcoming.

THE QUEEN   If it can — if it is really true — of course it makes a great difference.

BISMARCK   To your Majesty's mind? On that I had no doubt. But elsewhere it does not seem to have been regarded as important.

THE QUEEN   Prince Bismarck, I am greatly distressed to hear you say so. I shall speak to the Empress about it at once; and if that is the sort of man he is (of which I had no suspicion), I certainly do not think that he is a fit person to marry anyone belonging to *My* family.

BISMARCK   In that case, I can leave the matter in your Majesty's hands, with confidence that my cause for very grave anxiety is now over.

THE QUEEN   Your Excellency may, I think, be quite sure that, in a matter such as this, my Daughter, the Empress, will not persist in a course which would have my strongest disapproval.

BISMARCK   Again I express my deep gratitude for your Majesty's promised intervention. I am only sorry that duty forced me to speak to your Majesty on so painful a subject.

THE QUEEN   You were quite right to do so. I only wish I had known before (as I *ought* to have known), what you have just told me. That would have settled the matter ... And now, since your Excellency and I are in such fortunate agreement, I can speak with more confidence on another matter which is also painful and difficult. I have a great favour to ask of you.

BISMARCK   Anything within my power to serve your Majesty I will do — gratefully.

THE QUEEN   Prince Bismarck, when the Emperor dies my Daughter's position will be one of terrible loneliness.

BISMARCK   That, Ma'am, I fear may be true; but it will be largely of her Majesty's own making.

THE QUEEN   That may be so; perhaps I cannot judge, loving her as I do. But when that happens, it is your Excellency who can help most.

BISMARCK In what way, your Majesty?

THE QUEEN When he dies, she will be helpless, and without friends to protect her.

BISMARCK From what, Ma'am, or from whom?

THE QUEEN It is painful to say; but your Excellency knows it as well as I do — from her son, Prince Wilhelm, who will then be Emperor.

BISMARCK I fear your Majesty overrates any influence that I shall have in that direction. He means to be his own master — and hers.

THE QUEEN Yes, I fear that that is the position, and is what he intends. Oh, how he has changed! He was such a dear nice child.

BISMARCK He is a child still, Ma'am — a child who means to have his own way in everything.

THE QUEEN But for your Excellency he has always expressed the greatest admiration and devotion.

BISMARCK Yes, Ma'am; but he has not yet tasted power: that may make a difference.

THE QUEEN Nevertheless, your high State-office, and the great services you have done your Country, must confer on you a right to give counsel and advice. And what I ask of your Excellency is that, so far as it is in your power, you will protect the interests of the Empress, so that she may not be deprived of her legitimate rights.

BISMARCK (*measuring his promise carefully*) I assure your Majesty that, so far as I have power to prevent, the Empress shall be deprived of none of those rights which properly belong to her.

THE QUEEN Of course, if her position here became *too* difficult, she might return to England.

BISMARCK That, Ma'am, she would not be allowed to do except on conditions.

THE QUEEN Conditions? What does your Excellency mean?

BISMARCK I believe, Ma'am, I am right in saying that her son, when Emperor, would not allow her to leave the country without certain undertakings.

THE QUEEN   Pray, of what kind?

BISMARCK   If your Majesty will pardon me — your Majesty must already know that the Empress has very little discretion.

THE QUEEN   I know that she is sometimes rather ill-advised.

BISMARCK   That ill-advice, Ma'am, is her own. Her Majesty consults nobody whose advice she might find distasteful.

THE QUEEN   What is this matter on which your Excellency says she will have to give undertakings?

BISMARCK   Over the publication, your Majesty, of certain material now in her possession, which should properly belong to the State. I beg that your Majesty will not oblige me to say more.

THE QUEEN   I trust that I share with your Excellency the discretion which you say that my Daughter lacks. I have now only to thank your Excellency for having been so frank with me, and for showing me such confidence . . . I have only one more request to make. I have asked the Empress to join me here in order that she may meet you. She is probably already waiting. Before I return to my own country, may I see your Excellency give her your hand, and promise her the protection of which she will soon be so greatly in need?

(BISMARCK *bows.*)

BISMARCK   I am all at your Majesty's service. If the Empress is willing to trust me with the protection of her rights, I am willing to promise such service to the best of my ability.

THE QUEEN   I thank your Excellency.

(THE QUEEN *goes to the door, opens it, and goes through.* THE PRINCE *waits; within voices are heard, but not the words. Presently* THE QUEEN *returns, accompanied by* THE EMPRESS. THE EMPRESS *is wearing gloves.*)

THE QUEEN   Prince Bismarck, I have brought the Empress, my Daughter, in order that I may commend her to your care before I go. I have informed her of your Excellency's promise.

(BISMARCK *bows. There is a pause.*)

She wishes now to give you her hand in renewal of confidence and friendship.

(Slowly THE EMPRESS *extends her gloved hand.* THE QUEEN *takes, and presents it to* PRINCE BISMARCK. *He bends over it, and appears to kiss it, but does not quite do so.* THE EMPRESS *withdraws her hand, and stands rigidly waiting, saying nothing. There is another pause.)*

THE QUEEN I thank your Excellency for having given me this opportunity of meeting you, and for the great comfort and satisfaction of knowing that the interests of my dear Daughter, the Empress, are now safe in your hands. Our meeting has given me great pleasure. I wish your Excellency good-bye.

*(*THE QUEEN *gives him her hand. He kisses it, bows and retires.)*

THE EMPRESS Confidence! Friendship! Oh, Mamma! What a humiliation you have forced on me!

THE QUEEN Humiliation, my dear? What do you mean?

THE EMPRESS To give him my hand! As if I believed in any promise *he* could make! Safe? Never — never while he and Willy are alive!

*(*THE EMPRESS *turns and goes quickly out of the room, slamming the door behind her.)*

THE QUEEN *(soliloquizing)* 'He and Willy!' Well, well! Three obstinate people: and *you*, my dear Vicky, the worst of the lot. There's no pleasing some people!

(She follows THE EMPRESS *out.)*
(Meanwhile, passing from the audience chamber, BISMARCK *has returned to find* BUSCH *waiting for him.)*

BISMARCK *(rubbing his hands)* Well, so that's over!

BUSCH As your Excellency says 'Well', I trust that it means well.

BISMARCK Yes, Busch, it does — far more than I had ever expected.

BUSCH What impression did her Majesty make on your Excellency?

BISMARCK A packet of surprises; and biggest surprise of all — there's a woman one can do business with. All the same, thank

God it's over, for I tell you that, to begin with, she frightened me.

BUSCH   Perhaps until your Excellency frightened *her*.

BISMARCK   No, Busch, I didn't, not for one moment. I don't believe she's capable of being frightened — politically. That's the big thing about her: she's got a job, that she believes she knows how to do. And by God, she does do it, though maybe she doesn't know *how*, and maybe I don't either. It's her amazing confidence in herself, and without any conceit, which makes her the power she is.

BUSCH   Has not your Excellency the same confidence?

BISMARCK   Yes, in myself; but now there are others that have not. I'm serving a new master, and he serves an old mistress, damn her! And behind him, when he dies (as he's going to) I've another master — waiting — of a different sort . . . No, she's sure of herself in a way that *I* can't be. Europe has become so accustomed to her, that I doubt whether we could make war on her even if we wanted to; and that gives her power. She stopped *us* making war once (though we didn't let her know it) — on France. In '75 that was. And with that poor, dying fool on the throne, and the other Vicky behind him, she might do the same again. That's power, Busch, that's power!

BUSCH   Did she and your Excellency come to any agreement?

BISMARCK   Yes, we did. And then on the top of it she made me do something I didn't want to do at all — and didn't like doing: but I had to.

BUSCH   What was that, Excellency?

BISMARCK   Promise that I'd do everything I could to make things comfortable for my deadliest enemy — that daughter of hers; and I've given her my word for it — almost without the asking. For though she called it a favour, she made it the sort of favour one couldn't say no to — giving me to understand that she was quite sure of all the things I wasn't sure about myself, and how perfectly she trusted my honour and my nobility of character and all the rest of it: not in so many words, but just in her way of saying it . . . When I tussled with the Pope, over the Kulturkampf, *he* didn't trust any of it. This was a more spiritual battle; and on one point, at any rate, I got beaten.

BUSCH Beaten, your Excellency?

BISMARCK Well, I gave her my word. That was all I had to give her, being all she wanted . . . And then out she goes and fetches in the Empress — to effect a reconciliation between us, if you please. And I had to scrape and bow like a lackey — and no choice about it. Rather humiliating, you know.

BUSCH And the Empress, Excellency? How did she . . .?

BISMARCK She? — stood like a stone wall, with an eye that wished me dead; gave me a gloved hand to kiss; and not a word did either of us speak, the one to the other — not one word. Old Majesty did the talking — said how much she trusted and approved of me, and to finish gave me a warm hand-shake at parting. Busch, I shan't like having to go back on *her*, though I may have to if the Daughter doesn't behave herself. When I spoke of certain things which must not go out of the Country, *she* knew what I was talking of.

BUSCH The Emperor's Diaries, Excellency?

BISMARCK Yes; and there's correspondence as well . . . I'm not sure yet, so can't do anything. But I'm told . . . Well, we can't have a Queen's luggage searched; but I'm told on fairly reliable authority (we've had to keep a sharp watch, you know) that she's carrying away documents — letters and diaries — which will have to come back. That Daughter of hers — a traitor to her adopted country, if ever there was one — is reckoning to have them published after *his* death.

BUSCH But, Excellency, if the Queen herself is taking them, how can your Excellency trust her any further?

BISMARCK Because she thinks they are only private papers about family matters. But in Royal families, if private matters are made public they become political. That's why those diaries will have to come back, as old Vicky will see when we demand the return of them. But that's what *our* Vicky plans to do — as a slap in the eye for young Wilhelm and me. That we can stop; but we can't stop it *now*. And on top of that — though I know what's been done behind our backs — I've said I'll do all I can for that — well, that woman who calls herself Empress! Of course, I ought to have made it a condition of doing anything that those papers should not go out of the country at all. But I didn't. There's where she had the better of me. One can't do a stand-and-deliver of that sort to *her*; such beautiful manners — a plain face, nothing to look at, but so charming.

BUSCH   But Excellency, if those papers go out of the country, will not copies be made before the originals are returned?

BISMARCK   Very likely; but *she* won't let them be published; she's got a sense of honour — which the other hasn't. When she returns them there'll be no hanky panky about publishing the copies or keeping them, either.

BUSCH   But is there not, Excellency, the further possibility of the Empress herself going back to England, and then taking the matter into her own hands?

BISMARCK   She won't be allowed to return to England till she has given up everything — *and* a signed undertaking as well. Yes; we can trust the old Mother, but we can't trust the Daughter ... Busch, this has been a great encounter. You may call it a draw if you like: but I wasn't beaten — except when I had to kiss that gloved hand. A bit of a humiliation that was; but with the other thing settled, it was worth it.

THE SUPERLATIVE RELATIVE

3rd August 1889

It is a bright summer morning. THE QUEEN *sits in her small private
drawing-room at Osborne, from the windows of which the Solent
can be seen, now crowded with ships and pleasure-boats, all festively
decked in honour of the arrival of His Imperial Majesty the Kaiser
Wilhelm. An* ATTENDANT *has already announced His Royal
Highness* THE PRINCE OF WALES, *and as* THE PRINCE *enters, withdraws, closing the door behind him with courtly ceremony and
obeisance.*

THE PRINCE *is in yachting costume; and apparently relations between
Mother and Son are, for the time being, cordial; they embrace
amicably.*

THE PRINCE Good morning, Mama. I am sorry if I am late.
I was going out to my yacht when your message came that you
wished to see me.

THE QUEEN Yes, Bertie, I wanted a word with you before I have
my talk with William, whom I have arranged to see this morning —
alone — just our two selves.

THE PRINCE A very good arrangement, Mama. I hope that you
will be able to do him good.

THE QUEEN I have no doubt that I shall, Bertie; but I shall do it
quite kindly. How did your meeting with him go off yesterday?

THE PRINCE Quite properly, of course, as it was all done under
the public eye. When it is a matter of ceremony and State occasion,
he knows how to behave as well as I do. This morning's papers
say that our meeting was 'very friendly and cordial'.

THE QUEEN But have you not seen him since the State dinner
last night — more privately, I mean?

THE PRINCE I have not, Mama.

THE QUEEN But why not? Surely you have had the opportunity.

THE PRINCE Because he has not yet written to apologize to me for his bad behaviour last year; and I do not think that he intends to. Therefore I prefer that we do not meet more than we can help. And I have no doubt that he prefers it too.

THE QUEEN   But, Bertie, now that he *is* here, you must behave properly.

THE PRINCE   I always do behave properly, Mama, even when he does not.

THE QUEEN   You know quite well what I mean; being proper to one's near relatives is not the same as being proper to other people. You can't go on treating him as if he were a stranger, or as if he were not welcome.

THE PRINCE   I shall find it rather difficult. We did not ask him to come.

THE QUEEN   What do you mean by 'we'? The invitation did not come from you. It was *I* that asked him.

THE PRINCE   I do not think that you really did, Mama; he asked for himself, so often that at last you could not refuse.

THE QUEEN   I asked him when I thought right, and not before. I kept him waiting a long time, which was only what he deserved after the way he had been behaving. And I made him quite understand that it was his own fault that I did not let him come before. He knows it, and that is enough.

THE PRINCE   Are you going to make him apologize for his refusal to meet me in Vienna last year — for saying that I was not to come while he was there; that if I *did* come *he* would not?

THE QUEEN   As you know, Bertie, he denies having ever said so.

THE PRINCE   And as *you* know, Mama, when he says that, he is not telling the truth. It has come from three different sources that he did say so.

THE QUEEN   He may not have said it in so many words, Bertie. But you must remember that you had been rather indiscreet in discussing with others certain political matters about which you should have been more careful.

THE PRINCE   What I said was said quite privately to friends — merely of things which I hoped might be done for the peace of

Europe: and would have been done had his father lived long enough to be really Emperor.

THE QUEEN   Yes; but what you said got passed on to him.

THE PRINCE   Rather dishonourably, and very much altered in the way it was said.

THE QUEEN   Still, it was a mistake to talk about such burning questions as Alsace and Schleswig-Holstein still are, to anyone of another country, who could be capable of repeating it.

THE PRINCE   As I have already said, Mama, I thought that I was speaking confidentially to one who was my friend. In future he will not be.

THE QUEEN   We must all learn by experience, Bertie; and for you it is more important than for most people. In politics, and still more in foreign diplomacy, the less you rely on people's honour the better. Prince Bismarck, as you know, gave me his word that he would do all he possibly could to see that poor dear Vicky got her rights and was properly treated. And now you see what has happened.

THE PRINCE   I think that has been William's doing more than Bismarck's, Mama. Vicky told me that herself.

THE QUEEN   Yes; last year he even wanted to prevent her coming to me here for rest and change. Only think of it! So I put my foot down, and said that till she *had* been, it was no use *his* proposing to come, for I wouldn't have him. It's quite dreadful the way he has behaved to her.

THE PRINCE   I think, Mama, that his becoming Emperor is the most serious thing that could have happened, not only in regard to our family relations, but in the relations of our two countries. He means to make himself such a figure in the world that some day — if we are not careful — there will be war.

THE QUEEN   Between England and Germany? No, Bertie, impossible! That could never happen. France and Russia will always be there to prevent that; because Germany's making war on *us* would be *their* opportunity; and Bismarck knows it. He depends on us (he told me that himself) to keep the Triple Alliance going.

THE PRINCE Bismarck won't always be there, Mama; nor does Willie wish him to be; he has ideas of his own. And I don't think we shall have to wait long before he makes himself his own master — and a very bad one that is likely to be.

THE QUEEN Well, I am going to have a good talk with him; and he has never yet shown any lack of proper respect to *me* — even though, at times, he behaves foolishly — and, to his poor dear Mama, very badly, as I shall tell him.

THE PRINCE Then I hope, Mama, that in the course of your good talk with him, you will tell him to treat me, also, with proper respect before others. The last time that we met, before the Vienna affair, he slapped me on the back in the presence of several of his suite, and said, 'Uncle Bertie, you are getting fatter than ever! You must come to Homburg again.'

THE QUEEN Well, of course he ought not to have said that; but saying that you ought to come to Homburg was almost like an invitation, and showed that he spoke in a friendly spirit.

THE PRINCE (*st ffly*) I do not like that sort of friendliness.

THE QUEEN Well, you had nothing, you say, to complain of in the way he behaved to you when you went out to meet him on his arrival yesterday. ·

THE PRINCE No, he behaved then in the proper way, so far as the formalities were concerned; but of course he tried to convey by his manner that he was the more important person. That he cannot help doing; he does it wherever he goes.

THE QUEEN He does not dare do it to me.

THE PRINCE No, I think you are the only person whom he treats as an equal. And when I am representing you, Mama (as I was, when I received him yesterday), he should, I think, treat me exactly as he treats you.

THE QUEEN Well, I'll do what I can, Bertie, to make things pleasanter between you. Poor Willie! He has had such a bad bringing up under that man Bismarck, whom at one time he almost worshipped, as you know. If that infatuation is over so much the better . . . I have arranged this morning to receive him here, by himself, for though he wanted me to give him another formal

reception, with a lot more presentations, I said that after all I had done yesterday I was not up to it. So you need not be here either, nor Beatie, nor anybody.

THE PRINCE   Thank you, Mama. I am very glad to be so excused.

THE QUEEN   Yes; but don't go away, because when we have had our talk I shall send for you. And then, Bertie, do make an effort to be pleasant to him, and forget all past differences; though *I* shall still have a few things to say to him that he will not like. He does not quite like my only letting him come here; he wanted also to go to London. But I said that this time I did not wish it.

THE PRINCE   It is a good thing you did, Mama; for he might not have had a very good reception; there might even have been a hostile demonstration.

THE QUEEN   Yes, but I didn't tell him that; it might have been good for him if I had. But you know how, when he pays a State-visit, he always takes such a large suite with him — forty or fifty people — and we should have had to find room for them; but here he just stays on his own yacht, and we don't have to do anything about it, though I was going to offer to have him here at Osborne if he would like to come from his yacht for a few nights.

THE PRINCE   I do not think he will wish that, Mama.

THE QUEEN   Well, I rather hope he won't. And now, Bertie, you must go away, for he may be here at any moment; and you stay and be ready when I send for you.

THE PRINCE   I will do as you tell me, Mama.

THE QUEEN   I am sorry, Bertie, that you and he do not get on well together.

THE PRINCE   I am sorry too, Mama. But you may remember how, when he was quite a small boy, he bit my hand in a temper for nothing at all; and he has been biting me ever since, or trying to. So I prefer to keep out of his way.

THE QUEEN   Well, you can't do that always; and you can't do it now; and, of course, for seeing the yacht-racing you will have to invite him on to your own yacht.

THE PRINCE   That is all arranged, Mama. I asked him, and he accepted.

THE QUEEN Very well; then now go, my dear.

(THE PRINCE *goes.* THE QUEEN *returns to her letter-writing. Presently the door opens, and (announced by a* GENTLEMAN *of the Court with due formality)* THE KAISER *enters.*)

THE KAISER Good morning, Grandmama. I hope that I see you well.

THE QUEEN Good morning, Willie. Yes; but rather tired after yesterday. So to-day I am going to stay quiet, and see only those I want to see, of whom you, of course, are the first. How well you look! And you have brought such fine weather with you.

THE KAISER No, Grandmama, you had it waiting for me here, when I arrived. It was part of the splendid welcome which you gave me at Spithead on the meeting of our two fleets — a most magnificent spectacle. I wish you could have seen it.

THE QUEEN I saw it from here, Willie; and of course I heard all the saluting. And what a fine fleet you have brought with you.

THE KAISER Yes, Grandmama. I think that it really does us credit — at last. And now I want to thank you once more, for having made me an Admiral of your own fleet. It is of all honours the one which I most coveted, and hoped that I might earn through your good approval of me.

THE QUEEN I am very glad that I was able to give you such pleasure; it seemed to me that it was the best way of showing how safe and friendly are the relations of our two countries. For though Germany has now become a strong naval Power, we are never likely to be at war. Otherwise, of course, I could not have made you an Admiral.

THE KAISER It has had a very great and happy effect on the political feeling of my country. Everybody is very pleased about it.

THE QUEEN Then so am I. And now sit down, Willie. We have a great deal to talk about. When did you last see poor Mama?

THE KAISER I have not seen her for a long time, Grandmama.

THE QUEEN I think you ought to go and see her more often than you do. It is not right that you and she should keep so much apart: it makes people talk.

THE KAISER I don't think she wishes to see me, Grandmama, more than I wish to see her. She now has an establishment which seems to satisfy her; and can no longer complain of feeling deserted and alone, having contracted a few weeks ago the private marriage which I thought it proper that she should make.

THE QUEEN I was very much surprised, and rather sorry, when I heard of that, Willie.

THE KAISER I considered it to be necessary; and she herself had come to see that it was advisable. People were beginning to talk.

THE QUEEN Really, how abominable of them!

THE KAISER No, Grandmama, it was only to be expected. People cannot help talking scandal about Royalty if anything is given them to make it possible; and Mama having become on such intimate terms of friendship with her Court Chamberlain, it was necessary to put a stop to it.

THE QUEEN Well, we can only hope it was the best thing to do under the circumstances.

THE KAISER I am sure that it was, Grandmama.

THE QUEEN Then, as it has been done at your wish, I do ask you, Willie, to go and see your Mama again when you return. It will show that the marriage has your approval.

THE KAISER I will think about it. Perhaps I will. As you know, my wish is always to please you.

THE QUEEN Yes, Willie, I know that; but you do not always succeed.

THE KAISER I am sorry, Grandmama; but whose fault is it?

THE QUEEN Yours, Willie; and generally no one else's.

THE KAISER Will you tell me, Grandmama, in what way I have at any time failed to please you, or at least to try to?

THE QUEEN Well, I don't want to go into politics now; but you know quite well that you have lately been making things very difficult for my Ministers; and you have in consequence lost a great deal of your popularity in this country. Indeed, I don't mind telling you, now, that that is why I could not invite you to visit me in London, which otherwise I should have been so glad to do. But here at Osborne I am so much more at home, and can do things more independently. I did hope that when you had taken Prince Bismarck's measure (as you seem to have done) and had realized how much he was trying to make himself your master, things would become easier; but they have not. One trouble after another has been cropping up, and in all parts of the world you have been making difficulties, especially in Africa.

THE KAISER It is in Africa, Grandmama, that your Ministers have been making difficulties for *us*. They seem to think that Africa already belongs to them, or so much of it that they have the right to decide on the disposal, to whatever country they choose, of what they do not want for themselves.

THE QUEEN I do not think they do anything of the sort. In dealing with the claims of other countries, I have always found Lord Salisbury very fair and sensible.

THE KAISER Those are qualities which strike one differently, according to the country that one belongs to. But I am sure, dear Grandmama, that if you were either your own Prime Minister or your Minister for Foreign Affairs, there would be no difficulty at all; indeed I think there would have been an alliance between England and Germany long ago.

THE QUEEN Well, Germany is the country with which I would most like to see England in alliance — if there has to be any; for it was your dear Grandfather's constant wish also. But I must not discuss matters like that with you without first receiving the advice of my Ministers, whom — my present ones — I can trust, I am thankful to say; which has not always been the case — far from it. No, we won't go into that now; because this is only a family visit you are paying — not political; and I have not thought it necessary to ask any of my Ministers to meet you. But one of the things I do want to speak to you about more especially, Willie, is the way you behave to your Uncle Bertie.

THE KAISER How do you mean that I behave to him?

THE QUEEN For one thing, you do not treat him with proper respect; and he feels it.

THE KAISER For instance?

THE QUEEN Well, he gave me one instance which I am not surprised that he resented. He tells me that once in the presence of your own suite, you told him that he was getting fat.

THE KAISER I said that he was putting on weight, yes. In Germany that is a high compliment. One says it as a good joke.

THE QUEEN It is not a good joke here, Willie; and if you do say such things, you only say them in private.

THE KAISER I think Uncle Bertie does not like me.

THE QUEEN Perhaps that is because you do not like him. Why don't you? Have you anything to complain of in the way he behaves to *you*?

THE KAISER He behaves to me too much as my uncle, and forgets that while he is still only a Prince, I am now the German Emperor; and he would do better to remember it.

THE QUEEN (*tartly*) And you would also do better to remember, Willie (what I think you forget) that when he meets you in public, as he did when he received you yesterday, he does so as My representative, and is therefore your equal.

THE KAISER When we meet on State occasions, I have nothing to complain of him; but often when he has talked to me about Mama, I have been exceedingly annoyed at the sort of authority which he seems to assume over me; and *that* I am not going to allow.

THE QUEEN You know, Willie, that I myself think that, over your Mama, you have been a good deal to blame. But what makes me so anxious about you and your Uncle Bertie is that some day he will be in my place; and it may then matter very much indeed for both our countries if you and he are not on good terms. So do try this time to be more friendly, and, in a way, more respectful. For after all, he is your uncle, and very much the elder, and has had far more experience than you in all sorts of ways. Indeed he has, as I think you must know, a great reputation for his savoir-faire in all the countries that he has visited.

THE KAISER His savoir-faire goes down better in France than Germany, I find. His frequent visits to Paris are, I believe, far more political in character than you know, or would approve.

THE QUEEN Well, I do wish he would not go to Paris so often; but not for any reason such as you suppose, about which I am sure you are quite mistaken. But he has associates there of whom I cannot approve. King Leopold of the Belgians is one; and he, as you must know, has a very bad reputation — such a disappointment he would have been to his dear excellent father . . . But now, Willie, I must not keep you any longer. Your Uncle Bertie is here, waiting to take you on to his yacht for the races, and it is quite time you started; so I will send for him.

(*She rings. An* ATTENDANT *enters.*)

Will you ask the Prince to come?

(*The* ATTENDANT *bows and retires.*)

Well, I am very glad to have had this talk with you, Willie, just our two selves alone. And you will try, will you not, to be more kind to poor dear Mama?

THE KAISER I always wish to do everything possible to please you, Grandmama. But you must know, the difficulties have not always been of my making. Until Papa died she still tried to treat me like a child.

THE QUEEN Oh yes, I know, I know!

THE KAISER And to that I could not submit.

THE QUEEN No, of course not. Still . . .

(THE PRINCE *enters. And now with* THE QUEEN'S *eye upon them, they both become models of politeness.*)

THE PRINCE Good morning, William.

THE KAISER Good morning, Uncle Bertie.

THE PRINCE I think we are going to have a fine day, and the wind is in a good quarter for the races. Mama dear, you will be able to see them start from this window, and also the finish when they return.

THE QUEEN Yes; but I am afraid I shall not know which is which.

THE PRINCE You will know the *Meteor*, Mama. It is the largest, and it will be flying the German flag.

(*Gunfire is heard.*)

Ah, that's the signal of preparation for the first race. If we are to see it we must go. Your race, William, is the third; the event of the day.

THE QUEEN And I do hope that you win it, Willie.

THE KAISER Yes, Grandmama, so do I — that is, if Uncle Bertie's yacht is not also to be in it.

THE PRINCE Oh, no, I am not competing against *you*, William.

THE KAISER Thank you, that is very kind; and it gives me a better chance.

THE PRINCE Oh, I don't think that we have anything here that can beat your *Meteor*.

(*Which perhaps has been carefully arranged for* THE KAISER'S *better satisfaction*.)

THE KAISER Well, we shall see.

THE QUEEN Yes; and don't wait any longer, or you will be missing the first race.

THE KAISER Then good-bye for the present, Grandmama dear. (*He goes to her and kisses her*.) And thank you so much for asking me to come.

THE QUEEN Well, I hope it won't be for the last time, and that we shall see you here again before long. But I can't promise. I am not so young as I was.

THE KAISER You are as young as the two of us put together, Grandmama.

THE QUEEN As the two of you put together! I'm ten years younger than *that*. When you were born I was not as old as your Uncle Bertie is now.

THE PRINCE Good-bye, Mama.

(*He goes to the door and opens it, and stands aside for* WILLIAM *to go out first.* WILLIAM *clicks heels, and bows politely, declining the honour.* THE PRINCE *again makes a gesture for* THE KAISER *to precede him; but* THE KAISER *takes his arm, and says jovially:*)

THE KAISER Come along, Uncle Bertie, the door is wide enough for both of us!

(*And they go out side by side.*)

THE QUEEN Well, I seem to have done them both good; I only hope it will last. And now I must write to my poor Vicky . . . Oh dear! I wish she hadn't done it. Still, I do understand . . . oh yes, I *do* understand. . . .

PROMOTION COMETH

20th January 1891

THE QUEEN *and her Visitor are in seated conversation, but the conversation is not intimate. The new Canon's wife has come for inspection; and, much to Her Majesty's surprise and annoyance, the inspection is gradually being shifted to herself. This sort of thing has never happened before: not, at least, since her accession to the throne. But here we are! It is a test of dignity, for the Canon's wife has all the physical advantages! Tall, severe, magisterial, with self-confidence in every line, feature, and gesture; in any other company she would dominate the scene. But here she does not. How on earth that Other, so short, plump, and round-about, manages to do it, Heaven only knows! It is a secret she has made her own for over fifty years, and it will go on, through years of infirmity, to the day of her death. Now, feeling the masterful coils of this boa-constrictor closing round her,* THE QUEEN *tries to make shift of the conversation; and the two Ladies-in-Waiting, placed for dutiful attendance in the embrasure of the window, look on and say nothing, except to each other with their eyes. So much freedom of expression Court etiquette allows to them.*

THE QUEEN And I hope you find your house quite comfortable, Mrs. Clayton?

MRS. CLAYTON It will be, your Majesty, as soon as I have had time to make it so.

THE QUEEN Was anything the matter with it? Repairs — drains? The Canon, your husband's predecessor, lived in it to a good old age. He was quite hale and hearty, almost to the last, I believe.

MRS. CLAYTON No bathroom, or housemaid's closet, your Majesty.

THE QUEEN (*in chilled astonishment*) Housemaid's closet!

MRS. CLAYTON (*explaining*) For hot-water cans, brooms, and dustpans, your Majesty.

THE QUEEN I never heard of them!

427

MRS. CLAYTON Indeed? No, Ma'am?

THE QUEEN (*decisively*) We don't have them at Windsor.

MRS. CLAYTON That is a pity, Ma'am.

THE QUEEN Pity? You pity Windsor Castle, Mrs. Clayton!

MRS. CLAYTON (*courageously*) Castles sometimes need renovating, your Majesty.

THE QUEEN Windsor was thoroughly renovated, externally, by King George IV; and internally, by the Prince, my Husband . . . I will let you see over the Castle, if you like, Mrs. Clayton.

MRS. CLAYTON I shall be most happy, your Majesty. I may be able to suggest some improvements.

THE QUEEN (*incredulously*) Improvements? After what the Prince did himself, I allow nothing to be altered.

MRS. CLAYTON In that case, Ma'am, further suggestions will be useless.

THE QUEEN I am afraid so. You see, Mrs. Clayton, I have recollections. All the things that He did seem to me like yesterday. The Great Exhibition of 'fifty-one. So many new ideas came in then. It was the beginning of a new age; and all his own dear wonderful invention. The world doesn't know, even yet, what it owes to him.

MRS. CLAYTON (*incredulous*) The Prince Consort's invention, your Majesty?

THE QUEEN (*luxuriating sadly in the recollection*) Yes, he started it.

MRS. CLAYTON It didn't get to the Canon's residence, apparently, Ma'am. The kitchen is so dark that my cook can't see to cook without gaslight.

THE QUEEN Indeed? Very sad . . . Still, you *have* gaslight, I suppose?

MRS. CLAYTON Oh, yes, Ma'am. There *is* gas, of course; not as good as it might be. As soon as the meter is turned on, the whole house reeks of it.

THE QUEEN (*ignoring the complaint*) Then that meets the difficulty. And how do you like Windsor, Mrs. Clayton? . . . the people, I mean?

MRS. CLAYTON There are far too many poor people in Windsor, your Majesty.

THE QUEEN There are.

MRS. CLAYTON Deplorably, shamefully poor.

THE QUEEN Yes, I suppose so.

MRS. CLAYTON I am bound to tell your Majesty that I find they have been much neglected. The parish has not been properly worked, or organized as it should be.

THE QUEEN (*with a touch of ice*) Indeed!

MRS. CLAYTON Just think, Ma'am, there are no Mothers' Meetings. They have never heard of them.

THE QUEEN (*after just thinking*) Nor have I. What do Mothers meet for, Mrs. Clayton?

MRS. CLAYTON I might say — to become civilized, your Majesty. Some I find quite primitive in their notions . . . savages almost . . . certainly not Christian.

THE QUEEN Here in Windsor? Most extraordinary. How can that be possible?

MRS. CLAYTON Anything is possible if left to itself, your Majesty. In this case, it comes from neglect, and lack of education.

THE QUEEN But what is one to do? There are so many of them — far too many, as you say. And social conditions make it so difficult. You can't get rid of ignorance in a day, Mrs. Clayton.

MRS. CLAYTON No; your Majesty, nor in a lifetime, if one does nothing. Indifference, prejudice, class-distinction all help?

THE QUEEN *Help?*

MRS. CLAYTON *Have* helped most certainly to make Windsor what no self-respecting place ought to be.

THE QUEEN (*correctively, for these are wild socialistic notions, which ought not to be expressed*) Would you wish to get rid of class-distinction, Mrs. Clayton?

MRS. CLAYTON I would wish to get rid of anything, Ma'am, which prevents people from recognizing their responsibilities. It is what I am hoping to do here —

THE QUEEN Indeed!

MRS. CLAYTON (*continuing*) — as soon as I can find the time for it.

THE QUEEN (*grasping at a straw*) Ah, yes. You have your husband to look after.

MRS. CLAYTON I have, Ma'am. That, of course —

THE QUEEN (*completing the sentence as it should be completed*) — must be your *first* consideration.

MRS. CLAYTON It has always been so, your Majesty. But it is not my last, or only one. I have also my children.

THE QUEEN Ah, yes. You have a large family?

MRS. CLAYTON Only five . . . at present.

THE QUEEN (*deprecating the prospective suggestion*) Dear me! But your husband, the Canon. Is he not — rather delicate?

MRS. CLAYTON Oh, no, your Majesty — quite robust. Not delicate, but difficult. He is a scholar — as perhaps your Majesty knows — and needs quiet and retirement.

THE QUEEN (*with a touch of mischief*) I hope he gets it.

MRS. CLAYTON (*conscious of good management*) He does, Ma'am. I arrange that. During certain hours of the day, I allow him to see nobody. I had to make that rule for him.

THE QUEEN Indeed!

MRS. CLAYTON His regular writing hours, I mean, when he is not at home to anyone.

THE QUEEN Ah, yes. He is writing history, I believe?

MRS. CLAYTON He is, Ma'am.

THE QUEEN When will it be finished?

MRS. CLAYTON Before he dies, Ma'am, I hope . . . *he* hopes, also. Four volumes have already been published; and there are four more to come.

THE QUEEN Dear me! I should call that an Encyclopaedia, not a history.

MRS. CLAYTON (*instructively*) History, your Majesty, has become very complicated in these days. Modern research has brought so much more material to light, that it has almost to be rewritten.

THE QUEEN Now, that is rather a pity, when it has been so well done already. Lord Macaulay was a great writer of history, was he not?

MRS. CLAYTON Nobody reads Macaulay now, Ma'am, for facts; only for amusement.

THE QUEEN Dear me! How extraordinary! I used to know Lord Macaulay, Mrs. Clayton. I remember receiving him on his return from India. A most interesting man. In fact, almost all I know about India — the life and habits of the people, I mean, was told me by Lord Macaulay himself — personally!

MRS. CLAYTON Indeed, Ma'am. I wonder if it is still true.

THE QUEEN Oh, yes. For he told me that the East never changes, and never will.

MRS. CLAYTON I suppose that is because the missionaries don't do their duty.

THE QUEEN Oh, why should you say that, Mrs. Clayton?

MRS. CLAYTON Because, Ma'am, India is larger than Windsor. And when I find how much Windsor — the poor of Windsor — have been neglected, I imagine that India may be in a like state, or worse. I am starting a Mothers' Meeting, your Majesty, and I wondered if, for the opening of the first meeting, your —

THE QUEEN (*intervening, and oh! you should see now the eyes of the Ladies-in-Waiting*) Ah, yes. But you can't have Mothers' Meetings in India, Mrs. Clayton. Purdah makes that impossible.

MRS. CLAYTON I am not proposing to start Mothers' Meetings in India, your Majesty. I was speaking of Windsor; and I wondered —

(*We almost know what* MRS. CLAYTON *is going to say; and so does* THE QUEEN, *though it is difficult for her to believe it. With an instinct of self-preservation, she rises, and brings the conversation to an end. The Ladies-in-Waiting rise, and* MRS. CLAYTON, *robbed of her prey, has to rise also.*)

THE QUEEN I am so sorry, Mrs. Clayton; but I fear, now, I have an appointment. This has been a most interesting conversation;

you have given me much to think about. I believe we are to have the pleasure of hearing the Canon preach on Sunday?

MRS. CLAYTON I believe so, your Majesty.

THE QUEEN Has he yet begun writing his sermon?

MRS. CLAYTON I don't know, your Majesty. Sometimes he prefers preaching from notes.

THE QUEEN Oh, I prefer *written* sermons.

MRS. CLAYTON Shall I tell him that is your Majesty's wish?

THE QUEEN (*with a touch of pinprick in her voice*) Oh, no, no! Don't tell him anything. Just let him alone to do as he likes. Good-bye, Mrs. Clayton, and I hope that your house is going to be habitable, when you can find time to attend to it.

MRS. CLAYTON So good of your Majesty to wish it.

(MRS. CLAYTON *curtsies deeply over the hand graciously offered her.*)

THE QUEEN Good-bye. Lady Grace, will you see Mrs. Clayton safely out, please.

(MRS. CLAYTON *has made the proper Court passes. At the door she turns again, and, assisted through it by* LADY GRACE, *curtsies herself out. The door shuts. But there is the other Lady-in-Waiting still in attendance.*)

You can go, too, Miss Somers, now. I don't want you. And send Sir Henry Ponsonby to me — immediately.

(MISS SOMERS *makes her curtsy. Again the door shuts and* THE QUEEN *is alone. Taking up the stick, with which she now walks when troubled by rheumatism, she begins moving about the room; and the sharp tapping of her stick upon the carpet gives an emphasis to what she has now to say to herself.*)

Instant promotion! . . . Instant promotion! . . . Yes . . . yes . . . yes, indeed! . . . Instant . . . *instant* promotion!

(SIR HENRY PONSONBY *has entered, and stands, quietly observant. He sees plainly that something is amiss.*)

SIR HENRY Your Majesty wished to see me?

THE QUEEN (*turning sharply*) Sir Henry, will you please make a note that Canon Clayton is to have instant promotion . . . to the first vacancy that offers.

SIR HENRY Vacancy, Ma'am? What sort of vacancy?

THE QUEEN Dean, or Bishop . . . it does not matter which. Whichever comes first. For if that woman stays here, as long as she expects to stay, she will make me go and open her Mothers' Meetings. The women of Windsor, she informs me, are living in a very ignorant and neglected condition. *And I am one of them!*

SIR HENRY (*scandalized, yet amused*) Dear me! Dear me!

THE QUEEN Therefore I say . . . instant promotion! Isn't there a vacant Bishopric or Deanery just now? Any Deanery will do. Surely there is one?

SIR HENRY I saw in *The Times*, Ma'am, this morning, the death of the Bishop of Ballarat.

THE QUEEN Ah! . . . That will do. Where's Ballarat? Not in Scotland, I hope?

SIR HENRY Oh, no! Ballarat is somewhere in the Antipodes, I believe . . . Australia.

THE QUEEN Ah, that will do quite nicely! Will you please tell the Prime Minister not to begin making any appointment till he has seen *me*. You might mention Canon Clayton's name to him, as a preliminary.

SIR HENRY I doubt, Ma'am, whether we shall be able to persuade Canon Clayton to go out to the Colonies.

THE QUEEN Why not?

SIR HENRY It is hardly the kind of life that would suit him — he being so much a scholar, and a writer.

THE QUEEN Well, can't he write there?

SIR HENRY Not without books for reference, Ma'am . . . and a large library, I fear. He must have within reach some such institution as the British Museum.

THE QUEEN Haven't the Colonies got anything of the sort?

SIR HENRY Hardly yet! . . . only a few of them. Not in Ballarat, I'm afraid.

THE QUEEN Dear me! How extraordinary! How ignorant and neglected they must be, then. Surely a suitable place for Mrs. Clayton to go to. Suggest it to her, Sir Henry. See *her* first, and if she agrees . . . that will settle it.

SIR HENRY Well, your Majesty, I haven't much hopes; but I will try.

THE QUEEN (*suddenly remembering*) Oh, what about Peterborough, now that Bishop Magee is going to York?

SIR HENRY Ah, Peterborough! Yes, I had forgotten Peterborough.

THE QUEEN Tell the Prime Minister that if he won't take Ballarat, he is to have Peterborough.

SIR HENRY I will do my best to suggest it, Ma'am.

THE QUEEN Don't suggest it, Sir Henry, say I *wish* it.

SIR HENRY Did she . . . Was she . . . very . . .?

THE QUEEN Sir Henry, I was never so near being put in my place by anyone. Never! What do others think of her?

SIR HENRY Mrs. Clayton has only been here three months, Ma'am; but already she terrifies people.

(THE QUEEN *takes up her knitting.*)

THE QUEEN So I should imagine — unless they stand up to her, as *I* did.

SIR HENRY They found a name for her, which your Majesty might like to hear.

THE QUEEN Well, and what is it?

SIR HENRY They call her, Ma'am, the 'She-bear of Windsor'.

THE QUEEN And a very good name too! She almost got me in her hug to-day. I only just escaped.

(*At this point a* GENTLEMAN-IN-WAITING *enters, and stands drooping for permission to speak.*)

THE QUEEN Yes, what is it?

GENTLEMAN The Bishops, your Majesty, have arrived, and are waiting your Majesty's pleasure.

THE QUEEN Which Bishops?

GENTLEMAN There are six of them, your Majesty. The Bishop of London; the Bishop of —

SIR HENRY Your Majesty will remember that the appointment was made three weeks ago. Your Majesty wished to discuss with them the appointments to the Royal Commission on Church Discipline, which are now under your Majesty's consideration.

THE QUEEN Oh, yes, I knew I had some engagement for this afternoon, though I had forgotten what it was. Yes, I shall have a great deal to say to them about *that*! Tell them to come in. And order tea. They were asked to take tea, I believe, were they not?

GENTLEMAN Your Majesty did so command.

THE QUEEN Very well; let them come in at once. And see that tea follows immediately.

(*Exit the* GENTLEMAN-IN-WAITING.)

Sir Henry, I shall want you to stay. I shall have to talk to them seriously; and you must take notes of what any of them say. This lawlessness in the Church is nearly all their fault. They don't put their foot down as they should do. It doesn't happen in Scotland.

SIR HENRY In the Church of Scotland, Ma'am, there are no Bishops' feet to be put down.

THE QUEEN No. And the Church has done better without them. It has remained Protestant. I wish that the Church of England were Presbyterian, too.

SIR HENRY Indeed, Ma'am, that would be an interesting experiment.

THE QUEEN Yes; so much safer. Mr. Gladstone's appointments were sometimes terrible. Lord Salisbury's are almost worse. A ritualist at Lincoln, and Canons who have become Socialists in more places than one can name. What is religion coming to?

SIR HENRY Possibly to disestablishment, Ma'am.

THE QUEEN Yes. And, where, as Head of the Church, shall I be then? He wanted to make Canon Liddon Bishop of Oxford. I put my foot down on that . . . Yes?

(*The* GENTLEMAN-IN-WAITING *re-enters.*)

GENTLEMAN   The Lord Bishops, your Majesty, are here.

THE QUEEN   Let them come in.

(*The* GENTLEMAN-IN-WAITING *steps back to the door, and, with a gesture of 'line clear', stands back to admit the six invited* BISHOPS, *who advance into the room processionally, and bow. Like Noah negotiating the animals into the Ark, he names them as they enter.*)

GENTLEMAN   Your Majesty . . . The Bishop of London; the Bishop of Winchester; the Bishop of Rochester; the Bishop of Salisbury; the Bishop of Ely; the Bishop of Chichester.

(*Meantime, while its tail is still entering,* THE QUEEN *is graciously receiving the head of the procession, which murmurs appropriate response to her greetings.*)

THE QUEEN   My dear Bishop of London, how do you do? My dear Bishop of Winchester, so pleased to see you . . . My dear Bishop of Rochester, I hope dear Mrs. Brown is better? I hear she has been ill.

ROCHESTER   I thank your Majesty, much better.

THE QUEEN   How do you do, my dear Bishop? You have come up from Salisbury to-day?

SALISBURY   Only from London, your Majesty.

THE QUEEN   So you had not too long a journey?

SALISBURY   Oh, no, your Majesty.

LONDON   Winchester and Salisbury are staying with me at Fulham, Ma'am, for the night. We all came down together.

THE QUEEN   Very pleasant, I'm sure. So it has not been too inconvenient for you?

THE BISHOPS   Oh, no, your Majesty.

THE QUEEN   My dear Bishop of Ely, how do you do? And you, my dear Bishop of Chichester; it is a long time since I have seen you. I am so glad that you have all been able to come. Sir Henry, please say that we will have tea at once.

(*A mere gesture from* SIR HENRY *to the* GENTLEMAN-IN-WAITING *is sufficient. Tea enters automatically, already poured out, and sup-*

*ported on trays by liveried Footmen. Cake and bread and butter
follow. A Footman brings a separate tray to Her Majesty; but, with
monosyllabic No, she rejects it. She is going to do the talking;
and a tea-cup with its etceteras would be a hindrance. On the other
hand, that calculated hindrance is now being imposed on the* BISHOPS.
*They stand about, holding small saucers, with spoons and bread and
butter precariously balanced. With such accompaniments, it is
difficult to be sacerdotal, or argumentative. And argument her Majesty
does not mean to allow. For a while the servants are a protection from
the impending attack;* THE QUEEN *and her six* BISHOPS *talk of the
weather and things that do not matter; and* THE QUEEN, *in her regal
way, does it embracingly.*)

THE QUEEN   I hope you are all having good weather in your
dioceses?

(*They are; grateful appreciation of the fact flutters over the tea-
cups.*)

THE BISHOPS (*dispersedly*)   Quite excellent, Ma'am . . . during the
last week . . . Very seasonable . . . Oh, yes. Things are a little late,
under God . . . but one mustn't complain.

(*The* BISHOP OF LONDON, *however — the future Archbishop —
puts more personality into his response.*)

LONDON   There was a very high tide at Fulham, Ma'am, yesterday.

THE QUEEN   Ah, indeed? That sometimes happens, does it not?
Fulham is rather a damp place, I'm afraid.

LONDON   It is, Ma'am. But Lambeth is worse. Half the Arch-
bishops die of it.

THE QUEEN   Dear me, how sad! . . . and how extraordinary! I
hope, my Lords, that none of your palaces are damp?

LONDON   All of them, your Majesty. Like ourselves, they are old
and falling into decay. Slightly insanitary, most of them.

THE QUEEN   Dear me!

(*There is a pause. The other* BISHOPS *have been apprehensively
admiring the conversational powers of* BISHOP TEMPLE, *their leader.
But now he is finishing his bread and butter, and reaching out his hand
for cake, which a Footman stoopingly supplies.*)

THE QUEEN (*to* WINCHESTER) I hope, my dear Bishop, that you and the Bishop of Salisbury have had the opportunity, while at Fulham, of talking over with the Bishop of London the matter about which I wrote to him? . . . Tell the servants to go, Sir Henry! . . . It is very important that I should know your views on the subject, and that you should know *mine*. My Lord Bishops, I am referring to the Royal Commission on Church Discipline, which is about to be appointed.

(*The Footmen have departed.*)

LONDON Which *has* been appointed, Ma'am.

THE QUEEN But not yet confirmed by *me*. I wish to see it strengthened.

LONDON Indeed, Ma'am? With permission, I venture to think that it is already large enough.

THE QUEEN So do I. Certain persons have been included who ought not to be there: whose appointment I do not approve.

LONDON Indeed, Ma'am? As I am largely responsible for the clerical nominations, I am anxious to hear your Majesty's objections.

THE QUEEN There are too many of the High Church Party.

LONDON There must be some, Ma'am.

THE QUEEN Why?

LONDON They are representative, Ma'am. They form a very large, and learned, and influential part of the Church Established.

THE QUEEN Yes; and I want it stopped — put an end to, at once.

LONDON Extermination, Ma'am, in these days, is rather difficult.

THE QUEEN They ought not to be encouraged; they ought not to be officially recognized at all.

LONDON I'm afraid, Ma'am, that they have historical claims which cannot be entirely ignored.

THE QUEEN I am not talking about history, Dr. Temple; I am talking about *now*.

LONDON So am I, Ma'am.

THE QUEEN Oh? Then, why mention history? What I wish to

say is that all this Romish Ritual has got to be put down ...
I won't have it!

LONDON Nor will I, Madam — for myself; I have no use for it.

THE QUEEN But the Lincoln Judgment *allows* it. Most extraordinary!

LONDON The Lincoln Judgment, Ma'am, for which I am partly
responsible —

THE QUEEN (*interposing*) Yes, I *know*.

LONDON (*continuing*) — has greatly disappointed the High Church
Party. They find some of its conclusions very difficult to accept.
But the Bishop himself has bowed to the Judgment. That is a great
point to have achieved.

THE QUEEN Well, if he hadn't, he must have resigned.

LONDON But would he?

THE QUEEN He ought never to have been made a Bishop. I was
against it; and, you see, *I was right*.

LONDON He has made a very good Bishop.

THE QUEEN (*scandalized*) A *good* Bishop!

LONDON He is very much beloved in his own diocese — indeed
it would be a wonder were it otherwise. Dr. King of Lincoln is
more of a saint than all the rest of us put together.

THE QUEEN Indeed? I don't claim to be a judge of saints; but
are not saints sometimes superstitious?

LONDON They are, Ma'am, they are. That has been one of the
great troubles of Church history. But we are getting over it.

THE QUEEN We are not getting over *him*.

LONDON We are not, Ma'am.

THE QUEEN I consider the Lincoln Judgment most deplorable:
leaving him on the Bench at all is a great mistake.

LONDON I am afraid, Ma'am, that your disapproval is largely
due to history: it being mainly upon history that the Lincoln
Judgment was based.

THE QUEEN Indeed? Then no wonder.

LONDON   No wonder, as you say, Ma'am.

THE QUEEN   History? It reads to *me* as though it were trying to make out that at the Reformation nothing happened.

LONDON   Ah, no, Ma'am; it was only trying to make out what *did* happen.

THE QUEEN (*astonished*)   Don't you *know*?

LONDON   Not as clearly as I would like to know: none of us do.

THE QUEEN   Then I don't wonder!

LONDON   No, Ma'am; nor do I.

THE QUEEN   I am afraid that is our only point of agreement, Dr. Temple. It is very painful to me to have to speak to *Bishops* about how things are going in the Church, of which I am the Head. But, being in that position, I have to speak with authority. And I say, again, that all this flaunting Ritual has got to be put down: I won't have it! It does not happen in Scotland; so why should it happen here?

LONDON   Technically speaking, Ma'am, the Scottish Church is heretical: it is not Episcopal.

THE QUEEN   I am Head of the Scottish Church, Dr. Temple. Am I heretical?

LONDON   I should not like to say, Ma'am. I trust not.

THE QUEEN   *I* trust not. But it is not the Church of Scotland, but the Church of England which we are now discussing. Why, with so many Bishops in authority, is there so much disobedience?

(*To be out of this — a mere temporary expedient, indicative of a weak character — the* BISHOP OF CHICHESTER *tiptoes to the cake-stand, and helps himself.*)

ROCHESTER   The question is very difficult, Ma'am.

THE QUEEN   It is. But the difficulty must be met. It's no use temporizing about it. Delay is compromising the Church, and my position as Head of it . . . Things have got to be altered.

WINCHESTER   The question is, Ma'am, how can we get the clergy to obey?

THE QUEEN   If they don't, send them to prison!

LONDON We did that to one. It was no good.

THE QUEEN No, because he was let out again. If they had imprisoned a dozen —

LONDON Then, I fear, Ma'am, there would have been a large secession to Rome; and an increased circulation of the *Church Times*.

THE QUEEN Well, if they have Romish beliefs, let them go to Rome. Do any of you approve of such practices?

THE BISHOPS (*precipitately*) No. Oh, no . . . Very regrettable.

LONDON Also, in my opinion, superstitious and foolish. But the law can't do everything, Ma'am . . . It can't alter a stubborn mind.

THE QUEEN Well, if the law needs strengthening, strengthen it! . . . This has got to be put down! And the law *can* do something, at all events. My Lords, what are *you* going to do about it?

SALISBURY Your Majesty may be assured that we shall all do our best . . . to bring back to the Church the peace and unity which it needs.

THE QUEEN Yes; and drastic discipline is the only thing that will do it. Some of the Bishops have got so in the habit of being disobeyed, that they do nothing . . . nothing whatever!

WINCHESTER What, definitely, would your Majesty wish us to do? The circumstances are often very difficult.

THE QUEEN I wish you all to speak strongly for the strengthening of Church Discipline when the matter comes before your Lordships' House — as it will do presently. That is why I have sent for you to-day.

(*The* BISHOP OF CHICHESTER *jolts his tea-spoon, and upsets his cake.*)

Sir Henry, give the Bishop of Chichester another piece of cake. He has dropped his.

CHICHESTER I beg your Majesty's pardon; I did not perceive that I had done so.

(*In a paroxysm of nervousness, he recovers the fallen fragment, and is about to take a bite of it.*)

THE QUEEN Don't eat it! Take another!

CHICHESTER (*in an aside to* SIR HENRY, *who is now offering him the cake-stand*) No more, I thank you. I might repeat my clumsiness. These saucers . . . rather small, you know . . . for the cake. Relieve me of it . . . Thank you!

(*He gets rid of the cake.*)

THE QUEEN Why is there this difference, I want to know, between England and Scotland? In Scotland we have no trouble, none at all. And *they* manage without Bishops. Why is religion in Scotland so much better, and purer, and more Protestant, than in England?

LONDON That, Ma'am, is a very complicated matter of history. Hardly to be explained over a cup of tea . . . not thoroughly and satisfactorily.

THE QUEEN I don't require to have it explained, so long as you get it altered. Have you all had as much tea as you want?

THE BISHOPS Quite, your Majesty . . . Oh, quite.

CHICHESTER (*with his cake still on his mind*) Most refreshing!

WINCHESTER (*ingratiatingly*) And very good tea, too, Ma'am, if I may be allowed to say so.

THE QUEEN Oh, yes. I get all my tea from India. I hope *you* all get *your* tea from India as an encouragement to the Empire. I feel that we should all do so.

LONDON Really, Ma'am, I don't know where my tea comes from. I generally take green tea; and more of it, I am afraid, than is good for me.

THE QUEEN That is a pity. Too much green tea, I have heard, is quite dangerous. Tell Mrs. Temple from me, that she shouldn't allow it.

LONDON Mrs. Temple cannot interfere, Ma'am. I make it myself in my own study.

THE QUEEN What habits! Dear me! How extraordinary! . . . Well, my Lords, I thank you very much for coming. I have told you my mind on the subject; and when the matter comes before the House of Lords, I shall read with interest what you all have to say about it. And now, if any of you would like to go round the gardens and the conservatories before you leave, pray do so.

(*A murmur of thanks comes from the* BISHOPS. *Their ordeal over, the gardens will be a welcome change, both of scene and subject.*)

Sir Henry, will you please?

(*And* SIR HENRY *goes to call in the* GENTLEMAN-IN-WAITING, *who will be the Bishops' escort from now until their departure. And now, very graciously,* THE QUEEN *dismisses them back to their dioceses.*)

Good-bye, my dear Bishop of London. My dear Bishop of Winchester, good-bye. My dear Bishop of Rochester, remember me to your dear wife; I am so glad she is better. Good-bye, my dear Bishop; you go back to Salisbury to-day?

SALISBURY To-morrow, your Majesty.

THE QUEEN Ah, to-morrow. Good-bye, my dear Bishops.

(*This is to the* BISHOP OF CHICHESTER. *And now only the* BISHOP OF ELY *is left.*)

THE QUEEN Good-bye, my dear Bishop. I was so sorry to hear to-day of the death of the Bishop of Peterborough.

(SIR HENRY *is now back at her elbow, and almost inaudibly gives the prompting word.*)

SIR HENRY . . . Of Ballarat.

THE QUEEN Of Ballarat, I mean.

ELY (*somewhat astray*) Ah, yes . . . indeed, Ma'am.

THE QUEEN You knew him, of course?

ELY Hardly, Ma'am. I believe that I assisted at his consecration.

THE QUEEN A great loss to the Church, out in the Colonies, will it not be?

ELY Indeed, yes, Ma'am. Such a large diocese. Almost the size of England.

THE QUEEN Indeed? I hope his successor will be wisely chosen. A great responsibility.

ELY Yes, indeed, Ma'am.

THE QUEEN And there is the vacancy at Peterborough too. In all these cases — positions of such importance — it is so necessary to find just the right person.

ELY I am sure that your Majesty's choice — so far as it rests with your Majesty — can always be relied on.

THE QUEEN Very good of you to say so, my dear Bishop. These vacancies are always a great anxiety to me. Things in the Church, being as they are — and the appointments not always all that I could wish. Good-bye. Sir Henry will go with you, and see that you join the others. Good-bye.

(*The* BISHOP, *accompanied by* SIR HENRY PONSONBY, *bows himself out.* THE QUEEN *is left alone.*)

THE QUEEN Well, I hope that's all settled now. I've told them what I think. . . .

(*Then an earlier thought strikes her.*)

Ah, yes! That woman! . . . Ballarat . . . or Peterborough . . . Yes! . . . Instant promotion!

(*And, in less than a week, one of the two vacancies is offered — and is accepted.*)

'A GREAT RELIEF'

3rd March 1894

THE QUEEN *sits at a writing-table in her private Apartment at Bucking-*
ham Palace. With a brisk and pleased expression, she finishes and
signs a letter which she then hands over to SIR HENRY PONSONBY,
who stands in attendance.

THE QUEEN Sir Henry, will you see that this letter goes to Lord
Rosebery *at once.* And if, later, you could see him yourself, say I
should be glad to have his answer to-day — this morning, if possible;
before anything gets into the papers.

SIR HENRY I will do my best, Ma'am. Would your Majesty
prefer for me to go now? That would be the quickest way.

THE QUEEN No, no. You must wait until I have seen Mr.
Gladstone. I might want you again. I always find it so difficult to
understand what he really means; and still more so now that he has
become so deaf.

SIR HENRY I don't think your Majesty will have any difficulty
in understanding him on this occasion.

THE QUEEN Indeed, I hope not. Of course, it is going to be
painful; but oh, Sir Henry, such a relief!

SIR HENRY Quite so, Ma'am; that, I can fully appreciate.

THE QUEEN Then please see that that letter goes at once.

(SIR HENRY *goes out with the letter, but immediately returns.*)

SIR HENRY Mr. Gladstone is here, Ma'am.

THE QUEEN I will see him.

SIR HENRY Mrs. Gladstone also, I am told, has come with him.

THE QUEEN Poor thing, poor thing! What a life he has led her,
to be sure. Will you say that I will see her — afterwards.

(SIR HENRY *bows, and goes; and* THE QUEEN *continues her writing.*
Presently the door opens and a COURT ATTENDANT *makes announce-*
ment.)

ATTENDANT Mr. Gladstone, your Majesty.

(MR. GLADSTONE *enters, halts at the threshold, and bows low.* THE QUEEN *rises slowly,* MR. GLADSTONE *advances, and bows again over the hand which she raises toward him.*)

THE QUEEN Good morning, Mr. Gladstone. This was not too early for you, I hope?

GLADSTONE Far from it, your Majesty. For the purpose which brings me here, by your Majesty's gracious permission, the earlier the better — for all parties.

THE QUEEN I was not thinking of *parties*, Mr. Gladstone. But to-day I have much to do, which must be done at once — arrangements that cannot wait. My Government must be carried on by somebody. That was my reason for naming so early an hour.

GLADSTONE I thank your Majesty for so graciously explaining.

THE QUEEN (*seating herself*) I only wished you to know . . . And now, Mr. Gladstone, I am ready to hear anything that you have to tell me.

GLADSTONE (*left standing*) I have already received your Majesty's gracious permission to make resignation of my office as Prime Minister of your Majesty's Government. And your Majesty has granted me this interview for the express purpose of placing in your Majesty's hands this letter tendering that resignation, as, in humble duty, I now do.

(*He advances and presents the letter, which she takes and lays on the table at her side.*)

THE QUEEN Thank you. Thank you, Mr. Gladstone. Is there anything further you wish to say?

GLADSTONE (*after a pause*) On this last occasion, Ma'am, I feel myself under a deep obligation to express to your Majesty, my sense of the high honour that your Majesty has conferred on me in permitting me once more to be Prime Minister and Head of your Majesty's Government. That office it has been my honour to hold four times, at your Majesty's command, over a considerable period of years. Circumstances have now made it imperative that I can hold it no more.

THE QUEEN I think you have done right, Mr. Gladstone, your health not being what it was.

GLADSTONE •The reasons for my resignation, Ma'am, are given in that letter. They are not political, they are personal. The Government which, at your Majesty's command, I formed two years ago, has still, I believe, the confidence of the Country; and in the House of Commons it continues to have a majority. Elsewhere, it is not so fortunate. But so long as it stood for policies approved by the electorate, it would have been my duty, and my earnest endeavour, to remain responsible, under your Majesty's commission, for the carrying of those policies into law. But my physical powers have failed me. My eyesight and my hearing no longer enable me to fulfil adequately the duties which my office requires. I have not consciously delayed, Ma'am, in seeking the relief which has become necessary. The close of the session gave a natural opportunity, of which your Majesty has now graciously permitted me to avail myself.

THE QUEEN Thank you, Mr. Gladstone; you have explained the position very clearly. I quite understand. I am so sorry that you should have any trouble or anxiety about your eyes. Pray have them seen to at once; and do take a good rest. I may say at once that the reasons you have stated are quite sufficient. I accept your resignation.

(MR. GLADSTONE *bows.*)

It has been a long time, has it not, since you first took office?

GLADSTONE About fifty-three years ago, Ma'am, I first had the honour.

THE QUEEN How much has happened since then, has it not? What changes!

GLADSTONE We have indeed, Ma'am, seen great changes. In the life of the Nation, as well as in our own.

THE QUEEN Yes, and changes which have not always been for the better, I fear.

GLADSTONE There have been mistakes, Ma'am, no doubt. We all make them.

THE QUEEN   Yes . . . And then others have to pay for them — unfortunately . . . I understand, Mr. Gladstone, that you would not be willing to accept a peerage?

GLADSTONE   With your Majesty's permission, I would say no.

THE QUEEN   I would have been glad to offer it.

GLADSTONE   I thank your Majesty for so graciously saying.

THE QUEEN   It is the least I could do, in consideration of the many years during which you have held such high office, and so much responsibility. For that reason, had you felt able to accept it, I should have been more than willing.

GLADSTONE   Again I thank your Majesty . . . I . . .

(He pauses; and before the word comes that he wishes to say, THE QUEEN *has risen, and is once more speaking.)*

THE QUEEN   Good-bye, Mr. Gladstone. Will you, please, remember me very specially to dear Mrs. Gladstone . . . How is she?

GLADSTONE   Mrs. Gladstone is here, Ma'am.

THE QUEEN   Ah, yes. Sir Henry told me, I remember.

GLADSTONE   She asks very specially, if, by gracious permission? she may see your Majesty for a few moments before we leave.

THE QUEEN   Certainly. Would she, perhaps, like to see me alone.

GLADSTONE   I believe she hoped she might see you alone, Ma'am.

THE QUEEN   I shall be very pleased. Will you yourself take a message to her, and ask her to come in? And before you go, I have ordered that there shall be some refreshment for you. Good-bye.

(She extends her hand. He takes it, bowing low.)

GLADSTONE   With most humble duty, I thank your Majesty.

(He bows himself out. THE QUEEN *stands looking after him until the door closes. Then, as she returns to her seat, she speaks.)*

THE QUEEN   So that is over — at last!

(She takes up the letter of resignation, and looks at it. Then she rings a handbell. The door opens; an ATTENDANT *appears.)*

THE QUEEN   Tell Sir Henry to come.

(SIR HENRY *is apparently there in waiting. He enters.*)

Sir Henry, this is Mr. Gladstone's letter of resignation. See that it is put safely away.

(SIR HENRY *takes it, and moves to go. The door opens, the* ATTENDANT *announces.*)

ATTENDANT Mrs. Gladstone, your Majesty.

(THE QUEEN *rises, and the expression of her face is now quite different from that with which she met, a short while ago, the entry of her great Minister; her liking for the wife being almost as great as her dislike for the husband.*)

THE QUEEN Dear Mrs. Gladstone, I am so pleased to see you.

(MRS. GLADSTONE *curtsies, while* THE QUEEN *holds her hand with hardly any Court formality at all.*)

MRS. GLADSTONE How good of your Majesty to say so. I hoped you would forgive me. I felt I had to come — this last time.

THE QUEEN Oh, yes, of course, I understand. And do, please, sit down. This must be a very trying time for you.

MRS. GLADSTONE (*restraining her tears*) Oh, not for me! It's for him! To have him give up before — before — he has been able to finish what he so hoped, and lived for.

THE QUEEN But how much better, both for him, and for you. It was really the only thing to do. And you must see now that he takes a complete rest. You won't let him touch politics again, will you? Now, promise!

MRS. GLADSTONE (*speaking with difficulty*) Oh, your Majesty! It was to see you . . . so very specially to-day . . . that I came. I wanted . . . to say something.

THE QUEEN Yes?

MRS. GLADSTONE But so difficult!

THE QUEEN I am sure, dear Mrs. Gladstone, anything you wish to say, I shall be willing to hear.

MRS. GLADSTONE It is something, which *I* can say, but which he could not; but which I felt you ought to know. I am the only one who can tell you. So I have come. . . .

(*She is crying now; but she controls her voice.*)

It has always been, Ma'am, a great trouble to him — a great grief, that you could not approve of his policy.

THE QUEEN (*stiffening a little*) But his policy was his own choice, Mrs. Gladstone.

MRS. GLADSTONE Yes.

THE QUEEN When I told him — as I often did — how wrong and mistaken it all was, he would not believe me. I did my best. But he would go his own way.

MRS. GLADSTONE Of course, Ma'am, he could not do otherwise, feeling so sure that he was right.

THE QUEEN Whatever his feelings were, Mrs. Gladstone, he did not consult *mine*. If he had any himself, I do not know. But for any pain it may have caused him, *I* am not responsible.

MRS. GLADSTONE But you see, Ma'am, his difficulty. Trying for so many years to mend a great wrong; returning to office for that reason alone; and then — so many hindrances, disappointments, defeats, failures. It was difficult for him to be patient.

THE QUEEN I do not think patience has ever been your husband's strong point, Mrs. Gladstone. He could never stand contradiction. But he has often contradicted *me*.

MRS. GLADSTONE Oh, your Majesty, he has his faults, I know. Sometimes he is difficult. But — I have always believed in him, so absolutely! And with his great mind! . . . I know that he always meant well!

THE QUEEN I have never blamed *you*, Mrs. Gladstone, for agreeing with your husband. That is always a wife's duty — if possible.

MRS. GLADSTONE We have never quarrelled, Ma'am; never had any difference. Not once. Not once!

THE QUEEN Then I am sure, my dear Mrs. Gladstone, that *you* have nothing with which to reproach yourself. But you had not to meet him over politics, as I had. It has been very unfortunate, of course, and not as I wished. Twenty years ago he told me that he intended to retire from political life; and I advised him to do so.

How much happier he would have been had he taken my advice then. All that has happened since has made things so difficult.

MRS. GLADSTONE   Oh, yes; but believe me, Ma'am, his devotion to your Majesty, and the Crown, were very great. That *never* altered.

THE QUEEN   His political activities have sometimes made that difficult to believe.

MRS. GLADSTONE   But I do ask your Majesty to believe it! I do! I do! It is only that I have come to say. Indeed, indeed, Ma'am, his devotion to your Majesty was, and remains still, very great.

THE QUEEN   Since you say so, Mrs. Gladstone, I accept your word for it.

MRS. GLADSTONE   Will you let me tell him *that*? That you *do* believe?

THE QUEEN   If it is any comfort for you to tell him so — or for him to hear it — you may tell him that I *do*.

MRS. GLADSTONE   Oh, I am so grateful, so grateful, that you will let me tell him that. And that you *do* really believe it.

THE QUEEN   Then go now, and tell him at once; for he is waiting.
   (*She rises.*)

Good-bye! We shan't often meet again, I suppose? But it has always been a pleasure for me to see you. And I would like you to know that I shall always remember and think of you as a friend. Good-bye, dear Mrs. Gladstone.

   (*Speechless,* MRS. GLADSTONE *receives the kiss* THE QUEEN *bestows upon her, curtsies deeply, kisses her hand, and goes.* THE QUEEN *rings, and the Attendant enters for orders.*)

THE QUEEN   Send Sir Henry to me at once.

   (SIR HENRY *enters after only a moment or two.*)

THE QUEEN   Ah, there you are, Sir Henry. Have you been with Mr. Gladstone.?

SIR HENRY   No, Ma'am; I was waiting, in case your Majesty required me.

THE QUEEN   Have you any news yet from Lord Rosebery?

SIR HENRY I have just received a message to say that his answer will be here in a few hours. He indicates, Ma'am, that it may be 'Yes'.

THE QUEEN It could hardly be otherwise. I would not have had anyone else. Had he declined I should have insisted on a dissolution.

SIR HENRY How did you find Mr. Gladstone, Ma'am?

THE QUEEN Very deaf; but able to talk as much as ever . . . Poor Mrs. Gladstone! For her I am very sorry. Dear, nice creature! What a fate!

THE PRIMROSE WAY

18th May 1894

THE QUEEN *is giving audience to* LORD ROSEBERY, *her Prime Minister. Personally she likes him, but disapproving of his politics, her manner, while they are discussed, is stiff, and she does not invite him to sit down.* LORD ROSEBERY *is quite aware both of the personal liking and of the political disapproval; and he rather enjoys his ability to steer a deft course through a situation which others would find difficult. If only he can keep old Majesty in a fairly good temper, the position will not be so impossible as it became under his great predecessor of unhappy memory. But recently he has made a speech on the House of Lords question which she very much disapproves, and now he is hearing of it.* THE QUEEN, *whose increasing infirmities make walking difficult, keeps a stick by her side, and occasionally taps with it. It thus serves not only as a means to locomotion but as a symbol.*

THE QUEEN   Lord Rosebery, I have been reading the speech you made at Edinburgh last week.

ROSEBERY   Since your Majesty has done me that honour, I hope it was correctly reported.

THE QUEEN   I hope *not*.

ROSEBERY   Was there anything in it of which your Majesty does not approve?

THE QUEEN   I didn't approve of *any* of it, Lord Rosebery. To attack the House of Lords is to attack the British Constitution; if the one goes, the other goes with it.

ROSEBERY   But *I* don't want the House of Lords to go, Ma'am. I regard it as a most valuable adjunct to our legislative system, so am trying to save its life.

THE QUEEN   Oh, indeed? By riding over it rough-shod? If you do that, what will be left worth saving?

ROSEBERY   Riding over it rough-shod, Ma'am, is, to my mind, an apt expression of what the House of Lords, in recent years, has been doing to the House of Commons.

THE QUEEN And quite right too! — when it loses its head and tries to pass measures which would be the ruin of the Country.

ROSEBERY Measures, Ma'am, of which the Country has at General Elections expressed its approval.

THE QUEEN I doubt it. Often at a General Election the majority of people don't know what they are voting for.

ROSEBERY That, Ma'am, is a revolutionary statement, far more upsetting to the British Constitution than attack on the House of Lords. Yet, sometimes, I should almost agree. Democracy until we get equal education for all, remains an imperfect instrument.

THE QUEEN Equal education! You wouldn't have *everybody* well educated, would you, Lord Rosebery?

ROSEBERY I would, Ma'am.

THE QUEEN Dear me! What a very Radical notion. Most extraordinary! If you did, how would you get anyone to do all the necessary disagreeable work of the world?

ROSEBERY I do not know, Ma'am, whether *I* may claim to be well educated; but I can conceive of no work so disagreeable (under certain conditions) as that of Prime Minister.

THE QUEEN Ah! But that is a high honour, and is well paid for.

ROSEBERY Better than a dustman, or a roadsweeper? Yes, Ma'am, though the duties are somewhat similar. But it so happens, that in my case I have a competence of my own which makes even agreeable employment unnecessary. I can even afford to run horses for the Derby — an occupation which I greatly prefer.

THE QUEEN Then what made you take to politics, Lord Rosebery?

ROSEBERY A certain measure of conviction, Ma'am, coupled with a sense of duty. Unfortunately, my convictions tend to be temperate, and my sense of duty intermittent. It would be far easier for me to shoulder the burden of government were I a fanatic, or an enthusiast.

THE QUEEN It's the fanatics who do all the mischief.

ROSEBERY Half of it, Ma'am; the other half is done by the indifferent, and the dead-weights whom one can't move.

THE QUEEN If they do nothing, why need you trouble about them?

ROSEBERY Unfortunately, Ma'am, some of the most conspicuous examples have seats in the House of Lords. Usually they don't take them: but when some measure of outstanding importance goes up to their House, these back-woodsmen make their appearance: and after an effective display of rough-riding, they disappear again.

THE QUEEN Well, Lord Rosebery, I suppose that, like yourself, they have an intermittent sense of duty which is sometimes roused. Can you blame them?

ROSEBERY I'm afraid I do, Ma'am.

THE QUEEN I don't . . . As you know, Lo d Rosebery, personally I like you very much: but I don't like you politics.

ROSEBERY I am sorry, Ma'am; but is not that an almost unavoidable experience, for a constitutional Sovereign who has (to her country's benefit) outlived so many changes of Government? Party politics necessarily ring changes with which your Majesty's political convictions (based on an unbroken experience of over half a century) cannot be expected to be always in agreement.

THE QUEEN I have *no* politics, Lord Rosebery, except the welfare of my country.

ROSEBERY That is what we should all say, Ma'am; and Party divisions are the expression of it. And these Party divisions (on that in-and-out system we call popular government) present themselves alternately, at comparatively short intervals, to your Majesty's undivided mind for check and correction, which, I frankly admit, has often proved of great benefit to the counsels of the nation. But, Ma'am, when the popular mind continues to insist on making what your Majesty regards, perhaps rightly, as a mistake, it is a fundamental principle of the British Constitution that it should be allowed to make it.

THE QUEEN In that case, what is the use of the House of Lords?

ROSEBERY *Continues* to insist I said, Ma'am. The use of the House of Lords is to require evidence that the persistence exists. The House of Lords has had to yield in the past when the popular will was made manifest. Of late years it has been wasting time by being slow in recognizing the evidence of a firm popular demand for things which it dislikes.

THE QUEEN I think the House of Lords has been quite right. And it grieves me more than I can say, that a man of your high intelligence and character should have taken the wrong side.

ROSEBERY Should my services have ceased to give your Majesty satisfaction, I am very ready to give up my office.

THE QUEEN I don't like your way, Lord Rosebery, when I complain about anything, of threatening me with your resignation, which you know I don't wish.

ROSEBERY Indeed, Ma'am, I do not threaten it: I only offer it. So long as your Majesty wishes to keep me, I should greatly regret — were circumstances to force me to anticipate, for my own relief, the fate that is shortly awaiting us.

THE QUEEN What fate do you mean, Lord Rosebery?

ROSEBERY Your Majesty must be as well aware as I am, that at the next election we are going to be defeated. But our opponents are not yet ready to take our place; they would prefer that we should continue (in the phrase used by Sir William Harcourt before *he* became a Home Ruler) 'to stew in our own Parnellite juice'. Parnell has gone: but the juice remains. For the present Home Rule has dished the Liberal Party. Reforms are sometimes misdated: that mis-dated reform was my inheritance when, at your Majesty's command, I accepted office. I cannot go back on it, I have only tried to get round it. I have failed.

THE QUEEN And I don't wonder! Home Rule is an utterly mistaken notion. The Irish are not fit to govern themselves. They never have been, and they never will be. They are an ignorant, superstitious, and uneducated people.

ROSEBERY Of which, Ma'am, education is the only remedy; and we English have always held that self-government is the best of all possible educations. A country learns by its mistakes.

THE QUEEN For the English, that may have been true; but the English are so different. Would you give self-government to savages, Lord Rosebery?

ROSEBERY I would not take away from them, Ma'am, any form

of self-government with which their tribal traditions had provided them.

THE QUEEN Oh, indeed? Slavery, cannibalism, polygamy? You would allow those to go on?

ROSEBERY I should hardly define such tribal customs, Ma'am, as 'a form of self-government'. But polygamy I would certainly not interfere with; we never have, Ma'am. Had we done so the British Empire would not be what it now is. But if I may be allowed to revert to the Irish question: whatever the right solution may be, the Government of Ireland under British rule has been England's conspicuous failure, while elsewhere her rule has been an equally conspicuous success. Does not that in itself suggest, Ma'am, that a change is necessary?

THE QUEEN Yes, I think they've been given too much liberty — not too little. Ever since the last extension of the Franchise (one of Mr. Gladstone's many mistakes) sent eighty Home Rulers to Parliament, there's always been trouble. They haven't even known how to behave themselves.

ROSEBERY That trouble, Ma'am, was the symptom of a deep-rooted unrest which had become national.

THE QUEEN Well, I don't like symptoms; they are unhealthy things, and one shouldn't encourage them.

ROSEBERY Murder will out, Ma'am, without waiting for encouragement. And so also will certain symptoms in the body-politic, when Government ceases to be representative. We want to make Government in Ireland more representative than it has been in the past. When we have done that, we hope — we believe that the symptoms will disappear.

THE QUEEN Do you think, Lord Rosebery, it is constitutional to persist in a policy which you say you know is going to be defeated?

ROSEBERY I do, Ma'am, most certainly.

THE QUEEN Well, I don't.

ROSEBERY I am sorry to have so wide a difference from your Majesty; but if single defeats decide the matter, half the reforms which have made this country what it is could never have become law.

THE QUEEN A great many things have become law which had much better not.

ROSEBERY For instance, Ma'am?

THE QUEEN If I named them, Lord Rosebery, I fear it might only disclose a still further difference of opinion, over what is now past. When mistakes have been made, and can't be remedied, it is no use discussing them. What I have to do my best to prevent now is the making of any *more* mistakes.

ROSEBERY I am always deeply grateful for your Majesty's advice, even when circumstances stand in the way of its adoption. A Prime Minister who has inherited from his predecessor, as I have done, a Policy, a Cabinet, and a Parliament; a party divided into groups, and a leader in the Lower House bitterly hostile to himself and ostentatiously indifferent to the fate of the Government, such a Prime Minister has to regard himself rather as a prisoner of State than as a free agent: nothing could give me more personal satisfaction than to escape from such an entanglement. But it was, if I may be allowed to remind your Majesty, at your Majesty's most express wish that I got myself into it. And honour now forbids me to relinquish it, till some day in the division lobby the hour of my deliverance strikes. The time will not be long.

THE QUEEN And then, Lord Rosebery?

ROSEBERY Then, Ma'am, I shall thankfully retire to my stables, and there watch the training of a horse with which I am hoping to win the Derby.

THE QUEEN In *that*, I shall wish you every success, Lord Rosebery.

ROSEBERY Most kind of your Majesty to say so.

THE QUEEN So long as you don't call it '*Home Rule*'.

ROSEBERY Oh, no, Ma'am; it already has a far more fortunate name than *that*.

THE QUEEN What name?

ROSEBERY Ladas.

THE QUEEN Why Ladas?

ROSEBERY He was a runner in the service of Alexander the Great, whom nobody was ever able to beat.

THE QUEEN Well, then, I hope your horse will live up to his name ... I suppose you have to take great care of him?

ROSEBERY Very great care, Ma'am, not only of his health and training; he has also to be watched, day and night, to prevent his being got at before the race.

THE QUEEN Does that ever happen?

ROSEBERY Yes, Ma'am, it happens — not frequently: but it is always liable to happen. 'Doping' in racing circles has become a fine art; so has 'pulling', though that has to be very cleverly done to escape detection.

THE QUEEN What is 'pulling'?

ROSEBERY A trick by which a dishonest jockey, who has been bribed to it, prevents his horse from winning: he holds him back.

THE QUEEN Dear me: how very shocking!

ROSEBERY Has your Majesty ever heard the story of a horse called Pepper's Ghost? He won a race under very remarkable circumstances.

THE QUEEN No, never.

ROSEBERY He was a splendid horse, and a hot favourite for one of the big events. His jockey was offered £1000 on the condition of his not winning the race. Afraid to be caught 'pulling', what was this jockey to do? The horse's name may have suggested it. Just before mounting he went up to the horse's head, fondled it, and put a pinch of pepper up its nose. The race started, the horse sneezed all the way — and won.

THE QUEEN Dear me! Most extraordinary! And was it found out?

ROSEBERY Yes, Ma'am; directly the race was over, the trainer had the horse's nose examined, the pepper was found and traced; the jockey confessed.

THE QUEEN Was he prosecuted?

ROSEBERY No, Ma'am; he was too valuable. He wasn't even dismissed. They put some pepper up *his* nose as a lesson for him, and told nobody. After that he won several more races for its owner on the same horse. Pepper's Ghost, your Majesty may be interested to hear, came to Windsor on one occasion for stud purposes, and sired Peppercorn out of Cornucopia.

THE QUEEN Most interesting! I wish I had time to hear a great deal more. Do you know, Lord Rosebery, you are the first of my Prime Ministers to talk to me about horse-racing since Lord Melbourne. No doubt Lord Palmerston would have liked to: but I always kept him at a distance because of his bad behaviour to my dear husband, the Prince. But I find you always so pleasant and amusing, when we don't have to talk politics; and I wish we never had to.

ROSEBERY No one wishes that, Ma'am, more than I do. I only ask your Majesty to believe that though I am made responsible for a policy — not of my initiation — which has your Majesty's disapproval, you have no more loyal and devoted subject than your present Prime Minister. And if fate is propitious I may shortly be able to please your Majesty in two quite opposite ways.

THE QUEEN Oh? and what ways will those be?

ROSEBERY By winning the Derby, Ma'am, and by losing an election.

THE QUEEN (*appreciating the joke*) Well, about the last I won't say anything. As for the other, nothing would give me more pleasure. And I wish I could come and see you win it myself. Good-bye, Lord Rosebery.

(*She gives him her hand without rising.*)

ROSEBERY (*as he bows over it*) Your Majesty's most obedient and faithful servant.

(*And he retires well pleased with himself for management of a situation which had become difficult. By telling a quite untrue story of his own invention he has put* HER MAJESTY *into a good temper, and made himself once more as acceptable as under present adverse circumstances is possible. True to his family name, he has found that the Primrose Way is the one that he can always tread with natural grace and generally with good results when it takes him away from politics.*)

'PAINFUL NECESSITY'

1898

THE QUEEN *is seated in one of the Royal Apartments at Windsor. A door opens: a* GENTLEMAN *enters, and announces,* 'LORD KITCHENER OF KHARTOUM, *your Majesty'. And as this most recent and distinguished recipient of the Royal Favour enters,* THE QUEEN *does him the great honour of rising, and the further honour of presenting him with her hand, over which he jerks a bow.*

THE QUEEN   Lord Kitchener, we are very pleased to meet you.

KITCHENER   I thank your Majesty for the great honour. Also for the title which your Majesty has now conferred on me.

THE QUEEN   You have *quite* deserved it, Lord Kitchener: far more than others I could name, to whom — on the advice of my Ministers — I am obliged to give titles, and marks of distinction, for things which have *not* pleased me.

KITCHENER   Which means, I hope, that your Majesty is pleased with *me*?

THE QUEEN   Very pleased, Lord Kitchener! I don't think anyone else could have done better.

KITCHENER   If your Majesty is satisfied, so am I.

THE QUEEN   More than satisfied. You have not only upheld the honour of your Country, you have restored to it what it had *lost* . . . Well, we won't talk politics; but there was a great deal in the Egyptian policy of my Ministers which I could *not* approve. That is all over, thanks to *you*! And I hope we shall always *keep* Egypt — for the benefit of its native population, as well as for our own.

KITCHENER   I hope so, Ma'am: I think so. A little taste of possession goes a long way — settles it, makes it become a habit. After we've been in Egypt fifteen years, it's getting difficult to make a real Englishman believe that it's not just as much ours as India, or any of the other Colonies.

THE QUEEN Well, Lord Kitchener, you call that 'habit'. I call it experience, and the 'political instinct' for which the British race has always been famous. And (the Suez Canal being the way to India) so necessary. If we lost *that*, we might lose India, too.

KITCHENER We might, Ma'am.

THE QUEEN I don't mind telling you, Lord Kitchener, that there is every prospect of my sending you back to India, before long. *I* wish it; and my Ministers are beginning to agree that it will be the best thing possible for India, and for everybody concerned.

KITCHENER I shall always be at your Majesty's orders: a soldier's first duty.

THE QUEEN Yes; and you are a *real* soldier, Lord Kitchener: you don't merely *look* one. (*At this compliment, Lord Kitchener jerks a bow.*) . . . May I have your photograph?

KITCHENER Most honoured, your Majesty.

THE QUEEN Will you send it me — signed? A large and full-length one, please; because you are so tall — as a soldier ought to be.

KITCHENER To that, Ma'am, there are some good exceptions.

THE QUEEN Oh, yes; Lord Roberts is quite a little man, isn't he? But a thorough soldier. I always like meeting him — so loyal, and genuine, and such a good Christian.

KITCHENER He's a very good fellow, Ma'am. He has no jealousy; and that — in the higher ranks — is a rare quality.

THE QUEEN Very satisfactory. Then I hope you and he get on well together . . . Now do, please, sit down, Lord Kitchener; because there is something rather serious I want to talk to you about . . . (*With a bow, he seats himself.*) I am quite sure you did it for the best, and thought it necessary; and, of course, as far as *he* was concerned, just what he deserved, and a very good punishment, too! But I don't like it! . . . I mean this digging up of the Mahdi, and the destruction of his tomb. One doesn't like doing that to dead people — if it can be avoided. The Archbishop of Canterbury spoke to me about it, directly it was done. *He* didn't quite like it, either.

KITCHENER No, Ma'am, I daresay not. The Church has often to think and speak one way — for the sake of appearances — while the Army and the Politicians — for getting the thing done — have to think, speak, and act another way.

THE QUEEN (*doubtfully*)　Yes; I suppose so ... Still — to a dead body — was it necessary?

KITCHENER　As he had cut off Gordon's head, Ma'am, we had to cut off *his* — as an example.

(THE QUEEN *had not thought of this.*)

THE QUEEN　Yes; *that* I can understand. ...

KITCHENER　And after all, Ma'am, in this Country we've done the same.

THE QUEEN　Oh, but surely not!

KITCHENER　Yes, Ma'am; we dug up Oliver Cromwell — tarred and feathered him, and hung him up at Westminster, as a warning to others.

THE QUEEN (*approvingly*)　Ah, yes; but then, he'd killed his *King*!

KITCHENER　Yes, Ma'am; but we also took up Admiral Blake out of Westminster Abbey, and treated him much the same; though he himself had had no hand in killing the King. It was just a form of government which had to be put down, in such a way that it should never come up again. And that was the shortest and cheapest way to it.

THE QUEEN　In this case, it has caused more comment than I like.

KITCHENER　Yes, Ma'am; from ignorant people.

THE QUEEN　But some of them very highly placed, and of excellent character.

KITCHENER　Yes, Ma'am; but high place, and excellence do not preclude ignorance — especially when dealing with the customs and superstitions of the East. The Mahdi almost founded a new religion — or, anyway, revived the fanaticism of an old one; and his Tomb would have become the centre of it. Mohammedanism wouldn't be nearly so strong and fanatical as it is, Ma'am, if it hadn't Mohammed's Tomb, and the pilgrimages to it, year in, year out, to keep it going. It would have been just the same had we left the Mahdi where his followers had buried him in triumph —

a triumph which, for them, meant a triumph over Christianity, Ma'am.

THE QUEEN Yes; well, of course, that *had* to be prevented somehow. You cut off his head, you say? And what did you do with it?

KITCHENER Made it into an ink-pot, Ma'am.

THE QUEEN (*judicially*) I don't quite like that, Lord Kitchener.

KITCHENER You would, Ma'am, if you saw it. It looks very handsome mounted in silver.

THE QUEEN I mean, I'm rather sorry you should put it to such a use: rather gruesome, and a little — unkind.

KITCHENER It wasn't ever my duty to be kind to *him*, Ma'am. It makes an interesting souvenir for my study; and in helping me to write my official reports, is more usefully and honourably employed than it ever was in the lifetime of its late owner. I thought, Ma'am, I was doing him rather an honour.

THE QUEEN No, Lord Kitchener, please put it away!

KITCHENER I will, Ma'am, I will ... Your Majesty would not like to have it for the Windsor Museum?

THE QUEEN No, Lord Kitchener, I think not. Very kind of you to offer it.

KITCHENER It would have been a great honour for *him*, Ma'am.

THE QUEEN Yes: but I shouldn't like my Mohammedan subjects to know. It might give them a wrong impression. They might be hurt.

KITCHENER They might, Ma'am; I don't know. We should only be doing to him what the Roman Church has done all down the ages to its own Saints and Martyrs.

THE QUEEN The same thing? How do you mean, Lord Kitchener?

KITCHENER By cutting them up into small pieces, Ma'am, and packing them off, here, there, and everywhere, to be venerated.

THE QUEEN Yes; but to be *venerated*.

KITCHENER The breaking open of tombs, and the dismemberment of their occupants happens in both cases, Ma'am; but for different reasons. The Roman Church does it to encourage superstition; we've done it to put it down; and we've done it very successfully. That, Ma'am, by itself, I think, sufficiently justified the doing of it.

THE QUEEN (*still a little dubious*) Yes, I suppose it does, then. Though I wish it had not been necessary. It didn't seem quite Christian.

KITCHENER Christianity is rather thrown away, Ma'am, in dealing with false prophets, and people of that sort. It was a bloody tyranny, and it had to be put down. The Soudan is now under decent government: in a few years' time, at the present rate of progress, it will be self-supporting, and may even bring us in revenue.

THE QUEEN Very satisfactory. And is there any prospect of the natives becoming Christian, now that they see what Christianity really means?

KITCHENER The missionaries would say yes, Ma'am. They always do, in order to justify the expenditure of their missions, and their large families, for which they get a capitation grant ... I don't know. Gordon (who knew more about it than most people) said that if the Bishops would only allow polygamy among the natives, Christianity could sweep up the whole of North Africa.

THE QUEEN (*scandalized*) Gordon! General Gordon said that? And he such a good Christian! No, Lord Kitchener, that could never be allowed. Christian morals and principles must not be tampered with, however advantageous the results might seem. It would not be Christianity at all! It would be a reversion to paganism.

KITCHENER Only to the Old Testament, Ma'am.

THE QUEEN Ah! but the Old Testament tells us that polygamy was never a success. David, and Solomon, and even Abraham were examples of that.

KITCHENER Well, Ma'am, on those matters — being myself a bachelor — I am not an authority.

THE QUEEN Aren't you ever going to marry, Lord Kitchener?

KITCHENER I hope not, Ma'am; not, at any rate, till I have retired from active service.

THE QUEEN But won't that be too late?

KITCHENER Marriage takes up too much time, Ma'am, for a man of my profession.

THE QUEEN But are not most of the officers of my Army married, Lord Kitchener?

KITCHENER Yes, Ma'am, and in my estimation none the better for it. When on active service, it makes them mope, and spend a lot of time writing to their wives things that aren't true.

THE QUEEN Not true?

KITCHENER Nobody writes the truth, Ma'am — about War, in letters to his women at home. It couldn't be done.

THE QUEEN Well, of course, women don't *have* to know all the truth; so why should they? The details are too unpleasant.

KITCHENER The whole thing's too unpleasant, Ma'am: except what appears in the papers. That has to be done — to make War popular.

THE QUEEN Yes, I suppose so: a painful necessity; but it has to be. My Empire couldn't get on without occasional wars, I'm afraid; though I wish it could.

KITCHENER Nobody wishes that, Ma'am, more than the married men in the Army. That's why I prefer them unmarried.

THE QUEEN Oh, I see. Well, Lord Kitchener, you have interested me very much: and you have also set my mind at rest on a matter that was rather troubling me. I shall write, and tell the Archbishop all that you have said: and I am sure that he will now agree, and see how necessary it was ... (*She rises, and again offers him her hand.*) Good-bye, Lord Kitchener; I am so glad to have met you. And you will be sure to send me that photograph, to which I am looking forward, and shall always greatly value.

KITCHENER I will, Ma'am; indeed, I will.

(*And with no more grace of movement than of mind,* LORD KITCHENER *bows himself stiffly out.* THE QUEEN *watches him go, then settles back comfortably into her seat — tired, but quite pleased.*)

THE QUEEN What a *nice* man!

HAPPY AND GLORIOUS

20th June 1897

From the 'great relief', confirmed by the voice of the electorate two
years later, THE QUEEN passes serenely on to the culminating triumph
of her reign. The Diamond Jubilee provides material for a tableau
rather than a play; and it is as a tableau that we have here presented
to us this gathering together, at Buckingham Palace, of more than
fifty of THE QUEEN'S direct descendants, together with representatives
of all the crowned heads of a Europe still at peace.

The Triumphal Procession is over, and the large upper chamber
becomes filled with Royalty. Bonnets, costumes, uniforms mingle
in a moving clash of colours; Orders sparkle, sword-chains clink,
spurs jingle. Their owners step delicately, bowing their way from
group to group; and — some now encountering for the first time —
high form and ceremony are still the rule. But here and there Mem-
bers of the Royal Family, meeting each other, exchange remarks of a
familiar character, though sometimes in a foreign accent. And as all
(except an Official or two) who thus mix and converse are Royal
Highnesses — if nothing more — there is no need to trouble about
names. Nobody to-day, except THE QUEEN herself (and perhaps the
Heir-Apparent) is individually important. So, not as individuals
but in the group, we listen to their ROYAL HIGHNESSES chatting
among themselves over the events of the day, filling up time till the
Chief Character makes her appearance.

ROYAL HIGHNESSES Well! So that's over! ... How beautifully
everything went! ... Excellently! ... Very well indeed! ... Nothing could have been better! ... I hope Mamma enjoyed it as much
as we did ... Oh, I'm sure she did ... What crowds! What
cheering! And what perfect order! ... Yes, the English are a
wonderful people ... Have you seen Mamma, since she got back?
... Yes, I have just been with her ... How has she borne it? ...
Oh, she's all right. She will be up in a minute. They are getting
her into her chair.

AN IMPERIAL HIGHNESS My dear Uncle Bertie, congratulations!
What a glorious landmark in the annals of your great Nation!

HIS ROYAL HIGHNESS Thank you. Yes, very satisfactory, I think. I am so glad that you were able to be present.

AN IMPERIAL HIGHNESS Ach! I would not have missed it for anything!

HIS ROYAL HIGHNESS (*to an* OFFICIAL) Sir Arthur, will you please to give orders for the window to be ready?

(SIR ARTHUR *bows, and goes to give the order. Presently two Footmen enter, and undo the bolts of the centre window. A Court Official enters, comes to His Royal Highness, bows, and makes a communication.*)

HIS ROYAL HIGHNESS (*to* HIS IMPERIAL HIGHNESS) Excuse me for one moment.

SIR ARTHUR (*to the Footmen*) Do not go; remain.

(*They stand to attention on either side of the window. And now, from the corridor outside, comes an approaching sound — a mingling of voices, footsteps, and a low rolling of wheels; and* THE QUEEN *enters, seated in her wheeled chair, accompanied by her two Sons. The assembled Family and the Royal Guests, with the formality befitting a great occasion, bow low upon her entrance. The word 'Congratulations' emerges from the general hum of voices. Then expressions of affection take the place of ceremony.*)

A ROYAL PRINCESS Mamma, dear, how are you?

THE QUEEN Very tired, my dear; but oh, so happy! . . . To think now that it is all over! . . . So glad that I had the strength for it!

PRINCESS And the courage, Mamma, dear!

ANOTHER PRINCESS You were quite wonderful, Mamma!

THE QUEEN Yes, so the Doctor tells me. He has just felt my pulse and taken my temperature. And he says that he could not have believed it possible. Oh, I'm — I'm so thankful!

HIS ROYAL HIGHNESS So is everybody. And now, Mamma, I think you had better take a glass of wine. It will do you good.

THE QUEEN Thank you.

HIS ROYAL HIGHNESS And may we also drink to your good health, Mamma?

THE QUEEN Certainly; why, yes, certainly! Please, all of you!

(*In the background Attendants have already begun serving wine into glasses. A glass is brought to* THE QUEEN.)

THE QUEEN   What is it?

HIS ROYAL HIGHNESS   Champagne, Mamma.

THE QUEEN   No, no; I will have sherry. (*So sherry is brought.*) How long has it taken?

PRINCESS   Nearly three hours, Mamma.

THE QUEEN   Oh, dear me! And it seems like yesterday and tomorrow — almost! . . . Three hours!

HIS ROYAL HIGHNESS   Your Imperial and Royal Highnesses, I have great pleasure in asking you to drink to the health of Her Majesty, the Queen. May she continue long, in health and prosperity, to enjoy the love of her Children and her people.

(*The health is drunk with decorous enthusiasm.* THE QUEEN *sits bowing her acknowledgments to all the assembled Family, with tears and smiles.*)

THE QUEEN   Thank you! Oh, thank you!

PRINCESS   Won't you go and rest now, Mamma?

THE QUEEN   Not yet . . . That cheering that I hear means that my dear people are expecting to see me again. I must try not to disappoint them.

PRINCESS   It would be nice if you could, Mamma. You think you can?

THE QUEEN   Yes, but I can't get up. I must go as I am. Have the windows opened.

(*The windows are opened by the Footmen; the cheering swells.*)

THE QUEEN   Yes, but over the balustrade, they will not be able to see me. I must be raised. Tell them to bring in the sliding dais.

HIS ROYAL HIGHNESS   It is already there in position, Mamma.

THE QUEEN   Really! How thoughtful!

(*And so, when the window is opened, the sliding dais is let down from without into the window-frame. While this is being done with quiet efficiency by the well-trained Footmen, the* QUEEN *continues speaking.*)

Then, now, will you, Bertie, and some of the others go out, and let them know that I am coming? Not too many, just a few.

(*So six members of the Royal Family go out on to the balcony, and the cheering grows louder.* THE QUEEN, *seeing that the dais is now in position, makes a gesture of command, and the chair, slowly propelled, mounts the ramp prepared for it, and passes into the balcony. Immediately the cheering becomes tremendous, and would go on without abatement for much longer than exhausted old human nature can allow.* THE QUEEN *gives the signal for retirement; the chair is withdrawn, and backs into its former central position; and the Royal Family retire, bowing, from the public gaze. The dais is lifted, the window is closed again.*)

THE QUEEN It's very gratifying, very, to find — after all these years — that they do appreciate all that I have tried to do for them — for their good, and for this great Country of ours. We have been so near together to-day — they and I: all my dear people of England, and Scotland and Wales — *and* Ireland, and the dear Colonies, and India. From all round the world I have had messages. Such loyalty — such devotion! Most extraordinary! Tell Mr. Chamberlain how very much I approve of all the arrangements he made for the representation of all parts of my Empire in the Procession. Everything so perfectly in order. Most gratifying! . . . Well, I must go now and rest, or I shall not be able to take my place at dinner to-night, and that would never do! . . . So happy! . . . As we were coming back — you were in front, Bertie, so perhaps you didn't see — it was just by Hyde Park Corner, there was a great crowd there; and a lot of rough men — of course it ought not to have happened, but it didn't matter — broke right through the lines of the police and troops guarding the route; and they ran alongside the carriage, shouting and cheering me. And I heard them say: 'Go it, Old Girl! You've done it well! You've done it well!' Of course, very unsuitable — the words; but so gratifying! And oh, I hope it's true! I hope it's true! . . . Hark! They are still cheering . . . Albert! Ah! if only you could have been here!

(*And, having said her say, the great, wonderful, little old Lady gives the signal to her Attendants, and is wheeled slowly away.*)

RECOLLECTIONS

1900

It is afternoon, late in March. THE QUEEN, *in her private apartment at Windsor Castle, sits in an arm-chair at a small movable writing-table.* LADY JANE CHURCHILL, *one of the most intimate of her Ladies in Waiting, is in attendance.* THE QUEEN *lays down her pen and leans back, tired, in her chair.*

THE QUEEN There: that is finished! . . . It has taken me a long time.

LADY JANE I am afraid so much writing tires you, Ma'am — too much.

THE QUEEN Yes, I am tired. *(She makes a gesture for the table to be moved away. Her* LADY *moves it to one side.)* I don't think I shall go on writing my diary any more. Perhaps this is the last time. My eyes . . . I find it so difficult.

LADY JANE Your Majesty has kept a diary for a great many years?

THE QUEEN Yes; ever since I came to the throne. When I have had the health and strength for it, I have never missed a day.

LADY JANE I suppose, Ma'am, it has been a great help for reference, when your Majesty has wanted to remember things?

THE QUEEN Oh, no; I have never needed it for myself. I remember everything. No, I wrote it for others. There is nothing in it that may not be read — some day . . . not yet. There are some still living who might be hurt by what I have said about them.

LADY JANE Some of your Majesty's Ministers?

THE QUEEN Yes; *and* others. Oh yes, there is a great deal about my Ministers which some of them would not like at all — Ministers, *and* Ministries.

LADY JANE Can your Majesty remember *all* your Majesty's Ministers — of the past?

THE QUEEN　All that were of any importance, yes. All my Prime Ministers, of course.

LADY JANE　Some of them were great statesmen, were they not?

THE QUEEN　Yes, some: not all.

LADY JANE　What a wonderful Cabinet they would have made, if your Majesty could have had them all together.

THE QUEEN　No, indeed! A very bad Cabinet.

LADY JANE　Oh? but why, your Majesty?

THE QUEEN　Because Prime Ministers always want to have their own way. It would have been like the Kilkenny cats — nothing but tails left ... Yes, one of the greatest trials of my life has been my Prime Ministers wanting to have their own way. And of course, sometimes I had to let them. And then (when it was too late) they found out their mistake, and were sorry. Oh yes, Prime Ministers are very unteachable — most of them. Though, to be sure, some of them had to teach *me*, just a little, at first — before I had had experience.

LADY JANE　Lord Melbourne was the first, Ma'am, was he not?

THE QUEEN　Yes; he was very nice and kind to me; and I was fond of him; but I don't think *he* tried to teach me as much as he ought to have done. I was very young then, and I enjoyed being Queen; and he liked me to enjoy myself, because that gave him less trouble. Dear lazy man! he didn't like trouble; no. Sir Robert Peel, whom at first I did not care for, taught me much more; and he had such a respect for the Prince, my husband: he often consulted him. Of course, when I had the Prince to help me, everything was different: so much easier, especially when things were difficult.

LADY JANE　And after Sir Robert Peel, Ma'am; who was the next?

THE QUEEN　Let me see. Oh, Lord John Russell — Lord Russell as he became afterwards; a troublesome little man, very well-behaved and well-meaning, but not good as a Prime Minister. He couldn't keep Lord Palmerston in order. *We* had to do that for him — the Prince and I. Yes: in 1851, he behaved so badly that he had to

resign. But it wasn't much good; he had made himself so popular (it's what the bad politicians always manage to do), that four years later he was back as Prime Minister, with Lord John Russell serving under him. It was then that he tried to get us into war with America. The Prince saved us from that. It was the last thing he did — the very last.

LADY JANE That was a great thing to do, Ma'am. And what a mercy that the Prince *was* able to do it.

THE QUEEN Yes; oh, but I was forgetting. Of course before that — yes, before that — came the Crimean War. That was almost a defeat for us: it was the French who really won it; but we didn't let people know *that*. It wouldn't have done. You see, everybody had forgotten what war was like; no one knew anything about it: so it was all a dreadful muddle — so much unnecessary suffering and loss of life. It was so bad that the Ministry responsible for it had to resign. And at that time everybody was so jealous of the Prince that *he* could do nothing. One day a most shocking rumour was put about that he had been sent to the Tower — for treason; and I shouldn't wonder if it was Lord Palmerston who did it. He and the Prince never got on together. He wasn't considerate or properly respectful; indeed he was not quite a gentleman; three months after the Prince's death, he came for an audience wearing a coloured waistcoat and a tie with spots. I never forgave him that! Still, for all his faults, I liked him better than Mr. Gladstone.

LADY JANE But Mr. Gladstone was always respectful, was he not, Ma'am?

THE QUEEN Respectful? Oh yes. But he never seemed to hear what I said — not with any attention. He was a great talker: he just waited and went on — *would* have his way; there was no moving him. Home rule; such a mistake! Well, I was able to stop *that* at all events . . . and get a Ministry I could *trust*; though Lord Rosebery would have been a very good Prime Minister — if he hadn't been tied up with Mr. Gladstone . . . And now, will you ring, please? I must have my glass of wine.

LADY JANE Yes, Ma'am. And then do rest a little. You look so tired, Ma'am.

(*She rings: an* ATTENDANT *enters.*)

THE QUEEN I always am now. (*To* ATTENDANT.) Bring the wine ... Of course one of the things which made it difficult for me to like Mr. Gladstone was that he turned out Lord Beaconsfield. After that everything went wrong. So many new notions, and every one of them a mistake, when half the Liberals had become Radicals. Mr. Chamberlain's fault, that was; but he learned his mistake, and as a Liberal Unionist became quite a reformed character. (*The wine is brought, and served.*)

LADY JANE You mentioned Lord Beaconsfield, Ma'am; was he the greatest of your Ministers?

THE QUEEN No; he was a good and wise statesman; and always asked my advice about everything. But the greatest of all my Ministers was the Prince himself. Before the end he was really King Consort — not Prince; but nobody knew that — except myself ... Lord Beaconsfield was the last of my Ministers whom I could really call a friend. And now I have hardly any of my real friends — my old friends, left. Relatives too — all the old ones are gone. It's ten years now since anyone called me by my own name: it makes me feel so lonely sometimes, never to hear my name spoken. And the best thing I have to remember now is that England is so much greater — better too in *some* ways — than when I came to the throne: less poverty: less drunkenness; but in other ways — especially in politics — things have *not* improved ... There! I've talked too much. I must rest now.

LADY JANE Shall I read to you, Ma'am?

THE QUEEN Yes; if you can see without having any more light, and don't mind my going to sleep while you read, as I probably shall. Put that back (*points to her diary*) into its place. Lock it up safely, and bring me the key.

LADY JANE And then, Ma'am, what would you like me to read?

THE QUEEN Anything that's there. I shan't listen to you for long. And while you read, Jane, you may sit down.

(LADY JANE *curtseys her thanks, puts away the diary; locks the book-case, and then begins selecting a book from those lying on the table. Presently she chooses one; she brings back the key and lays it on the table beside* THE QUEEN; *then sits, turns the pages, takes out a marker, and prepares to start reading.*)

LADY JANE This is from *Lavengro*, Ma'am, by George Borrow, which I was reading to your Majesty yesterday: the part where he is speaking of the dead friend whom he still loves and remembers best of all.

THE QUEEN Ah, yes; yes. Read that!

LADY JANE (*reading*) '. . . How frequently does his form visit my mind's eye in slumber and in wakefulness, in the light of day, and in the night watches. But last night I saw him in his beauty and his strength; he was about to speak, and my ear was on the stretch, when all at once I awoke, and there was I alone, and the night storm was howling amidst the branches of the pines which surround my lonely dwelling. "Listen to the moaning of the pine, at whose root thy hut is fastened" — a saying that, of wild Finland, in which there is wisdom; I listened, and thought of life and death.'

Softly, from the Castle Yard, comes the stroke of six o'clock; the chimes follow. LADY JANE *waits and listens to the opening notes of 'Abide with me': then turns and sees that* THE QUEEN *is already asleep. She closes the book, lays it down, rises, and goes near: and now assured that* THE QUEEN *is really asleep, she says softly:*)

LADY JANE Oh, how I would like to kiss you now! But I mustn't do that — not without leave — *Victoria.*

(*With tender affection she speaks into the sleeping ear the name which has passed into history.*)